# Formulating Foster

# Formulating Foster

*Stephen C. Foster and the Creation of a National Musical Myth*

CHRISTOPHER LYNCH

# OXFORD
UNIVERSITY PRESS

Oxford University Press is a department of the University of Oxford.
It furthers the University's objective of excellence in research, scholarship,
and education by publishing worldwide. Oxford is a registered trade mark of
Oxford University Press in the UK and in certain other countries.

Published in the United States of America by Oxford University Press
198 Madison Avenue, New York, NY 10016, United States of America.

© Oxford University Press 2025

All rights reserved. No part of this publication may be reproduced, stored in a retrieval system, transmitted, used for text and data mining, or used for training artificial intelligence, in any form or by any means, without the prior permission in writing of Oxford University Press, or as expressly permitted by law, by license or under terms agreed with the appropriate reprographics rights organization. Inquiries concerning reproduction outside the scope of the above should be sent to the Rights Department, Oxford University Press, at the address above.

You must not circulate this work in any other form
and you must impose this same condition on any acquirer.

Library of Congress Cataloging-in-Publication Data
Names: Lynch, Christopher, 1984– author.
Title: Formulating Foster : Stephen C. Foster and the creation of a
national musical myth / Christopher Lynch.
Description: [1.] | New York : Oxford University Press, 2025. |
Includes bibliographical references and index.
Identifiers: LCCN 2025013428 | ISBN 9780197811696 (paperback) |
ISBN 9780197811689 (hardback) | ISBN 9780197811726 |
ISBN 9780197811702 (epub)
Subjects: LCSH: Foster, Stephen Collins, 1826–1864. | Foster, Stephen Collins,
1826–1864—Political and social views. | Lilly, Josiah Kirby, 1861–1948. |
Composers—United States—Biography. | Popular music—United States—
19th century—History and criticism. | Popular music—United States—
20th century—History and criticism. | Popular music—Political aspects—
United States—History.
Classification: LCC ML410.F78 L96 2025 | DDC 782.42164092 [B]—dc23/eng/20250401
LC record available at https://lccn.loc.gov/2025013428

DOI: 10.1093/9780197811726.001.0001

Paperback printed by Integrated Books International, United States of America
Hardback printed by Bridgeport National Bindery, Inc., United States of America

The manufacturer's authorized representative in the EU for product safety is
Oxford University Press España S.A., Parque Empresarial San Fernando de Henares,
Avenida de Castilla, 2 – 28830 Madrid (www.oup.es/en or product.safety@oup.com).
OUP España S.A. also acts as importer into Spain of products made by the manufacturer.

*To Deane and Kathy*

# Contents

Acknowledgments   xiii

Introductory Essay: Remembering the Life and Works of
Stephen C. Foster   1
    Stephen C. Foster: Life and Works, Revisited   15
    The Oral Histories   43

## PART I. COMPETING NARRATIVES AFTER FOSTER'S DEATH   49

1. An Obituary of Stephen C. Foster (1864)   61
    Introduction   61
    "Stephen C. Foster, the Composer," *Pittsburgh Evening Chronicle*,
        January 21, 1864.   62

2. Two Letters by Henry Baldwin Foster (1864)   66
    Introduction   66
    Henry Foster to Susan G. Beach, January 23, 1864,
        Foster Hall Collection, C934.   68
    Henry Baldwin Foster to Ann Eliza Buchanan,
        February 4, 1864, Foster Hall Collection, C935.   69

3. Reminiscences of George W. Birdseye (1867)   71
    Introduction   71
    George W. Birdseye, "A Reminiscence of the
        late Stephen C. Foster," *New York Musical Gazette*,
        January 1, 1867.   74

4. Reminiscences of Robert P. Nevin (1867)   84
    Introduction   84
    Robert P. Nevin, "Stephen C. Foster and Negro Minstrelsy,"
        *The Atlantic Monthly*, November 1867.   87

5. Reminiscences of John Mahon (1877)   102
    Introduction   102
    John Mahon, "The Last Years of Stephen C. Foster,"
        *New York Clipper*, March 24, 1877.   103

6. An Interview with an Anonymous Pittsburgh
   Acquaintance (1879) ................................................. 116
   Introduction ............................................................. 116
   *St. Louis Times-Journal*, February 22, 1879. ........... 118

7. An Interview with Rebecca Shiras Morris and
   Joan Sloan Shiras (1879) .......................................... 119
   Introduction ............................................................. 119
   "'Old Folks at Home': Is Pittsburg's Revered Song-writer its
   Author? A Strong Showing that he Did not Write all he is
   Credited With," *Pittsburg Leader*, February 23, 1879. ... 121

8. An Interview with Samuel S. Sanford (1882) ............ 125
   Introduction ............................................................. 125
   *Detroit Free Press*, October 5, 1882. ........................ 127

9. An "Anonymous" Interview with Morrison Foster and
   George C. Cooper (ca. 1888) ..................................... 131
   Introduction ............................................................. 131
   "Massa's in de Cold Ground: The Sad Ending of
   Stephen G. [sic] Foster's Career," unidentified clipping, ca. 1888. ... 133

10. An Interview with an Anonymous "Acquaintance" (1889) ... 136
    Introduction ............................................................. 136
    P. D. Haywood (a pseudonym for John H. Horton),
    *Philadelphia Times*, October 23, 1889. ................... 137

## PART II. MEMORIALIZING FOSTER AT THE TURN OF THE TWENTIETH CENTURY    141

11. Reminiscences of Kit Clarke (1893) ......................... 157
    Introduction ............................................................. 157
    *Brooklyn Daily Eagle*, October 2, 1893. ................... 159

12. An Interview with Jane Foster Wiley (1895) ........... 164
    Introduction ............................................................. 164
    *Pittsburg Press*, May 18, 1895. ................................ 166

13. An Interview with Frank Dumont and a Pittsburgh Lady (1895) ... 169
    Introduction ............................................................. 169
    *Pittsburg Press*, May 27, 1895. ................................ 171

14. Two Interviews with Susan Pentland Robinson (1895) ... 174
    Introduction ............................................................. 174
    *Pittsburg Press*, June 1, 1895. .................................. 175
    *Pittsburg Press*, June 5, 1895. .................................. 177

| | |
|---|---|
| 15. An Interview with John H. Cassidy (1895) | 179 |
|     Introduction | 179 |
|     *Pittsburg Press*, June 13, 1895. | 181 |
| 16. An Interview with J. William Pope (1895) | 182 |
|     Introduction | 182 |
|     *Pittsburg Press*, June 23, 1895. | 183 |
| 17. An Interview with a "Prosperous Merchant" (1895) | 185 |
|     Introduction | 185 |
|     *Pittsburg Press*, June 27, 1895. | 185 |
| 18. An Interview with Jehu Haworth (1895) | 188 |
|     Introduction | 188 |
|     *Pittsburg Press*, June 28, 1895. | 188 |
| 19. An Interview with Marion Foster Welch (1895) | 190 |
|     Introduction | 190 |
|     *Pittsburg Press*, July 2, 1895. | 190 |
| 20. Two Interviews with William Hamilton (1895) | 192 |
|     Introduction | 192 |
|     *Pittsburg Press,* July 11, 1895. | 195 |
|     *Pittsburg Press*, July 15, 1895. | 197 |
| 21. An Interview with an Art Dealer (1895) | 200 |
|     Introduction | 200 |
|     *Pittsburg Press,* July 31, 1895. | 201 |
| 22. An Interview with a St. Louis Businessman (1895) | 202 |
|     Introduction | 202 |
|     *Pittsburg Press*, August 9, 1895. | 202 |
| 23. An Interview with a "Prominent Pittsburgher" (1895) | 205 |
|     Introduction | 205 |
|     *Pittsburg Press,* August 11, 1895. | 208 |
| 24. Morrison Foster's Sketch of His Brother's Life (1896) | 210 |
|     Introduction | 210 |
|     Morrison Foster. "Stephen C. Foster." Pittsburgh, 1896. | 210 |
| 25. An Interview with the "Foster Serenaders" (1900) | 236 |
|     Introduction | 236 |
|     *Pittsburg Press,* July 22, 1900. | 237 |
| 26. An Interview with Rachel E. Woods (1900) | 240 |
|     Introduction | 240 |
|     *Pittsburg Press*, August 24, 1900. | 241 |

| | |
|---|---|
| 27. An Interview with the Daughter of a Friend (1900) | 243 |
| Introduction | 243 |
| *Pittsburg Press*, August 30, 1900. | 244 |
| 28. An Interview with William P. T. Jope (1900) | 245 |
| Introduction | 245 |
| *Pittsburg Press*, September 8, 1900. | 246 |
| 29. An Interview with Maria Beabout (1900) | 247 |
| Introduction | 247 |
| *Pittsburg Press*, September 12, 1900. | 247 |
| 30. Reminiscences of George C. Cooper (1902) | 249 |
| Introduction | 249 |
| George C. Cooper, "Stephen C. Foster," *Piano Music Magazine*, May 1902. | 250 |
| 31. Recollections from Classmates at the Athens Academy (1905/1911) | 253 |
| Introduction | 253 |
| R. M. Welles, "The Old Athens Academy," *Annual* 5 (1911). | 253 |

## PART III. REMEMBERING FOSTER AFTER THE NAACP'S 1914 PROTESTS — 255

| | |
|---|---|
| 32. Reminiscences of Susan McFarland Parkhurst (1916) | 269 |
| Introduction | 269 |
| Mrs. E. A. Parkhurst Duer, "Personal Recollections of the Last Days of Foster." *Etude*, September 1916. | 270 |
| 33. A "Letter" by W. W. Kingsbury (1905/1916) | 276 |
| Introduction | 276 |
| "Old Letter Is Found Praising S. C. Foster," *Pittsburgh Sun*, September 11, 1916. | 277 |
| 34. An Interview with B. D. M. Eaton (ca. 1916) | 279 |
| Introduction | 279 |
| Unidentified Clipping, Foster Hall Collection. | 279 |
| 35. Harry Houdini's Take on Kit Clarke's Memories of Foster (1916) | 281 |
| Introduction | 281 |
| *Etude*, November 1916. | 281 |
| 36. Reminiscences of John W. Robinson (1920) | 284 |
| Introduction | 284 |
| Harold Vincent Milligan. *Stephen Collins Foster*. | 284 |

| | |
|---|---|
| 37. More Reminiscences from George C. Cooper (1920) | 285 |
|     Introduction | 285 |
|     Harold Vincent Milligan, *Stephen Collins Foster*. | 286 |
| 38. An Interview with Marion Foster Welch (1924) | 290 |
|     Introduction | 290 |
|     *Pittsburgh Gazette Times*, January 10, 1924. | 290 |
| 39. An Interview with Marion Foster Welch (1929) | 293 |
|     Introduction | 293 |
|     *Kansas City Star*, April 11, 1929. | 293 |
| 40. Family Memories Relayed by the Grandson of Thomas "Daddy" Rice (1931) | 296 |
|     Introduction | 296 |
|     Dean J. Rice to Josiah Kirby Lilly, March 27, 1931. | 297 |
|     Excerpt from a Letter by Dean J. Rice to Josiah Kirby Lilly, April 14, 1931. | 300 |
| 41. An Interview with Katherine Schoenberger Mygatt and Martha Stough (1934) | 302 |
|     Introduction | 302 |
|     Esther Hamilton. "Sells Foster Picture from Attic for $200: Struthers Man's Discovery Revives Interest in Composer Who Wrote Songs at Warren." *Youngstown Telegram*, February 3, 1934. | 303 |
| 42. Jessie Welsh Rose Relays Her Grandmother's Memories (1926/1934) | 308 |
|     Introduction | 308 |
|     Jessie Welsh Rose. "My Grandmother's Memories." *Foster Hall Bulletin* 10 (May 1934): 9–14. | 309 |
| 43. Concluding Essay: After Archival Amnesty: Toward a New View of Stephen C. Foster | 322 |
|     Constructing the Foster Hall Collection | 324 |
|     The Narratives and Rituals of Foster Hall | 339 |
|     The Consequences of Archival Amnesty: Memory of Foster since 1954 | 351 |
|     Listening with New Ears | 370 |
| *Appendices* | 377 |
| *Bibliography* | 383 |
| *Index* | 393 |

# Acknowledgments

This book represents the culmination of the first chapter of my career. Searching for jobs, navigating the publishing world, and establishing myself as a scholar have not been easy tasks; and I feel I owe everything to three individuals who never gave up on me, even when I was ready to quit. My undergraduate music history professor, James A. Davis, inspired me to become a music historian and continues to offer invaluable mentorship. One of the happiest accidents of my life was getting hired at the Stephen Foster Memorial in 2018, causing me to pivot my scholarship to music of the Civil War era, which is Jim's area of study. Talking to Jim about my work has been greatly beneficial, and his fingerprints are all over this book. It has meant so much to me personally to have learned and grown with him for more than twenty years now.

Deane L. Root and Kathryn Miller Haines at the Foster Memorial took a chance on hiring me, a scholar of American music with little expertise at the time in Foster's music and no experience as an archivist. I like to think my "outsider" perspective helped me see new things in the Foster collection, but in order to do that I had to rely on their deep knowledge of the materials and American cultural history. Their encouragement and commitment to supporting me and other scholars as we question what we think we know about Foster and the collection, especially when those questions are uncomfortable, have been inspiring. Through their example they continue to teach me what it means to be a historian and caretaker of an archive, and I feel very lucky to call them friends.

# Introductory Essay

## Remembering the Life and Works of Stephen C. Foster

Just outside my former office in the ornate, Gothic-style Stephen Foster Memorial at the University of Pittsburgh, a stone wall bears an inscription "affectionately dedicated" to Josiah Kirby Lilly Sr. (1861–1948). It reads:

> As a boy he found comfort and courage
> and joy in the songs of
> STEPHEN COLLINS FOSTER
> In payment of this unpayable debt he
> gathered the facts of Foster's life
> and of his songs into
> THE FOSTER HALL COLLECTION
> and gave the collection in trust to the
> UNIVERSITY OF PITTSBURGH

The inscription immortalizes the assumption, widely shared when the building was dedicated in 1937, that the Foster Hall Collection represents an objective, exhaustive, and authoritative record of the life and legacy of a composer of uplifting music, Stephen C. Foster, who was born outside of Pittsburgh in 1826 and died in New York in 1864. Not tempered with words like "most of" or "many," the inscription lacks nuance. It plainly states that the building hosts "the facts," which has given the impression—in its most extreme interpretation—that no more data about Foster and his music exists outside the walls of the memorial.

Looking for a hobby upon his retirement as president of Lilly Pharmaceuticals in Indianapolis, Lilly initially set out to collect first editions of all of Foster's musical scores in late 1930 or early 1931. Needing assistance researching and identifying his compositions, he recruited Katharine Whittlesey Copley and her father, Walter R. Whittlesey. Whittlesey possessed valuable research experience as well as subject knowledge, having

*Formulating Foster*. Christopher Lynch, Oxford University Press. © Oxford University Press 2025.
DOI: 10.1093/9780197811726.003.0001

coauthored with Oscar Sonneck an annotated list of Foster's songs and recently retired as a music librarian at the Library of Congress.[1] Lilly also hired Fletcher Hodges Jr., a young man who had just received his undergraduate degree in English from Harvard, to arrange and describe new acquisitions and employed a team of assistants and typists to support the work. After about two years of circulating bulletins that enumerated to rare book dealers and private collectors the items they were looking for, the team had identified and acquired first editions of nearly all of Foster's compositions, including many more than Whittlesey had previously identified with Sonneck.

Lilly's collecting interests quickly expanded beyond scores. He formed relationships with many of Foster's relatives, friends, and their descendants, from whom he purchased items such as the composer's manuscripts, instruments, and account books, as well as photographs and thousands of pages of correspondence documenting the family's history. He also acquired a great deal of memorabilia and commissioned portraits, original artwork inspired by Foster's music, and recordings. He housed his materials in a building in Indiana called "Foster Hall" and named them the "Foster Hall Collection."

Lilly learned of the ongoing effort to erect the Stephen Foster Memorial at the University of Pittsburgh early in his collecting work. Initiated in 1927 by the Tuesday Musical Club, a women's group that sponsored performances in Pittsburgh, the effort had stalled amid the economic crisis of the 1930s. Lilly's much-needed financial contributions toward the project bought him considerable sway in the memorial's design.[2] Originally intended to house a theater, event space, and offices for the Tuesday Music Club, the evolving design sketches show the addition of a "shrine" to the composer, a reading room, a space to store the Foster Hall Collection, and an office for the collection's curator, Fletcher Hodges Jr., whom Lilly "donated" with the 10,000 items in the Foster Hall Collection when the building opened in 1937.[3] Lilly personally funded Foster Hall's activities at the University of Pittsburgh for about

---

[1] Walter R. Whittlesey and O. G. Sonneck, *Catalogue of First Editions of Stephen C. Foster* (Government Printing Office, 1915).

[2] For more on the Tuesday Musical Club's role in the founding of the Stephen Foster Memorial, see Geraldine Morris Bair, "Beautiful Dreamers: The Founding of the Stephen Foster Memorial in Pittsburgh, Pennsylvania, 1927–1937, the Working-in, and the Aftermath," Manuscript, 1997. Digital Collections, University of Pittsburgh Library System, Foster Hall Collection (FHC).

[3] "Preliminary Sketch of Stephen C. Foster Memorial," undated; "Tentative Plot Plan, University of Pittsburgh," January 5, 1934, Stephen Foster Memorial Building Blueprints and Plans, Center for American Music, University of Pittsburgh Library System.

**Figure I.1.** The Stephen Foster Memorial. Foster Hall Collection, Center for American Music, University of Pittsburgh Library System.

two years, at which point support was assumed by the Lilly Endowments (Figure I.1).

After Lilly's death in 1948, the Lilly Endowments continued to make annual payments to the Foster Hall Collection before making a final contribution to seed the memorial's own endowment in the early 1990s.[4] With the exit of the Lilly Endowments, the Foster Hall Collection transformed into the Center for American Music and was subsumed into the University of Pittsburgh Library System. The collection remained in the Stephen Foster Memorial, where it was curated by Hodges's successor, Deane L. Root. Soon after the creation of the center, Root hired Kathryn Miller Haines, and I joined the staff in 2018. Haines became head following Root's retirement in 2020, and three years later we decided the almost ninety-year-old Stephen Foster Memorial was no longer suitable for storing special collections and

---

[4] A financial report of the Lilly Endowments from 1952 indicates that the Stephen Foster Memorial was granted $25,000 per year. Funding increased over the following decades. A financial statement date June 30, 1980, indicates that Lilly Endowments granted the Stephen Foster Memorial $50,000 over the preceding year. See "Lilly Endowment, Inc.: A Report for 1952," FHC, unprocessed papers; and Financial Statement for the 1979–1980 Fiscal Year, June 30, 1980, FHC, unprocessed papers.

permanently moved the materials to an off-site archival facility, decreasing the collection's easy accessibility but vastly improving the stability of the environment in which it is preserved. I moved on to become head of the Music Library—a different branch of the University of Pittsburgh Library System—in 2024, shortly after the collection's removal.

In the collection's heyday in the Foster Memorial building, the assumption of its authority relied not only on its supposed completeness but also on the widespread agreement that archives were objective resources and, as such, were historians' best available sources. In the foundational book *A Manual for Archive Administration*, first published in 1922, Hilary Jenkinson explicated this view:

> Preserved oral tradition, contemporary narrative, comment and criticism, personal memoirs, official or semi-official compilations—these will no doubt continue to hold a position, often very important, among the sources upon which the ultimate historian draws for his final synthesis of the facts about any given period, movement, crisis, or relation. But it is more than doubtful if any authoritative historical work will ever again be published without copious notes referring to verifiable manuscript sources; and it has become a recognized fact that such a work must be preceded by and dependent on the cumulative effect of a quantity of studies by other hands in which settled opinion upon comparatively small points is based upon the laborious examination and analysis of details in Archives.[5]

Jenkinson reserved the word "archive" for official documents generated by government or administrative offices and asserted that "archives were not drawn up in the interest or for the information of Posterity."[6] The Foster Hall Collection, then, most definitely did not meet Jenkinson's criteria, and Lilly—or perhaps Whittlesey—seems to have been aware of this when naming the materials a "collection." They also aptly named them for *Foster Hall*, a name that suggests it is more informative about Foster Hall's interests and agendas than it is about the composer. Naming it the "Stephen Foster Collection" would have made Lilly's collecting focus more apparent, but it would have obscured his influence and departed from recommended practices for collection management.

---

[5] Hilary Jenkinson, *A Manual of Archive Administration* (Clarendon Press, 1922), 1–2.
[6] Jenkinson, *Manual of Archive Administration*, 11.

Even so, few people took notice that the Foster Hall Collection is a *collection* of Stephen Foster materials and an *archive* of Foster Hall's initiatives, programming, interests, and agendas. In application the collection's name meant very little to most people. Lilly still promoted Foster Hall's mission as objective and exhaustive, asserting that he sought to obtain "as complete data as possible concerning the life and work of Stephen Collins Foster."[7] As the inscription in the stone of the Stephen Foster Memorial indicates, this caught on with the public and researchers. In the end, the self-aware designation "Foster Hall Collection" made little difference, and the collection was generally assumed to be an archive of the composer's life and work that was as impartial as Jenkinson's ideal, amounting to what was perceived as a complete representation of the "facts of Foster's life and music."

For more than half a century, archivists and historians have repeatedly demonstrated that even collections Jenkinson would have labeled "archives" are not objective but are created, arranged, and described in specific, often intentional ways by creators, institutions, archivists, and other interested parties. Archives tell specific narratives and conceal others. Howard Zinn's 1970 provocation that "the most powerful, the richest elements in society have the greatest capacity to find documents, preserve them, and decide what is or is not available to the public" has become common knowledge in archival studies, inspiring investigations into other forms of power that shape archives and the knowledge they help create.[8] Studies reveal that archives have foregrounded the elite and marginalized the less privileged; erased people who were enslaved or oppressed, projecting past violence into the present day; portrayed oppressive governments as strong, competent, and well respected by their subjects; and projected noble motives onto exploitative enterprises.[9]

Despite these interventions into the assumption of archival objectivity, to this day the presumed impartiality of the Foster Hall Collection has largely escaped scrutiny. As recently as 2012, musicologist Mariana Whitmer celebrated the collection as "the most comprehensive documentation of [Foster's] life and music" and credited it with having "helped to clarify our

---

[7] *Foster Hall: A Reminder of the Life and Work of Stephen Collins Foster, 1826–1864* (Josiah Kirby Lilly, 1935).

[8] Howard Zinn, "Secrecy, Archives, and the Public Interest," *MidWestern Archivist* 2, no. 2 (1977): 20.

[9] See Marisa J. Fuentes, *Dispossessed Lives: Enslaved Women, Violence, and the Archive* (University of Pennsylvania Press, 2016); Ann Laura Stoler, *Along the Archival Grain: Epistemic Anxieties and Colonial Common Sense* (Princeton University Press, 2009).

understanding of Foster and amend some of the myths surrounding his life."[10] She positioned Lilly as something of a hero who, because he "knew there was more to be appreciated" about the composer, "devoted vast resources to collecting and preserving Foster's legacy."[11] To be clear, Whitmer is not wrong. Lilly's collection has enriched understandings of Foster immensely. But there is more to the story. His conscious and unconscious personal biases, agendas, and conflicts of interest that shaped what Jacques Derrida refers to as "archontic" practices—the depositing, unifying, identifying, classifying, and describing of an archive—remain mostly unexamined.[12]

In the five years I worked with the Foster Hall Collection before its removal from the Stephen Foster Memorial, I grew increasingly conflicted about the building and its contents. I never stopped being impressed by the artistry of the architecture by Charles Klauder, the interior and exterior stone carvings by Edward Ardilino, the windows with stained-glass medallions depicting scenes from Foster's songs designed by Frances Van Arsdale Skinner of the renowned Charles Connick Studio, the wrought-iron fixtures by Samuel Yellin, and the interior design and furniture by Gustav Ketterer. As I witnessed the temple-like building create a sense of awe and wonder that shaped visitors' perceptions of the composer, I also witnessed Foster's legacy undergo a reckoning outside the memorial's walls. Just prior to my arrival, a Pittsburgh statue of Foster seated above an enslaved man and transcribing a song he performs ("Uncle Ned," as indicated on the page the bronze Foster holds) was deemed "the most racist statue in America" by a blogging provocateur.[13] The city initiated a review of the statue, formed an advisory committee that included Deane L. Root, and established a period of public comment. Some residents derided Foster as a racist, while others defended him as an advocate for racial justice.[14] Ultimately, the committee unanimously recommended the removal of the statue, and the city agreed.

---

[10] Mariana Whitmer, "Josiah Kirby Lilly and the *Foster Hall Collection*," *American Music* 30, no. 3 (Fall 2012): 326.

[11] Whitmer, "Josiah Kirby Lilly," 328.

[12] Jacques Derrida, "Archive Fever: A Freudian Impression," *Diacritics* 25, no. 2 (Summer 1995): 10.

[13] Damon Young, "The Most Racist Statue in America Is in . . . Pittsburgh, and It's the Most Ridiculous Magical Negro You'll Ever See," *The Root*, August 17, 2017, https://www.theroot.com/the-most-racist-statue-in-america-is-in-pittsburgh-1797950305.

[14] Bill O'Driscoll, "Hearing Held on Possible Removal of Pittsburgh's Stephen Foster Statue," *Pittsburgh City Paper*, October 5, 2017, https://www.pghcitypaper.com/Blogh/archives/2017/10/05/hearing-held-on-possible-removal-of-pittsburghs-stephen-foster-statue; Chris Potter, "Consensus at Meeting: Remove Stephen Foster Statue," *Pittsburgh Post-Gazette*, October 4, 2017; Dan Majors, "City's Art Commission Unanimous: Statue of Stephen Foster Needs to Go," *Pittsburgh Post-Gazette*, October 25, 2017.

Then, in 2020, about two years after the statue's removal, activists motivated by the murder of Breonna Taylor, an innocent Black woman from Louisville, Kentucky, protested the annual performance of Foster's "My Old Kentucky Home" at the Kentucky Derby, arguing that the continued performance of the song perpetuated racial inequities.[15] As the dissonance between my experiences with Foster's music inside and outside the memorial grew stronger, I gradually came to think of the building and the Foster Hall Collection not as symbols of Foster and the "facts of his life" but as an archival object itself, an architectural document of how memory keeping at the height of Jim Crow could make a symbol of inclusivity and democracy out of a composer whose fame rested principally upon songs that invoke racist stereotypes in their depictions of enslavement (Figure I.2).

Archival theorist and activist Verne Harris suggests that both "archive and memory are best understood as genres of the trace."[16] Harris thus conceptualizes what Lilly intuitively understood: archival practices and memory are interrelated but not the same. As we will see in detail in this book's "Concluding Essay," Lilly worked closely with the Foster family to deliberately create an archive that told the story about Foster that they wanted to tell, a story that they mostly believed to be true—incorrectly, in some of its details—and that they were aware contained large generalizations and omissions. They constructed their story in response to counternarratives about Foster that had circulated since the composer's lifetime. Recognizing that archival practices alone were not enough to shape collective memory, Lilly also harnessed the power of public scholarship and ritual, sponsoring commemorative activities and funding the creation of a great amount of literature about the composer.

Lilly's approach to portraying Foster is concisely articulated in the biography he commissioned from John Tasker Howard. Contrasting him with his American predecessors in composition "who imitated foreign models," Howard cast Foster as "under the spell of the minstrel shows, the singing of the Negroes who came to Pittsburgh and Cincinnati on the river boats from the South, and of the Negro worshippers in a little church near his childhood home." In other words, Howard described Foster as a White man who

---

[15] Lauren Aratani, "'No Justice, No Derby': Breonna Taylor Demonstrators Protest Kentucky Race," *The Guardian*, September 5, 2020; Eleanor Bingham Miller and Keith L. Runyon, "At Kentucky Derby, Drop 'My Old Kentucky Home' Anthem and Weep for Breonna," *Louisville Courier Journal*, September 2, 2020.

[16] Verne Harris, *Ghosts of Archive: Deconstructive Intersectionality and Praxis* (Routledge, 2021), 10.

**Figure I.2.** The former Reading Room in the Stephen Foster Memorial. Foster Hall Collection, Center for American Music, University of Pittsburgh Library System.

embraced America's multiracialism, embodying openness and tolerance. Such views came to define American democracy, of course, only in the post–Civil War era. Having died more than one year before the end of the conflict, Howard positioned Foster as a progenitor to those ideals, a construction that suited his present-day geopolitical situation. He continued, "His songs are distinctly American, and yet the thoughts they express are so basically human that they are sung throughout the world. Foster achieved a nationalistic expression that is at the same time universal in its appeal."[17] Writing during the ascendancy of Adolf Hitler, Howard defined American nationalism in contradistinction to jingoistic nationalism in Germany, linking tolerance of the world's peoples (universalism) to American patriotism through the figure

---

[17] John Tasker Howard, *Stephen Foster, America's Troubadour*, Apollo ed. (Thomas Y. Crowell, 1964), 2–3.

of Foster in a construction I refer to as the "national-universal myth."[18] This construction inserts Foster into a common schema of mythology by offering a definition of the national character while centering him in a story about a formative moment in its development, ultimately positioning Foster as the first American composer. Howard and Foster Hall put to service the beauty of some of Foster's melodies and his brief dominance of the antebellum US commercial sheet music market to support the myth of the composer as America's first "troubadour" and a symbol of the nation's inclusivity.

Drawing on his vast resources, Lilly distributed literature espousing this myth to librarians, scholars, radio broadcasters, educators, the US military, and politicians; and he began supporting and participating in annual commemorations of the composer in Pittsburgh every January 13, the anniversary of Foster's death. Lilly elevated the myth to a level close to a national "collective memory." But, as historian Guy Beiner argues, "the construction of a completely collective memory is at best an aspiration of politicians, which is never entirely fulfilled and is always subject to contestations." Beiner argues for a historiographical model that acknowledges "the intricate and fluid dynamics of social remembrance, which constitute a multi-layered battleground of power struggles that undermine the possibility of uniformity implied by the adjective 'collective.'"[19] This model maps perfectly onto memory of Foster, which has always been contested. Even at the myth's peak, Lilly is best thought of as one voice—albeit a loud one—within a polyphony of remembering.

This book shows that Lilly propagated the Foster myth but did not invent it. It was present, though certainly not ubiquitous, more or less immediately following the composer's death. Over several generations it gradually became more accepted through a process that rested upon the longstanding and popular assumption that the meaning of a composer's life and their works are intertwined. This "predisposition to hear music as a form of

---

[18] The view that Americans defended the ideals of tolerance, democracy, and universalism in the face of German nationalism was common in the United States during the Second World War, particularly in the arts. See Annegret Fauser, *Sounds of War: Music in the United States during World War II* (Oxford University Press, 2013); Christopher Lynch, "Die Zauberflöte at the Metropolitan Opera House in 1941: The Mozart Revival, Broadway, and Exile," *Musical Quarterly* 100, no. 1 (Spring 2017): 33–84; and Christopher Lynch, "The Metropolitan Opera House and the 'War of Ideologies': The Politics of Opera Publicity in Wartime," in *Music in World War II: Coping with Wartime in Europe and the United States*, ed. Pamela M. Potter, Christina L. Baade, and Roberta Montemorra Marvin (Indiana University Press, 2020), 111–30.

[19] Guy Beiner, "Troubles with Remembering; or, the Seven Sins of Memory Studies," *Dublin Review of Books*, November 2017, accessed September 1, 2023, https://drb.ie/articles/troubles-with-remembering-or-the-seven-sins-of-memory-studies/.

autobiography," as musicologist Mark Evan Bonds describes it, grew so dominant within European and American musicologists' constructions of composer biographies that Bonds has given it a name, the "Beethoven Syndrome,"[20] owing to the centrality of Beethoven life-writing to the syndrome's development. Biographies portrayed Beethoven as a deaf composer whose genius was fully realized when his infirmity empowered him to compose music about heroes overcoming adversity. As K. M. Knittel writes, this Beethoven narrative

> reduces him to a cipher: within the myth, Beethoven is not a human being, but rather a symbol of a larger aesthetic doctrine or concern. The myth ignores anything—biographical facts, musical works, real suffering—that cannot reify the happy ending. Thus, it includes only a few biographical details ... and instead emphasizes primarily anecdotes ... that cannot be shown to be true, but which nevertheless seem to illustrate something "real". Musically, the myth restricts Beethoven's oeuvre to a mere handful of pieces that are valued for their ability to illustrate his strength ... ignoring those pieces that are too "happy" or that do not foreground conflict. This limited collection of pieces, facts and anecdotes is then overlaid with a Romantic plot of struggle and transcendence, suggesting not just a reading of Beethoven's life, but a reason and a way to value his works as well.[21]

Beethoven's life and works, according to the narrative, can only be understood in tandem.

Many nineteenth- and early twentieth-century biographies of canonical composers in the European tradition were constructed along these lines to anachronistically thrust nationalistic ideologies onto their subjects. In the period in which Germany became a modern nation state, Beethoven retrospectively became an expression of German nationalism, a symbol of the perceived advancement and superiority of the German nation.[22] When Russia dominated Poland, Chopin's music in Polish dance styles was recontextualized to portray him as a Polish nationalist.[23] And in the age of

---

[20] Mark Evan Bonds, *The Beethoven Syndrome: Hearing Music as Autobiography* (Oxford University Press, 2020), 1.
[21] K. M. Knittel, "The Construction of Beethoven." In *The Cambridge History of Nineteenth-Century Music*, ed. Jim Samson (Cambridge University Press, 2001), 120.
[22] Knittel, "Construction of Beethoven," 147.
[23] See Jim Samson, "Myth and Reality: A Biographical Introduction," in *The Cambridge Companion to Chopin*, ed. Jim Samson (Cambridge University Press, 1992), 1–8; and Jolanta

emancipation, Jim Crow, and US imperialism, Stephen C. Foster was retroactively portrayed as sympathetic to all who lived within the nation's borders, a trait that purportedly enabled him to compose songs that were representative of the American "crucible" and democratic ideals in their universally human themes. These myths rely on very few anecdotes and ignore all but a small subset of works. In Foster's case, the subset consisted of the songs that remained in public consciousness at the time of the myth's origins, and the myth's circular logic discouraged looking beyond Foster and those songs for more complete ways of understanding them: we "know" Foster was sympathetic because of the songs, and we "know" those songs are sympathetic because of his character. Whereas historians have debunked many myths about European composers, the stubbornly persistent reduction of Foster continues to do great injustice to our understandings of the complexities of the songwriter and his times today.

As my addition to the history of Foster's contested memory, this book comes down hard on Foster Hall's methods and agendas. Setting out to counter Foster Hall's narrative of the composer, I have refused to write another biography. Music historian Jolanta T. Pekacz notes that "musical biography typically develops in a way similar to a realistic novel: a coherent, unified voice claiming to present the truth about a life; omniscient narration, repeating themes and symbols; and a linear, chronological presentation of events provide readers with the illusion of totality and closure."[24] All of these elements of musical biography enabled Foster Hall's propagation of the national-universal myth. In contrast to their writings about Foster, I do not create a totalizing, chronological narrative of Foster's life but rather compile and contextualize all the remembrances of Foster that I have managed to find—including several that do not reside in the Foster Hall Collection and have been unknown to biographers—foregrounding new anecdotes, biographical details, and pieces of music and enabling a deeper, more humanizing understanding of the composer. Laying out the reminiscences side by side allows episodes from Foster's life to be revisited from different perspectives, shedding light on his multifaceted personality and legacy. It is

---

T. Pekacz, "Deconstructing a 'National Composer': Chopin and Polish Exiles in Paris, 1831–1849," *19th-Century Music* 24, no. 2 (2000): 161–72.

[24] Jolanta T. Pekacz, "Memory, History and Meaning: Musical Biography and Its Discontents," *Journal of Musicological Research* 23, no. 1 (2004): 42.

likely that more remembrances will come to light as more nineteenth- and early twentieth-century literature is digitized and made discoverable, but unlike Lilly, I have aimed for completeness rather than selectivity.

I also reject the omniscient voice that Foster Hall adopted in its literature. For the last revised edition of his Foster biography in 1953, Howard updated the section on memorials, combining an objective tone with the passive voice in a manner that obfuscates the actors behind memorialization. He writes, for example, that "a work by [Arturo] Ivone was presented to the city [of Cincinnati] in 1937"[25] instead of *Lilly commissioned a statue and presented it to the city of Cincinnati*. Elsewhere he informs readers that "a major national tribute was paid Foster in 1940" by the "hundred and eight electors of the Hall of Fame at New York University" when they selected him to become "the seventy-third American to join the gallery."[26] He should have written *Foster Hall and I orchestrated a campaign to have Foster elected to the Hall of Fame*. His rhetoric always creates the false impression that Foster's elevation to the position of "father of American music" resulted from people of all stripes and colors from across the United States expressing their admiration for the composer's songs. Of course, many people rallied around Foster in the 1930s and 1940s, but Howard hides the detractors and conceals the role of Lilly's machinations and pocketbook. I have a hard time reading his passively voiced words without thinking that he and Lilly feared that public knowledge of their influence would diminish the illusion of Foster's universal popularity.

In contrast to Foster Hall's tone, I foreground my own subjectivity. Of course, like Foster Hall, when constructing my arguments I make choices about what evidence to cite, and I propose some grand claims. But I confine my commentary to my introductions, footnotes, and concluding essay, separating it from the remembrances, which I present uncensored and in full, to offer my voice not as an omniscient narrator but as just one among many in this chronicle of the crooked trajectories of Foster memories over the last 160 years. I write my commentary from a certain point of view, strongly influenced by the questions about the history and persistence of racism in the United States that have informed much of our civic dialog in recent years, as well as my front-row seat to the

---

[25] Howard, *Stephen Foster*, 362.
[26] Howard, *Stephen Foster*, 367.

recent transformations of the Stephen Foster Memorial and Foster Hall Collection. But whereas Lilly and Howard hid their subjectivity, I show my work. I can do this, in part, because the evolution of the Stephen Foster Memorial over the last three decades has removed any institutional pressure to preserve Lilly's vision for the building. Unshackled from the influence of Lilly's money in the mid-1990s, the curators of the Foster Hall Collection began expanding the focus and activities of the archive. And as the building aged and standards for archival care rose, there was no compelling reason for keeping the Foster Hall Collection as Lilly had envisioned it. In 2023, the decision to remove the collection for preservation purposes felt like the logical next step in the building's evolution. And now, as a former curator of the collection in the Foster Memorial building, I feel like it makes sense to write honest commentary about my perspectives on Foster and memory.

The history of the building from 1937 to 2023 provides a lesson in the great power over knowledge creation held by archives, institutions, time, and individuals (from gatekeeping family members to billionaire enthusiasts, curators, biographers, provocateurs, protesters, building managers, and librarians). For almost ninety years, the easy access of the Foster Hall Collection in the Stephen Foster Memorial, located in the center of the university campus in one of the busiest sectors of Pennsylvania, helped preserve Foster at the center of narratives about US cultural history. On the one hand, the collection's removal will hasten processes already underway that are expanding our understandings of nineteenth-century American music history, which traditionally have been Foster-centric. Musicologist Lars Helgert, who has done much to excavate information about Foster's musical contemporary Herrman S. Saroni from its burial place underneath the immense literature on the more famous composer, laments the "great deal of valuable American music from the middle of the nineteenth century [that] has never been explored by historians." He rightly complains that despite (or, I would add, because of) the "fair amount of scholarship on some of the period's major figures . . . large gaps remain in our understanding of the musicians and the music."[27] Making it less easy to study Foster by removing the Foster Hall Collection from the memorial will undoubtedly encourage

---

[27] Lars Helgert, "Herrman S. Saroni: Paths to Success as a Composer in New York, 1844–52," *American Music* 40, no. 2 (Summer 2022): 141.

researchers to develop more inclusive histories of the nation's musical heritage, not erasing Foster or diminishing the brilliance and beauty of his music but weaving him into a richer historical tapestry that includes less famous figures such as Saroni and other neglected musicians. On the other hand, the process of removing the collection unearthed hundreds of documents that the original curators never processed—caches of files and loose papers that had never been considered archival materials, as well as documents that the original curators appear to have wanted to conceal. These materials, many of which are examined in this book for the first time, greatly enrich our understanding of Foster himself.

This book therefore straddles two impulses that may initially appear to be at odds: my aim is to elucidate the artificiality of the national-universal myth, but the act of writing a book about the canonical figure of Foster also further entrenches him in the collective psyche. Rather than contradicting each other, these impulses work together, ultimately undermining the national-universal myth that helps keep Foster centered in our understandings of music history while also demonstrating with more nuance and specificity the less grandiose but still significant ways in which Foster is an important figure in the nation's history. With the 200th anniversary of the composer's birth on July 4, 2026, which coincides with the 250th anniversary of the signing of the Declaration of Independence, this is an appropriate moment to pause and reflect on what we know and say about Foster and his legacy.

This book lays out how competing narratives about Foster gradually gave way to the national-universal myth, which was enshrined in the Foster Hall Collection. To understand the myth's relationship to the collection and other extant evidence of Foster's life and career, and to prepare for tracing the myth's emergence through the contested memories in this book, it is useful first to establish a baseline of what is known—or, I should say, what *I* have come to believe we can safely say we know—about Foster's relationship to his craft. By closely examining not just the basic facts of his life but also what he would have understood about the uses and functions of his music, I argue that his life cannot be reduced to a simple cipher for interpreting his songs. Breaking up the life–music circularity upon which most biographies rely allows for a more nuanced reading of what his art meant to him and the people in his world and begins to illuminate how it has meant so many different things to so many listeners, including his companions who wrote the reminiscences in this volume.

## Stephen C. Foster: Life and Works, Revisited

In the early 1850s, a young White woman named Lizzie Ogden, daughter of a prominent Pittsburgh pharmacist, carefully bundled the sheet music she had spent years collecting and brought it to a shop to be bound into a single book that would display her name on the cover and "Music" on the spine.[28] Binding music into a prized possession for home use was common among young, middle-class women in the United States. The wear and tear on Lizzie's volume's pages, cover, and spine suggest it did not merely sit on her piano as a display of her taste and accomplishments but was an object from which she performed frequently.

Since the daughters of the Ogden family were friends with the sons of the Foster family,[29] it is not surprising that Lizzie's bound volume carefully preserves five songs composed by Stephen C. Foster, who was almost exactly her age and—despite his Scots-Irish, Presbyterian heritage—attended the Episcopal church with her in Pittsburgh. He courted and married Jane McDowell in 1850, but earlier he may have flirtatiously given Lizzie some of his songs. It is tempting to think that he composed the waltz song "Turn Not Away," which contains the line "Turn not away/From the fond heart thou hast slighted," after Lizzie rejected him. Perhaps he gave her the song, which she bound in her volume, as a symbol of their continuing friendship following romantic rejection.

Lizzie also bound Foster's 1849 sentimental minstrel ballad "Nelly Was a Lady," an early hit for the young songwriter. Lizzie's pride in knowing the composer was probably deepened by her knowledge that Foster had written the song for people like her. With its moderate tempo and 4/4 meter, the song possesses an openness and expansiveness that enables strong emotional expression in performance, similar but no more difficult—easier, in some ways—than the operatic arias by Donizetti, Bellini, and Balfe that Lizzie also bound. She could probably play the piano part easily, and she likely found the vocal melody, falling within a relatively narrow range, manageable as

---

[28] Lizzie Ogden, vol. 52, bound volume of sheet music, Collection of Bound Volumes, Center for American Music, University of Pittsburgh Library System.

[29] The Ogden family is mentioned in a letter from Henry Baldwin Foster to Morrison Foster, March 16, 1846, FHC, C488. Evelyn Foster Morneweck mentions the Ogden daughters as "familiar friends." See Evelyn Foster Morneweck, *Chronicles of Stephen Foster's Family*, vol. 1 (University of Pittsburgh Press, 1944), 317. Morrison's second wife, Rebecca Snowden (Evelyn Foster Morneweck's mother), was Lizzie Ogden's cousin.

well. With a little work, she could impress visitors to her home by playing and singing this song well.

Although the song's technical demands are not great, we would be wrong to consider it a simple song, for it contains a universe of emotional expression. Like many of Foster's songs that would come to endear him to performers and listeners, it is sung from the perspective of an imagined enslaved man. The man's wife has died, and the song veers between intense sorrow and nostalgic reflection. The man works on the Mississippi River, toting cottonwood; but his thoughts never stray from his beloved. The opening words, "Down on de Mississippi," hop down and back up before stalling on the phrase's high note on the first syllable of the word "floating"—a natural stretching of the rhythm that captures the singer's aching for release from his inner pain. In later verses, the singer remembers his wife's smile as "like de light ob day a dawning" and recalls walking with her "in de meadow mong de clober." Now, he laments, she is buried "close by de margin ob de water,/Whar de lone weeping willow grows."

With one exception, Lizzie bound sentimental, patriotic, and religious songs featuring White, Black, or racially unspecific singing personas, often in the lyrical waltz or ballad styles of "Turn Not Away" and "Nelly Was a Lady." In contrast, the one exception in her volume—Foster's "Oh! Susanna"—is a bouncy comic minstrel song with snappy rhythms in the style of a polka. Foster wrote it less for the middle-class parlor, where young women like Lizzie entertained guests while adhering to strict codes of etiquette, than for his boyhood friends, with whom he blackened his face and performed minstrel songs in an amateur minstrel troupe. Although he has frequently been mischaracterized as the inventor of minstrelsy, he was far from it. He and his friends merely imitated professional blackface performers such as Thomas Rice, Nelson Kneass, Joseph Murphy, and others who toured the towns along the Ohio and Mississippi Rivers, performing acts that featured dehumanizing, often raucously bawdy caricatures of Blackness. The existing social and musical codes and conventions of the worlds of the parlor and the minstrel stage—and Foster's ability to write songs that straddled both worlds—were the primary forces shaping most of his music.

But "Oh! Susanna" did not really straddle both worlds. It highlights what Saidiya V. Hartman characterizes as the "terror and enjoyment" of minstrelsy.[30] In the first verse, the buffoonish and unintelligent blackface

---

[30] For Hartman's discussion of "terror and enjoyment" in minstrelsy, see *Scenes of Subjection: Terror, Slavery, and Self-Making in Nineteenth-Century America* (Oxford University Press, 1997), 25–32.

character can hardly string together two thoughts that do not contradict each other:

> It rain'd all night de day I left,
> De wedder it was dry;
> The sun so hot I froze to def,
> Susanna, dont you cry.

The second verse pokes fun at the difficulties of keeping pace with the mid-nineteenth century's new technologies: the telegraph, the steamboat, and the railroad.

> I jump'd aboard the telegraph
> And trabbled down de ribber,
> De lecktrick fluid magnified,
> And kill'd five hundred Nigga.
> De bulgine bust and de hoss ran off,
> I really thought I'd die;
> I shut my eyes to hold my bref
> Susanna dont you cry.

The character's confusion is conveyed through his incorrect belief that telegraphs use electricity and magnetism and that electricity is a fluid. He confuses an actual telegraph with a steamboat named *The Telegraph* and mistakenly states that the steamboat ran on a bull engine (i.e., the "bulgine"), which was an engine for a locomotive. Moreover, since bull engines generated their horsepower by burning coal, there would not have been actual horses to run off when *The Telegraph*'s engine malfunctioned. The non sequiturs and oxymorons, combined with the bouncy joviality of the music, portray the Black singing persona as carefree and happy regardless of the horrors to which he is subjected. Such infantilizing depictions played into White notions of Black people as emotionally simple and thus needing the paternalistic social structures of enslavement or Northern Jim Crow laws. The portrayal of Black people as impervious to physical harm could even justify the violence to which they were often subjected. The casual flippancy toward Black lives in the second verse of "Oh! Susanna" thus simultaneously entertained and enforced the White supremacist social order.

Many people of Lizzie's social status considered "Oh! Susanna" unsuitable for the rarefied atmosphere of the middle-class parlor, where behaviors and rituals were regulated by the rules laid out in etiquette manuals of the day.[31] The majority of surviving bound volumes like Lizzie's contain no minstrel songs, suggesting that many people considered the genre inappropriate for the parlor; and when minstrel songs do appear, they tend to be sentimental—as in "Nelly Was a Lady"—as opposed to comic songs like "Oh! Susanna."[32] For many years publishers struggled to inject minstrel songs into the genteel parlor. Blackface music failed to break into the parlor world in the 1830s, so throughout the 1840s publishers printed lithographic renderings of White minstrel performers dressed as gentlemen on sheet-music covers, softened minstrel lyrics, and increasingly published sentimental minstrel songs like "Nelly Was a Lady" that treated their subject matter more seriously.[33] These songs often still suggested racist messages but were more palatable to middle-class White consumers because they excised "offensive words" like the N-word and abandoned questionable attitudes such as flippancy toward death. "Oh! Susanna" was an immensely popular song in minstrel shows, around campfires, and on the frontier; but it is not common in bound volumes, suggesting that its content, language, and tone were broadly seen as inappropriate for the parlor. Lizzie probably included the song in her bound volume because she knew the composer. Perhaps for her and her family, this overrode its characteristics that were at odds with popular notions of gentility.

---

[31] A foundational text for parlor culture is Katherine C. Grier, *Culture and Comfort: Parlor Making and Middle Class Ideology, 1850–1930* (Smithsonian Institution Press, 1988). For general studies of etiquette as it relates to parlor music, see Candace Bailey, "Binder's Volumes as Musical Commonplace Books: The Transmission of Cultural Codes in the Antebellum South," *Journal of the Society for American Music* 10, no. 4 (2016): 446–69; Julia Eklund Koza, "Music and the Feminine Sphere: Images of Women as Musicians in *Godey's Lady's Book*, 1830–1877," *Musical Quarterly* 75, no. 2 (Summer 1991): 103–29; and Judith Tick, "Passed Away is the Piano Girl: Changes in American Musical Life, 1870–1900," in *Women Making Music: The Western Art Tradition (1150–1950)*, ed. Jane M. Bowers and Judith Tick (University of Illinois Press, 1986).

[32] See Petra Meyer Frazier, "American Women's Roles in Domestic Music Making as Revealed in Parlor Song Collections: 1820–1870," PhD diss., University of Colorado, 1999; Karen Stafford, "Binders' Volumes and the Culture of Music Collectorship in the United States, 1830–1870," PhD diss., Indiana University, 2020; Candace Bailey, *Unbinding Gentility: Women Making Music in the Nineteenth-Century South* (University of Illinois Press, 2021), 3; and Mark Slobin et al., eds. *Emily's Songbook: Music in 1850s Albany* (A-R Editions, 2011), 7–13. Bailey has begun to trace regional and evolving attitudes toward minstrelsy in binders' volumes. For example, she notes that after the Civil War the volumes of Southern women more often include minstrel songs in dialect. Candace Bailey, "Opera, Lieder, or Stephen Foster? Popular Song in the Antebellum US South," in *Popular Song in the 19th Century*, ed. Derek B. Scott (Brepols, 2022), 37–59.

[33] Stephanie Dunson, "The Minstrel in the Parlor: Nineteenth-Century Sheet Music and the Domestication of Blackface Minstrelsy," PhD diss., University of Massachusetts Amherst, 30–35. See also, Dunson, "The Minstrel in the Parlor: Nineteenth-Century Sheet Music and the Domestication of Blackface Minstrelsy," *ATQ* 16, no. 4 (December 2002): 241–56.

Foster was certainly familiar with the middle-class parlor and its practices, but when he wrote "Nelly Was a Lady" and "Oh! Susanna" he could not have imagined that he could make a living selling sheet music to young women such as Lizzie. Many of the reminiscences in the following pages portray a music industry that was maturing during Foster's youth and primed for his emergence in young adulthood as the nation's first songwriter to find success across multiple years. During his childhood, the Foster family played instruments, purchased sheet music, and studied with local music teachers, activities that were not as common even one generation prior. Piano ownership was rare in middle-class homes in Foster's boyhood, only gradually becoming more common after Jonas Chickering began manufacturing high-quality square pianos in Boston in 1838. Other piano makers quickly emulated Chickering. According to Richard Crawford, "By 1851, some 9,000 pianos per year were being made in the United States; Chickering, the leading firm, produced 10 percent of that total."[34]

At the same time, copyright laws—which had been recently amended in 1831—protected US composers for the first time. The law protected *written* and *published* melodies, a European-derived conception of music that greatly benefited White composers of the Euro-American tradition over musicians who practiced oral traditions, including those derived from Africa. The system, forged in the context of enslavement and Northern Jim Crow, favored White composers who notated approximations or mockeries of oral traditions, as found in the minstrel tradition and early transcriptions of spirituals. As Matthew D. Morrison writes, "Because performance was not deemed copyrightable in the foundational property laws that emerged in the eighteenth and nineteenth centuries, early black aesthetics—often transmitted through orality or corporeality—were left out of the realm of protection both in copyright and contract law."[35] Thus it was at mid-century—precisely when Foster decided to make a career of churning out songs for voice and piano—that the music industry was ready for a White

---

[34] Crawford, *America's Musical Life: A History* (Norton, 2001), 235. See also Cynthia Adams Hoover and Edwin M. Good, "Piano," Grove Music Online, Oxford Music Online, January 31, 2014, accessed November 24, 2021, https://doi.org/10.1093/gmo/9781561592630.article.A2257895; and Dale Yi-Cheng Tsang-Hall, "The Chickering Piano Company in the Nineteenth Century," doctor of musical arts thesis, Rice University, 2001, 7.

[35] Matthew D. Morrison, "Blacksound," in *The Oxford Handbook of Western Music and Philosophy*, ed. Tomás McAuley et al. (Oxford University Press, 2020), 558. For an overview of how Foster's career and legacy were shaped by copyright law, see Jason Lee Guthrie, "America's First Unprofessional Songwriter: Stephen Foster and the Ritual Economy of Copyright in Early American Popular Music," *Journal of the Music & Entertainment Industry Educators Association* 19, no. 1 (2019): 37–72.

composer to earn a living composing music for pianists and singers in White, middle-class parlors.

In 1849, after some of Foster's songs surprised the composer by earning great sums for their publisher, he signed contracts with two music publishers that ensured him royalties and committed himself to songwriting. Encouraged by the publishing firm Firth, Pond & Co. "to compose only such pieces as are likely both in the sentiment & melody to take the public taste,"[36] and soon needing to sell as much music as possible to support his young family—he married Jane in 1850 and welcomed a daughter, Marion, the next year—Foster turned away from dehumanizing songs like "Oh! Susanna" and embraced sentimental minstrel songs in the mold of "Nelly Was a Lady," which were better suited for straddling the worlds of the parlor and the minstrel stage.

It is not difficult to imagine the range of meanings "Nelly Was a Lady" had in its day. Playing and singing the song for amorous young gentlemen in her parlor, Lizzie probably tapped into the song's pathos, showing off both her skills of musical expression and her emotional maturity. She and her listeners may have taken the lyrics literally as a song of sadness following the loss of a loved one. Or perhaps, with smoke from Pittsburgh's early coal-burning mills wafting through the air, they heard the song's nature descriptions and similes—Nelly's smile like the light of day, her burial near the water's bank under the willow—as metaphorically linking the woman's death to a perceived vanishing natural world amid the Industrial Revolution. Such songs about modernization had, after all, swept across the United States in the popular Irish ballads of Thomas Moore and his imitators since the 1810s.[37] In one way of looking at Foster's songs, Foster Americanized the sentiments expressed in Moore's music by including people who were enslaved as emblems of what was lost in modernity.

Perhaps when Lizzie sang "Nelly Was a Lady" she smoothed out the dialect—which all antebellum Americans understood as indicating the song was sung from the perspective of a Black character—to minimize or negate the race of the character.[38] Or perhaps she highlighted race and leaned into

---

[36] Firth, Pond & Co. to Stephen Foster, September 12, 1849, FHC, C916.

[37] For the influence of Moore's songs on Foster, see Charles Hamm, *Yesterdays: Popular Song in America* (Norton, 1979), 205–206 and 214–19.

[38] Evelyn Foster Morneweck observed markings in a bound volume that indicated the dialect in Foster's "The Glendy Burk" was eliminated in the parlor. She writes, "Stephen's song is a spirited, rollicking steamboat ballad that has become a river classic. It is written in simple negro dialect, but inoffensive as it was, this dialect was considered quite too vulgar to be sung by a certain genteel young lady of the [18]60s whose bound volume of music I recently inspected. Her fastidious singing teacher in the young ladies' seminary at which he taught, had crossed out all the 'de's' and 'wid's' and 'dah's'

both the pathos and the dialect. Because abolitionists and supporters of racial equality often embraced humanizing portrayals of enslaved people, some people would have heard a performance like this as making a racially progressive statement. Under the headline "Who Write the Negro Songs?," White activist Linnaeus P. Noble wrote in his abolitionist newspaper *National Era* in 1857 that "the principal writer of our national music is said to be Stephen C. Foster."[39] Perhaps, then, as talk of abolition, disunion, and Civil War began to dominate national conversations, Lizzie and her guests understood "Nelly Was a Lady" as an expression of support for racial equality, humanizing and dignifying the female subject by placing her on the same level as Lizzie, an aspiring young *lady*, and in turn creating a new "national" song that laid out a new, progressive conception of citizenship and the nation.

But those with White supremacist or pro-slavery sensibilities often interpreted sympathetic portrayals of enslaved people as exhibiting a childlike demeanor that necessitated their subjection. Musicologist Candace Bailey has shown that "white gentility did not allow for the possibility of Black gentlewomen," even though "many Black women learned to read music as part of the cultural performance of parlor music—that is, singing and playing notated music as dictated in etiquette manuals, definitive guides to gentility, written for whites."[40] Perhaps, if Lizzie and her White guests were like most of their White American peers in believing that the White race sat atop the racial hierarchy, they would have let out a few chuckles at what they perceived as the silliness of the Black character in the song singing with the pathos and sentiment about his "wife," a Black "lady." Indeed, to many White Americans, Black people attaining gentility was literally a joke. In this sense, "Nelly Was a Lady" demonstrates one of the ways Hartman identified in which "the recognition of humanity and individuality acted to tether, bind, and oppress."[41] When the song was interpreted as demonstrating the unattainability of gentility for Blacks and thus justifying White paternalism, Foster's toned-down

---

and substituted the proper 'the's' and 'with's' and 'there's' which the elegance of the young pupil's social position demanded—her father was a senator" (*Chronicles*, vol. 2, pp. 520–21). For more on crude minstrel songs in the parlor, see Bailey, *Unbinding Gentility*; Katherine K. Preston, "Music in the McKissick Parlor," in *Emily's Songbook: Music in 1850s Albany*, ed. Mark Slobin, James Kimball, Katherine K. Preston, and Deane Root (A-R Editions, 2011), 17; Frazier, "American Women's Roles," 193–94; and Tick, "Passes Away," 93.

[39] L. P. Noble, "Who Write the Negro Song?," *National Era*, April 9, 1957.
[40] Candace Bailey, "Music and Black Gentility in the Antebellum and Civil War South," *Journal of the American Musicological Society* 74, no. 3 (Fall 2021): 601.
[41] Hartman, *Scenes of Subjection*, 5.

and sentimentalized language brought White supremacy into the parlor. As Jabari Asim writes, "Racist language once frowned on by men who aspired to be gentlemen acquired a cloak of respectability."[42]

Scholars interpreting the political messages of the song through rose-colored glasses have claimed that "Nelly" dignifies its title character by referring to her as a lady.[43] Musicologist Deane L. Root comments that he is unaware "of an earlier song ... in which a black woman is called a lady—a term that was usually reserved for well-born whites at the time" and suggests that Foster embarked on a "mission" to popularize a liberal, racially inclusive vision of the United States. Citing a letter he wrote to the world-famous minstrel performer Edwin P. Christy in which he asked him to perform one of his minstrel songs "in a pathetic, not a comic style,"[44] Root contends that Foster wanted songs like "Nelly Was a Lady" to dignify, not demean.

But by 1849 the "black lady" was an established minstrel stereotype that mocked "uppity" Black women. Foster, having performed in amateur minstrel shows and cavorted with minstrels since his youth, certainly knew the caricature well. The type appeared, for example, in the early minstrel song "Come Back Stephen," which was probably written by Daniel Decatur Emmett and appeared in an 1844 songster. The title character is depicted as a mischievous liar, and the chorus implores women not to believe him: "Sing, oh, lord *ladies* you mustn't mind Stephen,/For Stephen such a liar, dat de debil can't believe him" (emphasis added). A later verse has little to do with the liar Stephen but presents an opportunity for men to dress in drag and mock Black women with middle-class aspirations: "De ladies walk Broadway, All in dar curls an' ruffles,/But when dar comes a stormy day, Why den dey get de snuffles."[45]

At mid-century, the Black lady type frequently appeared in minstrel parodies of popular operas, which Renee Norris describes as "a comic debasement of opera's situations and characters via a blackface context ... to depict

---

[42] Jabari Asim, *The N Word: Who Can Say It, Who Shouldn't, and Why* (Houghton Mifflin, 2007), 82.

[43] Matthew Shaftel, "Singing a New Song: Stephen Foster and the New American Minstrelsy," *Music & Politics* 1, no. 2 (Summer 2007): 16; Dale Cockrell, "Nineteenth-Century Popular Music," in *The Cambridge History of American Music*, ed. David Nicholls (Cambridge University Press, 1998), 173; Deane L. Root, "Music and Community in the Civil War Era," in *Bugle Resounding: Music and Musicians of the Civil War Era*, ed. Mark A. Snell and Bruce C. Kelley (University of Missouri Press, 2004), 42.

[44] "The Mythtory of Stephen C. Foster or Why His True Story Remains Untold," *American Music Research Center Journal* 1 (1991): 31. Stephen C. Foster to Edwin P. Christy, June 20, 1851, FHC, C997.

[45] See Renee Norris, *Opera Parody Songs of Blackface Minstrels* (A-R Editions, forthcoming).

Blacks as unattractive, incompetent, poor, and uneducated in contrast with the elevated and aspirational characters in opera."[46] Christy, to whom Foster once wrote to express his desire "to unite with you in every effort to encourage a taste for this style of music so cried down by opera mongers,"[47] did much to popularize the type by having his troupe perform arias for operatic sopranos in falsetto and drag. A playbill for Christy's Minstrels from around 1850, for example, indicates that the falsettist Maximilian Zorer sang the aria "Casta Diva" from Vincenzo Bellini's opera *Norma*.[48] Revealing how adeptly Foster united with Christy's approach to minstrelsy, "Nelly Was a Lady" also appears on the playbill (Figure I.3). The verses, sung from the perspective of Nelly's husband, were probably sung in the low range Foster indicated. But Foster indicated that the whole troupe should join in for the chorus, and he wrote it in four-part harmony for soprano, alto, tenor, and bass. The upper parts were probably sung in falsetto by Zorer and the troupe's other famous falsettist, George Christy.

Zorer and George Christy not only sang "Nelly" in falsetto but also wore blackface and dressed in drag, perhaps mocking Nelly in their movements. It would not have required much hamming up to elicit laughter, which Foster must have known when he asked Christy to perform his sentimental minstrel songs "in a pathetic, not a comic style." The sight and sound of a man in Christy's troupe performing in falsetto, drag, and blackface while acting with a straight face—as depicted on Foster's own sheet music covers (Figure I.4)— would have been hilarious to many in the audience. Indeed, many people in White audiences were so conditioned at laughing at caricatures of straight-faced, pathos-expressing Black people as "uppity" that they initially laughed at the serious performances of Black operatic soprano Elizabeth Taylor Greenfield in the 1850s.[49]

My point is not that "Nelly Was a Lady" was a song that mocked Black women. My point is that it was a song that mocked Black women at the same time that it was the opposite and neither.[50] Foster wrote "Nelly Was a Lady"

---

[46] Norris, *Opera Parody Songs*, 138.
[47] Stephen Foster to Edwin P. Christy, February 23, 1850, FHC, C917. For more on how opera was harnessed to appeal to "opera mongers," see Renee Lapp Norris, "Opera and the Mainstreaming of Blackface Minstrelsy," *Journal of the Society for American Music* 1, no. 3 (August 2007): 341–65.
[48] Norris, *Opera Parody Songs*.
[49] Julia J. Chybowski, "Blackface Minstrelsy and the Reception of Elizabeth Taylor Greenfield," *Journal of the Society for American Music* 15, no. 3 (August 2021): 306–10.
[50] My conception of the political mutability of minstrelsy is indebted to a long lineage of previous scholarship. See Eric Lott, *Love & Theft: Blackface Minstrelsy & the American Working Class*, 20th anniversary ed. (Oxford University Press, 2013); W. T. Lhamon Jr., "Turning around Jim Crow," in *Burnt Cork: Traditions and Legacies of Blackface Minstrelsy*, ed. Stephen Johnson

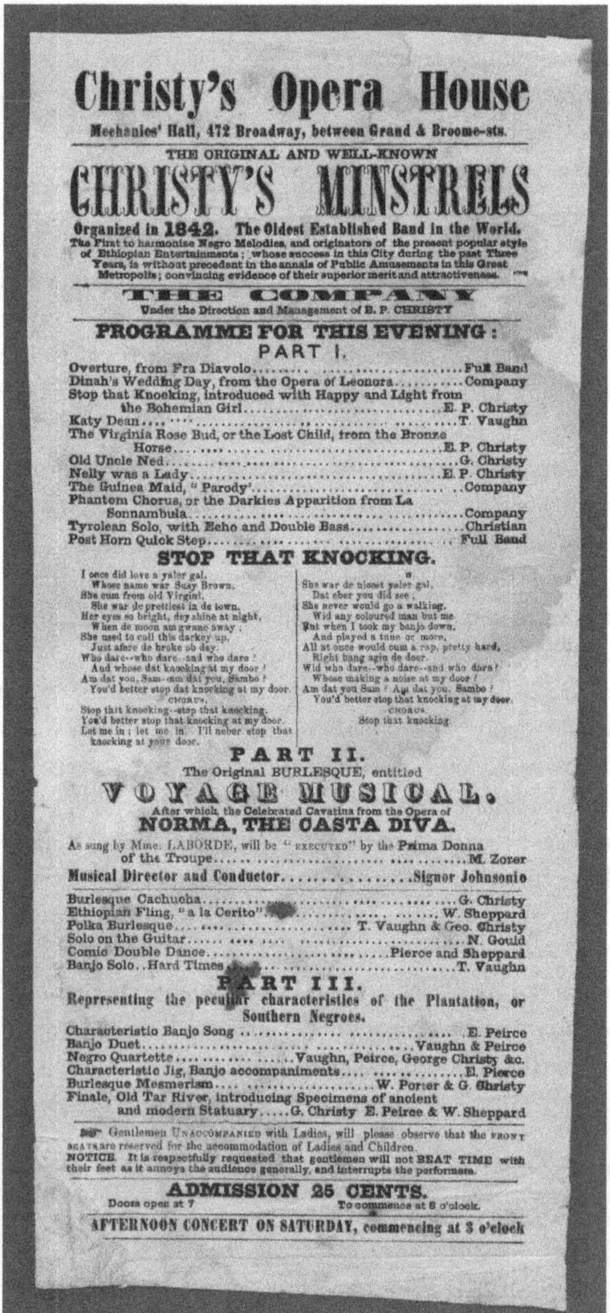

**Figure I.3.** Playbill for Christy's Minstrels. MS Thr 1848, Harvard Theatre Collection, Houghton Library, Harvard University.

**Figure I.4.** Cover of an early edition of "Oh! Susanna." Foster Hall Collection, Center for American Music, University of Pittsburgh Library System.

to straddle the worlds of the parlor and the minstrel stage and transcend political divisions over racial policies by keeping his lyrics tame and "respectable" by White, middle-class standards and leaning into sentimentality while hinting at the Black lady stereotypes present on the all-male, predominantly working-class blackface minstrel stage. To make it suitable to different performance contexts and maximize his profits, Foster wrote "Nelly Was a Lady" to mean whatever a potential performer or consumer wanted it to mean.

Although he would eventually come to realize that ambiguous songs like "Nelly Was a Lady" were very popular, early in his professional songwriting career he worried that even these sentimental minstrel songs would damage his reputation among middle-class consumers. In 1851, for $15 he sold minstrel performer Edwin P. Christy the right to premiere his song "Old Folks at Home" and list himself as author and composer on the sheet music. The minstrel ballad portrays a freed man wandering "sadly" and "longing for de old plantation" as he recollects about family and friends from his days when he was enslaved. Like "Nelly Was a Lady," it possesses a moderate tempo, 4/4 meter, and relatively wide melodic range, all of which give it a more expansive breadth of emotional expression than "Oh! Susanna." The melody is not strictly pentatonic but includes pentatonic sequences that nostalgically hearken back to the old Irish ballad style of Thomas Moore, invoking Anglo-American folksong and underscoring the song's theme of longing for days past.[51] For example, the opening phrase ("Way down upon de Swanee Ribber/ Far, far away") is purely pentatonic and contains a characteristically Fosterian upward leap of an octave between the syllables "Swa-" and "-nee," creating a sort of emotive wail that expresses the man's sadness. But, as historian Sarah Meer wonders, is his longing to return to family and friends a reflection of a normal, natural old-age nostalgia for youth? Is it an anti-slavery depiction of family separation? Or is it a pro-slavery expression of longing to return to enslavement itself?[52] Foster refused to pin down its meaning.

Still finding his way on the sheet music market, Foster allowed Christy's name to appear on the printed music. But when the song became a smash hit, he attempted to renege on their arrangement. He wrote to Christy,

---

(University of Massachusetts Press, 2012), 18–50; and Christopher J. Smith, *The Creolization of American Culture: William Sidney Mount and the Roots of Blackface Minstrelsy* (University of Illinois Press, 2013).

[51] Steven Saunders and Deane L. Root, *The Music of Stephen C. Foster: A Critical Edition* (Smithsonian Institution Press, 1990), xxxv–xxxvi.
[52] Sarah Meer, *Uncle Tom Mania: Slavery, Minstrelsy & Transatlantic Culture in the 1850s* (University of Georgia Press, 2005), 57.

As I once intimated to you, I had the intention of omitting my name on my Ethiopian songs, owing to the prejudice against them by some, which might injure my reputation as a writer of another style of music [parlor songs], but I find that by my efforts I have done a great deal to build up a taste for the Ethiopian songs among refined people, by making the words suitable to their taste, instead of the trashy and really offensive words which belong to some songs of that order. Therefore I have concluded to reinstate my name on my songs and to pursue the Ethiopian business without fear or shame, at the same time that I will wish to establish my name as the best Ethiopian song-writer. But I am not encouraged in undertaking this so long as "The Old Folks at Home" stare me in the face with another's name on it.[53]

As musicologist Steven Saunders observes, Foster's letter suggests that at issue for the composer was "his reputation, his sense of self as a composer, and his desire to project the proper image in the marketplace."[54] When he was afraid racialized songs would tarnish his reputation, he allowed Christy's name to appear on the sheet music instead of his own. But by the time Foster asked for his name to be reinstated, consumers had purchased thousands of copies of "Old Folks." Christy rejected his request, but Foster had learned a valuable lesson: sentimental minstrel songs did not offend the sensibilities of his middle-class target consumers; in fact, they were exceptionally lucrative.

Foster realized that by eliminating "trashy and really offensive words" and focusing on politically ambiguous sentimentality while retaining—perhaps more subtly—some of the racism of minstrelsy, he had stumbled upon a golden songwriting formula that allowed him to write songs for minstrel performers that would not tarnish his reputation "among refined people" and would continue to sell to sheet music buyers who would perform the music in their parlors.[55] When he wrote to Christy, he was already replicating several features of "Nelly Was a Lady" and "Old Folks" in other songs. "Massa's in de Cold Ground" similarly depicts an imagined enslaved man pouring out his heart at the loss of a loved one, but in this case, the loved one is his enslaver. The song has "respectable" lyrics, but to what end? Does it humanize the enslaved man in a gesture toward abolition, citizenship, and

---

[53] Stephen Foster to Edwin P. Christy, May 25, 1852, FHC, C869d.
[54] Steven Saunders, "The Social Agenda of Stephen Foster's Plantation Melodies," *American Music* 30, no. 3 (Fall 2012): 280.
[55] Although Foster's publishers exaggerated the number of copies of "Old Folks at Home" that they sold, Foster's royalties enumerated in his account book demonstrate that he sold hundreds of thousands of copies overall.

equality? Or does it portray a "happy slave" who benefits from the "benevolent" institution of enslavement?

"My Old Kentucky Home" is sung from the perspective of an enslaved man forcibly removed from his enslaved family in Kentucky to work in the Deep South, and the song discards "Black" dialect completely. The man longs to return to his family in Kentucky, but because he does not explicitly long for his freedom, the song could be understood as expressing the man's desire to return to enslavement in Kentucky. Does it make an anti-slavery statement by tapping into one of the atrocities of enslavement commonly cited by abolitionists—the cruelty of family separation? Or would this man be happy to be enslaved in Kentucky? Like "Nelly Was A Lady," "Old Folks at Home," and "Massa's in de Cold Ground," the meaning of the song resides in the minds and hearts of the performers and listeners.

By 1852, then, Foster had learned that the language of sentimentality, to borrow the words of historian Rebecca Bedell on the composer's contemporaries in the visual arts, was "a politically malleable rhetoric" that "is inherently neither progressive nor conservative."[56] He wrote sentimental songs that his abolitionist friend Charles Shiras would admire and that would also be cherished by his brother Henry, who worked in the Treasury Department under slavery-aligned Democratic presidents and once longed to marry into a family of enslavers on Maryland's eastern shore. He wrote "Old Folks at Home" so that it could be performed by the anti-slavery activist-singers the Hutchinson Family, which it was, but also so that it would be loved by his sister Henrietta, who sided with the South in the Civil War, and his sister Ann Eliza, who married the brother of the Democratic, pro-slavery president James Buchanan. He must have known that "Old Folks at Home," "My Old Kentucky Home," "Massa's in de Cold Ground," and some of his other sentimental minstrel songs were being inserted into stage adaptations of the abolitionist novel *Uncle Tom's Cabin*.[57] He also must have known that some of these adaptations conveyed anti-slavery messages while

---

[56] Rebecca Bedell, *Moved to Tears: Rethinking the Art of the Sentimental in the United States* (Princeton University Press, 2018), 44.

[57] For *Uncle Tom* shows, see Meer, *Uncle Tom Mania*; John L. Brooke, *There Is a North": Fugitive Slaves, Political Crisis, and Cultural Transformation in the Coming of the Civil War* (University of Massachusetts Press, 2019); John W. Frick, *Uncle Tom's Cabin on the American Stage and Screen* (Palgrave Macmillan, 2012); Joseph P. Roppolo, "Uncle Tom in New Orleans: Three Lost Plays," *New England Quarterly* 27, no. 2 (June 1954); Thomas Riis, ed., *Uncle Tom's Cabin (1852) by George L. Aiken and George C. Howard* (Garland, 1994); Riis, "The Music and Musicians in Nineteenth-Century Productions of *Uncle Tom's Cabin*," *American Music* 4, no. 3 (Autumn 1986): 268–86; and Lott, *Love & Theft*, 218–41.

others perverted the novel to convey pro-slavery sentiments. This must have been how he wanted it. He wrote his sentimental minstrel songs to appeal to—that is, to sell to—this broad spectrum of politically affiliated people within his personal circle and beyond.

He also wrote them to satisfy his publishers' desire to sell his songs to a diverse *national* audience, that is, to consumers in both the North and South. In 1849, he signed his first publishing contracts with the New York firm Firth, Pond & Co. and F. D. Benteen, based south of the Mason–Dixon Line in Baltimore, Maryland. Although Bailey has shown that the reach of his music was limited in the Deep South, dealers' newspaper advertisements and seller information stamped on early editions reveal that the music of both publishers circulated across the nation's sections, primarily in the North and Upper South (Figure I.5).[58]

It was not unusual for artists and publishers to try to cast a wide net by avoiding stances on divisive issues, particularly enslavement and racial equality. As Maurie D. McInnis points out, due to the business ties between cotton plantations and New York's bankers, insurers, and merchants, commercial art dealers in New York refused to carry art that expressed abolitionist sentiments, such as John Rogers's 1859 sculpture *The Slave Auction*, which depicted the horrors of enslavement in a scene of family separation on the auction block, a common abolitionist image (Figure I.6). Rogers had success selling the cast to abolitionists, and it was praised in abolitionist publications; but this still proved a disappointment to the artist. He wrote, "By taking a subject on which there is divided opinion, of course, I lose half my customers." McInnis concludes, "Rogers learned that in America, a topic as politically controversial as slavery, and especially slave auctions, did not sell well. His experience explains why so few American artists touched the subject before the war."[59]

Even after the war began, publishers of newspapers were reluctant about displaying a sectional bias. As historian Joshua Brown observes,

> With a combined circulation of more than four hundred thousand nationwide, the three New York–based papers eagerly dispatched artist-correspondents to accompany federal troops and report on the war, but

---

[58] Bailey, "Opera, Lieder, or Stephen Foster?," 37–59.
[59] Maurie D. McInnis, *Slaves Waiting for Sale: Abolitionist Art and the American Slave Trade* (University of Chicago Press, 2011), Kindle, chap. 5.

**Figure I.5.** Signed carte de visite featuring a portrait of a young Stephen Foster, perhaps from early in his songwriting career. Foster Hall Collection, Center for American Music, University of Pittsburgh Library System.

**Figure I.6.** A stereograph of John Rogers's *The Slave Auction* (1859), published by H. Wood, Jr., 639 Broadway, NY, 1868. Library of Congress.

they also harbored lingering illusions about maintaining a southern readership (or rapidly reengaging it at the end of what was projected initially to be a short war). *Harper's Weekly, Frank Leslie's Illustrated Newspaper*, and the *New York Illustrated News* refrained from presenting news pictures that might be construed as critical of slavery.[60]

It was not until the embargo of trade and mail with the South, which was enforced beginning in the summer of 1861, that publishers, dealers, and artists began to demonstrate more confidence presenting a sectional bias in the conflict.

The political ambiguity of Foster's songs allowed them to have some appeal across racial lines. It is often pointed out that Frederick Douglass, one of the leading Black abolitionists and racial justice activists of the antebellum period, who grew up on and escaped from a plantation adjacent to one owned by Foster's cousins in Maryland, saw Foster's songs as useful to his cause. In an 1855 address to the Rochester Ladies Anti-Slavery Society, he said that Foster's songs "awaken the sympathies for the slave, in which antislavery principles take root, grow, and flourish."[61] Not surprisingly,

---

[60] Joshua Brown, "Re-visions of war," in Eric Foner and Joshua Brown, *Forever Free: The Story of Emancipation and Reconstruction*, with illustrations edited and commentary by Joshua Brown (Vintage Books, 2006).

[61] Frederick Douglass, "The Anti-Slavery Movement, Lecture Delivered before the Rochester Ladies' Anti-Slavery Society, March 19, 1955," in *Frederick Douglass: Selected Speeches and Writings*,

though, other Black contemporaries of Foster responded more negatively to his songs. Joshua McCarter Simpson, an Ohioan and former indentured servant—a form of unpaid labor in the North, often indistinguishable from enslavement for Black people at the time—became an ardent abolitionist in the 1850s. His "To the White People of America," which he indicates should be sung to the tune of Foster's "Massa's in de Cold Ground," denounces White hypocrisy: "See the white man sway his sceptre,/In one hand he holds the rod—/In the other hand the Scripture,/And says that he's a man of God." Unlike in Foster's version, Simpson's White man is no "massa" to weep about when he dies. In "Away to Canada," to the tune of "Oh! Susanna," Simpson rejects White sympathy toward the people whom they enslave: "O! old master,/While you pray for me,/I'm doing all I can to reach/The land of Liberty."

Simpson *intentionally* rejected Foster's lyrics. In the preface to his songster *Original Anti-Slavery Songs*, he writes that he used the tunes of minstrel songs to "kill the degrading influence of these comic Negro Songs . . . and change the flow of these sweet melodies into more appropriate and useful channels."[62] Simpson heard Foster's minstrel lyrics as degrading attempts at humor, and therefore as unsuitable to abolitionism. He harnessed their tunes to undermine their original messages through biting irony.

Simpson's verses were admired by Foster's fellow Pittsburgher Martin Delany, a Black nationalist who in the 1830s had apprenticed with Foster's future wife's father, the medical doctor Andrew McDowell. Delany included three of Simpson's revisions of Foster's songs in his 1859 novel *Blake; or the Huts of America*. The novel's title character escapes enslavement and travels the South in search of his family, learning the stories of other enslaved people he encounters and recruiting many of them to join him along the way. Blake meets a character who sings Simpson's version of "Old Folks at Home," which maintains the sentiments of Foster's original but clarifies its meaning.

> Way down upon the Mobile river,
> Close to Mobile bay;
> There's where my thoughts is running ever,

---

ed. Philip S. Foner (Lawrence Hill Book, 2000), 329; and Douglass, "The Anti-Slavery Movement," in *My Bondage and My Freedom* (Miller, Orton & Mulligan, 1855), 462.

[62] Joshua McCarter Simpson, *Original Anti-Slavery Songs* (J. McC. Simpson, 1852).

> All through the livelong day:
> There I've a good and fond old mother,
> Though she is a slave;
> There I've a sister and a brother,
> Lying in their peaceful graves.
> O, could I somehow a'nother,
> Drive these tears way;
> When I think about my poor old mother,
> Down upon the Mobile bay.[63]

Unlike Foster's song, Simpson's is not open to interpretation. Because this enslaved man does not sing that he is "still longing for de old plantation," it is not possible to interpret his words as suggesting that he longs to return to enslavement. He pines only for his loved ones.

One of the men Blake rouses to action sings Simpson's version of Foster's sentimental minstrel song "Uncle Ned." Foster's version depicts a group of enslaved people lamenting the death of "old Uncle Ned," whom the lyrics portray as a "good" slave because he enjoyed working hard for his master and is now in heaven. The song exhibits classic Fosterian ambiguity, portraying Ned in a humanizing, dignifying manner *and* as the "happy slave" stereotype, opening it up to pro-slavery, anti-slavery, and neutral interpretations. Simpson's lyrics, on the other hand, no longer describe a "good slave" but portray enslavers as evil and deserving of death:

> Old master's dead and lying in his grave;
> And our blood will now cease to flow;
> He will no more tramp on the neck of the slave,
> For he's gone where slaveholders go!
> Hang up the shovel and the hoe—o—o—o!
> I don't care whether I work or no!
> Old master's gone to the slaveholders rest—
> He's gone where they all ought to go![64]

---

[63] Martin Delany, *Blake; or, the Huts of America*, corrected ed., ed. Jerome McGann (Harvard University Press, 2017), 101–102.

[64] Delany, *Blake*, 106.

Blake ultimately leads a group of people to freedom in Canada. As they escape, a member of the group breaks into Simpson's rewritten version of "Oh! Susanna" and is joined by his fellow fugitives.[65]

I find it perplexing that William W. Austin interprets Delany's repudiation of Foster's lyrics as "a remarkable tribute" to Foster that shows that "Delany's attitude . . . is as favorable toward Foster's songs as any of the American attitudes."[66] I am equally perplexed that Foster scholars would imagine that the composer's father-in-law Andrew McDowell wrote a letter of recommendation for Delany to attend Harvard to study medicine—not only is there no evidence but McDowell had died by the time Delany went to Cambridge, Massachusetts—and that they would draw on the real and imagined aspects of the relationship between Delany and McDowell to link Foster to Delany's racially progressive views.[67] What the actual evidence seems to suggest is that Foster's ambiguous language that nods toward White supremacy was unacceptable to Delany, who "corrected" the songs by using Simpson's obvious and direct anti-racist lyrics. The technique of writing new words to songs—contrafact technique—was common the United States since the colonial era, often employed to communicate political messages.[68] Christopher Smith refers to the technique as "a portable, adaptable, and resilient political tool" in which a melody "acquires layer upon layer of communicative associations when each new set of words is inscribed . . . upon the recollected connotations of the tune's prior usages."[69] Given the ubiquity of this technique in the mid-nineteenth century, Delany likely expected at least some of the people who encountered the new texts in his novel to notice the differences between the versions and appreciate the ways in which the contrafact texts subverted the meaning of the original lyrics. This was, in fact, precisely what Simpson described when he wrote about killing the degrading influence of minstrelsy.

And, as it turns out, Frederick Douglass's complete statement to the Rochester Ladies Anti-Slavery Society about Foster's songs is more nuanced than historians and musicologists have recognized. He qualified his words

---

[65] Delany, *Blake*, 144–45.

[66] William W. Austin, *"Susanna," "Jeanie," and "The Old Folks at Home": The Songs of Stephen C. Foster from His Time to Ours*, 2nd ed. (University of Illinois Press, 1989), 70.

[67] Root, "Mythtory," 28; Shaftel, "Singing a New Song," 17; and JoAnne O'Connell, *The Life and Songs of Stephen Foster* (Rowman & Littlefield, 2016), 124–25.

[68] See Glenda Goodman, "Transatlantic Contrafacta, Musical Formats, and the Creation of Political Culture in Revolutionary America," *Journal of the Society for American Music* 11, no. 4 (November 2017): 392–419.

[69] Christopher J. Smith, "We Have Fed You All 1000 Years: Nineteenth-Century Radical Song and the Rise of North American Labor," *American Nineteenth Century History* 24, no. 3 (2023): 258.

of praise, saying "it would seem almost absurd to say it, considering the use that has been made of them, that we have allies in the Ethiopian songs," in order to acknowledge the horribly racist uses of the songs *as well as* their potential to "awaken the sympathies for the slave, in which antislavery principles take root, grow, and flourish."[70] In other words, Douglass knew that some of Foster's songs could encourage White listeners to sympathize with the slave and bring them into the abolition movement, but he also knew that the very same songs could be put to opposing uses in degrading minstrel shows and other performances that denigrated Black people. In another article, Douglass called White minstrels "the filthy scum of white society, who have stolen from us a complexion denied to them by nature, in which to make money, and pander to the corrupt taste of their white fellow citizens."[71] He understood that the ambiguity of Foster's songs allowed them to be put to competing uses to either dignify or degrade people of African descent.

Although Douglass's nuanced words suggest that Foster's songs may have appealed to some Black consumers, a note that appeared in 1853 in the *Musical World and New York Musical Times* confirms that Foster and his publishers thought of his consumers as White. The *Musical World* was edited by the White Richard Storrs Willis, an associate of Firth, Pond & Co. Willis informed his readers that he had told Foster in a meeting in his office that "much of his music is now excellent, but being wedded to negro idioms it is, of course, discarded by many who would otherwise gladly welcome it to their pianos." In other words, Willis harbored the same fears about minstrel songs as unsellable for parlor use that Foster had only recently overcome. Willis assured his readers that "we were glad to learn from Mr. F. that he intends to devote himself principally hereafter to the production of 'white men's' music."[72] As Saunders notes, "Foster ultimately followed exactly the path outlined in the *Musical World* . . . largely turning away from minstrel song" for the remainder of the 1850s.[73]

Many biographers and scholars have relied on Foster's shift away from explicitly racialized songs to construct a narrative about the composer embracing a more racially tolerant attitude as he matured in adulthood.

---

[70] Douglass, "Anti-Slavery Movement," in *Frederick Douglass*, 329; and Douglass, "Anti-Slavery Movement," in *My Bondage and My Freedom*, 462.
[71] Frederick Douglass, "The Hutchinson Family," *North Star*, October 27, 1848.
[72] Richard Storrs Willis, ed., "Pittsburgh," *Musical World and New York Musical Times* 5, no. 5 (January 29, 1853): 75.
[73] Saunders, "Social Agenda," 283.

This is wishful thinking. Christy retired in 1854, but the broadening of minstrel audiences to include middle-class White women and children—"refined people," as Foster had put it—was taken up by other troupe leaders, including Samuel Sanford, a leader of one of the first minstrel troupes in the mid-1840s. Throughout the 1850s and 1860s, when Sanford's Philadelphia-based troupe came to Foster's Pittsburgh, newspapers advertised to women and promoted special matinee performances as appropriate for families. One performance included a giveaway of "$50 worth of jewelry,"[74] and the local clothier Van Gorder tried to capitalize on local women's interest in Sanford's troupe by taking out an ad that encouraged "ladies visiting Sanford's Opera Troupe" to "call at Van Gorder's and buy a Rigolette, Head Dress" and other accessories.[75] Sanford won over genteel Pittsburghers who were once skeptical of minstrelsy. In 1862, a reviewer in the *Pittsburgh Post* admitted that the paper was "slow to recognize the true merit" of Sanford's troupe, but, because "nothing that will offend the ear of modesty or chastity is permitted on the boards," the *Post* took the opportunity to "commend them [the troupe] to the public."[76]

After 1853, Foster's new, completely "race-less" songs figured into these performances, in which Sanford's troupe added racial specificity to them by performing in blackface. In his remembrance reproduced in this volume, Sanford claimed his troupe introduced several of Foster's songs in the composer's hometown, including "Hard Times Come Again No More," which was published in early 1855. "Hard Times" is not typically thought of as a minstrel song today; but, in addition to Sanford's comment, playbills and sheet music covers indicate minstrels frequently performed it in blackface, and the remembrances of Robert Peebles Nevin and Foster's own brother Morrison characterize it as a minstrel song.[77] Its 4/4 meter, moderate tempo, flowing and expressive melody, and sentimentality expressed in the lyrics were certainly commensurate with his earlier sentimental minstrel ballads, simultaneously allowing minstrels to perform the song as a Black caricature

---

[74] Advertisement for the "Farewell nights of the New Orleans Opera Troupe" at the Athenaeum on Liberty Street, *Pittsburgh Post*, January 7, 1853.
[75] Advertisement, *Pittsburgh Gazette*, January 5, 1855.
[76] "Sanford's Troupe," *Pittsburgh Daily Post*, July 2, 1862.
[77] The covers of London sheet music editions state the song was "sung by Christy's minstrels." Foster wrote other songs without explicit references to race that were published with sheet music covers that indicated they were performed by minstrels, including "Old Dog Tray" ("Sung by Christy's Minstrels") and "Ellen Bayne" ("Sung by Edwin P. Christy").

and enabling White genteel consumers to imagine in their parlors that the song was about people like them.

The opening line invites listeners to think of the plight of those who are less fortunate: "Let us pause in life's pleasures and count its many tears/ While we all sup sorrow with the poor." The "poor" is a vague term that, if enacted in blackface, could refer to enslaved people or free Black people, or, if not performed in blackface, could be understood to refer to the White working class. It could also, of course, be understood as referring to all poor people, regardless of race. The chorus is a plea but not to an enslaver or capitalist oppressor. It is a plea to unspecified "Hard Times" themselves:

> 'Tis the song, the sigh of the weary;
> Hard Times, Hard Times, come again no more;
> Many days you have lingered around my cabin door;
> Oh! Hard Times, come again no more.

Foster had written of "hard times," which come "knocking at the door," in one other song—the sentimental minstrel song "My Old Kentucky Home." Some "Hard Times Come Again No More" listeners in Foster's day—especially at minstrel shows—probably therefore pictured enslaved people in Kentucky and the Deep South. But other listeners would have thought of Charles Dickens's novel *Hard Times*. Published serially between April and August of 1854—just a few months before the publication of Foster's song—the novel critiques many aspects of life in a socially striated industrial English city. "Hard Times" thus invoked race and did not invoke race. It both was and was not a minstrel song. The song still exhibited Foster's penchant for ambiguity but in a new form. At this stage, he embraced total racial ambiguity, allowing his songs to be performed in differently racialized contexts and even further broadening his White target audience. He did not embrace a more progressive racial view that he came to see as at odds with the genre of minstrelsy. He disguised his minstrel songs but never stopped writing them.

In spite of all this, I must advise caution. We would be wise to avoid creating a new myth by reducing Foster to a one-dimensional writer of ambiguous commercial songs. As demonstrated in his pre-professional comic songs such as "Oh! Susanna," his embrace of political ambiguity in his sentimental minstrel songs in the early 1850s, and his shift away from racialized songs to unracialized parlor ballads in 1853, he was much more than this. Overall, he was *adaptable*, receptive to market trends, business pressures, and the needs and tastes of different audiences and consumers. He was willing to shift his song style in different contexts and over time.

We see another dimension of Foster as a songwriter in the noncommercial songs he wrote throughout the 1850s for political rallies in Pittsburgh that came down decisively on the anti-abolitionist, Democratic side. In 1856 he and his brother Morrison cofounded a glee club that the songwriter directed in public performances in support of his sister's brother-in-law James Buchanan's presidential campaign. In his unpublished songs in support of Buchanan, Foster was openly partisan. In "The White House Chair," for example, his lyrics proclaim,

> Let all our hearts for union be,
> For the North and South are one;
> They've worked together manfully,
> And together they will work on.

In contrast to his politically ambiguous commercial songs, with these words Foster tethered himself to the Democratic Party's alliance with the Southern planter class and the doctrine of states' rights, that is, the right of Southern states to continue the practice of enslavement. In response to a Republican parade in Pittsburgh, Foster and his brother Morrison cowrote verses for a song called "The Abolition Show," which were sung to the tune of "Villikins and His Dinah." The brothers' verses mocked Republicans and abolitionists—including some of their friends—as young, simple-minded, weak, and shallow "babies" with no respect for the Constitution. Abolition, the song posited, would violate states' rights and lead to the dissolution of the Union. In all, on a local level and at a safe distance from the national market, Foster had no problem embracing partisanship and overt racism.

His unrivaled ability in his sentimental songs to straddle the worlds of the parlor and the minstrel stage, feminine and masculine, middle class and working class, North and South, White supremacy and equality, Black and White, and Republican and Democrat enabled him to sell hundreds of thousands of copies of sheet music. But his fortunes began to change in the second half of the 1850s. Struggling with alcoholism and probably depression, he put out few new songs between 1856 and 1860. Regaining some momentum in 1859 and 1860, he again tried to adapt. In 1860, he moved his family to New York, presumably to be in a bigger music market and closer to publishers and performers. It seems he was willing to compose anything that would sell. He returned to the sentimental minstrel song with "Old Black Joe" and to comic minstrelsy in such songs as "Don't Bet Your Money on de Shanghai." He dabbled for the first time in nonracialized comic songs, such as "If You've Only Got a Moustache." He entered into an extensive collaborative relationship for the first time in his career with lyricist and friend George Cooper.

The Civil War's disruption of sheet music distribution and political norms caused Foster to shift his songwriting approach once again. Some of his songs circulated in the Confederacy in pirated editions after Southern markets were cut off by Lincoln's trade embargo with the South.[78] But Foster no longer received royalties from Southern sales, which meant that he now wrote only for Union consumers, so he began writing songs that were vociferously supportive of the Union and antagonistic toward secessionists, setting, for example, the recruitment poem "We Are Coming Father Abraam." But he probably did not leave the Democratic Party and never supported abolition. As Emerson notes, his lyrics "do not oppose slavery; in fact, they never mention it."[79] In their focus on the Union, his songs could appeal to pro-Union conservatives as well as Republicans and abolitionists.[80] Some of his war songs continued to be ambiguous. In "For the Dear Old Flag I Die," for example, he never mentions which flag is being fought for. In "That's What's the Matter" he proclaimed with music more martial than anything he had ever written that "the rebels have to scatter" and "we'll make them flee by land and sea." The first edition of the sheet music, however, indicates the song was regularly performed by minstrel Dan Bryant (Figure I.7), and newspaper ads demonstrate Bryant sang the song in dialect as "Dat's What's de Matter."[81] This suggests the song's lyrics were understood in some contexts

---

[78] Morneweck, *Chronicles*, vol. 2, 541.

[79] Ken Emerson, *Doo-Dah!: Stephen Foster and the Rise of American Popular Culture* (Simon & Schuster, 1997), 277.

[80] By appealing to the widespread desire to preserve the Union, Abraham Lincoln built an interparty coalition of supporters for the war effort. See Eric Foner, *The Fiery Trial: Abraham Lincoln and American Slavery* (Norton, 2010), 166–205; Adam I. P. Smith, *No Party Now: Politics in the Civil War North* (Oxford University Press, 2006); and Mark E. Neely, *Lincoln and the Democrats* (Cambridge University Press, 2018). Candace Bailey has documented a case of music being gifted across political lines by friends who bonded over their shared pro-Unionism. Bailey, "'Remember Those Beautiful Songs': Preserving Antebellum Cultural Practices through Music Collection during the Civil War," *American Music* 38, no. 3 (Fall 2020): 281.

[81] Ad for Dan Bryant's Minstrels, *New York Daily Herald*, October 8, 1863.

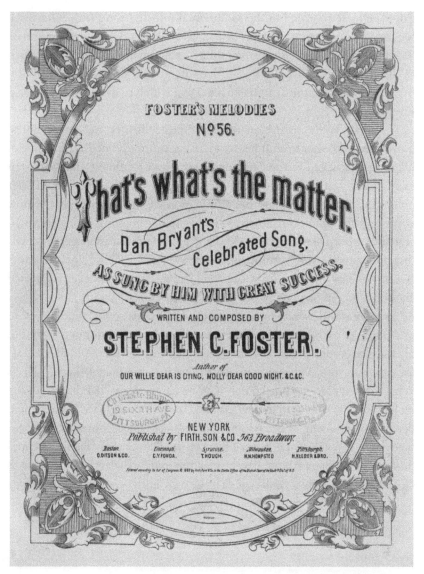

**Figure I.7.** The cover of "That's What's the Matter." Foster Hall Collection, Center for American Music, University of Pittsburgh Library System.

as genuine and in others as ironic. In other words, it seems Foster continued to try to have it all ways in his songs.

Although Foster's own lyrics never mention enslavement, he did set Cooper's minstrel text "A Soldier in de Colored Brigade," which explicitly states a pro-slavery opinion:

> Some say dey lub de darkey and dey want him to be free,
> I s'pec dey only fooling and dey better let him be.
> For him dey'd brake dis Union which de're forefadders hab made,
> Worth more dan twenty millions ob de Colored Brigade.

Cooper's lyrics seem to express a view that Foster appears to have always held, that preserving the Union was more important than liberating people who were enslaved. But it also seems that as the market shifted and Foster's old ambiguous approach to songwriting faltered, and as he grew increasingly desperate for income and spiraled in an alcoholic decline, he became willing to publish an explicitly political song of a kind he had once taken great pains to avoid.

Foster's struggles ran so deep that either he could not support his family or his family grew unwilling to put up with him. His wife Jane and daughter Marion, about 10 years old, moved back to Pennsylvania, where Jane eventually worked as a telegrapher. He remained in New York and struggled. He drank. We can see his physical decline in photographs from this period (Figures I.8 and I.9). On January 11, 1864, he wounded his neck in his hotel room, in what was probably an illness-induced fall but that some people have claimed was suicide. When he died three days later in the hospital, his wallet contained only thirty-eight cents, the only money to his name. For the three decades following his death, his widow Jane's receipts from his sheet music royalties reveal negligible sales.[82] Only a handful of his sentimental minstrel songs remained in public consciousness. "Old Folks at Home," "Massa's in de Cold Ground," "My Old Kentucky Home," and "Old Black Joe" persisted in *Uncle Tom* shows and the repertoires of opera divas and Black ensembles such as the Fisk Jubilee Singers. Eventually, these songs would form the foundation of how the composer would be remembered. As Austin notes, "There can be no doubt that all four of Foster's most characteristic 'plantation songs' owe much of their fame to *Uncle Tom*."[83] But for decades, he was mostly forgotten.

Overall, Foster was never one kind of songwriter, and his biography is not easily reduced to a cipher for interpreting his songs. When we look at the totality of his career, we see a composer who wrote sentimental songs

---

[82] These records are found in FHC, Series I, Subseries 5, Post-Mortem Royalty Statements & Correspondence, 1864–1900. For an analysis, see Howard, *Stephen Foster*, 353–57.

[83] Austin, *"Susanna," "Jeanie," and "The Old Folks at Home,"* 235.

**Figure I.8.** Portrait of Stephen Foster, tintype, 1850s. Foster Hall Collection, Center for American Music, University of Pittsburgh Library System.

and comic songs; a composer of racist, race-neutral, and racially progressive songs; a politically active and politically neutral Foster; a sectional and nonsectional Foster; a composer whose notion of the Union changed. He was adaptable over time and across different contexts. Through his most successful songs in the early 1850s—the sentimental minstrel songs—he crafted an image somewhat like a musical statesman, standing above partisanship, sectionalism, and, to a degree, racial divisions. Based on these songs, anyone—regardless of their views—could believe he sympathized with their situation and outlook. But this image—perpetuated long after his death by the national-universal myth—was a mirage. Foster was complicated. He had strong, conservative personal opinions that evolved over time. Until the last chapter of his life, he was careful about where he expressed those opinions. Musically, he was always willing to experiment. He went where the commercial winds pushed him. His music and lyrics evolved.

**Figure I.9.** Portrait of Stephen Foster, tintype, 1860s. Foster Hall Collection, Center for American Music, University of Pittsburgh Library System.

## The Oral Histories

The chronological arrangement of all the oral histories of Foster, including reminiscences previously unknown to biographers, greatly enhances our understanding of the composer. They introduce new anecdotes, enable the authentication of a new Foster song ("Hurrah for Buchanan, of the Keystone State," see Appendix A), and illuminate his personality. As a whole, the reminiscences paint a rich, though still incomplete, portrait. His memorialists consistently portray him as shorter than average, not unattractive, and social yet introverted and deeply sensitive. John Mahon describes Foster as modest, maybe even shy, usually not wanting to reveal to strangers that he was the writer of songs they undoubtedly knew. Multiple friends recall him as emotional, tearing up when greeted with kindnesses, performing sentimental music, or remembering loved ones. According to numerous accounts, he was "moody" or "melancholy," and an anonymous friend suggests that he could be "melancholy, then again cheerful and vivacious." He may have lived with depression or bipolar disorder.

Taken together, the reminiscences also provide a relatively complete outline of Foster's life. They sketch important events in his childhood, including his birthday in Lawrenceville on July 4, 1826; and they document the family's move across the Allegheny River to the town (soon thereafter city) of Allegheny, his visits with relatives in eastern Ohio, his schooling, and his first compositional experiences for school performances and amateur entertainments among friends in parlors and minstrel shows. They provide an overview of his early professional life, starting with his move to Cincinnati in 1846 to work for his brother Dunning McNair Foster, and documenting the surprise success of "Oh! Susanna," which led to publishing contracts in 1849 and inspired his return to the Pittsburgh area in 1850. Many of the reminiscences mention his marriage to Jane in 1850 and the birth of their daughter, Marion, in 1851, but they provide few details of his family life. They do, however, document his prodigious compositional output in this period, as well as his struggles with addiction, mental health, and poverty beginning in the latter half of the 1850s. His family and friends from Pittsburgh appear to have known little of his life in New York, where he moved in 1860. But his friends Birdseye, Mahon, Kit Clarke, and Cooper fill in many of the blanks about his social life, career, struggles, and, ultimately, tragic death in 1864.

The oral histories also contain intriguing points of disagreement. Some of the early reflections describe Foster in the terms in which he would become mythologized. He was described (probably by his brother Morrison writing anonymously) as a national figure right after his death, and in 1867 Robert Nevin introduced the notion that he taught White people how to sympathize with people who were enslaved, thus playing a role in the nation's racial progress. We see this idea becoming more widely embraced beginning in the 1890s, notably in qualified terms in Morrison's reminiscence. But all along there were always alternative interpretations. P. F. Kane's description of Foster's minstrel shows reveals that the composer was conscious of the stereotypes he invoked in songs featuring caricatures of African Americans as buffoonish, foolishly aspirational, and happy slaves. And the accounts of Clarke, Sam Sanford, and others reveal that Foster remained closely linked to the genre of minstrelsy throughout his career, even as songs such as "Hard Times Come Again No More" became less overtly rooted in the conventions of the genre. By dwelling on his drinking, poor working habits, and tragic end, Birdseye, Mahon, and Cooper portray him far less heroically than the myth. Cooper, in written comments to biographer Harold Vincent Milligan, outright stated that Foster opposed the heroic fight for emancipation, saying that "he scorned to see the disruption of the ties that held the negroes to their masters & of which ties he had written so many songs."[84] Overall, the reminiscences reveal that the national-universal myth took decades to coalesce and gain widespread acceptance.

I have arranged the reminiscences chronologically and grouped them into three periods that reflect this evolution. Part I, "Competing Narratives after Foster's Death," includes private letters and articles dating to between 1864 and 1889. These are the "freshest" recorded memories of the composer, and placing them side by side exposes strong differences. Overall, memory of Foster and his songs faded to near oblivion for about thirty years following his death. As documented in Part II, "Memorializing Foster at the Turn of the Twentieth Century," interest in Foster began to re-emerge in the 1890s. In this period, Morrison collaborated with the editor of the *Pittsburg Press*, Thomas Keenan Jr., to engineer a radical reversal of the declining interest in his music. Building on Nevin's portrayal of Foster, they championed him as a composer who expressed "universal" human emotions, laying the groundwork for him to be accepted as a composer whose attitudes toward his diverse musical and textual sources were representative of American democracy, embracing all the nation's races, genders, and sections. Their work highlights the mutability of the national-universal myth, transcending political divisions while also fitting nicely within the Democratic Party's 1890s identity politics and platforms on race relations and gender roles. Morrison and Keenan placed the myth on solid ground in these years; but some of the remembrances still offered interesting counternarratives, and it would be decades before the myth was broadly accepted. Even during the musical nationalism of the First World War Foster would be largely overlooked.

Part III, "Remembering Foster after the 1914 NAACP's Protests," includes the most distant recollections of Foster, all of which were published in the years after the National Association for the Advancement of Colored People (NAACP) successfully organized to have a songbook including some of his minstrel songs banned from the Boston Public Schools in 1914. The myth gained prominence following the NAACP incident as White intellectuals defended Foster and dismissed the NAACP's actions by asserting that his music was representative of the entire nation, not one of the nation's races.

---

[84] George Cooper to Harold Vincent Milligan, July 2, 1917, FHC, C929.

This thinking would come to greatly influence Lilly, the consequences of which ultimately enshrined the myth in respected academic and government institutions.

It would be going too far to simply dismiss the national-universal myth as *memory* as opposed to *history*, which Pierre Nora characterizes as "in fundamental opposition":

> Memory is life, borne by living societies founded in its name. It remains in permanent evolution, open to the dialectic of remembering and forgetting, unconscious of its successive deformations, vulnerable to manipulation and appropriation, susceptible to being long dormant and periodically revived. History, on the other hand, is the reconstruction, always problematic and incomplete, of what is no longer.[85]

Nora's construction, commonly accepted by historians and musicologists, views memory as "deforming" the objectivity of history—the "what is no longer"—by being overly *imaginative* and susceptible to outside influence. Foster scholarship has certainly sometimes fallen prey to those forces, but the reminiscences expose that just as often—if not more often—historians have failed to adequately exercise their imaginations, resulting in conjecture that is partial, biased, or both. The reminiscences present an argument for historians to shed their skepticism of memory and eschew positivism by embracing the imaginative, which would open up our understanding of Foster rather than restrict it to narrow and at times agenda-driven conjectures.

Overall, I seek consensus. Taking memory and history seriously, this book encourages us to weigh memories against each other and other surviving documents. We also must account for the incompleteness of the corpus of remembrances. Most obviously and significantly, although Foster's fame is based on his songs about Black people and enslavement, Jim Crow largely segregated Black people from Foster memory keeping. No firsthand accounts of Foster from Black people were recorded or preserved, at least none that I have managed to find, so all the remembrances in this volume exemplify what sociologist Joe Feagin terms the "white racial frame," in which understandings and experiences of the world are scripted by the agendas of

---

[85] Pierre Nora, "Between Memory and History: Les Lieux de Mémoire," *Representations* 26 (Spring 1989): 9–10.

Whiteness.[86] Taking this into account, in my commentary and essays I attempt to shine a light on the diversity of Black thought regarding Foster and his music. Although they do not come in the form of firsthand remembrances, these perspectives are nonetheless integral to understanding Foster as a cultural phenomenon from his time to ours. I hope this book points toward richer, more nuanced, and more complete ways of understanding Foster, his music, and his legacies.

Foster's intentions and his songs' original social functions are only part of the story of his music's significance. The reminiscences teach us as much about Foster's intentions as they do about the various agendas of people who used his music from his time to ours. This book thus illuminates varied interpretations of his songs, avoiding what musicologist Richard Taruskin refers to as the "poietic fallacy," or "the conviction that what matters most (or more strongly yet, that all that matters) in a work of art is the making of it, the maker's input."[87] And yet one of the things I find most fascinating about Foster is his deliberate embrace of art's ability to be used in ways that depart from its creators' intentions; in most of his commercial songs, he promoted varied uses and applications by maximizing openness and ambiguity. In other words, Foster's input—his intention to de-emphasize his own views—really matters.

Because of the ambiguous content of his best-known songs, today Foster is often made out to be a racial-justice hero or a racist monster. More accurately, as this volume shows, his songs have served both purposes and much more. He held unambiguous political views and on occasion wrote unambiguous racist and sectional songs. He also wrote an abundance of ambiguous songs that suit a variety of situations, some of them unpleasant to modern sensibilities about inclusivity. His brilliance shines bright in these songs, which he wrote to mean whatever people want them to mean and which have always eschewed singular, easy ways to read them. Even though people have long argued about the "right" interpretations of his songs, with Foster there are no simple narratives. It is my hope that by critically examining the mythology this volume humanizes Foster, showing him to be adaptable, complex, and far from perfect.

---

[86] Joe Feagin, *The White Racial Frame: Centuries of Racial Framing and Counter-Framing* (Routledge, 2013). For an application of this framework to music historiography and theory, see Philip Ewell, *On Music Theory and Making Music More Welcoming for Everyone* (University of Michigan Press, 2023), esp. 24–27.
[87] Richard Taruskin, "The Poietic Fallacy," *Musical Times* 145, no. 1886 (Spring 2004): 10.

# PART I

# COMPETING NARRATIVES AFTER FOSTER'S DEATH

## Introduction

Scholars have been prone to overgeneralize about the reception history of Foster's music. For example, in Grove Music Online musicologist Deane L. Root writes that Foster's songs "have circulated globally with unprecedented persistence from his time to ours."[1] To be sure, Foster's music did spread far and wide starting in his lifetime and continuing after his death, and we can confirm from Foster's royalty payments that he sold hundreds of thousands of pieces of sheet music in the 1850s. But the evidence of his songs' global persistence in the nineteenth century only consists of a small number of anecdotes, such as travel writer Bayard Taylor's reports from the 1850s of encountering some of Foster's songs in Panama and Delhi,[2] the reports of traveling minstrel troupes and *Uncle Tom* shows performing Foster's music in England throughout the second half of the nineteenth century,[3] and the publication of some of Foster's songs by English and German publishers.[4] Based on such a small amount of geographically limited evidence, broad claims about Foster's global reception fail to address the ebbs and flows of his music's circulation and the particular routes it took to specific locations around the world.

---

[1] Deane L. Root, "Foster, Stephen C(ollins)," Grove Music Online, Oxford Music Online, 2013, accessed June 20, 2023, https://doi.org/10.1093/gmo/9781561592630.article.A2252809.
[2] Bayard Taylor, *Eldorado; or, Adventures in the Path of Empire* (G. P. Putnam, 1882), 13; and Taylor, *A Visit to India, China, and Japan in the Year 1853* (G. P. Putnam, 1855), 155. See also Austin, "Susanna," "Jeanie," and "The Old Folks at Home," 28 and 31; and Emerson, *Doo-Dah!*, 10.
[3] See Meer, *Uncle Tom Mania*, 133–60; and Michael Pickering, *Blackface Minstrelsy in Britain* (Ashgate, 2008).
[4] In London in the 1850s, "My Old Kentucky Home" was issued by Jullien & Co., Musical Bouquet, and Boosey & Hawkes.

In a very influential monograph, William W. Austin misrepresents one of Bayard Taylor's accounts. Claiming to summarize Taylor, Austin states that Taylor "heard 'Uncle Ned' among Arabs in North Africa," citing this as evidence of Foster's music traveling to "some astonishingly remote places" where it "entered traditional repertories."[5] But Taylor's original words suggest none of this. In fact, he reported that *he* performed the song for North Africans who otherwise did not know it, and he provides no indication that it remained in their "repertory."[6] The assumption of the universality of Foster's music seems to have led scholars astray. Quick to accept his music's global presence, they have inflated his fame.

Candace Bailey has begun to tell a more complex story, noting that in surviving bound volumes belonging to Southern women in the 1850s and 1860s, Foster's music "is strangely obscure ... not missing altogether, but hardly ubiquitous."[7] She concludes that "the rise of Foster's compositions as the epitome of American song aligns with a new spirit of the nation that arose in the last third of the nineteenth century."[8] In other words, in his lifetime Foster's music was not "national," and it did not come to be seen as national—that is, as representative of all the nation's peoples and sections—until late in the nineteenth century. This fits with what we have already seen about the precipitous decline in popularity of Foster's songs in the United States in the last three years of his life, exacerbated by the Civil War's impact on musical dissemination and antebellum cultural practices. When he died nearly penniless in 1864, most of his well-known songs had been written in the previous decade and were considered old and out of step with the day's cultural trends.

Over the next thirty years in the United States, a few of Foster's songs were kept alive in performances by minstrels, opera divas, and theater troupes; but in general his music continued to decline in popularity. Its popularity shifted across the Atlantic, where it was published in large quantities in England, and "My Old Kentucky Home" was published in German translation. Its decline and eventual resurgence in the United States provide essential context for the first reminiscences. Written between 1864 and 1889, these reminiscences responded in different ways to fading memory of the composer.

---

[5] Austin, *"Susanna," "Jeanie," and "The Old Folks at Home,"* 31.
[6] Bayard Taylor, "Magic of Music," *National Intelligencer*, reprinted in *Dwight's Journal of Music* 3 [1853], 131.
[7] Bailey, "Opera, Lieder, or Stephen Foster?," 39.
[8] Bailey, "Opera, Lieder, or Stephen Foster?," 53.

## Fading Away

The story of Foster's music's declining popularity is detailed in the royalty statements and correspondence between his heirs and publishers. Strapped for cash in 1857, Foster asked Firth, Pond & Co. and F. D. Benteen to buy him out of future royalties with one-time cash payments, which they gladly did. From this point, he and his heirs did not receive royalties on existing songs until the original copyrights ran out—which in those years was twenty-eight years after a song was registered for copyright at a district court. At that point, his heirs renewed the copyright and reasserted a royalty claim for an additional fourteen years. By the time the initial copyrights began to expire, most of Foster's song rights had been acquired by two publishers: William A. Pond & Co. (formerly the Pond of Firth, Pond & Co.) and Oliver Ditson & Co.[9] In anticipation of their claims expiring and Foster's heirs renewing the copyright of "Old Folks at Home," Ditson wrote to Jane, Foster's widow, proposing terms for a new contract.[10] They informed Jane that "Old Folks" had been given new life when it entered the recital repertoire of operatic soprano Christine Nilsson, indicating that the song was "dying out when Nilsson revived it." Tellingly, they did not inquire about renewing any other songs, suggesting that "Old Folks" was the only song by Foster that had seen a resurgence of sales.

With the composer's brother Morrison acting as intermediary, Jane agreed to allow Ditson to continue to publish all the music to which they had the rights in exchange for a three-cent royalty on every copy sold.[11] Morrison negotiated the same deal with William A. Pond & Co.[12] From Jane's royalty statements, which survive in the Foster Hall Collection, we can calculate exactly how many non-pirated copies of Foster's sheet music were sold between 1879 and the expiration of the last renewed copyright in 1898. With Nilsson continuing to perform "Old Folks," and with her operatic

---

[9] Howard, *Stephen Foster*, 351.
[10] Oliver Ditson & Co. to Jane Foster, March 29, 1879, FHC, D252; and Oliver Ditson & Co. to Jane Foster, April 22, 1879, FHC, D253.
[11] Morrison Foster to Ditson & Co., May 5, 1879, FHC, D256; Ditson & Co. to Morrison Foster, May 7, 1879, FHC, D259; Morrison Foster to Ditson & Co., May 10, 1879, FHC, D255.
[12] The negotiations with William A. Pond & Co. did not go as smoothly. Pond was reluctant to accept Morrison's terms because he claimed Foster owed the firm $1,000 when he died. The negotiations are documented in a series of letters: William A. Pond & Co. to Morrison Foster, June 21, 1879, FHC, D207; William A. Pond & Co. to Morrison Foster, August 8, 1879, FHC, D208; William A. Pond to Morrison Foster, September 2, 1879, FHC, D209; Morrison Foster to William A. Pond & Co., September 4, 1879, FHC, D210; and William A. Pond & Co. to Morrison Foster, September 9, 1879, FHC, D211.

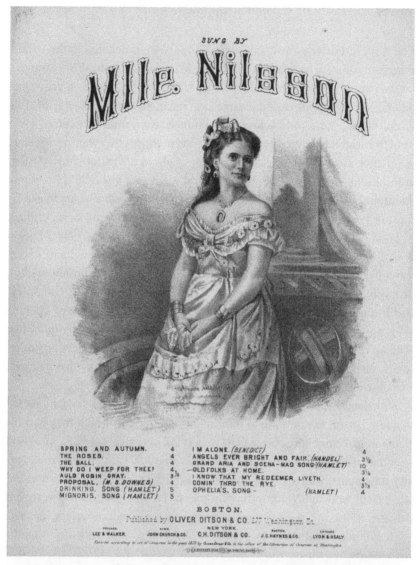

**Figure PI.1.** Sheet Music for "Old Folks at Home" with Christine Nilsson on the cover. Foster Hall Collection, Center for American Music, University of Pittsburgh Library System.

rival Adelina Patti adding it to her repertoire as well, it is not surprising that "Old Folks" earned the most. Ditson worked hard to capitalize on Nilsson's and Patti's performances, issuing special editions of the song featuring the divas on their covers (Figures PI.1 and PI.2). The song was also in the repertoire of Elizabeth Taylor Greenfield, an African American soprano whose performances probably helped drive sales of "Old Folks." Ditson was uninterested in placing her name or likeness on covers of the song, and the publisher never mentioned her in correspondence with Morrison or Jane. Ditson catered to a White consumer base.

Jane received the largest check for "Old Folks"—$220.80—in 1882, from which we can calculate that 7,360 copies were sold that year. Declining sales after this were linked to how much Nilsson and Patti sang the song. In 1887, Ditson wrote to Morrison that "we feel ashamed to send so small a royalty for last 6 months—but 'Old Folks' has had no lift from Nilsson or Patti, for a year or two, & without their aid, the sales fall off."[13] Nevertheless, across the fourteen years in which "Old Folks" was renewed for copyright, Jane received checks totaling $1,923.09 (the equivalent of $67,853.10 today using the Consumer Price Index to calculate inflation, or the equivalent of $509,547.62 in compensation today[14]) for the song, indicating that a modest 64,103 copies had sold.

"Old Folks" accounted for roughly half of all sales of Foster's sheet music in this period. The next best-selling song, "My Old Kentucky Home," peaked in 1886, earning Jane $85.50 from the sale of 2,850 copies that year. "Hard Times Come Again No More" peaked in 1888 with $16.50 earned from the sale of 550 copies. Jane received royalty checks for "Nelly Was a Lady" in only six years, in which a meager 350 copies were sold; in eight of the fourteen years Jane collected royalties, no copies of "Nelly Was a Lady" were sold at all. Jane's royalties for "Some Folks" indicate only a total of fifty copies sold across two of the fourteen years. In all years, only a handful of Foster's songs sold at all. Hundreds of Foster's compositions earned nothing, and of the songs that did sell, most earned less than $1 each year. All told, when "Old Folks" is removed from the figures, Jane earned $1,892.40, indicating that only 63,080 copies of all of Foster's songs except for "Old Folks" were purchased between 1881 and 1898. With "Old Folks" included, a total of 127,183 copies of Foster's music were sold. At the other end of the spectrum

---

[13] Oliver Ditson & Co. to Morrison Foster, February 3, 1887, FHC, D275.
[14] Inflation calculated using www.measuringworth.com.

54  FORMULATING FOSTER

Figure PI.2. Sheet Music for "Old Folks at Home" with Adelina Patti on the cover. Foster Hall Collection, Center for American Music, University of Pittsburgh Library System.

in this period was Charles K. Harris's smash hit "After the Ball," which sold more than 5,000 copies a day and earned the composer over $25,000 a month in the first months following its publication in 1892. In the first years it sold more than 2 million copies.[15]

## Minstrelsy, *Uncle Tom* Shows, Vaudeville, and Jubilee Singers

Given Foster's lifelong professional relationship with minstrelsy, it is somewhat surprising that there is relatively little evidence of Foster's music living on in minstrel performances after his death. Foster's songs almost exclusively figured into minstrel shows featuring older performers, notably Dan Bryant, with whom Foster appears to have had a close personal relationship. Firth, Pond & Co. published "That's What's the Matter" with "Dan Bryant's Celebrated Song, as sung by him with great success" artfully written on the cover, and after the dissolution of Firth, Pond & Co., William A. Pond issued "Old Black Joe" with Bryant's name prominently placed below the title.[16] Further suggesting an intimate relationship between the two are playbills that indicate that every time Bryant's troupe performed "Jeanie with the Light Brown Hair" they used not the published title and lyrics but the version that Foster and his family sang, which featured Foster's nickname for his wife: "*Jenny* with the Light Brown Hair."[17] Bryant's troupe was based in the Bowery in New York, a short walk from Foster's residences in the last years of his life; and the troupe briefly counted among its ranks the renowned Dan Emmett, whom we learn from Kit Clarke's remembrances was friendly with Foster.

Surviving playbills and programs for Bryant's Minstrels reveal that up to Bryant's death in 1875 the troupe performed Foster's "Why Have My Loved Ones Gone?," "Linger in Blissful Repose," "Lula Is Gone," "Camptown Races," "Hard Times Come Again No More," "Jenny With the Light Brown Hair," "Nelly Was a Lady," and "Don't Bet Your Money on de

---

[15] Russell Sanjek, *American Popular Music and Its Business: The First Four Hundred Years*, vol. 2, *From 1790 to 1909* (Oxford University Press, 1988), 310; Hamm, *Yesterdays*, 285; and Jon W. Finson, *The Voices That Are Gone: Themes in 19th-Century Popular Songs* (Oxford University Press, 1994), 69.

[16] Stephen C. Foster, "That's What's the Matter" (Firth, Pond & Co., 1862); Stephen C. Foster, "Old Black Joe" (William A. Pond, ca. 1863).

[17] "Jenny with the Light Brown Hair" appears on playbills from April 11, 1874, and May 19, 1874, both of which are found in the Harvard Theatre Collection of Blackface Minstrelsy, series 3, Playbills, Bryant's Minstrels Playbills, 1875–1876.

Shanghai."[18] The California Minstrels also performed from Foster's day through the 1870s and retained Foster's music in their repertoire. In 1866, Ben Cotton led the troupe with Joe Murphy, for whom Foster had written "Lou'siana Bell." Surviving playbills for Cotton & Murphy's California Minstrels reveal the troupe performed Foster's "Hard Times Come Again No More," "Beautiful Dreamer," "Come with Thy Sweet Voice Again," "Why Have My Loved Ones Gone," "Willie's Gone to the War," "Lula's Gone," "I'll Be True to Thee," and "Lilly Dale." Following Bryant's death in 1875, the California Minstrels took residence in Bryant's old theater. Their shows included Foster's "Kiss Me Mother Ere I Die," "There's No Such Girl As Mine," and, when Billy Emerson joined the troupe, "Old Black Joe."[19] Emerson was known for his performances of "Old Black Joe"; an edition of the song appeared without Foster's name on it in the mid-1870s, the cover of which labeled the song "Billy Emerson's Last Character Song."[20]

Besides the playbills of Bryant's Minstrels and the California Minstrels, Foster's music is virtually absent in surviving minstrel playbills from the 1870s and 1880s. It is worth adding, however, that minstrel programs typically list only the songs performed in the show's first two parts. In the 1870s and 1880s, the third and final part of the show was often a comical play or lampoon of a popular opera. Since playbills do not list the musical numbers in such plays, it is unknown the degree to which Foster's songs were included. It is known, however, that one popular kind of play—the *Uncle Tom* show, which was a play that lampooned the novel *Uncle Tom's Cabin*—regularly featured Foster's sentimental minstrel songs, especially "Old Folks at Home," "My Old Kentucky Home," "Massa's in de Cold Ground," and "Old Black Joe." We can safely assume, then, that these and similar songs lived on in other minstrel plays as well but, given their absence in programs and decline in sales, probably not with great frequency.

Perhaps inspired by the opera divas, "Old Folks at Home" and a couple other sentimental minstrel songs were performed in these years by touring ensembles of Black musicians, such as the Fisk Jubilee Singers and the Hampton Singers.[21] Beginning in 1872, the Fisk Jubilee Singers performed

---

[18] Harvard Theatre Collection of Blackface Minstrelsy, series 3, Playbills, Bryant's Minstrels Playbills, Box 24.
[19] Harvard Theatre Collection of Blackface Minstrelsy, series 3, Playbills, California Minstrels, box 8 and folder 106.
[20] "Old Black Joe," arranged by George T. Evans (M. Gray, 1873). The sheet music indicates this edition was published "by special arrangement with W. A. Pond & Co."
[21] Harvard Theatre Collection of Blackface Minstrelsy, series 3, Playbills, Jubilee Singers, box 14.

spirituals throughout the nation and abroad to raise money for Fisk University, and they were soon emulated by the Hampton Institute. Both schools, founded after the Civil War to educate freed people and their descendants, found themselves needing monetary contributions. The programs of other, nonacademic ensembles who emulated them, such as the Louisiana Jubilee Singers, the C. H. Perkins Celebrated Colored Virginia and Texas Jubilee Singers, and the North Carolina Jubilee Singers, also include "Old Folks at Home," as well as "Old Black Joe" and "Massa's in de Cold Ground."[22]

There are many reasons why jubilee singers performed Foster's songs. As Sandra Graham points out, "Old Folks" was experiencing the first peak of its revival following Nilsson's and Patti's performance of it in the 1870s. Additionally, Foster's lyrics offered descriptions of landscapes and people—inauthentic as they are—that are lacking in authentic spirituals, providing the jubilee singers' predominantly White audiences with contextual specificity to understand the new-to-their-ears spirituals that were programmed on the same concerts.[23] As multiple accounts of the musicians and people associated with the group attest, the singers were also eager to "prove" themselves to the White world by singing White music.[24] They were probably further encouraged to perform these songs because of the role they played in bringing in audiences (and contributions) and probably because they realized that, despite lines such as "still longing for de old plantation" in "Old Folks at Home," the sympathetic and humanizing portrayals made them more interracially sensitive than average minstrel songs.

Significantly, the programs from minstrel shows and jubilee ensembles rarely credit Foster as composer (Figure I.3). Thus, even though they kept a small number of his *songs* alive, these performances helped erase Foster himself from popular consciousness. In fact, by the end of the century, many Americans came to understand the songs that survived as authorless folk songs. And even though minstrelsy and *Uncle Tom* shows retained the songs' racist connotations, jubilee performances and Elizabeth Taylor Greenfield portrayed them as "authentic" Black songs, and the performances of White opera divas shed the songs' racial connotations altogether. Thus,

---

[22] Harvard Theatre Collection of Blackface Minstrelsy, series 3, Playbills, Jubilee Singers, box 14.
[23] Sandra Graham, "The Fisk Jubilee Singers and the Concert Spiritual: The Beginnings of an American Tradition" (PhD diss., New York University, 2001), 214.
[24] Sandra Graham, *Spirituals and the Birth of a Black Entertainment Industry* (University of Illinois Press, 2018), 30–31.

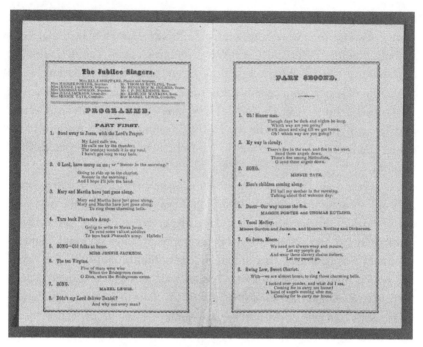

**Figure PI.3.** A program of the Fisk Jubilee Singers. MS Thr 1848, Harvard Theatre Collection, Houghton Library, Harvard University.

the ambiguities that Foster wrote into the songs enabled them to accrue new meanings after his death. As Graham writes, "Foster's plantation songs . . . came to be seen not in the narrow sense of Ethiopian [minstrel] delineations but in the broader sense of representations of America. It was the performance of these songs by artists as different as Christine Nilsson and the Jubilee Singers that helped generate this new interpretation."[25]

But, importantly, it would take time for these new meanings to be widely embraced. For the most part, from the 1860s to the 1890s, Foster and his music did not figure into popular culture in the United States to a very large degree. With few exceptions, the composer and his music were all but forgotten until the very end of the century, which explains why some of the first reminiscences portray him as underappreciated or forgotten and why some commentators felt they could take credit for his achievements. With so few

---

[25] Graham, "Fisk Jubilee Singers," 214.

people caring about Foster or his music, there was no widespread acceptance of a myth about the composer in these years. Some of the first reminiscences joined opera divas and jubilee singers in laying the groundwork for the national-universal myth, but as a whole the period is characterized by disagreements over Foster's memory.

# 1
# An Obituary of Stephen C. Foster (1864)

## Introduction

*At the time of his death, Foster was not a celebrity, and his music's popularity had significantly declined. But enough people remembered his earlier songs to warrant announcements and obituaries in periodicals across the country.[1] The following sketch of his life, which appeared in the* Pittsburgh Evening Chronicle *on the night of his funeral, was often reprinted and summarized.[2]*

*Though the article is unsigned, its initial publication in Pittsburgh and strong resemblance to Morrison Foster's later writings strongly suggest that Morrison was the author. Like Morrison's later writings, this article portrays the Foster family as elite and emphasizes their patriotism, asserts Foster as a national figure, and assures readers that Foster's links to minstrelsy do not affect his "high" social standing. Also like Morrison's later writings, the article makes no mention of Foster's alcoholism, racism, mental health, or marital troubles.*

*The article contains the earliest reference I have found to Foster as a painter of watercolors, and it also is the only source to offer the anecdote about a youthful Foster leading his friends in a parade through a park in Allegheny.*

---

[1] Examples include announcement, *Alexandria Gazette* (Virginia), January 19, 1864; "Funeral of Stephen C. Foster," *Philadelphia Inquirer*, January 22, 1864; "The News," *Chicago Tribune*, January 22, 1864; "Funeral of Stephen C. Foster," *Daily Ohio Statesman*, January 23, 1864; "Funeral of Stephen C. Foster," *Baltimore Sun*, January 23, 1864; announcement, *Buffalo Weekly Express*, January 26, 1864; announcement, *Liverpool Mercury* (England), February 6, 1864; announcement, *Placer Herald* (California), February 20, 1864; announcement, *Gold Hill Daily News*, February 27, 1864.

[2] Examples include "The Late S. C. Foster," *Washington National Republican*, February 1, 1864; "The Late Stephen C. Foster," *Dwight's Journal of Music*, February 6, 1864; "The Late Stephen C. Foster," *Burlington Times*, February 6, 1864; "The Late Stephen C. Foster," *Luzerne Union*, February 24, 1864; "Death of Stephen C. Foster," *American Citizen* (Butler, PA), February 24, 1864.

*Formulating Foster.* Christopher Lynch, Oxford University Press. © Oxford University Press 2025.
DOI: 10.1093/9780197811726.003.0002

## "Stephen C. Foster, the Composer," *Pittsburgh Evening Chronicle*, January 21, 1864.

This afternoon the mortal remains of STEPHEN C. FOSTER were carried to their last abode. As the incidents connected with one who has added so much to the musical fame of our country are of interest to all at home, as well as abroad, we propose to give a brief biographical sketch of our townsman,-- to tell who he was,--and what he did. STEPHEN C. FOSTER was born on the Fourth of July, 1826, the same day on which THOMAS JEFFERSON and JOHN ADAMS died. His father, WILLIAM B. FOSTER, Sr., was a native of Virginia, who settled in Pittsburgh in the year 1796, and entered into business with Major EBENEZER DENNY and ANTHONY BEELEN, Esq. In 1811 he laid out his farm (including the ground on which the United States Arsenal now stands, two and a half miles from Pittsburgh, and the surrounding premises) into a town, intending to call it Fosterville.[3] Soon afterwards, however, the gallant Captain LAWRENCE was killed, fighting his ship, the "Chesapeake," and Mr. FOSTER patriotically changed the name of his town to Lawrenceville, adopting as the motto on the corporation seal the dying words of LAWRENCE, "Don't give up the ship."

STEPHEN, at a very early age, manifested musical talents of an unusual order. At the age of seven years a flageolet was placed in his hands, and within a wonderfully short time he had, unaided, mastered its stops and sounds, so as to play with effect several familiar airs of the day. He never, however, aspired to greatness as a performer either vocal or instrumental, though the taste and sweetness with which he brought forth the most touching tones of the piano and flute could fix his audience in wrapt attention. And when he sang *his own* songs (accompanying himself on the piano or guitar) there was a plaintive sadness in his voice, and a magic in his touch that brought tears to listener's eyes. Not the most accomplished public singers could ever equal the effect with which he himself sang his own popular strains.

It was in a higher sphere than that of a *performer* of music that Mr. FOSTER sought and won fame. He zealously aimed to master music as a science, and earnestly devoted himself for years to the study of harmonies. The works of MOZART, BEETHOVEN and WEBER were his chief delight and frequent theme of conversation. His melodies were the spontaneous and original emanations of his own peculiar musical taste, but at an early

---

[3] William Foster Sr. acquired the land to lay out the town in 1814. See Howard, *Stephen Foster*, 6.

age he had so cultivated that taste in the true science of harmony, that those melodies came forth refined as gold, and when he reduced them to printed notes and launched them on the world, he knew they would be successful and would strike a popular chord. His talent for writing the poetry, as well as the music of his songs, (a combination rarely met with) gave him an advantage in setting the notes of music to words of corresponding euphony and accent. This advantage can only be realized by one who has experienced the great difficulty which a composer, who does *not* write his own lines, meets with in seeking to harmonize words and sounds.

Mr. FOSTER was an ardent student in other branches of learning. He taught himself many of the languages. In French and German he was quite proficient, and some of the water-color paintings of his youth are still the admiration of his friends. At no time, however, could he be induced to submit regularly to the restraints of the school room. From childhood he loved to wander alone among the beautiful hills and woods that surround his native city, and with his book and pencil, seat himself where the rustling of the leaves, the rippling water, the falling twigs and the twittering of birds, fell peacefully and harmoniously upon his sensitive ear. For years he pursued his studies in this quiet harmless way, and his parents finding that he always progressed favorably, soon ceased to insist on his confining himself, like other boys, to the schoolroom, but allowed him to pursue his studies in his own way.

As he approached manhood, Mr. FOSTER entered the counting house of his brother, DUNNING M. FOSTER, in Cincinnati, and was always notable for his accuracy and neatness. He was, however, not long permitted to devote his time to business pursuits. He had already composed many beautiful songs and pieces of instrumental music, which had, for years, been the delight and pride of his home circle. A few of them had been published, but had been a gratuity to the publishers, as he had not at that time any idea of asking pecuniary compensation for his musical productions.

His first published song, called "Open thy lattice, Love," was issued about the year 1842, by GEO. WILLIG, in Baltimore.[4] "Old Uncle Ned" and "Oh Susanna" were not long afterwards issued by W. C. PETERS in Cincinnati. No remuneration was asked or thought of by Mr. FOSTER for these, though

---

[4] "Open Thy Lattice Love" was published in 1844. After this article appeared, the incorrected date was repeated by Birdseye, Nevin, the anonymous source in 1889, Morrison in 1896, and Jessie Welsh Rose.

they proved immensely profitable to the publisher. Returning to Pittsburgh, Mr. FOSTER produced successively the "Louisiana Belle," "Nelly was a Lady," "Camptown Races," "My Old Kentucky Home," "Master's in the cold, cold ground," "Nelly Bly," "Oh, Boys, carry me 'long," and the world-renowned "Old Folks at Home," together with a large number of other songs suitable for the performances of the Ethiopian Minstrels. He was induced to compose his songs at this time in the shape of negro melodies on account of the wonderful interest all classes then took in that style of music.

For the past ten years, however, he confined his productions to airs and words of a sentimental or devotional character. Among these are "Willie, we have missed you;" "Ellen Bayne;" "Maggie by my side;" "Come where my love lies dreaming;" "Little Ella;" "Jennie with the light brown hair;" "Willie, my brave;" "Fare well, my Lillie dear;" "Oh, comrades, fill no glass for me;" "Old Dog Tray;" "Mollie do you love me?" "Summer breath;" "Ah, may the Red Rose live always;" "Come with thy sweet voice again;" "I see her still in my dreams;" "Suffer little children to come unto me;" "Ella is an Angel;" and some hundred others. There has been recently a book of Hymns published in New York, with beautiful airs, composed by Mr. FOSTER expressly for each hymn.

As we previously remarked, Mr. FOSTER for a long period allowed his works to be published without thought of pecuniary compensation; but the demand for them became so great, and before long so many flattering offers were made to him that he found himself impelled to abandon all other pursuits, and devote himself *entirely* to musical composition as a profession. He entered into an arrangement with FIRTH, POND & Co., the well-known New York publishers, which continued many years, and was the source of immense income to Mr. FOSTER, and also of large profits to the publishers. The commissions paid Mr. F. by them on the "Old Folks at Home" alone amounted to over $15,000.[5] Many other of his songs were nearly as profitable, but the "Old Folks at Home" reached a larger issue than *any song ever published in America*. For the privilege of having his name printed on one edition of this song, the late E. P. CHRISTY paid Mr. FOSTER Five hundred dollars.[6]

---

[5] This number is inaccurate. By Foster's own accounting, "Old Folks" and all its arrangements earned him a total of $1,647.46. At that point he sold future royalties to Firth, Pond & Co. Account Book, FHC, A230.

[6] This figure is inaccurate. John Mahon and the anonymous interviewee (who was likely George Cooper) in 1888 state that the fee was $15, a fee that John Tasker Howard shows was the correct amount. See Howard, *Stephen Foster*, 197–200.

During the past three years, Mr. FOSTER has resided in New York city, and his Pittsburgh friends, though they have missed his face, have continued to be reminded of him by the sounds of his familiar airs heard on every occasion. There are many of them who well remember the time when, at the age of seven years, dressed in paper cap and tin sword, he led his admiring playmates around the Allegheny common, marching to the notes of his juvenile flageolet. His death took place on the 13th inst., in New York city. With praise-worthy state pride, the President of the Pennsylvania Railroad Company gave orders that his remains and the party in charge of them should be passed over the road free of charge.[7] The Adams' Express Company also declined to take any pay for conveying his remains from New York to Harrisburg.

As stated in the previous notice given of the deceased, he married a daughter of the late Doctor McDowell, who, with an interesting daughter of twelve years, survive him. Some of his friends here, and other lovers of music who acknowledge his numerous and valuable contributions to musical science and literature, have united in having impressive and appropriate ceremonies at his funeral. At Trinity Church, the exercises were vocal, led by Mr. Kleber; at the grave they were instrumental, some of Mr. F's most popular airs having been introduced. Mr. FOSTER has won a fame which is undying. His influence extends over every land where there are voices to hymn forth sweet notes, and hearts to be moved by them. His numerous melodies will be the delight of millions yet unborn.

"Let me make the ballads of a nation," says a well-known writer, "and I care not who makes their laws," thus recognizing the familiar and homely ballads of a people as a paramount influence in moulding their wills and tastes, and influencing their destinies. In this view, then, Mr. F. occupies a high national position, but still greater honors ought to be his, for he has not only composed many of the most familiar and treasured *ballads* of our people, but has linked them to airs that can never die—which have a sad and plaintive melody so peculiar and fascinating that they will forever have a place in the human heart. Many of them have already been incorporated in books of Christian praise, and many more will follow. Short, then, as has been this gifted life, it has not been in vain, and both Poetry and Music will long mourn one who was, at the same time, their worshipper and fittest interpreter.

---

[7] It is worth noting that Foster's brother William B. Foster Jr. was the vice president of the Pennsylvania Railroad.

# 2
# Two Letters by Henry Baldwin Foster (1864)

**Introduction**

*Two days after Foster's funeral and the publication of the sketch of his life that Morrison Foster had probably written, the composer's other surviving brother, Henry Baldwin Foster, wrote the first of these two letters explaining the circumstances of his death. The second letter is dated two weeks later. Ten years Foster's senior, Henry B. Foster was the fourth eldest of the Foster children who lived into adulthood. He began his career as a clerk for a Pittsburgh firm, and in 1841 he went to work at the Land Office in the US Treasury Department, where he was hired by Walter Forward, a family friend from Pittsburgh who had been newly appointed as secretary of the Treasury. Henry worked in the Land Office, reorganized as part of the Department of the Interior in 1849, until he was dismissed during the Whig administration of Zachary Taylor. Henry and his wife, Ann Burgess, whom he married in 1847, moved back to Allegheny, where they lived with his parents, Morrison, and the composer in a house owned by William Jr. Henry died in 1870 in a fire caused by lightning striking the building in which he was working.*

*Several references in Foster's and Henry's letters indicate that they had a close bond. In his youth, while visiting a relative's farm in Ohio, Foster wrote to his father to encourage him to ask his brothers Henry and Dunning to come visit. "Tell them bothh [sic] to try to come for I should like to see them both most," he wrote.*[1] *One of Foster's last surviving letters is to Henry. He writes,*

My dear brother,
Send the money for the pictures to care of John J. Daly 419, Grand Street.

---

[1] Stephen Foster to William B. Foster Sr., January 14, 1837, FHC, A343.

*Formulating Foster*. Christopher Lynch, Oxford University Press. © Oxford University Press 2025.
DOI: 10.1093/9780197811726.003.0003

*I received a nice letter from Willie Foster but have not yet answered him. When you write, tell me all the news you can think of. You must remember it is nearly three years since I was in Pittsburgh.*

*I am very well and have been working quite industriously, but pay, these times, especially in music, is very poor.*

*Your affec. bro.*

*S. C. Foster*[2]

It is possible that the pictures for which Foster asked Henry to pay included the photograph he had taken around this time of him and his friend George Cooper.

As Foster lay in Bellevue Hospital in New York, having suffered a bad fall that left him severely wounded, he had Cooper write to both Morrison and Henry. The telegraph to Morrison survives. Cooper wrote, "Your brother Stephen I am sorry to inform you is lying in Bellevue Hospital in this city very sick. He desires me to ask you to send him some pecuniary assistance as his means are very low. If possible he would like to see you in person."[3] Two days later, on January 14, Cooper sent Morrison and Henry another telegraph: "Stephen is dead."[4]

It is possible that the January 21 sketch led to inquiries for more information about the composer's death, for the dearth of information in the article is contrasted in the following letters, in which Henry detailed what he knew of his brother's death and described the journey that he, Morrison, and Jane took to New York to retrieve Foster's body for burial in Pittsburgh. The exact nature of Henry's relationship with the first letter's recipient, Susan G. Beach, is uncertain, although he does refer to her as a "dear friend." In the second letter, which is more intimate, he wrote to his sister Ann Eliza, who lived in Paradise, Pennsylvania. Together the sketch and the letters show the family's different degrees of openness about their brother's final chapter in the days following his death. They were nearly silent to the public, more open to acquaintances, and most open only with each other.

---

[2] Stephen Foster to Henry Foster, December 6, 1862, FHC, A309.
[3] George Cooper to Morrison Foster, January 12, 1864, FHC, A361.
[4] Telegraph from George Cooper to Morrison Foster, January 14, 1864, FHC, A362.

## Henry Foster to Susan G. Beach, January 23, 1864, Foster Hall Collection, C934.

Mrs. Susan G Beach—

Dr Friend—I had resumed business but a few days after the severe attack of Soar throat, when I received three Telegraphic despatches *all at once,* two of them from Mr Geo Cooper of New York, and one from my brother in Cleveland, Oh.—one of Mr Coopers date NY Dec 11. Read.

"Your Brother Stephen is very sick and wishes to see you".
The other dated the 14th Dec was.
*"Stephen is dead"*

My brothers read "Stephen is dead, meet me in New York on Saturday"[5]

I left on Friday afternoon at four o'clock and arrived in N York on Saturday at noon with a severe head ache, Met my brother at St Nicholas Hotel, who informed me we would return the same evening, by way of the Allentown route. Fortunately by a misunderstanding between the undertaker and ourselves, we missed the train which was the one that met with that terrible accident at one of the bridges of Spruce Creek on the Pa Rail Road. We took the Phila train and remained at Phila on Sunday, when we heard of the accident & congratulated ourselves upon our fortunate escape.

From the interest you manifested to have my brothers songs, I know you will be gratified by a statement from me of the particulars of his death. He had been going about feeling quite unwell for several days, when on Saturday evening he retired early and requested the Landlord of the Hotel not to have him disturbed in the morning, about ten o'clock the next morning he opened his door and spoke to the chamber maid to bring him a glass of water, and turned to go back, when he fell as if he had been shot, and cut his head badly, a surgeon was sent for immediately, who dressed his wounds, on Monday & Tuesday he improved and spoke of being out again in a few days, on Wednesday he was proped up in his bed and was having his wounds dressed when he fainted away and *never revived again.* I have no doubt that owing to the state of his system, and the loss of blood, there was not strength sufficient left him to rally after fainting away.

Owing to the desire of his musical friends to manifest their appreciation of his talents, we had him buried from Trinity Church where the ceremonies

---

[5] Henry mistakenly recalls the correspondence as arriving in December, but it was January.

were exceedingly solemn, & at his grave I was completely overcome by *his loss*, and the beautiful music of the Brass Band performing his quartett, called "Come where my love lies dreaming"

My anxiety about him is *now all over,* He was a firm belivere in the gospel of Christ, & ever had an abiding confidence in his mercy.

In hopes you are all well,—

I remain your friend

Henry. B. Foster

## Henry Baldwin Foster to Ann Eliza Buchanan, February 4, 1864, Foster Hall Collection, C935.

My Dear Sister

I received your very welcom letter of the 1st inst to day and hasten to reply, in hopes I may in some measure relieve your sorrow by the assurance that we found everything connected with Stevey's life and death in New York much better than we had expected, he had been boarding at a very respectable Hotel and did not owe the Landlord a cent or any one else that we knew of, had retired early to bed on Saturday evening, the following morning opened his door and spoke to the chambermaid and turned to go back to his bed when he fell as if he had been shot striking his head on the chamber, a surgeon was procured immediately and his wounds dressed, he then sent for his friend Mr. Geo Cooper (as fine a little gentleman as I ever met) who telegraphed to Morrison and I, and persuaded Stevey to go with him in a carriage to the Hospital where he would be better attended to. On Tuesday he was much better, and Mr. Cooper was with him, on Wednesday, he was proped up and after having taken some soup was quite cheerful. When they commenced dressing his wounds and just as the person was washing out the rag, without Stevey saying a word he fainted away and never came to again.

There is something particularly sad about his life and death, yes! Poetically Sad, and I shall never again admire the beauties of nature without being reminded of some of his beautiful songs, such as

> When Spring time comes Gentle Annie,
>     And the wild flower scatter oe'r the plain,
> We shall never more behold thee
> Or see they lovely face again.

or
"I see her still in my dreams,
in my dreams,
By the meadow and the streams.

Our dear Mother said she could not endure it, in case Stevey was taken from her, to hear his songs, and we now realize what she sadly anticipated, oh! my dear sister it was heart rending to hear the band play "Come where my love lies dreaming as they lowered him into his grave, oh! I hope he is now happy, and that our prayers in his behalf have been heard in Heaven.

# 3
# Reminiscences of George W. Birdseye (1867)

## Introduction

*The biographical sketch and Henry's two letters demonstrate that the Foster family wanted to limit the information about the end of the composer's life that made it to the public, so it is not surprising that Morrison Foster also shaped the following reminiscence, written by one of Foster's closest friends in his final years, George Washington Birdseye (1844–19?). Birdseye probably met Foster while studying law at Columbia College in New York. According to a Columbia directory, in 1864–65 he was a junior living at 81 E. Fourth Street, not far from where Foster resided at the time of his death.*[1] *He appears to have transferred to Harvard, from which he graduated in 1866. He wrote and published articles and poetry beginning in his student days and practiced law into at least the early 1870s. But he eventually returned to journalism and publishing. His writings appeared in numerous periodicals, and composers such as Matthias Keller set several of his texts to music.*

*Before Birdseye's article about Foster appeared in the* Musical Gazette, *the editors sent a copy to Morrison for comments and corrections. In his reply to the editors, Morrison took exception to Birdseye's portrayal of his brother, responding negatively to his "reference to the only failing he ever had" and asking the editors not to publish anything about his brother's "peculiarities of habit." He claimed that Birdseye did not know his brother and was a "fraud."*[2] *Morrison indicated that he "made some corrections and a few expurgations" and requested that they not make "reference to certain*

---

[1] *Catalogue of the Officers and Students of Columbia College, 1864–65* (D. Van Nostrand, 1864), 49. Birdseye appears to have transferred that year to Harvard University, where he graduated with a law degree in 1866. *A Catalogue of the Law School of the University at Cambridge for the Academical year 1864–65* (Sever and Francis, 1865), 9. *Quinquennial Catalogue of the Officers and Graduates of Harvard University 1636–1905* (Harvard University, 1905), 438.

[2] Mason Brothers to Morrison Foster, February 2, 1867, FHC. Morrison's response is preserved in a draft written on the back of the Mason Brothers' letter.

*Formulating Foster*. Christopher Lynch, Oxford University Press. © Oxford University Press 2025.
DOI: 10.1093/9780197811726.003.0004

peculiarities."³ We know this only because he sketched out his reply on the initial letter from the editors, which survives among Morrison's papers in the Foster Hall Collection. But because his actual response and his marked copy of Birdseye's draft do not survive, we do not know what references to "peculiarities" Morrison struck from the article. All we know is that when the editor responded, he informed Morrison that "we agree with you in your remarks and the article is indeed in better taste with the prepared changes."⁴ Scholars have long assumed that Morrison excised mentions of Foster's alcoholism, but this assumption is dubious because the published article still made multiple references to alcohol consumption. We have no idea what content Morrison removed.

Contradicting Morrison's belief that Birdseye did not know his brother, in the 1930s Foster Hall staff discovered a letter by Foster to Birdseye, the only surviving letter from the last year of his life. The brief missive reveals little about their relationship:

Dear Sir
I will arrange Mr. Cooper's melody when my hand gets well.
Very Respy Yours
S. C. Foster⁵

The formal tone of the letter's salutation might suggest that Foster may not have been on a friendly, first-name basis with Birdseye. But the letter nonetheless confirms that they knew each other and that their relationship somehow involved their artistic interests and Foster's friend and collaborator George Cooper. It seems that Cooper had composed a melody, perhaps to a text by Birdseye, and Foster was to write the piano accompaniment. They probably never completed this project, for none of Foster's published songs credit Cooper as melodist or Birdseye as lyricist.

A manuscript in Foster's hand survives, however, in which he began to compose music for Birdseye's text "Meet Me Tonight Dearest Down by the Gate" (Figure 3.1).⁶ It is not the melody by Cooper that Foster wrote to Birdseye about, for Foster clearly wrote on the page below the music "Melody by Stephen Foster in his autograph." Like the melody by Cooper, though, Foster apparently never completed an accompaniment, and Birdseye's text

---
[3] Mason Brothers, Publishers to Morrison Foster, February 2, 1867, FHC, C899a.
[4] Mason Brothers, Publishers to Morrison Foster, February 7, 1867, FHC, C899b.
[5] Stephen Foster to George W. Birdseye, February 11, 1863, FHC, A334.
[6] Stephen Foster, "Meet Me Tonight Dearest," FHC, A333.

ultimately appeared in songwriter J. R. Thomas's "Down by the Gate," which was registered for copyright in Boston in 1863. Thomas's setting bears no resemblance to Foster's, and Foster's melody was eventually published as "Dearer than Life," with a text by Cooper, in 1869.

**Figure 3.1.** "Meet Me Tonight, Dearest, Down by the Gate," manuscript. Foster Hall Collection, Center for American Music, University of Pittsburgh Library System.

*Because of Morrison's reaction to Birdseye's article, Foster's biographers have largely discounted the account.[7] But despite minor factual inaccuracies, there is no reason to doubt its general claims. Many aspects of*

---

[7] Howard, *Stephen Foster*, 312–13.

*Birdseye's portrayal are affirmed in Cooper's recollections and an account by Foster's friend John Mahon. In fact, the scant details about Foster's last years in Morrison's biography of his brother suggest that it was Morrison, not Birdseye, who knew little about the last chapter of the songwriter's life or that what he did know he did not want made public.*

*Birdseye struggled in the years after Foster's death. He married Julia Jones in 1872, with whom he had a son in 1875. They separated by the end of the decade, after which he moved to Philadelphia and then Boston. He wrote to Julia in 1903, informing her that he had a "troublesome and painful" leg condition that left him unable to "walk any great distance" or "go up and down stairs unprovided with railings." Failing to find good-paying work, he relied on the charity of others and small receipts from his writing.[8] In 1898 he moved to Lynn, where he probably died in the 1910s. The last known record of his life is in the 1916 Lynn directory.*

---

## George W. Birdseye, "A Reminiscence of the late Stephen C. Foster," *New York Musical Gazette*, January 1, 1867.

### I.

"If a man were permitted to make all the ballads, he need not care who should make all the laws of a nation."

FLETCHER OF SALTOUN

It was my pleasure, a somewhat sad one it must be confessed, to be personally acquainted with Stephen C. Foster during the last year of his brief existence. It was in the latter part of the year 1862 that I saw him for the first time; and his appearance was so very different from what I had anticipated, that I was, to say the least, disappointed. The occasion is still fresh in my memory. "I was introduced to Foster, the composer, last night," said a friend to me; "would you like to know him?" I had for a long time greatly desired such an opportunity, and signified as much; while the songs I had loved from my very babyhood, almost all associated with Foster's name, bubbled up from my heart, and murmured in my ear, and I already imagined myself before

---

[8] George W. Birdseye to Julia, May 28, 1903, FHC, C946.

a hale, merry old man, with long white hair, his head bald at the top, and a kindly smile ever upon his lips—the man for whom I had long felt a sort of reverence. Talking of him and his melodies, we walked some distance down the Bowery, and turned into Hester Street. On the north-west corner of Christie and Hester Streets stands an old tumble-down Dutch grocery, and into this we entered. I followed my friend into the dingy bar-room at the back of the store, and a moment afterward was introduced to Stephen Foster. Let me briefly describe him as he then appeared to me. A figure slight, and a little below the medium stature, apparelled in clothing so well worn as to betoken "the seedy gentleman who had seen better days;" his face long and closely shaven; the mouth of Silenus; soft brown eyes, somewhat dimmed by dissipation, shaded by

"Downfalling eyelids, full of dreams and slumber;"

a rather high forehead, disfigured by the peak of an old glazed cap that hung closely to his head, scarcely allowing his short-cut brown hair to be seen. His appearance was at once so youthful and so aged, that it was difficult to determine at a casual glance if he were twenty years old or fifty. An anxious, startled expression hovered over his face that was painful to witness. It was hard for me to force myself to believe that that poor, wretched-looking object was at that moment the most popular song-composer in the world; but it was Foster indeed! He seemed as embarrassed as a child in the presence of a stranger, and this diffidence never entirely wore off. As I afterward discovered, he would walk, talk, eat and drink with you, and yet always seem distant, maintaining an awkward dignity, if I may so term it. Whether it was a natural bashfulness, or a voluntary reserve, I cannot say, but those who knew him most intimately were never familiar. His conversation, made up mostly of musical reminiscences, was profitable as well as interesting; and, at his kind and pressing invitation, I took many an opportunity to visit him. He slept in an old lodging-house in the Bowery as a general thing; but that dark grocery bar-room was for a long time his sole head-quarters, and many an exquisite melody has had its birth in that uncongenial place. In his latter years he seldom wrote, unless he found himself without means to indulge his insatiable appetite for liquor. At such a time I have seen him take a sheet of brown wrapping-paper from the counter, and, seating himself at a little drinking-table, or more probably a bean-box, rapidly dot down a few bars of some sweet air that had been haunting him perhaps for many days, meantime whistling the passage over and over again, modifying it until he felt satisfied. Then would follow simple, liquid words, appropriate in sentiment—then a few more bars of melody—then more words, and thus music and words would develop themselves together, and form literally "one harmonious whole."[9] He was not one to haggle about the price when selling his songs; and it was not seldom, in consequence, that a publisher would take advantage of his miserable condition, paying him a paltry sum for what other composers would demand and receive a fair remuneration. It may be that such small transactions were deemed to be all for his good, in order not to minister to his well-known passion for drink, and not for any pecuniary profit to his publishers; it is at least charitable to believe so. Some petty meannesses, however, he could not forget. He entered the store of one of his Broadway publishers, one evening, and asked him personally for a few copies of one of his songs, ("Why have my loved-ones gone?" if I remember rightly), as he had an opportunity to dispose of them. They were refused him, and he left the store with the tears rolling down his cheeks, for he was very sensitive, and weeping came to him far more easily than smiling. This is but a single instance from many to show how unkindly those acted toward him who had good reason to be among his best friends; and, after some such harsh rebuff as this, he would often seek refuge in his old haunt, and there gloom over it for hours together. It is sad to think that he, who was forever singing of home and loved-ones, should have no dearer place that he could call a home, and no fond friend to comfort him; yet here he was, alone, in this great cold city, and writing of "love, love and only love." He might have said of his songs as Mrs. Browning said of her works:—

> "To have our books
> Appraised by love, associated with love,
> While we sit loveless,—it is hard, you think?
> At least, 'tis mournful!"

Yet he chose love as his favorite theme from the very first song that he ever wrote. He used often to talk of his earliest efforts, and how he first happened to write for the minstrels. At a very early age he had managed to attain, unaided, a moderate proficiency in playing upon the flageolet, flute, and pianoforte, and through their instrumentality he composed many a pleasant melody, to the delight of his boyhood's friends, and to his own no small gratification.

---

[9] His drafts of lyrics in his sketchbook suggest that he generally wrote his lyrics and music separately. Sketchbook, 1851–63, FHC, A298.

Stephen's voice was then clear and beautiful in tone, and of course he became quite a leading spirit in serenading expeditions; and in these his own songs were always the favorites. He sometimes said that he believed that it was in these parties, and the feelings of social good-fellowship generated by them, that the germs of his love for strong drink were first planted, to be the bane of his whole future existence. A travelling minstrel troupe, passing through Pittsburg, Pa., his native place, gave a few performances at which he chanced to be present. He was immediately fired with a desire to have one of his own songs brought before the public. "Oh! Susanna," was submitted by him, accepted, and sung, and shortly afterward was published by Peters, of Cincinnati, meeting with a decided success, but for which Stephen received twenty-five copies, or thereabouts, of the song. This was in the year 1842,[10] when Stephen, who was born on Independence Day, 1826, was a mere boy of sixteen. In that same year, "Open thy Lattice, Love!" a serenade, was published by George Willig, of Baltimore, and "Uncle Ned," by the publisher of his first composition, both songs becoming rapidly popular.[11] He saw and felt that he was appreciated, and needed no other incitement to exertion. Song after song he taught the people, each new one to be loved by them better only than the last; for he had acquired the secret of translating the thoughts, feelings, and sympathies of every-day life into melody. Whenever an opportunity offered itself he would visit Methodist Camp Meetings, both white and black, and, listening to their weird chantings, which he loved to do, he would gather many an idea for his folk-songs; and in this fact, perhaps, lies the secret of his wonderful success in writing negro melodies.[12] One song of Foster's in particular, sprang from this source, and that is "Hard Times, Come Again no more!"[13] And here I might mention, that on more than one occasion, in that self-same grocery bar-room, I have heard him sing that good old song of his, with a pathos that a state of semi-inebriation often lends the voice; while his pockets were in the peculiarly appropriate condition of emptiness not unusual to them, and the forlorn-looking *habitues* of the place joined dismally in the chorus.

---

[10] It is possible that Foster wrote "Oh! Susanna" in the early 1840s, when he was performing with his friends in an amateur minstrel troupe, but he did not give the song to Peters until 1848.

[11] This incorrect publication date for "Open Thy Lattice Love" was a common error. The song was actually published by Willig in 1844. "Uncle Ned" was first published by Peters in 1848.

[12] Beyond Birdseye's account, no evidence exists of Foster attending camp meetings.

[13] Given the similarity to Morrison's claims about the origins of "Hard Times" (see Chapter 24), one wonders if Morrison was Birdseye's source here.

It would be unnecessary to give a list of all of Foster's songs; they are so numerous, and mostly so well known: but the following table of sales of but a half-dozen of them, taken from a Catalogue of the publications of Firth, Pond & Co., issued over twelve years ago, will give some faint idea of their wonderful popularity:—

Old Folks at Home, ...... 200,000
My Old Kentucky Home, ...... 150,000
Massa's in the Cold, Cold Ground, ...... 75,000
Old Dog Tray, (six months,) ...... 75,000
Willie, We Have Missed You, ...... 125,000
Ellen Bayne, ...... 75,000[14]

During the last twelve years these figures must have greatly increased, for even at this day the demand has not ceased.

In writing "The Old Folks at Home" Foster hoped, and even expected, as he himself told me, to rival "Home, Sweet Home," the air of which he thought contrary to all the rules of pure melody. He could never account for its popularity and the enthusiasm and emotion with which it was received on every occasion. Perhaps had he not made his song local, by the mention of the Swanee River, it might have had a less ephemeral existence, and have equaled the song it was intended to eclipse; for it is a simple, touching and beautiful composition. But few have dared to follow where Foster failed, and "Home, Sweet Home" still stands secure, the home-song of the world. In looking over the titles of his pieces, it is curious and pleasant to notice how often the name *Jenny* occurs. As many as ten of them are woven about that loved name—the name of his wife. She was the daughter of the late Dr. McDowell, of Pittsburg,—"Little Jenny Dow" as he calls her in one of his songs. He not only sang his wife's praises, but always spoke of her in the fondest terms; yet why they thus lived separated he never mentioned, avoiding the subject whenever it was approached. During the years he spent in New-York, until his death, she was employed as a telegraph operator at Greensburg, and she

---

[14] Firth, Pond & Co. inflated sales figures. In Foster's accounting, he earned $1,647.46 in royalties from sales of "Old Folks at Home" between October 1851 and January 1857. Because his contracts stipulated that he earned a $0.02 royalty on every copy sold, $0.015 on every copy sold of an arrangement he made, and $0.01 on every copy sold of an arrangement made by other composers, it can be reasonably estimated that something in the ballpark of 100,000 non-pirated copies of all arrangements of "Old Folks" were purchased in the United States in a little more than five years. "Old Folks" was Foster's most popular song.

is, in all probability, holding the position at this present time.[15] He often used to say, in his tender moments, that she it was who, then a bright-eyed merry little girl, first inspired his soul with song, and made him long to attune it to the music of her voice.

"Jenny's Coming o'er the Green," recalling the happy time when he waited for her coming, seemed to be his favorite above all his compositions; and, when asked to sing, if he yielded at all, which was but rarely, he would almost invariably choose that. He used sometimes to come to my room, and sing in plaintive tones, to his simple chord accompaniments, his own sweet songs. His voice was of small compass, and but little power—ruined by dissipation—yet he sang so tenderly and so earnestly that the effect was always pleasing.

II.

"—Nay, nothing; all is said,
His tongue is now a stringless instrument;
Words, life, and all, old Lancaster hath spent."
RICHARD II, Act. II, Sc. 1

When a boy, Foster was considered a moderately fair draughtsman; though in after life, he made but a single attempt to show to the world the talent he possessed in that department of the fine arts, and that was unappreciated. "Willie, we have missed you," that fond outpouring of longing and welcome, was written, and in the printer's hands, when its author was struck by a brilliant idea for an illustrated title-page. After some considerable labor, not unaccompanied with pleasure, he produced what he then thought to be an excellent representation of the scene of Willie's return. A new sensation tickling his heart-strings, he hastened to the engraver, and, handing him his effort, waited with conscious pride for the praise he felt sure it would call forth. The artist looked at it for a moment, then turned to him with an inquiring gaze: "Ah! Another *comic* song, Mr. Foster?" This was too much; and, in an instant, the design was snatched from his hand, and lay in fragments on

---

[15] Jane probably worked as a telegraph operator until about 1869, when she married Matthew D. Wiley.

the floor. "And never after that," added he, when relating the incident, "did I essay to show my versatility of talent."

In speaking of the "Old Folks at Home,"—the best-selling song that he ever composed, and in fact the most profitable piece of music published in this country prior to the Rebellion,—I failed to state that on the title-page to the Tenth Edition the name of E. P. Christy, of minstrel notoriety, appears as its composer. For this privilege he paid Foster a considerable sum.[16]

The verses, as well as the music, of nearly all of his songs were Foster's own; and it is interesting to notice how much he loved to use *"melody"* and *"dreaming"* above all other words, in writing them. In all of his many serenades they both occur; and even in his daily conversation he was wont to show this favoritism.

George Cooper, the friend of whom I spoke at the opening of my former paper, and to whom I was indebted for my introduction to him, was, I believe, one of the few who prevailed upon him to wed his music to the words of another than himself. He offered him some verses entitled "Jenny June." The "Jenny" was more than he could resist; so the song was composed, and from that time forth Mr. Cooper furnished him with words whenever required.

It was at an early hour on the morning of the tenth of January, 1864, that the strange and fatal accident occurred that terminated poor Foster's life. He was lodging at the time, as had latterly been his custom, at the American Hotel.[17] Rising from his bed, his feet had scarcely touched the floor, when suddenly, and for the first time in his life, he fainted; and, falling face downward, struck upon a piece of crockery with such force as to break it, cutting his head and lacerating his throat in a most shocking manner. The proprietor of the hotel, happening to know Mr. Cooper's residence, immediately sent for

---

[16] Birdseye did not specify the amount that Foster received from Christy. Nevin and Morrison later claimed he was paid $500, but John Mahon and the anonymous interviewee in 1888 both claimed that Foster was paid only $15, which is confirmed in the composer's account book and was further corroborated by Howard (see Howard, *Stephen Foster*, 197–200). When offering comments on Birdseye's article, Morrison may have pushed Birdseye toward vague language about the fee; he certainly enlisted Nevin (perhaps without Nevin's awareness) in helping him greatly exaggerate his brother's income.

[17] In addition to Birdseye, the American Hotel was mentioned by Cooper and Morrison (see Chapter 9) and Harry Houdini (see Chapter 35), and Cooper indicated the address was 15 Bowery (see Chapters 9 and 37). Mahon incorrectly referred to the establishment as the New England Hotel (see Chapter 5), and Howard later incorrectly reasoned that Foster was in fact staying at the New England Hotel at 30 Bowery because it had previously been called the North American Hotel (Howard, *Stephen Foster*, 343). However, newspaper reports refer to 15 Bowery as the "American House." For example, on December 9, 1864, the *New York Daily Herald* ran an article about two men who swindled a man out of "one hundred and sixty five dollars in gold coin and a watch and chain valued at one hundred dollars... in the saloon attached to the American House, No. 15 Bowery." This must have been where Foster was living.

him; and on his coming, in answer to the summons, he found him covered with gore, lying on a mattrass [sic], in the hall by the door of the room he had been occupying. It needed but a glance to show that his condition was a critical one; so he was immediately carried to the Hospital, where he was kindly cared for, receiving every attention it was possible to give. Here he lingered but three days.[18] In his waking hours he was scarcely ever unconscious as to what was passing around him, but even conversed easily, and on customary topics. He laid out plans for the future, just as he had often done before, and as often failed to follow them;—but it would not be his fault, poor fellow, that they were this time to be for nought. He seemed to have no idea that he was dying; and if any one thinking it better that he should know his hopeless condition, ventured to suggest it, he would put it from him with a laugh.

On the morning of the 13th the attendant came to him to wash and bathe his head and throat where the blood coagulated. In answer to some objections, he told him that he would be very careful not to hurt him. "Oh! wait till to-morrow," whispered Foster. A gasp followed, his head fell back, and he sank dead into the attendant's arms.

It is sad, indeed, to think that no loved one was near to bid him farewell, or to take his last words and thoughts from his poor dying lips; and that the last scene upon which his eye rested upon earth was the weary hospital-ward, and not the "home" of which he so often and so fondly sang.

At first it was proposed to bury him by subscription, and many kindly came forward with liberal offers for the purpose. Before accepting any assistance, however, Mr. Cooper telegraphed to Cleveland, Ohio, to his brother, Morrison Foster:—"Your brother, Stephen Foster, is dead." His family had previously no intimation that he was even ill, as several messages failed to reach them.

This message reached its destination, carrying sorrow with it, as such tidings ever will. The answer was, "Procure a metallic coffin, and have every attention paid to Stephen's remains. I start for New York to-night." Mr. Foster's directions were immediately followed; and when, accompanied by Mrs. Stephen Foster, he arrived in the city, the body was already enclosed in its coffin, and prepared for removal to the home he had loved when life and hope were young. For one day it remained with the undertaker, at his rooms in Spring street; and there I went to take a last look of all that remained of Stephen Collins Foster, the "Song-writer of America." His face, though

---

[18] Hospital records indicate that he was admitted on January 10 and died on January 13.

somewhat changed, was easily recognizable; and I experienced a genuine sorrow, as I gazed on the motionless form before me, and thought what he might have been had he lived "the days of a man's life," and taken the position to which his heaven-sent gift of melody entitled him. I recalled, with pleasurable emotions, my acquaintanceship with him, slight though it had been, and, at that moment, I could see in him nothing but what was beautiful and good; and this seemed to be the feeling, not only of myself, but of each one of the few who had known him, then gathered around his coffin.

At length that cold, calm face,—ruffled only by that agonized expression that ever leaves its trace, even after life is fled,

> "When minds of heavenly tone
> Jar in the music that was born their own,"—

Was covered, and I saw it no more. Adams' Express Company kindly offered their services to convey the remains to Pittsburg, which were thankfully accepted. Here interesting and imposing ceremonies were held in his honor. A large concourse of people, eager to do homage to the memory of their gifted fellow-townsman, attended the funeral, accompanying the body to the grave. Many of his popular melodies were there performed, among them that exquisite four-part serenade, "Come where my love lies dreaming,"—his most elaborate and artistic composition.[19]

On both sides of the great water the news of Foster's death was nowhere lightly written nor lightly read; for the world does not soon forget him who had added even a single ray to the joys of home; and around nearly every fireside where the English language is spoken, his songs have been, and will be, not only familiar, but loved.

There is no class of composers to whom the meed [sic] of praise is more readily and cheerfully given, by the masses of the people, than to the songwriter. His fame may be comparatively an humble one; but how much greater, to a sensitive nature, must be his joy and satisfaction to feel that the blessed offices of his words and melodies are to gild sentiment, to excite sociality, to soften recollection, to waken anticipation, to bind closer the family circle, and to mediate between lovers. Foster's songs have done all these; for, though the writings of others may be more polished and refined, his are of

---

[19] Death announcements indicate that "Come Where My Love Lies Dreaming" and "Old Folks at Home" were performed at Foster's funeral. Living in New York, Birdseye would have had easy access to *Frank Leslie's Illustrated Newspaper*, which published its announcement on February 6, 1864.

a character pre-eminently calculated to take and to hold the popular fancy, having enough of grace, freshness, and feeling to stimulate and impress the heart of the hearer; but they exhibit their author rather as one who instinctively adopted that manner of expression, than one who made music a study and a religion.

It seems strange that the songs of a native American ever should have become so well and widely known. Our country boasts no ancient legend-wreathed ruins and castles, no moldering abbeys, no relics of royalty, no records of departed greatness, nothing that either age or tradition can call its own; and these, in older lands that live in memory alone, have been ever the soul of song. Yet Foster, singing of friendship, home, and love, and of a native land young enough to live in the hope of a future, has made his melodies loved throughout the world, and

> "The spinsters and the knitters in the sun,
> And the free maids that weave their thread with bones,
> Do use to chaunt them."

# 4
# Reminiscences of Robert P. Nevin (1867)

## Introduction

It is unknown when Robert Peebles Nevin (1820–1908) first met Foster. Perhaps he was among the "old acquaintances" about whom the composer wrote when he attended Jefferson College in Canonsburg, Pennsylvania, before withdrawing after only one week in 1841.[1] But it is also possible that they did not meet until later. Nevin's letters to the composer's brother Morrison, on whom he relied for information about the composer for the following article, suggest that they did not know each other well.

After graduating from Jefferson in 1842, Nevin operated numerous businesses in the Pittsburgh area, including a store where he sold medicines, paints, and, for a time, petroleum that he refined. He became active in politics in 1844, writing for the Washington Reporter (in Washington, Pennsylvania) and penning the song "Our Nominee," which was published in newspapers across the country. Many historians and obituarists have failed to grasp the song's satirical tone, claiming it helped propel Democrat James K. Polk to the presidency. However, the memoir of William G. Johnston, a Pittsburgher and Whig, demonstrates that the song was understood at the time as mocking Democrats and supporting Whig candidate Henry Clay:

> The most pleasing song of that time was a humorous one composed by Mr. Robert [P.] Nevin, and sung by him on a number of occasions.... The roisterers [Democratic characters in the song] when they began their bout did not know who the nominee was to be, but as the song proceeds the news came that his name was James K. Polk of Tennessee, of whom they had never heard; but fidelity to their party led them still to drink to him, though melancholy largely supplied the place of joviality.[2]

---

[1] Stephen Foster to William Foster Jr., July 24, 1841, FHC, A346.
[2] William Graham Johnston, *Life and Reminiscences from Birth to Manhood of Wm. G. Johnston* (Knickerbocker Press, 1901), 255.

*Formulating Foster*. Christopher Lynch, Oxford University Press. © Oxford University Press 2025.
DOI: 10.1093/9780197811726.003.0005

Like many Whigs, following the dissolution of his party Nevin joined the newly formed Republican Party, thus standing across the partisan divide from Foster. His reminiscence of Foster, which he published in the Atlantic in 1867, helped him pivot to a career in journalism. In 1870 he left his previous business ventures and became a co-owner and editor of the Pittsburg Weekly Leader, quickly transforming it into a daily newspaper. A decade later he founded the Pittsburg Times. Over the course of his career, he published three books, and two of his poems were set to music by his son, the composer Ethelbert Nevin.

Nevin slowly wrote his account of Foster's life over the three years following the songwriter's death. When he wrote to Morrison about his intention to write about his brother, he recalled being present at an "Ethiopian" song competition at the Eagle Ice Cream Saloon, where "Oh! Susanna" was greeted with great enthusiasm in 1848. He wrote,

> Do you remember . . . that your brother Stephen produced one of his earliest compositions on that occasion, which was received with rapturous applause? I can't recall all the circumstances, but recollect well the fact that you were present, from your stating to me at the time that you thought I was in the list of competitors, altho I was not. . . . Was not the song "Uncle Ned"? What was the prize offered? I know a good deal of your brother, and have long intended to write an article about him, but in consequence of the pressure of other demands on my time have never yet accomplished my purpose. I think of doing so now, and will be much indebted to you for your recollections of the occasion I refer to—down to the smallest particulars, together with any other facts and incidents in his life, which you will think may tend to illustrate it properly. Steve and I were always good friends, and I don't think that he has received the attention due him in consequence of his peculiarly remarkable talents.[3]

Morrison corrected Nevin's mistakes and filled in the blanks. Several months later Nevin asked him for "a <u>detailed</u> account of that old musical club arrangement of yours you told me of, when Steve first conceived the idea of writing songs. I think you said it was about the time I brought out 'Our Nominee.'"[4]

---

[3] Robert P. Nevin to Morrison Foster, July 21, 1865, FHC, C473a.
[4] Robert P. Nevin to Morrison Foster, March 29, 1866, FHC, C473b.

86  FORMULATING FOSTER

*It is unclear if Morrison steered Nevin toward a portrayal of Foster as a national symbol or if they shared the general view of the composer's national significance. But Nevin's Republicanism appears to have shaped his portrayal of Foster as a transformative American figure, musically and politically. He presented him as a "reformer of his art," erroneously crediting him with popularizing the ensemble minstrel show in the early 1840s and linking his "reforms" to the nation's story of racial progress in the Civil War era. Despite standing across the political aisle from Nevin, Morrison came to appreciate Nevin's characterization of his brother's role in the redefinition of the nation in the Civil War era, adopting the general premise in his later writings.*

*Morrison, however, was not pleased with several aspects of Nevin's article when it was published. On his copy he scribbled "there are many inaccuracies in this sketch," and he crossed out and corrected factual errors and descriptions of his brother that he disagreed with.[5] When he expressed his dissatisfaction to Nevin, Nevin explained one of the errors as a mistake introduced by the editors and defended his description of the composer's alcoholism, writing, "I have tried to give a true picture of Steve's life and character. To do this I had to refer to certain facts which I aimed to express in the most delicate terms. I hope I have done it without occasion of offense to any of his friends."[6] Nevin had probably carefully worded his brief and vague reference to Foster's drinking out of respect for Morrison's wishes. In private, he was more direct. His nephew remembered his uncle telling him that "the last time he saw 'the poor fellow' Foster was in a rather disreputable joint in Second Avenue, Pittsburgh, seated alone at a small table, staring at a bottle of whiskey."[7]*

*Although Nevin was a Republican and supported emancipation, the article exposes his sense of White racial superiority. His portrayal of African Americans consists of racist stereotypes and a reductive racial essentialism, referring to "idiosyncrasies of the negro" that can be humorously enacted on the stage. Writing as the nation reeled from the destruction caused by the Civil War, Nevin indirectly expressed the dual beliefs, common among Whites, that emancipation was morally necessary and that African Americans were not equal to Whites. By the end of the*

---

[5] Robert Peebles Nevin, "Stephen C. Foster and Negro Minstrelsy," *Atlantic Monthly*, November 1867, 608, FHC, C473d.
[6] Robert P. Nevin to Foster, October 24, 1867, FHC, C473c.
[7] Franklin T. Nevin to John Tasker Howard, October 27, 1934, FHC, Letters Catalogued (I–Z), box A-2.

*century, many White Americans from competing factions would unite behind this view. Foster's music, in all its ambiguity, was strongly situated to support this reconciliation, and Nevin's article—errors and all—was frequently drawn on by writers such as Morrison celebrating his music as a national symbol.*

---

## Robert P. Nevin, "Stephen C. Foster and Negro Minstrelsy," *The Atlantic Monthly,* November 1867.

Thirty-six years ago a young man, about twenty-five years of age, of a commanding height,—six feet full, the heels of his boots not included in the reckoning,—and dressed in scrupulous keeping with the fashion of the time, might have been seen sauntering idly along one of the principal streets of Cincinnati. To the few who could claim acquaintance with him he was known as an actor, playing at the time referred to a short engagement as light comedian in a theatre of that city. He does not seem to have attained to any noticeable degree of eminence in his profession, but he had established for himself a reputation among jolly fellows in a social way. He could tell a story, sing a song, and dance a hornpipe, after a style which, however unequal to complete success on the stage, proved, in private performance to select circles rendered appreciative by accessory refreshments, famously triumphant always. If it must be confessed that he was deficient in the more profound qualities, it is not to be inferred that he was destitute of all the distinguishing, though shallower, virtues of character. He had the merit, too, of a proper appreciation of his own capacity; and his arms never rose above that capacity. As a superficial man he dealt with superficial things, and his dealings were marked by tact and shrewdness. In his sphere he was proficient, and he kept his wits upon the alert for everything that might be turned to professional and profitable use. Thus it was that, as he sauntered along one of the main thoroughfares of Cincinnati, as has been written, his attention was suddenly arrested by a voice ringing clear and full above the noises of the street, and giving utterance, in an unmistakable dialect, to the refrain of a song to this effect:—

> Turn about an' wheel about an' do jis so,
> An' ebery time I turn about I jump Jim Crow.

Struck by the peculiarities of the performance, so unique in style, matter, and "character" of delivery, the player listened on. Were not these elements—was the suggestion of the instant—which might admit of higher than mere street or stable-yard development? As a national or "race" illustration, behind the footlights, might not "Jim Crow" and a black face tickle the fancy of pit and circle, as well as the "Sprig of Shillalah" and a red nose? Out of the suggestion leaped the determination; and so it chanced that the casual hearing of a song trolled by a negro stage-driver, lolling lazily on the box of his vehicle, gave origin to a school of music destined to excel in popularity all others, and to make the name of the obscure actor, T. D. Rice, famous.[8]

As his engagement at Cincinnati had nearly expired, Rice deemed it expedient to postpone a public venture in the newly projected line until the opening of a fresh engagement should assure him opportunity to share fairly the benefit expected to grow out of the experiment. This engagement had already been entered into; and accordingly, shortly after, in the autumn of 1830, he left Cincinnati for Pittsburg.[9]

The old theatre of Pittsburg occupied the site of the present one, on Fifth Street. It was an unpretending structure, rudely built of boards, and of moderate proportions, but sufficient, nevertheless, to satisfy the taste and secure the comfort of the few who dared to face consequences and lend patronage to an establishment under the ban of the Scotch-Irish Calvinists. Entering upon duty at the "Old Drury" of the "Birmingham of America," Rice prepared to take advantage of his opportunity. There was a negro in attendance of Griffith's Hotel, on Wood Street, named Cuff,—an exquisite specimen of his sort,—who won a precarious subsistence by letting his open mouth as a mark for boys to pitch pennies into, at three paces, and by carrying the trunks of passengers from the steamboats to the hotels. Cuff was precisely the subject for Rice's purpose. Slight persuasion induced him to accompany the actor to the theatre, where he was led through the private entrance, and

---

[8] Nevin overemphasizes Rice's role in the origins of blackface performance. While it is true that his performance of "Jim Crow" created a sensation, blackface was common for centuries in the theatrical and folk traditions of Europe and the United States. Rice also had immediate predecessors in the theater who performed solo acts in blackface, including Charles Matthews, Thomas Blakeley, and George Washington Dixon.

[9] Historical accounts disagree on when and where Rice first performed "Jump Jim Crow," claiming that it occurred in Louisville, Cincinnati, Pittsburgh, and Baltimore sometime between 1828 and 1831. Pointing to contemporaneous newspaper accounts and the earliest surviving concert program that denotes Rice's performance of the song, Dale Cockrell suggests Rice introduced the song in mid-1830 in Louisville (*Demons of Disorder: Early Blackface Minstrels and Their World* [Cambridge University Press, 1997], 63–64).

quietly ensconced behind the scenes. After the play, Rice, having shaded his own countenance to the "contraband" hue, ordered Cuff to disrobe, and proceeded to invest himself in the cast-off apparel. When the arrangements were complete, the bell rang, and Rice, habited in an old coat forlornly dilapidated, with a pair of shoes composed equally of patches and places for patches on his feet, and wearing a coarse straw hat in a melancholy condition of rent and collapse over a dense black wig of matted moss, waddled into view. The extraordinary apparition produced an instant effect. The crash of peanuts ceased in the pit, and through the circles passed a murmur and a bustle of liveliest expectation. The orchestra opened with a short prelude, and to its accompaniment Rice began to sing, delivering the first line by way of introductory recitative:—

> O, Jim Crow's come to town, as you all must know,
> An' he wheel about, he turn about, he do jis so,
> An' ebery time he wheel about he jump Jim Crow.

The effect was electric. Such a thunder of applause as followed was never heard before within the shell of that old theatre. With each succeeding couplet and refrain the uproar was renewed, until presently, when the performer, gathering courage from the favorable temper of his audience, ventured to improvise matter for his distiches from familiarly known local incidents, the demonstration were deafening.

Now it happened that Cuff, who meanwhile was crouching in dishabille under concealment of a projecting flat behind the performer, by some means received intelligence, at this point, of the near approach of a steamer to the Monongahela Wharf. Between himself and others of his color in the same line of business, and especially as regarded a certain formidable competitor called Ginger, there existed an active rivalry in the baggage-carrying business. For Cuff to allow Ginger the advantage of an undisputed descent upon the luggage of the approaching vessel would be not only to forfeit all "considerations" from the passengers, but, by proving him a laggard in his calling, to cast a damaging blemish upon his reputation. Liberally as he might lend himself to a friend, it could not be done at that sacrifice. After a minute or two of fidgety waiting for the song to end, Cuff's patience could endure no longer, and, cautiously hazarding a glimpse of his profile beyond the edge of the flat, he called in a hurried whisper: "Massa Rice, Massa Rice, must have my clo'se! Massa Griffif wants me,—steamboat's comin'!"

A still more successful couplet brought a still more tempestuous response and the invocation of the baggage-carrier was unheard and unheeded. Driven to desperation, and forgetful in the emergency of every sense of propriety, Cuff, in ludicrous undress as he was, started from his place, rushed upon the stage, and, laying his hand upon the performer's shoulder, called out excitedly: "Massa Rice, Massa Rice, gi' me nigga's hat,—nigga's coat,—nigga's shoes,—gi' me nigga's t'ings! Massa Griffif wants 'im,—steamboat's comin'!!"

The incident was the touch, in the mirthful experience of that night, that passed endurance. Pit and circles were one scene of such convulsive merriment that it was impossible to proceed in the performance; and the extinguishment of the footlights, the fall of the curtain, and the throwing wide of the doors for exit, indicated that the entertainment was ended. Such were the circumstances—authentic in every particular—under which the first work of the distinct art of Negro Minstrelsy was presented.

Next day found the song of Jim Crow, in one style of delivery or another, on everybody's tongue. Clerks hummed it serving customers at shop counters, artisans thundered it at their toils, to the time-beat of sledge and of tilt-hammer, boys whistled it on the streets, ladies warbled it in parlors, and house-maids repeated it to the clink of crockery in kitchens. Rice made up his mind to profit further by its popularity: he determined to publish it. Mr. W. C. Peters, afterwards of Cincinnati, and well known as a composer and publisher, was at that time a music-dealer on Market Street in Pittsburg.[10] Rice, ignorant himself of the simplest elements of musical science, waited upon Mr. Peters, and solicited his co-operation in the preparation of his song for the press. Some difficulty was experienced before Rice could be induced to consent to the correction of certain trifling informalities, rhythmical mainly, in his melody; but, yielding finally, the air as it now stands, with a pianoforte accompaniment by Mr. Peters, was put upon paper.[11] The

[10] William Cummings Peters was active as a musician and merchant in Pittsburgh between 1827 and 1832, at which point he moved to Louisville. He entered the music publishing business in 1838, with branches in Louisville, Baltimore, Cincinnati, New York, and St. Louis. While Foster was living in Cincinnati, Peters published "Oh! Susanna" and "Uncle Ned," the popularity of which inspired Foster to pursue songwriting as a career.

[11] The "awkwardness" of the melody and rhythm—the way it broke the established rules of European-based musical composition—was typical of blackface songs. Cockrell writes, "Early minstrelsy's music (or, its noise) jangled the nerves of those who believed in music that was proper, respectable, polished, and harmonic, with recognizable melodies. 'Jim Crow' was not at all the way music was supposed to be: It was music for the croaking voice and the wild fiddle; the tune is awkward, repetitive, and even boring; the texts are disjointed, generally nonnarrative, and unrealistic. This music assaulted sensibilities, challenged the roots of respectability, and promised subversion, a world undone, and, concomitantly, a new set of codes" (*Demons of Disorder*, 80–82).

manuscript was put into the hands of Mr. John Newton, who reproduced it on stone with an elaborately embellished title-page, including a portrait of the subject of the song, precisely as it has been copied through succeeding editions to the present time. It was the first specimen of lithography ever executed in Pittsburg.[12]

Jim Crow was repeated nightly throughout the season at the theatre; and when that was ended, Beale's Long Room, at the corner of Third and Market streets, was engaged for rehearsals exclusively in the Ethiopian line. "Clar de Kitchen" soon appeared as a companion piece, followed speedily by "Lucy Long." "Sich a Gittin' up Stairs," "Long-Tail Blue," and so on, until quite a repertoire was at command from which to select for an evening's entertainment.

Rice remained in Pittsburg some two years. He then visited Philadelphia, Boston, and New York, whence he sailed for England, where he met with high favor in his novel character, married, and remained for some time. He then returned to New York, and shortly afterwards died.[13]

With Rice's retirement his art seems to have dropped into disuse as a feature of theatrical entertainment, and thenceforward, for many years, to have survived only in the performances of circuses and menageries. Between acts the extravaganzaist in cork and wool would appear, and to the song of "Coal-Black Rose," or "Jim along Joe," or "Sittin' on a Rail," command with the clown and monkey, full share of admiration in the arena. At first he performed solos, and to the accompaniment of the "show" band; but the school was progressive; couples presently appeared, and, dispensing with the aid of foreign instruments, delivered their melodies to the more appropriate music of the banjo. To the banjo, in a short time, were added the bones. The art had now outgrown its infancy, and, disdaining a subordinate existence, boldly seceded from the society of harlequin and the tumblers, and met the world as an independent institution. Singers organized themselves into quartet bands; added a fiddle and tambourine to their instruments—perhaps we should say implements—of music; introduced the hoe-down and the conundrum to fill up the intervals of performance; rented halls, and, peregrinating from city to city and from town to town, went on and prospered.[14]

---

[12] "Jump Jim Crow" was first published by E. Reilly in New York, not in Pittsburgh and not by Peters. The well-known lithograph was not created by John Newton but by an unnamed lithographer.

[13] Leading up to his 1832 debut at the Bowery Theatre in New York, Rice was in and out of Pittsburgh, developing his act in cities and towns along the Ohio River. He first appeared in London in 1836. He died in 1860. Rice's grandson, Dean J. Rice, took exception to Nevin's characterization of his grandfather as retiring upon his return from London. See Chapter 40.

[14] These ensemble performances would be the first performances to be labeled "minstrelsy." The first troupe in the East to use the moniker was the Virginia Minstrels, led by Dan Emmett, which

One of the earliest companies of this sort was organized and sustained under the leadership of Nelson Kneass, who, while skillful in his manipulations of the banjo, was quite an accomplished pianist besides, as well as a favorite ballad-singer. He had some pretensions as a composer, but has left his name identified with no work of any interest. His company met with such success in Pittsburg, that its visits were repeated from season to season, until about the year 1845, when Mr. Murphy, the leading caricaturist, determining to resume the business in private life which he had laid aside on going upon the stage, the company was disbanded.[15]

Up to this period, if negro minstrelsy had made some progress, it was not marked by much improvement. Its charm lay essentially in its simplicity, and to give it full development, retaining unimpaired meanwhile such original excellences as Nature in Sambo shapes and inspires, was the task of the time. But the task fell into bungling hands. The intuitive utterance of the arts was misapprehended or perverted altogether. Its naïve misconceits were construed into coarse blunders; its pleasing incongruities were resolved into meaningless jargon. Gibberish became the staple of its composition. Slang phrases and crude jests, all odds and ends of vulgar sentiment, without regard to the idiosyncrasies of the negro, were caught up, jumbled together into rhyme, and, rendered into the lingo presumed to be genuine, were ready for the stage. The wit of the performance was made to consist in quibble and equivoke, and in the misuse of language, after the fashion, but without the refinement, of Mrs. Partington. The character of the music underwent a change. Original airs were composed from time to time, but the songs were more generally adaptations of tunes in vogue among Hard-Shell Baptists in Tennessee and at Methodist camp-meetings in Kentucky, and of backwoods, melodies, such as had been invented for native ballads by "settlement" masters and brought into general circulation by stage-drivers, wagoners, cattle-drovers, and other such itinerants of earlier days. Music of the concert-room was also drafted into the service, and selections from the inferior operas, with the necessary mutilations of the text, of course; so that the whole school

first performed in 1843. It was quickly imitated by performers such as Edwin P. Christy, founder of Christy's Minstrels. Concomitantly, along the river towns of what was then the West, troupes such as the Sable Harmonists led by Nelson Kneass were formed.

[15] "Mr. Murphy" is Joseph Murphy. The first edition of Foster's "Lou'siana Bell," issued by Peters in 1847, indicates it was "written for and sung by Joseph Murphy of the Sable Harmonists," and playbills indicate that Murphy performed Foster's music through at least the 1870s. Murphy would later claim that his brother James Murphy wrote "Old Folks at Home" (see Chapter 6, Introduction).

of negro minstrelsy threatened a lapse, when its course of decline was suddenly and effectually arrested.[16]

A certain Mr. Andrews, dealer in confections, cakes, and ices, being stirred by a spirit of enterprise, rented in the year 1845; a second-floor hall on Wood Street, Pittsburg, supplied it with seats and small tables, advertised largely, employed cheap attractions,—living statues, songs, dances, &c.,—erected a stage, hired a piano, and, upon the dissolution of his band, engaged the services of Nelson Kneass as musician and manager. Admittance was free, the ten-cent ticket required at the door being received at its cost value within towards the payment of whatever might be called for at the tables. To keep alive the interest of the enterprise, premiums were offered, from time to time, of a bracelet for the best conundrum, a ring with a ruby setting for the best comic song, and a golden chain for the best sentimental song. The most and perhaps only really valuable reward—a genuine and very pretty silver cup, exhibited night after night, beforehand—was promised to the author of the best original negro song, to be presented before a certain date, and to be decided upon by a committee designated for the purpose by the audience at that time.

Quite a large array of competitors entered the lists; but the contest would be hardly worthy of mention, save as it was the occasion of the first appearance of him who was to prove the reformer of his art, and to a sketch of whose career the foregoing pages are chiefly preliminary.[17]

Stephen Collins Foster was born in Alleghany [sic], Pennsylvania, on the 4th of July, 1826.[18] He was the youngest child of his father, William B. Foster,—originally a merchant of Pittsburg, and afterwards Mayor of his native city, member of the State Legislature, and a Federal officer under President Buchanan, with whom he was closely connected by marriage.[19]

---

[16] Minstrelsy dominated American popular culture throughout the 1840s. It did not decline, nor did it need to be rescued by Foster, as Nevin suggests.

[17] In his annotations, Morrison crossed out the word "first," indicating that Foster's songs had already made a public appearance. It is possible that the first public performance of Foster's music was in a performance mentioned in an article published on January 22, 1857, in the *Cincinnati Gazette*. Editor and friend of Foster John B. Russell wrote, "Foster's earliest song was 'Uncle Ned,' which was first sung in Cincinnati, at a concert by Pond, McCann, and others, in 1845, and enthusiastically encored. It was soon published by Mr. Peters, and reached a sale till then unknown in the music-publishing business."

[18] Foster was born in Lawrenceville, two-and-a-half miles upriver from Pittsburgh (annexed by the city after the Civil War). In the 1840s and 1850s, when Nevin knew Foster, the songwriter lived in the city of Allegheny, across the river from Pittsburgh. These locations are all in Allegheny County.

[19] On his own copy of this article, Morrison notes that his father worked under presidents Madison, Monroe, Jackson, and Tyler but not Buchanan. Under Madison, he was appointed deputy commissioner of purchases based in Pittsburgh for the US Army. If Morrison is to be believed, he held this post into the Monroe administration. It is unclear what he did, if anything, under Jackson. Under

The evidences of a musical capacity of no common order were apparent in Stephen at an early period. Going into a shop, one day, when about seven years old, he picked up a flageolet, the first he had ever seen, and comprehending, after an experiment or two, the order of the scale of the instrument, was able in a few minutes, uninstructed, to play any of the simple tunes within the octave with which he was acquainted. A Thespian society, composed of boys in their higher teens, was organized in Alleghany, into which Stephen, although but in his ninth year, was admitted, and of which, from his agreeable rendering of the favorite airs of the day, he soon became the leading attraction.

At thirteen years of age, he made his first attempt at composition, producing for a public occasion at the seminary in Athens, Ohio, where he was a student at the time, the "Tioga Waltz," which, although quite a pretty affair, he never thought worthy of preservation.[20] In the same year, shortly afterwards, he composed music to the song commencing, "Sadly to mine heart appealing," now embraced in the list of his publications, but not brought out until many years later.[21]

Stephen was a boy of delicate constitution, not addicted to the active sports or any of the more vigorous habits of boys of his age. His only companions were a few intimate friends, and, thus secluded, his character naturally took a sensitive, meditative cast, and his growing disrelish for severer tasks was confirmed. As has been intimated, he entered as a pupil at Athens; but as the course of instruction in that institution was not in harmony with his tastes, he soon withdrew, applying himself afterwards to the study of the French and

---

Tyler he briefly worked as a clerk in the Treasury Department in 1841 in the District of Columbia, but he resigned after only a few weeks when he was elected mayor of Allegheny City. In 1833, his daughter Ann Eliza, Stephen Foster's sister, married Edward Buchanan, brother of politician and future president James Buchanan.

[20] Foster attended school at Athens in Pennsylvania, not Ohio. Morrison recalled the tune from memory in 1896. According to a letter Morneweck wrote to Hodges, "Father whistled it to one of the men in Mellor's Music Store, and he jotted it down." The letter and the manuscript, presumably in the hand of the man from the music store, are found in FHC. Evelyn Foster Morneweck to Fletcher Hodges Jr., February 11, 1953, FHC, unprocessed folder labeled "Morrison Foster's draft 'From Memory' of Tioga Waltz."

[21] Foster did not write "Sadly to Mine Heart Appealing" at the age of 13 in 1839–40. The poem, by Eliza Sheridan Carey, was first published in Littell's Living Age in October of 1844. Foster may have written an early version of the song upon encountering the poem in the magazine, but the only evidence pertaining to the composition of the song is a letter he wrote to Morrison in 1858 from New York, asking him to send "the book containing scotch melodies." He explained, "I have sent to F. P. & Co. the song 'Sadly to mine heart appealing'... and would like to select an old tune for the introductory symphony." After Morrison sent him the book, he selected the tune "Robin Adair" for the piano introduction and closing. Firth, Pond & Co. published the song that year.

German languages (a ready fluency in both of which he finally acquired), and especially to the art dearer than all other studies.[22] A recluse, owning and soliciting no guidance but that of his text-book, in the quiet of the woods, or, if that were inaccessible, the retirement of his chamber, he devoted himself to this art.

At the age of sixteen he composed and published the song, "Open thy Lattice, Love," which was admired, but did not meet with extraordinary success.[23] In the year following he went to Cincinnati, entering the counting-room of his brother, and discharging the duties of his place with faithfulness and ability. His spare hours were still devoted, however, to his favorite pursuit, although his productions were chiefly preserved in manuscript, and kept for the private entertainment of his friends. He continued with his brother nearly three years.[24]

At the time Mr. Andrews of Pittsburg offered a silver cup for the best original negro song, Mr. Morrison Foster sent to his brother Stephen a copy of the advertisement announcing the fact, with a letter urging him to become a competitor for the prize.[25] These saloon entertainments occupied a neutral ground, upon which eschewers of theatrical delights could meet with the abetters of play-house amusements,—a consideration of ruling importance in Pittsburg, where so many of the sterling population carry with them to this day, by legitimate inheritance, the stanch old Cameronian fidelity to Presbyterian creed and practice. Morrison, believing that these concerts would afford an excellent opportunity for the genius of his brother to appeal to the public, persisted in urging him to compete for the prize, until Stephen, who at first expressed a dislike to appear under such circumstances, finally yielded, and in due time forwarded a melody entitled, "'Way down South, whar de Corn grows."[26] When the eventful night came, the various pieces

---

[22] After Foster completed his studies in Athens, he attended Jefferson College but withdrew after only one week.

[23] It was often incorrectly stated that "Open Thy Lattice Love" was published in 1842. But it actually appeared in 1844, the year Foster turned 18.

[24] Morrison annotated that it was in 1846 that Foster went to work for his brother Dunning McNair Foster in Cincinnati. Family letters corroborate that it was around this time. The last record of Foster in Allegheny City is a letter from William Sr. dated October 31, 1846, and the first record of him in Cincinnati is a letter from his mother Eliza dated August 23, 1847. Although he shuttled back and forth between Cincinnati and Allegheny, he remained a resident of Cincinnati until early 1850.

[25] Nevin's chronology suggests this competition occurred between 1842 and 1844, but it actually took place on September 11, 1847.

[26] The published title is "Away Down Souf, Whar de Corn Grows." According to an advertisement in the *Pittsburgh Commercial Journal* on September 11, 1847, "Oh! Susanna" was also performed at the competition.

in competition were rendered to the audience by Nelson Kneass to his own accompaniment on the piano. The audience expressed by their applause a decided preference for Stephen's melody; but the committee appointed to sit in judgment decided in favor of some one else, himself and his song never heard of afterwards, and the author of "Way down South" forfeited the cup. But Mr. Kneass appreciated the merit of the composition, and promptly, next morning, made application at the proper office for a copyright in his own name as author, when Mr. Morrison Foster, happening in at the moment, interposed, and frustrated the discreditable intention.

This experiment of Foster's, if it fell short of the expectation of his friends, served, notwithstanding, a profitable purpose, for it led him to a critical investigation of the school of music to which it belonged. This school had been—was yet—unquestionably popular. To what, then, was it indebted for its captivating points? It was to its truth to Nature in her simplest and most childlike mood.

Settled as to theory, Foster applied himself to the task of its exemplification. Two attempts were made while he yet remained in Cincinnati, the pencil-drafts of which, however, were laid aside for the time being in his portfolio. His shrinking nature held timidly back at the thought of a venture before the public; and so the case stood until he reappeared in Pittsburg.

The Presidential campaign of 1844 was distinguished by political song-singing. Clubs for that purpose were organized in all the cities and towns and hamlets,—clubs for the platform, clubs for the street, clubs for the parlor, Whig clubs, Democratic clubs. Ballads innumerable to airs indefinite, new and old, filled the hand,—Irish ballads, German ballads, Yankee ballads, and, preferred over all, negro ballads. So enthusiastic grew the popular feeling in this direction, that, when the November crisis was come and gone, the peculiar institution, would not succumb to the limitation, but lived on. Partisan temper faded out; the fires of strife died down, but clubs sat perseveringly in their places, and in sounds, if not in sentiment, attuned to the old melodies, kept up the practice of the mad and merry time.

Among other organizations that thus lingered on was one, composed of half a dozen young men, since grown into graver habits, with Foster—home again, and a link once more in the circle of his intimates—at its head. The negro airs were still the favorites; but the collection, from frequent repetition, at length began to grow stale. One night, as a revival measure for the club, and as an opportunity for himself, Foster hinted that, with their permission, he would offer for trial an effort of his own. Accordingly he set to work; and at their next meeting laid before them a song entitled "Louisiana Belle." The piece elicited unanimous applause. Its success in the club-room opened to it a wider field, each member acting as an agent of dissemination outside, so that in the course of a few nights the song was sung in almost every parlor in Pittsburg. Foster then brought to light his portfolio specimens, since universally known as "Uncle Ned," and "O Susanna!" The favor with which these latter were received surpassed even that rewarding the "Louisiana Belle." Although limited to the one slow process of communication,—from mouth to ear,—their fame spread far and wide, until from the drawing-rooms of Cincinnati they were introduced into its concert-halls, and there became known to Mr. W. C. Peters, who at once addressed letters requesting copies for publication. These were cheerfully furnished by the author. He did not look for remuneration. For "Uncle Ned," which first appeared (in 1847), he received none; "O Susanna!" soon followed, and "imagine my delight," he writes, "in receiving one hundred dollars in cash!"[27] Though this song was not successful," he continues, "yet the two fifty-dollar bills I received for it had the effect of starting me on my present vocation of song-writer." In pursuance of this decision, he entered into arrangements with new publishers, chiefly with Firth, Pond, & Co. of New York, set himself to work, and began to pour out his productions with astonishing rapidity.

Out of the list, embracing about one hundred and fifty of his songs, the most flattering received among his negro melodies were those already enumerated, followed by "Nelly was a Lady," in 1849; "My Old Kentucky Home" [1853] and "Camptown Races," in 1850; "Old Folks at Home," in 1851; "Massa's in the Cold Ground," in 1852; "O Boys, carry me 'long," in 1853; "Hard Times come again no more," in 1854; "Way down South," and "O Lemuel," in 1858 [1849]; "Old Black Joe," in 1860; and (noticeable only as his last in that line) "Don't bet your Money on the Shanghai," in 1861.[28]

In all these compositions Foster adheres scrupulously to his theory adopted at the outset. His verses are distinguished by a naïveté characteristic and appropriate, but consistent at the same time with common sense. Enough of the negro dialect is retained to preserve distinction, but not to offend. The sentiment is given in plain phrase and under homely illustration; but it is a sentiment nevertheless. The melodies are of twin birth literally

---

[27] W. C. Peters published both "Uncle Ned" and "Oh! Susanna" in 1848.

[28] Although "Hard Times Come Again No More" is not often thought of as a minstrel song today, Nevin's inclusion of the song in this list of minstrel songs indicates it was considered a minstrel song in Foster's day.

with the verses, for Foster thought in tune as he traced in rhyme, and traced in rhyme as he thought in tune. Of easy modulation, severely simple in their structure, his airs have yet the graceful proportions, animated with the fervor, unostentatious but all-subduing, of certain of the old hymns (not the chorals) derived from our fathers of a hundred years ago.

That he had struck upon the true way to the common heart, the successes attending his efforts surely demonstrate. His songs had an unparalleled circulation. The commissions accruing to the author on the sales of "Old Folks" alone amounted to fifteen thousand dollars.[29] For permission to have his name printed on its title-page, as an advertising scheme, Mr. Christy paid five hundred dollars.[30] Applications were unceasing from the various publishers of the country for some share, at least, of his patronage, and upon terms that might have seduced almost any one else; but the publishers with whom he originally engaged had won his esteem and Foster adhered to them faithfully. Artists of the highest distinction favored him with their friendship; and [Henri] Herz, [Camillo] Sivori, Ole Bull, [Sigismond] Thalberg, were alike ready to approve his genius, and to testify that approval in the choice of his melodies as themes about which to weave their witcheries of embellishment. Complimentary letters from men of literary note poured in upon him; among others, one full of generous encouragement from Washington Irving, dearly prized and carefully treasured to the day of Foster's death. Similar missives reached him from across the seas,—from strangers and from travellers in lands far remote; and he learned that while "O Susanna!" was the familiar song of the cottager of the Clyde, "Uncle Ned" was known to the dweller in tents among the Pyramids.[31]

Of his sentimental songs, "Ah, may the Red Rose live always!" "Maggie by my Side," "Jennie with the Light-Brown Hair," "Willie, we may have missed you," "I see her still in my Dreams," "Wilt thou be gone, Love" (a duet, the words adapted from a well-known scene in Romeo and Juliet), and "Come where my Love lies dreaming" (quartet), are among the leading favorites. "I

---

[29] According to Foster's account book, shortly before he sold away future royalties from "Old Folks at Home" to Firth, Pond & Co., he had earned a total of $1,647.46 in royalties from sales of the song.

[30] Foster received $15, not $500, from Christy.

[31] Probably because of Morrison's influence, Nevin misleadingly suggests that Foster had personal relationships with "artists of the highest distinction." Morrison would echo these words in his own reminiscence (see Chapter 24). But Foster almost certainly did not have relationships with these artists. Mahon's response to these claims is more believable (see Chapter 5).

see her still in my Dreams" appeared in 1861,[32] shortly after the death of his mother, and is a tribute to the memory of her to whom he was devotedly attached. The verses to most of these airs—to the successful ones—were of his own composition. Indeed, he could seldom satisfy himself in his "settings" of the stanzas of others.[33] If the metrical and symmetrical features of the lines in hand chanced to disagree with his conception of the motion and proportion befitting in a musical interpretation; if the sentiment were one that failed, whether from lack of appreciation or of sympathy on his part, to command absolute approval; or if the terms employed were not of a precise thread and tension,—if they were wanting, however minutely, in vibratory qualities,—of commensurate extent would be the failure attending the translation.

The last three years of his life Mr. Foster passed in New York. During all that time, his efforts, with perhaps one exception, were limited to the production of songs of a pensive character.[34] The loss of his mother seems to have left an ineffaceable impression of melancholy upon his mind, and inspired such songs as "I dream of my Mother," "I'll be Home To-Morrow," "Leave me with my Mother," and "Bury me in the Morning." He died after a brief illness, on the 13th of January, 1864. His remains reached Pittsburg on the 20th, and were conveyed to Trinity Church, where on the day following, in the presence of a large assembly, appropriate and impressive ceremonies took place, the choral services being sustained by a company of his former friends and associates. His body was then carried to the Alleghany [sic] Cemetery, and, to the music of "Old Folks at Home," finally committed to the grave.

Mr. Foster was married, on the 22d of July, 1850, to Miss Jane D. McDowell of Pittsburg, who, with her daughter and only child, Marian [sic], twelve years of age at the date of his death, still survives him. He was of rather less

---

[32] Foster's mother died in 1855, and "I See Her Still in My Dreams" was first published in 1857.

[33] After moving to New York in 1860, Foster wrote music for other people's words more frequently than he had earlier. But Nevin did not realize how many times Foster had set other people's words in the 1840s and 1850s. These songs include "Open Thy Lattice Love," "There's a Good Time Coming," "Summer Longings," "The Spirit of My Song," "Eulalie," "Once I Loved Thee, Mary Dear," "I Cannot Sing To-night," "Annie My Own Love," "Sadly to Mine Heart Appealing," "My Angel Boy," "Linda Has Departed," "Parthenia to Ingomar," "For Thee, Love, For Thee," and "None Shall Weep a Tear for Me."

[34] Nevin knew little of Foster's compositional activities in New York. In truth, in New York Foster wrote lively minstrel songs (e.g., "Don't Bet Your Money on de Shanghai" and "A Soldier in the Colored Brigade"), comic songs (e.g., "Mr. and Mrs. Brown," "My Wife Is a Most Knowing Woman," "If You've Only Got a Moustache"), and war songs (e.g., "We Are Coming, Father Abraam, 300,000 More," "We've a Million in the Field," and "That's What's the Matter").

than medium height, of slight frame, with parts well proportioned, and showing to advantage in repose, although not entirely so in action. His shoulders were marked by a slight droop,—the result of a habit of walking with his eyes fixed upon the ground a pace or two in advance of his feet. He nearly always when he ventured out, which was not often, walked alone. Arrived at the street-crossings, he would frequently pause, raise himself, cast a glance at the surroundings, and if he saw an acquaintance nod to him in token of recognition, and then, relapsing into the old posture, resume his way. At such times,—while he did not repel, he took no pains to invite society. He was entertaining in conversation, although a certain hesitancy, from want of words and not from any organic defect, gave a broken style to his speech. For his study he selected a room in the top-most story of his house, farthest removed from the street, and was careful to have the floor of the apartment, and the avenues of approach to it, thickly carpeted, to exclude as effectually as possible all noises, inside as well as outside of his own premises. The furniture of this room consisted of a chair, a lounge, a table, a music-rack, and a piano. From the sanctum so chosen, seldom opened to others, and never allowed upon any pretence [sic] to be disarranged, came his choicest compositions. His disposition was naturally amiable, although, from the tax imposed by close application to study upon his nervous system, he was liable to fits of fretfulness and scepticism that, only occasional and transient as they were, told with disturbing effect upon his temper. In the same unfortunate direction was the tendency of a habit grown insidiously upon him,—a habit against the damning control of which (as no one better than the writer of this article knows) he wrestled with an earnestness indescribable, resorting to all the remedial expedients which professional skill or his own experience could suggest, but never entirely delivering himself from its inexorable mastery.

In the true estimate of genius, its achievements only approximate the highest standard of excellence as they are representative, or illustrative, of important truth. They are only great as they are good. If Mr. Foster's art embodied no higher idea than the vulgar notion of the negro as a man-monkey,—a thing of tricks and antics,—a funny specimen of superior gorilla,—then it might have proved a tolerable catch-penny affair, and commanded an admiration among boys of various growths until its novelty wore off. But the art in his hands teemed with a nobler significance. It dealt, in its simplicity, with universal sympathies, and taught us all to feel with the slaves the lowly joys and sorrows it celebrated.[35]

May the time be far in the future ere lips fail to move to its music, or hearts to respond to its influence, and may we who owe him so much preserve gratefully the memory of the master, STEPHEN COLLINS FOSTER.

---

[35] Nevin echoes Frederick Douglass's statement that two of Foster's songs can "awaken the sympathies for the slave, in which anti-slavery principles take root, grow and flourish." Nevin, a Republican, most likely read Douglass's autobiography *My Bondage and My Freedom*, in which these words were published in 1855. But he tamped down the radicalism of Douglass's rhetoric, referring only to sympathy rather than abolition and omitting Douglass's qualification that Foster's songs were also performed in dehumanizing ways. He also extended Douglass's favorable words about two of Foster's songs to everything Foster composed.

# 5
# Reminiscences of John Mahon (1877)

## Introduction

*John Mahon was born around 1815 in Ireland. After serving in the British Army in Malta and living in Greece, he immigrated to New York in 1853. He worked as a newspaper reporter, joined Masonic Lodge 227, and, later, befriended Foster, who moved to New York in 1860. By the end of the decade, Mahon was working for the Masons as the official reporter to the Grand Lodge of New York, preparing proceedings and reporting in periodicals on their activities. He may have died in early 1877, around the time this reminiscence appeared in the* New York Clipper. *He is listed in* Trow's New York City Directory for the Year Ending May 1, 1877, *but his name does not appear in later directories, nor does it appear in the 1880 US Census.*

*Like Foster, Mahon wrote and composed songs that were published by William A. Pond & Co. (formed in 1863 after the dissolution of Firth, Pond & Co.) and John Daly. Also like Foster, Mahon wrote a "Jenny" song, "Jennie Lives but for Thee," and he wrote war songs that addressed wartime issues without being divisive, such as "The Standard of the Free," "Corcoran's Ball" (which demonstrates his pride in his Irish heritage),[1] and "A Soldier Is My Beau." He also wrote more general sentimental songs, such as "The Heart That Pines for Thee." It is not surprising, then, that Foster and Mahon were close friends and that Foster gave to Mahon two silhouettes of himself, which he inscribed "to my friend" and signed (Figure 5.1) Despite their closeness, however, Foster and Mahon collaborated on only one song, "Our Darling Kate," which consists of melody and lyrics by Mahon and piano arrangement by Foster.*

*Mahon wrote the following remarkable account in direct reply to an article titled "The Minstrel Melodist" that appeared in the* New York Clipper

---

[1] According to historian Catherine V. Bateson, "Of all the Irish-born and descended officers, soldiers, and sailors whose wartime service was written into songs, arguably Michael Corcoran stands above all others." Catherine V. Bateson, *Irish American Civil War Songs* (Louisiana State University Press, 2022), 86.

on March 3, 1877. That article is a reworking of Nevin's reminiscence, with more flowery embellishments and a few added mistakes. That Nevin's article was the source is confirmed by the repetition of some of Nevin's mistakes—for example, the statement that Foster studied in Athens, Ohio, when in fact he studied in Athens, Pennsylvania—as well as by the inclusion of a long quotation of Nevin's article. Thus, Mahon's account is an indirect rebuke of Nevin's reminiscence and the information that had been fed to him by Morrison (and that would later reappear in Morrison's biography).

Mahon amplifies some of the Clipper author's statements. He buttresses the idea that Foster's "songs had an unparalleled circulation" by recollecting his first encounter with Foster's music in Greece. And he supports the statement that the songwriter was "connected by marriage with the late President James Buchanan." Yet more often Mahon disputes the author's claims. He refutes that "'Old Folks at Home' brought him over $15,000 from Firth, Pond & Co." and that "Christy paid $500" to advertise his name on the cover. He also refutes that Foster "seldom went out of doors, and in his few walks never sought companionship" by offering anecdotes of their socializing together and about town. And, finally, he disputes the article's claims—regurgitated from Nevin, who almost definitely got it from Morrison—that mail poured in from famous people, including Washington Irving, and that Foster cherished those letters until his death.

## John Mahon, "The Last Years of Stephen C. Foster," *New York Clipper*, March 24, 1877.

The sketch entitled "The Minstrel Melodist" in THE CLIPPER of March 3, though extremely well written, contains a few inaccuracies, which, with the permission of the editor, I propose to correct in this article, and also to add some reminiscences of the last two or three years of the life of Stephen Collins Foster which came under my own personal observation.

The first time I heard say of the melodies of this truly gifted man was in the Autumn of the year 1852, in Patras (the Mores), Greece. I had retired from the 69th Regiment of the British Infantry in 1850, in Malta, and, after some struggle in civil life, I was offered a position as clerk to a ship-chandler in Patras, at a salary which in New York would scarcely keep me in shoe-leather, but which in Patras or Malta was considered princely. The captain and owner of one of the English schooners which were consigned to my employer was a

**Figure 5.1.** Silhouettes of Stephen Foster, made for his friend John Mahon. Foster Hall Collection, Center for American Music, University of Pittsburgh Library System.

wealthy man, and had his wife and family, with a lady's maid, on board. One evening the captain and his family were invited to tea by my employer—who was also an Englishman—and during the evening the captain's wife, who was an excellent pianist, entertained us with some good music. Suddenly, turning to his two sons, who were about the ages of ten and twelve, he said:

**Figure 5.1.** Continued

"Come, sing one of those beautiful melodies which came out in London before we sailed."

The boys obeyed, and, accompanied by their mother, struck up "O Susannah, Don't You Cry for Me," and on being encored by the company they sang "Uncle Ned." Some months after, when the current season was over, I returned to Malta, and one day strolled up the Plazza Reale to see the guard-trooping, which always took place in front of the Governor's palace, and which is similar to that you call "beating off" in the United States. The quick march by the band on that occasion was "O Susanna!" and I wrote the air down afterwards from memory, and kept it by me, really believing it to be an English song, for all poor Foster's melodies were republished in England without even his name on the title-page. I arrived in America in 1853, and during the voyage from Malta, on board the bark Wildfire of Boston, heard the sailors sing many of Foster's songs, especially "Way Down upon the Swanee River," a song which impressed itself upon my memory ever after from hearing it sung in 1854 by the late James Lingard, at Purdy's National Theatre, in Chatham street, in the character of Uncle Tom, when Miss Cordelia Howard was Little Eva, her mother Topsy, and her father St. Clair.

In 1861, I think it was, I was standing in Windust's restaurant, in Park row,[2] one day, with one or two other journalists, when my attention was attracted by a short man, such as is described in THE CLIPPER article, who was very neatly dressed in a blue swallow-tailed coat, high silk hat, and-so-forth (the and-so-forth I forget). This gentleman walked up to the bar, took his drink, and was turning away, when Mr. E. P. Barcy, the barkeeper, whispered to me: "That is Stephen C. Foster, the great song-writer!"

I was enthusiastic about the man, as I had done something in his line myself, though at that time I had not published any music. I followed him out and introduced myself, and I must say that I found him most social and conversational. He enjoyed my enthusiasm very much, was pleased when I introduced him to people of note; but agreed with me on a signal, by which I understood when he did not wish to be known. This signal was a careless clapping of the hands three times, and when I heard that I simply introduced him as Mr. Foster. I took him to my residence and introduced him to my family and nearly all his latest songs were composed upon my piano. At that time he boarded at (I think) No. 83 Greene street, with his wife and little daughter Marian [sic], who was about eight years old. The boarding-house was kept by a Mr. and Mrs. Stewart.[3]

From that time until about a month before his death Foster and I were almost inseparable. In 1863 he was at the wedding of my oldest daughter, and played and sang several of his own pieces on that occasion, at which several theatrical lights were present, including George C. Boniface, Mrs. Boniface, and her sister (the late Kate Newton), and others whose names I now forget,

---

[2] Windust's was a restaurant and saloon located at 5-11 Park Row. According to Cindy R. Lobel, "Its walls [were] lined with playbills, clippings, and theater images," which made it "the headquarters of New York's theater crowd for years." Lobel, "'Out to Eat': The Emergence and Evolution of the Restaurant in Nineteenth-Century New York City," *Winterthur Portfolio* 44, nos. 2–3 (Summer-Autumn 2010): 205.

[3] Consulting city directories, Howard identifies a boardinghouse under the name Stuart at 113 Greene in 1859–60 and at 97 Greene in 1863–64. See Howard, *Stephen Foster*, 320.

except that the late John Nunan was one, and Mr. Joseph P. Beach of *The Sun* another.[4] He told me a great deal of his early career, and here I regret that I must tear away the veil of romance, and show the naked reality. The article says:

"'The Old Folks at Home' brought him in over $15,000 from Firth, Pond & Co. It has been said that E. P. Christy paid him liberally to allow that minstrel's name to appear on the latter's bills as the author of some of the songs written by Foster. We have no proof at hand that Christy's name ever so appeared except in the equivocal and ambiguous way in which any singer's name is liable to appear in connection with the song he is called upon to sing." (Well, I will furnish good and sufficient proof concerning one song at least.) "E. P. Christy's name was, however, on the title-page of one edition of the music of 'Old Folks at Home,' and for this advertisement, whether or not it was so worded as to imply authorship, it is admitted by the friends of Foster that Christy paid $500."

Well, "the friends of Foster" "admitted" more than ever did Foster himself. Long before I knew Foster I saw a song in Firth & Pond's (then on Franklin square) called "The Old Folks at Home, words and music by E. P. Christy" (it might be, perhaps, "Written and composed by E. P. Christy"), but, as I read it, it certainly "implied" not only "authorship," but "composership" also (if I may use the term), to my unsophisticated mind.

One night, while sitting in my apartments, then at 311 Henry street, my wife asked Stephen if he knew "The Old Folks at Home."

"By ------," he replied. "I should think I ought, for I got $2,000 (not $15,000, mind) for it from Firth, Pond & Co."

"Why," said I, "how could that be? Was not E. P. Christy the author and composer?"

"Oh, no, John," replied he, laughing. "Christy paid me fifteen dollars (not $500) for allowing his name to appear as the author and composer. I did so on condition that after a certain time his name should be superseded by my own. One hundred thousand copies of the first edition were soon sold, for which I received a royalty of two cents per copy, and received $1,400 in the same way for 'Willie, We Have Missed You.' Subsequently I sold out my royalties, and have now a contract to furnish Pond with twelve songs a year, for which I received $800 per annum, payable monthly at $66.66, and I have

---

[4] According to the 1860 US Census, his eldest daughter's name was Mary J. Mahon.

permission to furnish six songs per annum to Lee & Walker of Philadelphia for $400; so my income now is $1,200 per annum."[5]

In confirmation of a portion of the above, I remember having a conversation with Mr. Pond afterwards, in which that gentleman said to me:

"Why, I paid him *two thousand dollars* for 'The Old Folks at Home.'"[6]

One of the pieces composed for Lee & Walker was a duet called "The Mourning Heart," which he taught my youngest daughter (then about ten years old) to sing with him. This girl, who was afterwards the wife of an actor named W. J. Gross of Langrishe's company, now in the Black Hills, died on March 11, 1875, in Mexico. An obituary notice of her, written by one of the company, appeared about May of that year in THE CLIPPER. She was known professionally as Annie Mahon.[7]

THE CLIPPER speaks of Christine Nilsson singing "The Old Folks at Home" at Steinway Hall. At one of her concerts in the same hall, M. Vieuxtemps played "Willie, We Have Missed You" (another of his pieces), with splendid variations on the violin.

He once told me the history of "Comrades, Fill No Glass for Me." It was very interesting, but I regret I have forgotten it. Later in life, poor fellow, he, perhaps, had too many filled for him. But *"Nil mortuis nisi bonum."*

The history of "Jennie's Coming O'er the Green" he also told me. It was somewhat funny. It appears that he admired a young girl named Jennie (platonic, of course), and promised to write a song for her. He did so, and began it thus:

> Little Jennie's seventeen;
> Fairer form was never seen,
> Life and grace are in her mien.
> Why do I love her so?

---

[5] For more on the fee Foster received from Christy for "Old Folks," see Howard, *Stephen Foster*, 197–200.

[6] It appears to be accurate that Foster received $2,000 from "Old Folks." We know from Foster's account book that he earned a total of $1,647.46 in royalties from the song between 1851 and 1857. Furthermore, Firth, Pond & Co. bought out Foster from his future royalties to all songs published by them up that point for $1,872.28. They may have figured that $352.54 of the buy-out fee went toward "Old Folks" alone, which would have brought Foster's total earnings from the song to exactly $2,000.

[7] According to the 1860 US Census, her name was Adelaide A. Mahon, and she was 10 years old at the time of the Census. The duet for tenor and soprano "Mine Is the Mourning Heart" was published in *Clark's School Visitor* on January 17, 1861, and was issued as sheet music by Root & Cady in 1863.

But Mrs. Foster did not like such a pointed allusion to the young lady's age, so he changed the first line to

'Jennie's coming o er the green."[8]

I heard Mrs. W. J. Florence sing this song beautifully one night at Wallack's Old Theatre, on Broadway.

I now have to come to a turn in the tide of poor Foster's life. I believe I have already stated that he wrote and composed most of his latest songs in my rooms, in Henry street. One of these, and a most beautiful one—"Our Bright, Bright Summerdays are Gone"—he took to Pond, who refused it for some reason or other, and it made him feel very despondent; for about this time Lee & Walker had ceased employing him in consequence of hard times. I was then "under the weather" myself, and I remember one evening, when we were both pretty "hard up"—indeed, neither of us had a cent, and I had a family besides—suddenly he sat down to the piano.

"John," said he, "I haven't time to write a new song, but I think I can write 'Our Bright, Bright Summer-days are Gone' from memory."

He sat down, and wrote the words and music from memory in about an hour and a half.

"Take this round to Daly," said he, "and take what he will give you."

Mr. John J. Daly, now of 944 Eighth avenue, was then my publisher, and was at 419 Grand street. I took the song to Mr. Daly. He was proud to get a song from Foster. He tried it over, and it was really beautiful. He offered a sum which, though not a tithe of what Foster got in his better days, was still considered very handsome: and this "stone which the builders (Pond & Co.) rejected" became very popular. Subsequently the late Thomas D. Sullivan composed brilliant variations for this song, and it is a favorite to this day. His next was one of his finest, and was named "Our Willie dear Is Dying;" next "Little Belle Blair": and then followed "When the Bowl Goes Round," "A Thousand Miles from Home," and many others, some of which have been but recently published by Daly, and which were not published during his lifetime. "There Is No Such Girl as Mine," and others were also among his latest productions.

---

[8] Mahon correctly recalls the text of the published song. In 1895 Jane Foster Wiley recited the words Mahon claims Foster had originally written, and she claimed the song was never published. It appears she was unaware that Foster followed her advice about the text and published the song. See Jane's account in Chapter 12.

I have seen him stop in the street, take a pencil out of his pocket, mark a stave on his left thumb-nail, and write three or four starting notes.

"What are you doing?" I would say.

"Why, John," he would reply, "there is so much music running through my brain that I will miss it unless I put a note or two down to jog my memory."[9]

Yes, and some of his most beautiful songs were composed from such reminders.

But the money thus picked up did not last forever, and I was still without steady employment. One day, when we were down again (for in the meantime I did my best for him, his wife and child having been sent home), he sent me to his boarding-house to bring a package of letters from his trunk. One of these was from Ditson & Co. of Boston, to whom he had written some years before offering to write for them, although he was then in the service of Pond & Co. and of Lee & Walker. A portion of that letter ran thus, as nearly as I can remember: "We would gladly accept your offer, *for you are the best song-writer of this or any other country;* but it is contrary to professional etiquette to do so when you are exclusively engaged by another firm." Another letter showed him to be in Pond & Co.'s debt to a comparatively large amount. Another was an autograph letter from Alice Cary, and another from Washington Irving, all of which he gave me to read, for he had no secrets from me. Indeed, at one time he mentioned some delicate matters at Windust's, as I thought too publicly, and both myself and Thomas D. Sullivan rebuked him therefor. But the letter he wanted was one from George Washington to Professor McDowell (Mrs. Foster's grandfather or granduncle, I forget which), in relation to Mr. Custis, who was under that gentleman's tuition.[10] This letter, and those from Alice Cary and Washington Irving, he requested me to sell. I took them first to Mr. Greenwood, Barnum's manager; but he made me no offer, and I walked into Windust's. While there I got into conversation with an Episcopal clergyman, who invited me to drink something; and while sitting in one of the boxes I showed him the letters. He was most enthusiastic, and at once offered me $10 for Washington's letter and $3 for Washington Irving's, but would not take Alice Cary's. I took the money and brought it to Foster, who was much pleased. Some time after his death his brother-in-law wrote to me claiming

---

[9] That Foster notated small phrases and sub-phrases like this is corroborated by his sketchbook of lyrics, most of which date to his time in Pittsburgh and Allegheny in the 1850s.

[10] Morrison mentions this letter in his biography of Foster. He was probably embarrassed—or perhaps in disbelief—that his brother sold it and claims that it was still treasured. The George Washington letter is now part of National Archives.

the letter as his property, and I deeply regret that I could not remember even the name (a German one) of the clergyman.[11] All I know now is that Foster told me he sent the money to his wife. It may be so, although I do not think she needed it, for I learned she was doing well somewhere in Pennsylvania as a telegraph-operator.

One evening, after I got into business again, I was sent to report a temperance reception in the Bowery, which was held under the auspices of Mr. Daniel Walford of this city. I took Foster with me, and he gave me the signal agreed on; so I simply introduced him as Mr. Foster. One peculiarity of his was that, while he could remember the music of all his songs, he could never remember the words. During the evening singing was in order. Now, Foster had not a *primo-tenore* voice. His voice was not certainly first-class, but his singing was fair; so I asked him to sing the only song whose words he could recollect—"Hard Times Come Again No More." He commenced. Very little notice was taken of the first few bars, but as he proceeded he threw such pathos into his voice, especially when he came to the words: "There's a poor little maiden who weeps her life away," that there wasn't a dry eye in the room. Every voice was hushed. All crowded round him; and, as he came to the chorus:

> "'Tis the song, 'tis the sigh of the weary,
> Hard times! Hard times come again no more;
> Many days you have lingered around my cabin door—
> Oh, hard times come again no more,"

there arose such a burst of melody from the untutored (musically, I mean) male and female voices present as I never heard before or since. It pleased him.

"John," said he to me, "I release you from your promise; you may introduce me in my true character." I introduced him to Mr. Walford and one or two ladies, and by his permission Mr. Walford introduced him to all in these words:

Ladies and gentlemen, you have heard that beautiful song to-night sung with a depth of feeling to which we have been unaccustomed; but you will cease to wonder why it so moved us all when I tell you that he who sang it

---

[11] This was most likely Morrison inquiring about this letter, not a brother-in-law.

is the author and composer not only of that, but of some of the finest songs ever written, of which "The Old Folks at Home," "Willie, We Have Missed You," and others will never cease to stir the hearers' hearts. Permit me to introduce the celebrated American poet and musical composer Stephen C. Foster.

One moment of silence, amounting almost to astonishment, ensued, and then such a deafening cheer arose, both from men and women, as my pen cannot describe. Handkerchiefs waved, and cheer after cheer followed, while the numbers who rushed to grasp him by the hand seemed to embarrass him considerably. It was, in fact, a perfect ovation; and, although the people were all temperate, I believe that something stronger than lemonade was improvised somewhere for Foster and myself during the recess.

I should have stated that the letters above alluded to from Alice Cary and Washington Irving were mere answers to an offer, apparently made to each of them, to send them Washington's letter. Irving's letter ran somewhat like this:

MY DEAR SIR: I received yours of the --, and shall be very happy indeed to receive the original letter of Geo. Washington, which you so kindly offer to send me.
                            Yours truly, WASHINGTON IRVING.

That of Miss Cary was similar in style. If he had any other letter from Irving, he never showed or even spoke of it to me.

As regards his being connected with President Buchanan, I can confirm that from his own lips, for he often boasted of the relationship to me.

Some people have stated to me that Foster could not write music—that he merely whistled his airs, and got others to write them down. Nothing could be farther from the truth. He not only wrote, but arranged his music, and also wrote his words. *I know*, for I have seen him do so. Perhaps the last music he ever wrote was the piano accompaniments to a piece of mine called "Our Darling Kate," which was written (words and music) for the late Miss Kate Newton. The circumstances under which he requested me to let him arrange the accompaniment were very painful indeed. He was suffering from sheer want at the time; and, although I offered him money for what he wanted (a bed at the New England Hotel, where he was seized with the illness which proved unexpectedly fatal), he refused it unless I would let him arrange the song, which I gladly did. Madam Demorest, the celebrated *modiste*, paid me a handsome sum for it, and published it in her magazine for March, 1865.[12]

Some, too, have accused Foster of plagiarism. The late Sam Sharpley once told me that his wife was an excellent musician, and had an old book of Scotch songs, which they used to dress up in such a manner as to make them appear original. If Mrs. Foster was a musician, I never knew it. More, from my short acquaintance with her, I do not believe she knew a note of music. At all events, I *know* his later songs were *not* composed from any book, but were certainly penned down in my poor apartments, and some in my very presence. Still there was a great similarity between some of his pieces and some English and Scotch songs, as for instance "Willie, We Have Missed You," and "Jock of Hazledeane (Scotch)"; "Uncle Ned" and "The Tired Soldier" (English), this latter "Adagio;" "Gentle Annie" and "Annie Laurie," and others. Even "The Old Folks at Home," it was charged to his face at one time, was extremely like an old sacred piece of Haydn. But he assured me that he never heard the pieces in question. On the contrary, he claimed that the war song "John Brown" was his "Ellen Bayne" revamped, and that the idea of Root's "Old Folks Are Gone" was taken from his "Old Folks at Home."

In his early career he never (so he told me) wrote music to any other person's words, or vice versa; and, bosom friends as we were, he would not put music to words of mine. On one occasion only did he deviate from this rule, and that was in composing music for the song "Parthenia to Ingomar," commencing

> Deal with me kindly, cheer my young heart.[13]

In his latter days, however, he departed considerably from this rule, on the principle of *Necessitas non habet legem*; and there are many pieces extant written by some poets of the day which bear the legend

## "MUSIC BY STEPHEN C. FOSTER."

In January, 1864, I was compelled, in consequence of severe illness, to part with Foster and enter the pay-ward of Bellevue Hospital. On the 10th of that

---

[12] Mahon probably confused the names of two nearby hotels. The New England Hotel was located at 30 Bowery, a few doors away from the American House, which was located at 15 Bowery. See Chapter 3, n17.

[13] Mahon's claim that before moving to New York Foster set words by another poet only on one occasion is an exaggeration. While it is true that most of his songs from that period have words he wrote, many of his songs have texts by others. See Chapter 4, n33.

month I lost my wife, the mother of my children. On the 13th my friend died in the same hospital, and I knew not that he was even in there, the first intimation I had of his death being a short account of his funeral in the papers. I certainly was sorry, for I liked him much. But I knew not that he was there, and I saw him not. Well, "peace to his manes! We could have better spared a better man."

One of the most beautiful songs which Foster ever wrote was "Under the Willow She's Sleeping." Its history, as often told me by himself, is as follows: His little daughter, Marian [sic], had her mother's auburn hair and fair complexion, and he dearly loved the child. One day she was missed from the domestic circle for several hours, and considerable alarm was manifested by the parents. Search was made in every direction, and at length the father found her, sleeping under a willow-tree at some distance from their residence. He stood a few moments, as if spellbound, watching "the beautiful vision," as he called it, and exclaimed:

"Under the willows she's laid with care!"

and before awaking her sketched the first notes of the melody on his thumbnail, as was his wont. Aye, and often he sang that melody in my rooms, being particularly pathetic in the first line of the chorus: "Fair, fair, and golden hair." Once my wife[14] said to him:

"Well, I think, Mr. Foster, it was a strange thing for you to write that song as if it were a lament for a dead child."

"Ah!" said he, "I then for the first time realized the extraordinary beauty of my little darling, and thought what a horror it would be to me if I had found her dead instead of asleep. But in the line 'There's where my darling lies dreaming' I show my feelings. The words are poetical, and my be understood either of death or of sleep, or of both."

One night he and I went to Newark and dropped into a variety show, which was under the management of a New York gentleman named McCarthy, who had merely got the thing up for his own amusement. Shortly after we arrived a young lady entered and sang "Fairy Belle." Foster was actually wild with delight.

---

[14] According to the 1860 US Census, Mahon's wife's name was Ellen Mahon, and she had been born in Ireland around 1821.

"Why, John," said he to me, "there; she is singing one of my songs—no signal to-night, John," alluding to our agreement with regard to introduction. "You must introduce me."

I happened to know the manager, and did introduce him behind the scenes, where, I need not say, his reception was most enthusiastic.

Many of Foster's songs will never be known. He was constantly getting up something new, some of which never got beyond his "thumb-nail." But, really, neither the author of "Clipper Series No. VII" nor myself has given the titles of a tithe of them. I write simply from memory, but I have written nothing for the truth of which I cannot personally vouch.

# 6

# An Interview with an Anonymous Pittsburgh Acquaintance (1879)

## Introduction

*Shortly after John Mahon published his account in the* New York Clipper, *a performer named Joseph Murphy penned a letter to the paper asserting that his brother, not Foster, had written "Old Folks at Home." He wrote, "This song was written in 1851 by James Murphy, at his home in Bloomingdale, New York. He was at the time a well known glee singer, and composed the song for his own use, but afterwards sold it to the late E. P. Christy."[1] Joseph Murphy was acquainted with Foster. The first edition of Foster's song "Lou'siana Belle" indicates that it was "written for and sung by Joseph Murphy of the Sable Harmonists," and Nevin mentioned that a "Mr. Murphy" frequently appeared with the Sable Harmonists in Pittsburgh. But even though he knew Foster, his claims about "Old Folks" are demonstrably false.*

*When the* Clipper *asked Mahon to respond to Murphy, Mahon replied that he inquired about the matter with William A. Pond, a former partner in the publishing firm Firth, Pond & Co., who showed him a letter the firm had written to Foster dated September 22, 1851. According to Mahon, the letter (which I do not believe survives) read:*

> "Nelly Bly" goes like hot cakes. "Willie the Brave" is also doing well. Draw on us at once for $---. Christy has not yet sung "Old Folks at Home." He therefore desires us to delay the publication for a week or two.[2]

*Mahon added that "Mr. Pond fears he lost Foster's original letter in the fire of 1863 [the Draft Riots of 1863], but he has all the original contracts;*

---

[1] "Another Author of 'Old Folks at Home,'" *New York Clipper*, May 12, 1877.
[2] "Old Folks at Home," *New York Clipper*, May 26, 1877.

*Formulating Foster*. Christopher Lynch, Oxford University Press. © Oxford University Press 2025.
DOI: 10.1093/9780197811726.003.0007

*and anyone who is interested can see the above letter and the contracts at the store."* The Clipper *concluded that "this must close the case."*

But Murphy persisted. In an interview published in the St. Louis Times-Journal on February 21, 1879, Murphy again claimed that his brother James wrote "Old Folks at Home," but he now claimed it was in 1850, not 1851. He elaborated, "My brother played the tambourine, and one night while he and Colonel Keating were sitting in their room, he wrote this song on the parchment on the inside of the tambourine." We know Murphy's story is not true because drafts of the lyrics exist in Foster's handwriting, Foster mentions the song and his arrangement with Christy in his correspondence, and Foster enumerated the royalties he collected from the song in his account book. Murphy's story, moreover, is riddled with holes. His brother James could not testify on his own behalf because he was dead, and Joseph was unable to produce the tambourine because, he claimed, it resided with his sister in San Francisco. Joseph claimed that he had "considerable correspondence with parties who knew the circumstances of the case and who corroborated" his story, but he did not provide the identities of those parties, nor did he produce the correspondence because his wife "left it in San Francisco when we came away from there." Murphy's intransigence appears to be a publicity stunt. He was in St. Louis performing in a show when he issued these statements.

Although his story does not add up, it nevertheless sowed doubts about the authenticity of Foster's songs. According to Murphy, "There were a great many songs published under Foster's name that he never saw, and probably never knew who the parties were that wrote them." The Foster family bristled for decades as doubts about authorship persisted; they were only definitively laid to rest by the documentation of Foster's career conducted by Foster Hall in the 1930s. Despite these doubts, though, when the original copyright expired on "Old Folks at Home" in 1879, the publisher correctly began to list Stephen C. Foster as author and composer.

Two responses to Murphy's interview were published. The first, which appeared in the St. Louis Times-Journal *the day after Murphy's interview, was a statement by an anonymous newspaperman that is not found in the* Foster Hall Collection. The newsman—possibly B. D. M Eaton, who published another Foster memory many years later—claims to have heard Foster perform the song in a parlor in Pittsburgh's premier hotel, the Monongahela House, during the 1848 election. We know that Foster wrote campaign songs and gave musical performances in elections in 1851 and

*1856, but we know nothing of earlier political involvement. Moreover, it is all but certain "Old Folks" was not performed in 1848 because Foster's drafts of the lyrics clearly date to 1850. If this newsman heard the composer sing "Old Folks" at the Monongahela House, he is confused about the date of the performance.*

## St. Louis Times-Journal, February 22, 1879.

"So Joe Murphy claims that his brother wrote 'Old Folks at Home?' I call that robbing one dead man of his laurels to bestow them on another."

It was an old newspaper man who expressed this opinion as he laid down the Times-Journal yesterday.

"What do you know about it?" queried a reporter.

"This much: I heard Steve Foster sing that song the first time it was ever sung in public. That was in 1848, two years before Murphy says his brother wrote it. Foster sang it in the parlor of the Monongahela house in Pittsburg. It was during the Presidential campaign of '48, and I was then a reporter on the Pittsburg Post. I was present when Foster sang it, sitting at the piano and playing his own accompaniment. After that 'Swanee River' became a favorite song. Why, it was sang here in St. Louis in 1849, and Murphy says his brother wrote it in 1850. Sher. Campbell or Joe Murphy, I forget which, sang it here. No, not this Murphy, but a noted tenor singer of the same name. It was while the Campbell or the Buckley minstrels were here, I forget which. As long as he lived Stephen G. [sic] Foster got a royalty from a Boston house for every copy of that song that was sold. Murphy talks about 'No, Mary Blaine.' There was a very popular song in those days called 'Mary Blaine,' and that was written by Foster, too.[3] I never heard of 'No, Mary Blaine.' It wouldn't do for Murphy to go to Pittsburg and claim there that his brother wrote 'Swanee River.'"

---

[3] The song "Mary Blane," a popular minstrel song in the late 1840s, was published in 1846 by C. G. Christman of New York. The sheet music indicated the song was "composed and sung by" William "Billy" Whitlock, who was a founding member of the Virginia Minstrels with Dan Emmett, Dick Pelham, and Frank Brower.

# 7
# An Interview with Rebecca Shiras Morris and Joan Sloan Shiras (1879)

**Introduction**

*Joseph Murphy's interview inspired the following article, which appeared two days later in the* Pittsburg Leader, *edited by Robert P. Nevin (see Nevin's reminiscence of Foster in Chapter 4). Like Murphy, the author casts doubt on whether Foster had written his songs. The anonymous author interviewed Rebecca Shiras Morris and Joan Sloan Shiras, the daughter and mother of Charles P. Shiras, who had been a writer, editor, poet, and close friend of Foster. The Foster family struggled to quash and counter this kind of salacious commentary in these years. Later generations of Fosters would finally override it only when they joined forces with the wealthy and powerful Lilly. Given Lilly's alignment with the Fosters, it is not surprising that this article and a related letter by Morris are found in the Foster Hall Collection but were never publicized or made discoverable in the card catalog. Foster Hall, in other words, buried them.*

*Shiras was a member of Foster's close circle of friends, which the group called the Knights of the Square Table. Foster wrote a poem about these friends, beginning with a verse about Shiras:*

> First, there's Charley the elder, the Sunday-School teacher,
> Who laughs with a groan,
> In an unearthly tone,
> Without moving a bone
> Or a feature.[1]

*As boys, Shiras and Foster are known to have attended a performance of the singer William Dempster together. There they heard Dempster's*

---

[1] "The Five Nice Young Men, May 6, 1845," FHC, A329.

*Formulating Foster*. Christopher Lynch, Oxford University Press. © Oxford University Press 2025.
DOI: 10.1093/9780197811726.003.0008

*rendition of Tennyson's "The May Queen," which, according to Morrison, Foster often performed in private settings with tears in his eyes. Perhaps in these settings he sang the verses that he and Shiras added to the poem, which survive in manuscript.*[2]

*Although they were close, their professional relationship was minimal. Foster and Shiras are known to have written only one song together, "Annie My Own Love," although an anonymous friend and his widow, Jane, later mentioned that Foster also set Shiras's poem "The Popular Credo" (first line: "Dimes and Dollars! Dollars and Dimes!"). While Foster was living in New York, Shiras interpolated some of his friend's songs into his play "The Invisible Prince," which was produced in Pittsburgh in 1853. The play was a benefit for the ailing Shiras, who died in 1854.*

*Foster Hall probably felt justified burying the following article because its claims are highly dubious. The fact that Shiras's daughter, Rebecca Shiras Morris, was only two years old at the time of his death casts doubt on the family memories of Foster that she recounted to the reporter twenty-five years later. Also dubious are most of the claims of Shiras's mother, who was not well at the time of the interview. Her gravestone reveals that she died just weeks later. Her assertion that Shiras wrote the words to many of Foster's songs is disproven by the existence of Foster's handwritten drafts of most of the songs she mentions, as well as the fact that many of the songs were written after Shiras's death. Perhaps her many false claims are owed to an aging and failing memory.*

*But in addition to the dubious claims, Foster Hall probably buried the article because of its general negative portrayal of Foster. After all, they also declined to catalog a letter that Rebecca wrote around 1900 to her son, Charles Shiras Morris, in which she expressed regret about the interview and described Foster in harsh terms:*

> *I am enclosing a clipping which I have saved all these years. You can keep it, or destroy it as you wish. I cried my eyes out at the time for I did not know the man was a reporter. It raised quite a talk and as I had no proof of my father having written the things, I could not do anything. Still we all knew and Cousin George thinks he undoubtedly did. Something might turn up some time very unexpectedly that would throw more light on it. Foster drank very hard and died an inebriate and my father was always trying to help him, and*

---

[2] "The May Queen," FHC, A332.

*my grandmother, like all mothers, did not want my father to associate with him nor put his name on the "N---- Song." He lived a long time after my father, and separated from his wife. I can faintly remember him coaxing me to call him Uncle, and I still have a toy he brought for me, all these things you can have if you wish for Junior.*[3]

These sentiments did not fit the narrative of Foster the family or Foster Hall wanted to present.

Later scholars, however, overlooked the dubious claims and seized the Shiras family's assertions to suggest that Foster and Shiras worked closely. This line of reasoning first emerged in the 1970s following criticism of Foster's music during the civil rights movement. Linking Foster to Shiras, who expressed progressive and abolitionist sentiments, shielded Foster from criticism.

---

## "'Old Folks at Home': Is Pittsburg's Revered Song-writer its Author? A Strong Showing that he Did not Write all he is Credited With," *Pittsburg Leader*, February 23, 1879.

One day during the past week a few persons stood in front of a small picture hanging in the art gallery at the Loan exhibition, gazing at it very intently. Attracted by the crowd, a LEADER reporter nosed into the party in time to overhear the following conversation, the first speaker being an elderly gentleman with eye-glasses over his nose and a smile rather of the *Pecksniffian* order on his countenance:

"Charles P. Shiras," he read from the slip under the portrait. "Shiras! Shiras!"

"Oh, yes, I remember about him—a local poet—who wrote very excellently in his time, but died too young for fame."

"Yes," said the second speaker, a sharp-featured, gray hair, slim-built lady. "Yes, too young for the fame that was deservedly his, but which somebody else got."

"And who was this somebody else, my dear madam?"

---

[3] Rebecca Shiras Morris to Charles Shiras Morris, about 1900, transcribed for the Foster Hall Collection on June 18, 1938.

"Who was it?—why Stephen C. Foster, of course. Is not his name famous all over this and many other lands, because people think he wrote 'Old Folks at Home'?"

"And didn't he write it?"

"Not a bit of it. Every line of the words were composed by Charles P. Shiras, who lived and died in Allegheny."

With this remark, the couple moved on, still talking about the matter, but not within reportorial ear shot, and the [illeg.] was left to ponder over what he had heard.

Did Chas. P. Shiras leave any proof of what had been uttered? The lady who had made the statement would perhaps know, but alas! she could not be found again in the crowd. At last inquiry brought out the information that when Shiras died he left an infant daughter, who had grown to womanhood and married a gentleman in Allegheny named Morris. A directory was sought, the address of every Morris obtained, and armed with this clue the news man started on his errand. Morris after Morris was visited, but the daughter of the departed poet was not found. There was but one other name in the list—"Captain J. H. Morris, riverman, 31 Pearl street." The reporter proceeded on his way across the commons, along Federal street, half way up the hill, until he arrived at a not uninviting little street taking its origin at and running east from Federal street. Thirty-one was near the other end of the street, and as the reporter plowed his way through the snow he breathed a sigh of relief and congratulating himself that the precious "Pearl" had been found. The house was a modest looking one, two stories in height, with a basement. Ascending the steps the bell was rang and soon a lady of very pleasing features, looking not more than twenty-five years of age, stood before the scribe.

"Does Captain J. H. Morris live here?"

"Yes, sir."

"Has he a wife?"

"He has;" with a slight smile.

"And is her name Rebecca?"

"It is."

"And are you the lady, and was your father Charles P. Shiras?"

"Yes, sir; I am the daughter of Charles P. Shiras."

The LEADER envoy, with difficulty, suppressed a "Hooray," and introducing himself, explained the meaning of the visit.

Mrs. Morris invited him into a cozy little parlor, but said she did not desire any publicity in the matter, and for that reason felt averse to telling what she knew and thought about the authorship of the songs.

"My father died when I was but two years of age," said Mrs. Morris, who was a lady evidently of refinement and intelligence, "and what knowledge I possess of him, is but very limited. My mother died even before father, and what I have learned about him was principally from his mother. She remembers a great deal."

"And where is she?"

"Up stairs, but you cannot see her today. She is eighty-seven years of age, blind and can hear with difficulty. Tomorrow I will try and arouse her, and then you may talk to her if you will come."

"Do you know anything relative to the authorship of 'Old Folks at Home?'"

"I know that it was composed in this very house, between the years 1850 and 1852. My father had written 'Dimes and Dollars,' 'Redemption of Labor,' the 'Iron City,' and many other poems that had gained him celebrity. He and Foster were fast friends, the latter spending nearly all his time at our house. Foster would compose the music and my father the words, but in all cases Foster was forbidden in any way to attach my father's name to the songs, as father, or, in fact, no one else, at that time considered them worth anything, and he would not allow his name to appear in connection with any such trash, as it was deemed.

"Such good friends were they," said the lady, "that I am sure if they were both living, no one would be more ready to give my father credit for his part of the work than Foster. They are both dead now, and it is no use to stir the matter up any more."

Mrs. Morris stated she had a book in her possession, a collection of poems and prose extracts, first published in 1826. "It was in father's library. He certainly composed the music, but the words of his songs, in more than one instance, came from that book." The lady handed the reporter a scrapbook, containing the obituary of father, written by Mrs. Jane Swisshelm, telling of his poetic genius and ability as an editor. He was connected with the *Commercial Journal* at the time of his death.

Mrs. Morris did not wish to converse further on the subject, but invited a return the next day, which invitation was accepted, and the way was shown to the rooms of Mrs. Shiras, the mother of the dead poet. She was bed-ridden and blind, and her hair was silvery gray. The old lady heard with difficulty, but when her memory was quickened she talked along just as lively as a cricket. "Bless your soul, I know my son wrote many of the songs and helped to write many more. Right in that front room yonder him and Stephen would sit night after night. It was there they composed together 'Gentle Annie.' There was a young lady named Annie Evans they both knew and liked. She died and then that song was written. I heard them talk about it. The first money Steph got for any song was 'Old Uncle Ned.' He got $100 for it and then went and bought a piano. I remember that because my Charles laughed so much about it. 'Susannah Don't You Cry,'" and the old lady hummed a stanza of the song in as clear a tone as a young girl. "Well Stephen composed that song anyhow, because Charles thought it was so foolish; he told me about it and said it was great trash."[4]

Her son had died when he was but twenty-nine years of age, in 1854, when he was just becoming known to fame, and she felt confident if the truth was known, or rather if every one knew the relations existing between Foster and Charles Shiras, her son would have the credit of many of the songs credited to Stephen C. Foster.

In connection with these circumstances, it may be stated that she who was the wife of Foster is still alive, and is now the wife of Mr. Wylie, of Montgomery avenue, Allegheny.

There was a youth named James Harbison, whose mother still lived next door, who was wont to carry notes, messages and the manuscript of songs for her son and Stephen. That lad was now a gentleman doing business at Beaver Falls, and he asserts positively that Shiras is the author of "Old Folks at Home." Her son was a man who disdained at that time to father such effusions as those ballads were then considered. Mrs. Jane Swisshelm, she thought, might throw some light on the subject.

[The article quotes Joseph Murphy's claims in the *St. Louis Times-Journal*.]

A man named McLaughlin said to a LEADER man some years ago that he knew Foster composed "Old Folks at Home" in a Diamond alley saloon, where he composed many of his most popular melodies.

---

[4] The sketches to "Gentle Annie" exist in Foster's handwriting and date to after Shiras's death.

# 8
# An Interview with Samuel S. Sanford (1882)

### Introduction

*Samuel S. Sanford was a blackface performer, who according to his own account in an interview in 1874 began performing "as a boy in 1835." He added, "Afterwards I organized a company consisting of Dan Rice, Von Bonhurst, Master Roston and others, and we traveled through Pennsylvania."[1] It is possible that Sanford first met Foster at this time as Dan Rice was friends with Morrison.[2]*

*The following interview with Sanford is not in the Foster Hall Collection. Sanford claims to have been a member of the Virginia Minstrels with Dan Emmett, Frank Brower, Richard Pelham, and Billy Whitlock, who are said to have initiated the onstage positioning of a minstrel troupe's members in a semicircle, with tambourine and bones players at the ends and an interlocutor in the middle. Sanford's membership in this group cannot be confirmed, but he was certainly a member of one of the first troupes to emulate the Virginia Minstrels, the Buckley Family. As a percussionist, Sanford was one of the "end men."*

*After leaving the Buckleys, he formed his own minstrel troupes, variously called the New Orleans Opera Troupe, New Orleans Serenaders, and Sanford's Opera Troupe, which performed in Pittsburgh almost every year in the 1850s. In the early 1850s, he performed many songs by Nelson Kneass, who also performed in his group. He referred to Kneass and Foster as "the two bards of the minstrels."[3] He also became an important impresario in*

---

[1] "Old-Time Minstrelsy: An Interview with the Veteran Sam. S. Sanford," *Washington National Republican*, September 11, 1874.
[2] Their relationship is documented in several letters in the Foster Hall Collection: Dan Rice to Morrison Foster, June 17, 1843, FHC, D190; Dan Rice to Morrison Foster, July 24, 1843, FHC, D 191; Dan Rice to Morrison Foster, November 15, 1859, FHC, D192; Dan Rice to Morrison Foster, September 28, 1883, FHC, D193; Dan Rice to Morrison Foster, September 20, 1883, FHC, D194; Dan Rice to Morrison Foster, January 21, 1884, FHC, D195.
[3] "Old-Time Minstrelsy."

*Formulating Foster*. Christopher Lynch, Oxford University Press. © Oxford University Press 2025.
DOI: 10.1093/9780197811726.003.0009

*Philadelphia. Later in the century, acts such as the Carncross and Dixey's Minstrels and Frank Dumont's Minstrels performed at his theaters (Figures 8.1 and 8.2).*

**Figure 8.1.** Sam Sanford in costume. MS Thr 1848, Harvard Theatre Collection, Houghton Library, Harvard University.

**Figure 8.2.** Sam Sanford out of costume. MS Thr 1848, Harvard Theatre Collection, Houghton Library, Harvard University.

## *Detroit Free Press,* October 5, 1882.

"How long have you been in the minstrel business?" asked a reporter for THE FREE PRESS of Samuel S. Sanford, who is now filling an engagement at the Park Theater.

"I made my debut on New Year's eve, in 1832."

"Where did this event take place?"

"At a Philadelphia theater (then in the suburbs) which stood at the present corner of Eighth and Callowhill streets."

"What was your act?"

"I was a boy comedian and sang 'Boy, Harry Bluff,' and danced a sailors' hornpipe."

"How did you happen to get into the business?"

"How? Why I was born in the dramatic business. My mother, Mrs. Lindsay, was leading lady at the old Park Theater, New York, when the boy Edwin Forrest made his metropolitan debut. So you see I took to the stage naturally."

"Tell me something about old-time original negro minstrelsy."

"Well, I guess I can take you back as far as anybody. I remember the late famous Irish comedian Barney Williams as a jig dancer and comic singer, and I remember John E. Owens as a negro comedian. By the way, Mr. Owens is the original 'Uncle Tom,' and I remember when he acted the part for the first time—it was in Baltimore—he did it at the risk of his life. It was not fifty or a hundred persons who threatened to shoot him if he played the part, but a mob of 600 or 800 who gathered in the street and threatened to sack the theater."

"What was the minstrel party you first joined?"

"It was a party of five men known as the Virginia Minstrels. The names were Whitlock, Emmett, Brower, Pelham and myself. Recollect, this was forty-two years ago, before the days of mastodonic forties, railroads and 200 mile jumps. We had a violin, bones, tambourine, jawbone and triangle."

Manager C. O. White here interpolated: "Yes, and your triangle was a horse-shoe held by a piece of violin string and struck with a ten-penny nail."

Mr. Sanford—"That's true, but we were popular and made money."

"How long a performance did you usually give?"

"From an hour and a half to two hours long. But we worked. We not only doubled, but we each did four or five acts. Minstrelsy in those days was popular and a minstrel was respected. Why, when, a few years later I joined a party known as Dumbleton's Minstrels, we went to England and carried letters of introduction and recommendation from James K. Polk, then President of the United States, and I counted among my warm personal friends such men as Henry Clay, and Presidents Polk and Tyler. When President Tyler married Miss Gardner, I was invited by Henry Clay to take a minstrel party of my own to White Sulphur Springs, Va., and give a series of entertainments as a compliment to the bridal party.

"We remained there a week, giving performances each evening, and at the end of the engagement I received, beside the stipulated pay, a purse of $1,000.

To this day I do not know positively the donor of the purse, although I always credited it to Mr. Clay."

"Who were the members of that band?"

"They were G. Swayne Buckley, Fred. Buckley, a man named Crogin, whom I christened Dan. Raynor, one other, and myself."

"Where did you go at the close of that engagement?"

"We traveled in a carriage placed at our disposal by President Tyler from White Sulphur Springs to Vicksburg, Tenn., stopping by request (and, in fact, that was the main object of the trip), at Columbus, Tenn., to play and sing for James K. Polk and his wife. Of course we played at all the towns on the way. There were no halls then, and we played in hotel dining rooms, charging a dollar a ticket. We were few in number and our expenses were light."

"Give me an idea, Mr. Sanford, of the style of performance you used to give."

"Well, we had two settings for the 'first part.' In the first, we appeared according to our bills as 'Dandy Northern Nigs,' wearing white pants, ruffled shirt fronts, blue coats and brass buttons. We sang solos, duets and quartettes from operas, with accompaniments on our limited list of instruments. After an interval of ten minutes we reappeared as 'Plantation Darks of the South,' and sang Lucy Long, Dandy Jim, Aunt Sally, Dan Tucker and the like. After the 'first part' came our olio of specialties, in which we did dancing, farces and musical acts."

"You gave the first minstrel show ever given in Philadelphia, did you not?"

"Yes, sir, and the first ever given in Pennsylvania. I opened a negro minstrel hall on Chestnut street adjoining the Chestnut Street Theater. John E. Owens had just closed a wonderfully successful season with 'Uncle Tom's Cabin,' and I put on a piece called 'Rebuke to Uncle Tom,' in which I tried to depict slave life as I knew it and as it actually existed at that time.[4] I took in $11,000 in nine weeks and made such a hit that a grand torchlight parade was made in my honor by a body known as the Southern Students. They were young men from all parts of the South attending college at Philadelphia and Baltimore. They marched to my hall in a body, and during the performance

---

[4] In his 1852 version of *Uncle Tom's Cabin*, which he describes here as a *rebuke* of the abolitionist novel on which it was based, he portrayed enslavement as a benevolent institution that was mutually beneficial to enslavers and the people they enslaved. In a demonstration of the ambiguity of Foster's sentimental minstrel songs, his play featured Foster's songs, as did versions of the play that were more faithful to the novel's abolitionist message.

presented me with a set of solid silver, thirty pieces. After the performance they escorted me to my home and later in the night gave me a serenade."

"How has minstrelsy grown to proportions so great?"

"Naturally, and the growth has not yet stopped. Years ago when Stephen C. Foster, the greatest writer of ballads ever known, first came before the public, I was repeatedly laughed at for innovations. I was the first to introduce the cornet and the double bass into the instrumental feature of negro minstrelsy. Everybody said it wouldn't go, because it wasn't in keeping with the negro character, and I told them we couldn't get too much music into the show."

"Were you personally acquainted with Stephen C. Foster?"

"Yes, indeed; and I admired him almost to idolatry. By the way, the first time his songs 'Old Kentucky Home,' 'Hard Times Will Come Again No More,' and 'Come Where My Love Lies Dreaming,' were ever sung in public, they were sung by my minstrels. I paid him $50 for the three songs and they were all sung for the first time on the same night."[5]

"Where did this happen?"

"At Library Hall, Pittsburgh, and we had Jenny Lind as opposition."[6]

---

[5] As Sanford's words suggest, Foster's contemporaries thought of his sentimental songs such as "Hard Times Come Again No More" and "Come Where My Love Lies Dreaming" as minstrel songs.

[6] Contrary to Sanford's recollections, newspapers indicate his troupes appeared at Pittsburgh's Masonic Hall and City Hall in the 1850s. Library Hall did not open until 1870. When Jenny Lind appeared in Pittsburgh in April 1851 and November 1851, Sanford's troupe was not in town. However, in December 1852 his troupe performed at Masonic Hall while the operatic soprano and child prodigy Adelina Patti gave a concert at Lafayette Hall. It is possible that Sanford misremembered the soprano he competed against in Pittsburgh.

# 9

# An "Anonymous" Interview with Morrison Foster and George C. Cooper (ca. 1888)

### Introduction

*There was not much writing about Foster in the 1880s. After Sanford's interview, an article appeared in the* Pittsburgh Dispatch *on September 20, 1885, which provided an overview of the composer's life. In addition to including a previously unpublished song by Foster, "The White House Chair," the article included an interesting quote from "one of his most intimate friends":*

> He was the best natured man in the world, quiet, inoffensive and unobtrusive. He had but few intimate friends, but to these he was deeply attached. Like most geniuses he was more or less moody, at times being melancholy, then again cheerful and vivacious. He never seemed better pleased than when surrounded by the members of the singing club, of which he was director and accompanist. A good many thought him offish and selfish because he would not run with them, but he wasn't. One of his most genial associates was Charlie Shiras, the author of that immensely popular song: "Dimes and Dollars, Dollars and Dimes."

In anticipation of the publication of this article, Morrison registered the song "The White House Chair" for copyright on September 4, 1885. Because of his connection to the writing of the article, it is possible that he was the "intimate friend" quoted.

The following article was probably the next to appear that contained firsthand reminiscences of the composer, for it is found in a file in the Foster Hall Collection where it is dated 1888. The anonymous "Pittsburg gentleman who is about to write the life of Stephen G. [sic] Foster" referred to in the article is almost definitely Morrison. In 1888 Morrison wrote to Oliver Ditson, a music publisher who had obtained the rights

*Formulating Foster*. Christopher Lynch, Oxford University Press. © Oxford University Press 2025.
DOI: 10.1093/9780197811726.003.0010

to most of Foster's compositions, inquiring about reproducing some of his brother's songs in a biography he was writing. According to the article, the "Pittsburg gentleman" was conducting research and met with a friend of his brother in New York who took him to places Foster frequented. Given the similarity of the account to George Cooper's later writings, and given that Morrison and Cooper are known to have corresponded around the time of Foster's death, the "friend" who met with the "gentleman" is almost certainly Cooper. Ultimately, Ditson denied Morrison's request for including copyrighted songs in his biography, forcing him to wait until Foster's songs entered the public domain. His Biography, Songs and Musical Compositions of Stephen C. Foster *did not appear until 1896* (Figure 9.1).

**Figure 9.1.** Stephen C. Foster and George Cooper. Foster Hall Collection, Center for American Music, University of Pittsburgh Library System.

## "Massa's in de Cold Ground: The Sad Ending of Stephen G. [*sic*] Foster's Career," unidentified clipping, ca. 1888.

A Pittsburg gentleman who is about to write the life of Stephen G. [*sic*] Foster, the celebrated song writer, arrived in town yesterday. He was piloted by the only friend whom the composer had while in this city to the site of some of the places frequented by Foster previous to his untimely death, with the view of collecting material for his book. The heartrending tale of genius dethroned is told below.

Mr. Foster was the author, it will be remembered, of "Come Where My Love Lies Dreaming," "Massa's in de Cold, Cold Ground," "Old Dog Tray," the incomparable "Old Folks at Home," which has brought the tears to thousands of eyes when sung by Mme. Christine Nilsson and other divas equally celebrated, and many other melodies which still ring in the ears of millions of lovers of harmony in this and other countries.

When Mr. Foster came to this city from his home in Pittsburg he had written all his famous songs and there was a change in the taste of the capricious public. Foster tried to conform to the change, but on account of its superficial nature and also because his powers were failing because of his habits he was unable to do so. He came to this city in the year 1859 and spent the most of his time in a mean little grocery and liquor store combined at the corner of Hester and Christy streets.[1] He slept at what was then known as the American Hotel, 15 Bowery,[2] upon a bed consisting of a mattress and a single blanket. There was no carpet upon the floor and but one chair in the room. A picture of greater destitution could hardly be imagined than the quarters of this charming singer. If Foster's love had found him dreaming amid such squalid surroundings she would undoubtedly have fled in disgust.

His songs were written on the top of a bean box with a pencil. The melodies were always simple and needed careful revision, for he was not a musician in the technical sense of the term. At this time his main dependence was in writing Sunday school hymns for Horace Waters. Probably not one of the thousands of children who have sung his "Suffer Little Children," etc., ever dreamed that the little gem was written in a Hester street liquor saloon of the lowest type upon the top of a common bean box.

---

[1] Foster moved to New York in 1860.
[2] This is the same address that Cooper later provided Milligan. The name of the place of residence was the American House. See Chapter 3, n17.

His personal appearance at this stage of his career was disreputable and unkempt in the extreme. He rarely wore a shirt, and his coat was buttoned up to the neck to hide the deficiency. His clothing was of the meanest description. Upon his head he wore a glazed cap, which was the fashion of the time. Our informant is positive that during the three years of his residence in this city he never went to bed sober, and he never was in a fit condition to work until he had drank two glasses of the most villainous Jamaica rum ever concocted with the aid of adulteration. But, with the weakness of a sympathetic nature, so much did he regret the hold that liquor had upon him that foolish tears would roll down his cheeks and mingle with the poison he was drinking.

Foster's inspiration was quickened in a very novel manner. A tinkling, out-of-tune piano, upon which he used to drum out chords—for he was an indifferent player—furnished him with many a theme. He was in the habit, also, of following brass bands for miles, urging as an excuse for his idiosyncrasy that the music stimulated his creative faculty. The jolting of a Broadway stage almost invariably jogged a charming melody out of him. He was one of the most tender-hearted of men, and an agreeable comrade. He carried with him in the breast pocket of his coat a picture of his daughter Marion, and often when roaming about the streets of this city he would seat himself upon the curbstone, take the picture from his pocket and cry over it.

Gradually his powers left him and he became careless. His publishers began to look askance at him. Such an utter wreck did he become that three days previous to his death the tin boiler which stood on the stove in the grocery, and which was used to make hot drinks, was overturned, and a portion of its heated contents was spilled over one of Foster's legs, scalding him terribly. His friend tells the conclusion of Foster's miserable three years in the following manner:

"I think it was in the year 1861 that early one morning a messenger came to my residence and informed me that Foster had sent for me.[3] I hastened to his lodging house and found him lying upon a mattress upon the floor with his throat cut. A physician was sewing up the wound in his neck with a black thread. I kicked the physician down stairs, and then Stephen, who was as rational as I had ever seen him, told me that when he had tried to get

---

[3] Foster died in January, 1864.

out of bed he had fainted for the first time in his life, and that he had fallen and struck his face upon the jagged edges of a broken spittoon. He had a severe cut across the bridge of his nose, and the cut in his throat already referred to.

"But I do not think his injuries would have resulted seriously had he been in good health. The fact is that he was worn out. He was carried down stairs in a blanket and taken to Bellevue Hospital where he died two days later. In my last interview with him he said:

"'Frank, see what these people are giving me to eat,' pointing to a plate of roast beef and potatoes. 'I can't eat such hearty food as that. I wish you would get me some raspberry vinegar to cool my mouth.'

"After his death he was placed in the deadhouse, where I found him under three other coffins, wrapped in a piece of muslin for a shroud. I telegraphed to his brother, who was afterward killed in an explosion, and he telegraphed me to have Stephen's body placed in a metallic coffin and to spare no expense. The body of the sweetest song writer who ever wrote upon the American continent was taken to Pittsburg and buried, and the band at his funeral played as his dirge his most romantic creation, 'Come where my love lies dreaming.'"

"What was Foster's physical appearance?" said the reporter.

"He was an undersized man weighing about 140 pounds. His face was long and pale, and it bore a melancholy expression. His eyes were dark hazel in color. He wore no beard nor mustache, and upon his upper lip was a sear which he received when a youth in a very singular manner. He was out with a serenading party one night, and in putting a bottle up to his mouth a jagged edge of the bottle's lip inflicted a scar which he bore to his grave."

"Is it a fact, as reported, that E. P. Christy, the minstrel, tried to rob Foster of the credit of writing his songs?"

"No, it is not. Christy paid Foster $15 to permit that latter to print his name as author upon the title page of 'Camp Town Race,' 'Glendy Bark,' and many other of his most famous songs, but the public were well aware that Foster was the author. Foster's songs were sold on commission by Forth, Hall & Pond [sic], who were then doing business on Park place, and for a number of years Foster's royalties amounted to between $1,400 and $1,500 a year, an unprecedented sum for those days. A monument stands over Foster's grave in the Pittsburg cemetery. I don't know what the inscription upon it is, but it seems to me an appropriate one would be:

"'Massa's in de cold, cold ground.'"

# 10
# An Interview with an Anonymous "Acquaintance" (1889)

**Introduction**

*The following article, first republished here, is not in the Foster Hall Collection. Many of the details contradict other sources, and all its confirmable details were readily available at the time of the interview, suggesting the interviewee was a fraud. However, if this account is not fraudulent, it is the only firsthand testimony providing an explanation for Foster's separation from Jane and the only firsthand account that portrays him as dying by suicide.*

Only five people are known to have firsthand knowledge of Foster's last days: John Mahon, George Cooper, George W. Birdseye, Susan McFarland Parkhurst, and Kit Clarke. Mahon was dead when the article appeared, and none of the others fit the source's claims that he first met Foster in Cincinnati in 1857 when he worked for the Enquirer, was reacquainted with him in New York in the 1860s when he worked for the Times, and then was living in Philadelphia at the time of this interview in 1889.

Perhaps the closest fit to the description is Birdseye, whose occupation in an 1885 Philadelphia directory is "publisher."[1] Also, his descriptions of where and how he met Foster in New York strongly resemble Birdseye's 1867 account. But Birdseye is unlikely to be the interviewee. In his 1867 article, Birdseye claimed to have first met Foster in New York in 1862, not Cincinnati in 1857. Moreover, Birdseye no longer resided in Philadelphia in 1889. He appears in the 1886 Boston city directory, and an announcement appeared in the Boston Evening Transcript on September 22, 1886, indicating that "George Birdseye, formerly of Philadelphia, now a resident of Boston, is preparing a volume of poems entitled 'Vanities in Verse,' to be issued the coming winter by a Boston firm."[2]

---

[1] *Gopsill's Philadelphia City Directory, 1885* (James Gopsill's Sons, 1885), 194.
[2] "Literary Items," *Boston Evening Transcript*, September 22, 1886.

*Formulating Foster*. Christopher Lynch, Oxford University Press. © Oxford University Press 2025.
DOI: 10.1093/9780197811726.003.0011

*It is possible that the source could have been another, unknown friend of Foster's who knew similar details about his life as Birdseye and Cooper. But given what appear to be distorted similarities with the accounts by Birdseye, Nevin, and the anonymous interviewees the year before, it seems more likely that this interviewee was a fraud who took information from other sources and posed as a witness to Foster's last years.*

## P. D. Haywood (a pseudonym for John H. Horton), *Philadelphia Times*, October 23, 1889.

One gloomy day in January, 1864, two men were groping around in the deadhouse of the Bellevue Hospital, a hideous place. Finally a coffin was dragged from under several others and the lid removed. "That's him," said the rough attendant. Yes, there lay all that was mortal of Stephen Collins Foster, the sweetest song-writer that America ever produced.

The body was fearfully emaciated, and a gash in the throat was evidence that he had tried to end his weary life by suicide. He had been brought to the hospital from a wretched room in Washington Street near the Battery,[3] suffering from hunger and cold and the wound he had made, and in two days was dead, thus ending his life, like his prototype, Edgar Allen Poe, in the pauper ward of a hospital.

Foster was born in Pittsburg, July 4, 1826. He had only a common-school education and became a clerk in an iron foundry.[4] Although passionately fond of music, he had neither perseverance or force of character enough to study the notes thoroughly and to the last, although always practicing on the piano, could not play at sight. It was his habit to write out the words of his songs with many revisions, and then pick out on the piano a tune to suit him, and so retentive was his ear and memory that he could carry the melody until it was technically set to music. A young Irishman named Shanly, an excellent

---

[3] There is no additional source that suggests Foster ever lived in this location. The claim is probably false.

[4] Foster never worked in an iron foundry. As a young man, he briefly worked at a cotton mill and then worked as a bookkeeper for his brother Dunning's steamboat business. After that he earned his living only through the sale of sheet music, though he often depended on his family's generosity.

musician who lived in Allegheny City when not on tramp, used to do this for Foster.[5] He, too, was a hapless child of song and died in the almshouse here.

Foster published his first song, "Open Thy Lattice, Love," in 1842 and got $5 for it.[6] From this on to 1853 his career was prosperous, and he made his reputation world-wide as the writer of "O, Susannah," "Uncle Ned," "Old Folks at Home." George Christy paid him $500 for the latter.[7] "Old Black Joe" was his last negro melody. Then he tried a higher flight, composing sentimental songs, such as "My Old Kentucky Home," "Nellie Bly," and the best of his melodies of this class, "Come Where My Love Lies Dreaming." At this time he was in receipt of an income of not less than $1,500 per annum from royalties on his songs and his invention seemed inexhaustible. But he was surrounded by a crowd of sycophants that spent his money and led him into excesses that finally broke him down.

He was married and had one child, a daughter, whom he passionately loved, but his wife became weary of his excesses and left him, and henceforth his downward course was fearfully rapid. He sought inspiration in the bottle, and only composed when he wanted money to fill what he termed "his best friend."

His subsequent career can best be told by one who was with him to the sad ending. This gentleman is at present a resident of Philadelphia and these are his words: "I am a printer and was acquainted with Foster in 1857 when I worked on the *Enquirer*. He was living in Cincinnati then. He was a helpless, harmless fellow, more like a woman than a man. His only vice was his love of liquor, and his habitual associates were not calculated to reform him in this respect. Although not a trained musician he could bring melody out of a tin-pan, and was forever drumming with his fingers and humming snatches of song, and so he composed.

---

[5] I cannot find other references to Shanly, and the suggestion that he or anyone else regularly wrote piano accompaniments for Foster's melodies is difficult to assess because few of Foster's manuscripts survive. The manuscript of Foster's first published song, "Open Thy Lattice Love," has an accompaniment that is much more awkward than the version that was published, suggesting that the publisher had someone improve the accompaniment before it went to print. (This manuscript has been lost, but Morneweck reproduces it in *Chronicles*, vol. 1, p. 267.) On the other hand, Foster's surviving manuscripts from when he was older and more experienced were not altered before publication, and, as Steven Saunders has shown, Foster even corrected mistakes that publishers introduced (Saunders, "Stephen Foster and His Publishers, Revisited," *College Music Symposium* 28 [1998]: 53–69).

[6] This incorrect publication date for "Open Thy Lattice Love" was a common error. The song was actually published by Willig in 1844.

[7] Nevin claimed that E. P. Christy—not George Christy—paid Foster $500 for the song (see Chapter 4). In truth, E. P. Christy paid Foster only $15 for the song. George Christy performed in E. P. Christy's minstrel troupe before starting his own when E. P. retired.

"In 1860 I went to New-York to work on the *Times*. One cold, gusty night in March I was coming up Greenwich Street from the Battery and stopped in a grocery and liquor store to get a glass of cider. The proprietor was a German named Halb. It was rather rough inside, but I could hear behind a partition the tinkling notes of a piano marvelously out of tune. The German laughed as he said: 'That's a poor fellow what makes songs for a living and he uses my piano.' I stepped back, curious to see the song writer. A thin little man was bending over the instrument, striking out chords and humming to himself. I knew him at once—it was Stephen C. Foster—but how changed. He was fairly wasted away, and his clothing was tattered and filthy, with shattered low shoes and no stockings, and this in March. His story was soon told.

"'I am utterly lost, without a friend in the world, and I believe I am losing my mind,' and then he began to cry. It was a painful sight; I got him away; gave him some money, and left him at Duane Street. He went towards the river.

"I hunted him up again and again, with the same result. If I gave him money to buy a shirt, he drank it. He ate nothing. Several times, finding him shivering in the morning, I took him to a restaurant, but he wanted a cup of coffee only. Once I found him in a Cherry-street den surrounded by murderous-looking ruffians. He was playing the fiddle and two longshoremen were dancing to the music. At length I missed him, and after much inquiry found his lodging-house—a terrible place on West Street.[8] The keeper was a powerful Irishwoman and she said: 'Ah, the poor little man, he tried to kill himself and he is in the Bailyvoo Hospital. The copper took him there.' When I got there Foster was dead. His relatives reclaimed his body and he lies in a cemetery in his native city, and his epitaph should be: 'Life's fitful fever o'er, he sleeps well.'"

---

[8] This is the only source suggesting he lived on West Street. Like this person's earlier claim about where Foster lived, this is probably false.

# PART II
# MEMORIALIZING FOSTER AT THE TURN OF THE TWENTIETH CENTURY

## Introduction

Historian Christian McWhirter observes that "although the songs of the Civil War never disappeared entirely, they declined enough after Appomattox that their rediscovery in the mid-1880s constituted a revival."[1] Written in the Civil War era, Foster's songs followed a similar trajectory. Kept alive by opera divas and jubilee singers during the long period of decline that began during the Civil War, Foster's songs slowly began to make a comeback in the late 1880s. In 1887 a brief biography of the composer and several of his songs were included in a Civil War retrospective songbook called *Our War Songs North and South*.[2] This collection appeared amid a revival of general interest in the Civil War, and from this moment Foster's music would figure more prominently into memorialization of the war.[3] Like war songs, the rediscovery of Foster's songs at the end of the century constituted a revival.

Outside of memorialization of the war, interest in Foster's music was especially slow to increase. In 1889 the Boston-based publisher Ticknor &

---

[1] Christian McWhirter, *Battle Hymns: The Power and Popularity of Music in the Civil War* (University of North Carolina Press, 2023), 186.

[2] *Our War Songs North and South* (S. Brainards' Sons, 1887). Foster's songs appeared in a small number of other Grand Army of the Republic (GAR) songsters in the 1880s. See William Henry Smith, *Complete GAR Song Book* (R. W. Haskin, 1887); James Henry Kyner, *Odes, Hymns and Songs of the GAR* (H. Gibson, 1880); and S. H. Birdsall, *The Latest Songs for the Grand Army and for the Sons of Veterans* (L. Kimball & Co., 1884).

[3] See Rossiter Johnson, *Campfire and Battlefield: A History of the Conflicts and Campaigns of the Great Civil War in the United States* (Bryan, Taylor & Company, 1894), 134; *The Old Songs: A Collection of National Airs, Hymns of Patriotism, and Camp-Fire Melodies Compiled for the St. Paul Grand Army of the Republic* (McGill Printing Co., 1986).

Co. published a set of books with lavish illustrations by Charles Copeland depicting scenes from four of Foster's sentimental minstrel songs, "Old Folks at Home," "My Old Kentucky Home," "Massa's in de Cold Ground," and "Nelly Was a Lady."[4] In 1892, the large-scale musical theatrical extravaganza *The South before the War* toured the nation with its romantic tableaus of plantation life enriched by a performance of "My Old Kentucky Home."[5] The ballad also made an impression on many visitors at the Columbian Exposition in Chicago the following year, after which it quickly entered Kentucky lore as Kentuckians fabricated the legend of the composer writing the song in the Bluegrass State.[6]

The remembrances recorded during the early period of Foster's re-emergence form a unique grouping, characterized by the re-remembering of the composer after a long period of forgetting. Almost all the remembrances were first published in Pittsburgh while Morrison Foster worked to seize control of his brother's memory with his own biography and partnered with Thomas Keenan Jr., editor of the *Pittsburg Press*, to raise funds to erect a statue of his brother. Throughout 1895 and 1896, and again in 1900 leading up to the statue's unveiling, Keenan published praise-filled articles about Foster almost every day. Included among them were the majority of remembrances of the composer. Not surprisingly, many adhere to the way Morrison wanted his brother remembered, but the several remembrances that do not support Morrison's story speak to the lack of general acceptance of the Foster myth still at the turn of the century. The myth would not be widely accepted until Foster Hall's efforts in the 1930s, and not surprisingly Foster Hall declined to preserve the reminiscences from the 1890s that did not comport with Morrison's narrative.

As we have seen, Morrison had long been frustrated with the spread of misinformation about his brother and unseemly details about his alcoholism and character. He influenced Birdseye's article and expressed his dissatisfaction about Nevin's *Atlantic* article to the author. In addition, when the songwriter Will S. Hays wrote an article in 1875 claiming Foster did not have a

---

[4] Stephen Foster, *The Swanee River* [Old Folks at Home], illustrated by Charles Copeland (Ticknor & Co., 1889); Foster, *My Old Kentucky Home*, illustrated by Charles Copeland (Ticknor & Co., 1889); Foster, *Massa's in the Cold, Cold Ground*, illustrated by Charles Copeland (Ticknor & Co., 1889); and Foster, *Nelly Was a Lady*, illustrated by Charles Copeland (Ticknor & Co., 1889).

[5] See Emily Bingham, *My Old Kentucky Home: The Astonishing Life and Reckoning of an Iconic American Song* (Alfred A. Knopf, 2022), 56–60.

[6] The earliest reference to the Kentucky myth I have found is Will S. Hays, "Melody His Monument," *Louisville Courier-Journal*, June 18, 1893.

grave, Morrison wrote to the newspaper to correct the mistake.[7] Following the 1879 claims by Joseph Murphy, Rebecca Shiras Morris, and Joan Sloan Shiras, doubts about the authorship of Foster's songs resurfaced in 1884, and Morrison again refuted them.[8] In 1886 similar claims appeared in the *Chicago News*, and when S. Reed Johnston forwarded Morrison the article, Morrison responded forcefully that "Shiras was an intimate friend of ours" but "the only words of Shiras published to which Stephen ever wrote music were a song called 'Annie My Own Love.'"[9] After authorship questions appeared again in the *Chicago Times* in 1890, Walter Welsh, who was married to Foster's daughter, Marion, wrote to Morrison from the Windy City that "Marion wanted to go over and scalp the entire Times force this morning."[10]

By 1890, Morrison had attempted on numerous occasions to reframe his brother's memory. He gave an interview to the *Philadelphia Times* in 1883, and he helped his nephew write about Foster for the *East End Bulletin*—a small Pittsburgh paper—in 1887. In 1888 Morrison wrote to the publisher Oliver Ditson, who had acquired the rights to many of Foster's songs, requesting permission to reproduce Foster's music in a comprehensive songbook and biography.[11] Ditson denied his request, and Morrison waited until 1893—the year "Old Folks" entered the public domain—before starting the project. He first reached out to writer George Alfred Townsend about writing the biography, but when Townsend declined his proposal he set out to write it himself.[12] It was also in 1893 that Morrison launched the project with Keenan to erect the statue of Foster, which he probably hoped to complete by the 1894 encampment of the Grand Army of the Republic (the Union veterans' organization) in Pittsburgh. Both Morrison and Keenan served on the event's planning committee, and they probably pictured veterans buying Morrison's book and singing Foster's songs around the statue. But their plans were thwarted by a severe economic downturn in 1893, and the statue was further delayed by the Spanish-American War in 1898. Morrison's book

---

[7] Will S. Hays, "A Monument for Foster," *Brainard's Musical World*, December 1875; Morrison's response appeared in "Foster's Grave," *Pittsburgh Daily Gazette*, October 29, 1875.

[8] An 1883 interview appeared in the *Philadelphia Times* and all over the country. In 1884 he wrote to the *Philadelphia Times* to correct mistakes in an article.

[9] S. Reed Johnston to Morrison Foster, February 12, 1886, FHC, C918; and Morrison Foster to S. Reed Johnston, February 14, 1886, FHC, C919.

[10] Walter Welsh to Morrison Foster, April 7, 1890, FHC, D133.

[11] Oliver Ditson & Co. to Morrison Foster, May 5, 1888, FHC, C852.

[12] George Alfred Townsend to Morrison Foster, undated, FHC, C862c; George Alfred Townsend to Morrison Foster, July 16, 1893, FHC, C862a; George Alfred Townsend to Morrison Foster, January 2, 1894, FHC, C862b.

appeared as *Biography, Songs and Musical Compositions of Stephen C. Foster* in 1896, and the statue was not completed until 1900.

Because only twenty-five anodyne letters by Foster survive, some scholars have conjectured that Morrison destroyed most of his brother's correspondence.[13] As evidence, scholars point to Morrison's admission in his biography of "burning a lot of old letters" following his parents' deaths in 1855 and to an 1853 letter that he censored. That year he wrote a letter (which no longer survives) to his sister Henrietta informing her that Foster had separated from his wife, Jane. Her written response survives, but someone—possibly Morrison, who probably owned the letter before giving it to his daughter who ultimately donated it to the Foster Hall Collection—scribbled in black ink over some of the lines in an unsuccessful attempt to hide their content:

> How sorry I feel for dear Stevie. Though when I read your letter I was not at all surprised of the news it contained in regard to him and ~~Jane~~. I last winter felt convinced ~~that she would either have to change her course of conduct or a separation was inevitable~~ though I never wrote a word of the kind to Stevie.[14]

Some scholars have concluded from this that Morrison was the prime culprit behind erasing information about Foster. Perhaps. Or maybe Morrison was simply hiding Henrietta's comments about Stephen's marriage from Stephen—after all, Henrietta indicated she did not want him to know what she thought. The letter does not prove any archival malfeasance on Morrison's part, and it is possible that a later member of the Foster family—such as Evelyn Foster Morneweck, whom we will see distorting the historical record in this book's concluding essay—was behind the censorship of material. Or maybe, as Foster's name faded from memory, the letters were not censored by anyone so much as discarded by their various owners (and their descendants), who no longer saw any significance to them. Ultimately, Foster's missing letters are highly suspicious, but the mystery of how they failed to be preserved will probably remain unsolved.

---

[13] See Calvin Elliker, "The Collector and Reception History: The Case of Josiah Kirby Lilly," in *Music Publishing and Collecting: Essays in Honor of Donald W. Krummel*, ed. David Hunter (Graduate School of Library and Information Science, University of Illinois at Urbana-Champaign, 1994), 190 and 201; Emerson, *Doo-Dah!*, 313; and Root, "Mythtory," 26–28.

[14] Henrietta Thornton to Morrison Foster, June 21, 1853, FHC, C532.

It could be that Morneweck carried out the destruction of certain materials in the archive in keeping with how Morrison wanted his brother to be remembered. Morrison was transparent about what information he wanted made public and what information he wanted kept private when responding to the editors of Birdseye's reminiscence. He wrote to the editor, "The people generally of his native land [of Pittsburgh] love to know of him only as the ideal imaged [etched?] on their minds by his own strains of melody and simple unaffected poetry," adding, "I sincerely trust that my brother's memory may be kept identified solely with his work as an author, not his peculiarities of habit, and that no further attempt will be made by any one to 'draw his frailties from their dread abode.'"[15] Morrison did not want his brother's personal life to be known. He wanted public memory to be shaped only by the image projected by his songs. Did he destroy his brother's letters while compiling his brother's songs in his book to do this? Maybe. When the archive was being compiled in the 1930s, did Morneweck destroy letters to honor her father's wishes about Foster's memory? Maybe.

Morrison probably wanted his brother's memory shaped mostly by his music because he understood that in his brother's songs that were remembered at that time—his sentimental minstrel songs—Foster had chosen not to voice partisan views but to transcend sectionalism, ideology, and, to an extent, race. Throughout his life, Morrison was a conservative Democrat, politically and economically aligned with the Southern planter class. As a young man in the 1840s and 1850s, he built his wealth on enslavement, traveling to Southern plantations about twice a year to purchase raw cotton that he shipped back to Pennsylvania to be manufactured into various products.[16] After he left the cotton business, he remained linked to the Southern economy through his father-in-law Isaac Lightner Sr., brother-in-law Isaac Lightner Jr., and wife's cousin James S. Lightner, who lived in Missouri and worked in the hemp business. Isaac Jr. would fight for the Confederate Army and die at Lost Mountain, Georgia, in 1864.[17] Aware of the complex economic relationship between the North and South, Morrison publicly opposed abolition and supported the doctrine of states' rights, which allowed the voters (i.e., White, male citizens) of each state to determine to

---

[15] Mason Bros. to Morrison Foster, February 2, 1867, FHC, C899a.
[16] For more, see Christopher Lynch, "Stephen Foster and the Slavery Question," *American Music* 40, no. 1 (2022): 19–22.
[17] Morneweck, *Chronicles*, vol. 2, 537–38.

be slave or free.[18] Thus, Morrison embraced a decidedly White supremacist and misogynist vision of the nation as a union of states in which White male residents decided issues of enslavement and Blacks were not granted full citizenship. His brother's sentimental minstrel songs, which he loved, did not offend his political sensibilities.

But Morrison also knew that these songs spoke to people with vastly different views too. On July 10, 1884, he received a letter from Isaac Craig, who included a passage pertaining to "Old Folks at Home" excerpted from Anna Davis Hallowell's recent book about her grandparents, *James and Lucretia Mott: Life and Letters*. Hallowell identifies "Old Folks" as one of Lucretia's favorite songs:

> The year before [Lucretia] died [1880], when she was obliged to give up her life-long habit of early rising, and to spend weary hours in bed, she used to get a sweet-voiced little great-grandson to sing to her every morning, while he was dressing in the next room. The song was always "Old Folks at Home," over and over again. Then the little fellow would be called to her bedside to receive the penny that she had ready for him under her pillow.[19]

Lucretia Mott stood apart from Morrison as one of the foremost abolitionists of their day. There is no doubt, then, that Morrison grasped the significance of her standing united with him in admiration of his brother's music. Morrison knew that his brother's music could cut through social divisions.

As one of his brother's closest companions, Morrison knew that Foster shared some of his conservative ideas, including his general adherence to a White supremacist order. But he also knew they differed on decisive issues. Although they both opposed abolition and favored states' rights, during the Civil War Morrison was a "peace Democrat" who supported negotiations

---

[18] Morrison Foster, "The Uses of the Slave States," *Cleveland Plain Dealer*, February 28, 1861, in Morrison Foster Scrapbook 1855–1898, FHC, A287. His argument echoes a common argument against abolition, articulated by David Christy in *Cotton Is King; Or, the Culture of Cotton, and Its Relation to the Agriculture, Manufactures and Commerce* (Moore, Wilstach, Keys & Co., 1855). The intersectional antebellum economy has been a recent topic of considerable interest among historians. See Edward E. Baptist, *The Half Has Never Been Told: Slavery and the Making of American Capitalism* (Basic Books, 2014); David R. Meyer, *The Roots of American Industrialization* (Johns Hopkins University Press, 2003); Sven Beckert and Seth Rockman, eds., *Slavery's Capitalism: A New History of American Economic Development* (University of Pennsylvania Press, 2016); and Calvin Schermerhorn, *The Business of Slavery and the Rise of American Capitalism* (Yale University Press, 2015).

[19] Anna Davis Hallowell, *James and Lucretia Mott: Life and Letters* (Houghton, Mifflin and Co., 1884), 242.

with secessionists to preserve the union, while Foster was a "war Democrat" who supported preserving the union by defeating the insurrectionists militarily, a view he expressed in songs such as "We Are Coming Father Abra'am." But after Foster's death, and after the Civil War, Morrison found common ground in his brother's pre-war, sentimental minstrel songs, that is, the songs in which Foster chose *not* to overtly express his personal views and instead to appeal to people like Morrison and Mott simultaneously. Morrison probably believed that the potential for his brother to secure national fame rested on his sentimental minstrel songs' ability to cut across political, ideological, and racial divisions. So he wanted his brother's memory to be built upon "his own strains of melody and simple unaffected poetry," not his more narrow, personal opinions, "peculiarities of habit," or "frailties."

Morrison's configuration ignored songs such as the overtly racist "Oh! Susanna," the sectional "That's What's the Matter," the anti-abolition "A Soldier in de Colored Brigade," and the partisan "The Abolition Show." He included most of these songs in his book, but he did not dwell on them or focus on their controversial meanings. Morrison's biography followed the outline he had made when responding to Birdseye's article, ignoring certain biographical details and focusing on a subset of Foster's music to recast him in a purely positive, idealistic light. Ignoring certain details mattered little to the public. Not only were the controversial songs largely unknown at the time, but the construction of simple composer biographies upon superficial interpretations of only a composer's best-known pieces and a few carefully selected anecdotes was the norm in nineteenth-century musicology.

While Morrison worked on *Biography, Songs and Musical Compositions*, Keenan promoted the statue effort in the *Press* with articles full of bluster about Foster's historical significance. As founder of the International League of Press Clubs, Keenan probably facilitated the reprinting of the articles in newspapers across the country, spreading the idea that Foster was "first in the ranks of the song writers of America,"[20] "the first song writer of America,"[21] and the author of "the first distinctively American songs."[22] It cannot be serendipitous that by the end of 1895, after spending three years in residence in the United States, Czech composer Antonín Dvořák recommended that

---

[20] "Foster Memorial," *Pittsburg Press*, July 8, 1895.
[21] "Foster Memorial," *Pittsburg Press*, July 29, 1895.
[22] "Foster Memorial," *Pittsburg Press*, April 27, 1896.

American classical composers develop a national style by drawing on "the so-called plantation melodies and slave songs... like those of Foster."[23]

The *Pittsburg Press* also went to great lengths to portray Foster's music as expressive of universally shared human emotions. Drawing only on his sentimental songs to construct this portrayal, the paper wrote:

> It was this universality that made Foster's songs next to John Howard Payne's "Home, Sweet Home," the best known melodies of the age. Their simplicity made them understood of all; their pathos touched every heart, their melody appealed to every ear, cultivated or uncultivated. These wild flowers of song were so beautiful that they were given a premier place in every garden.[24]

Doubling down on universality, the *Press* routinely "reported" that Foster's songs "have made him famous in almost every country on the globe."[25] Keenan and the *Press* did not erase race in Foster's music. That was not possible. So instead they minimized it. Subsuming race into their discourse of universalism, they whitewashed the composer and his music.

A prominent Democrat, Morrison timed the release of his biography to be near the Democratic National Convention in July of 1896, shortly before he announced his own candidacy for Congress as a Democrat in a heavily Republican district. As a senior party figure in Allegheny County, Morrison was tasked that summer with hosting the Democratic presidential nominee William Jennings Bryan on his visit to Pittsburgh. On August 10, he and leading Democrats rendezvoused with Bryan in Canton, Ohio, where they called on Bryan's Republican opponent, William McKinley, who resided there. Then they headed to Pittsburgh, where hordes greeted them at the train station. Morrison and Bryan paraded in a coach along a highly publicized route populated by thousands of Pittsburghers. He also accompanied Bryan to dinner and escorted him—once again before thousands—to the city's theater district, where the nominee addressed two packed theaters.[26] In September, Morrison accepted his party's nomination

---

[23] Antonín Dvořák, "Music in America," *Harper's New Monthly Magazine*, February 1895, 432. For more on Dvořák and Foster, see Root, Deane L. "The Stephen Foster–Antonín Dvořák Connection," in *Dvořák in America 1892–1895*, ed. John C. Tibbetts (Amadeus Press, 1993), 242–54.
[24] "Story of the Stephen C. Foster Memorial: How the Fund Was Raised by the Pittsburg Press to Honor Pittsburg's Poet Whose Songs Are Sung Around the World," *Pittsburg Press*, August 5, 1900.
[25] "A. Carnegie, $1,000," *Pittsburg Press*, June 10, 1895.
[26] "Howley Laughs Last," *Pittsburgh Commercial Gazette*, August 7, 1896; "Reception to Bryan," *Pittsburg Press*, August 10, 1896; "A Vast Throng Cheered Bryan," *Pittsburg Post*, August 11, 1896;

to run for Congress[27] with a partisan speech that echoed Bryan's opposition to the gold standard.[28] He gave similar speeches in September and October, prominently participated in parades in Allegheny City and Pittsburgh, and served on the committee charged with distributing Democratic campaign literature.[29]

Morrison's biography played into his campaign. Making his family and brother look good also improved his own image. He stretched the truth (claiming, for example, that Foster was paid $500 by Edwin P. Christy when it was really $15), and he misled through omission (referring to his brother attending Jefferson College but declining to mention that he stayed only one week). Similarly, he referred to Foster's marriage to Jane but not their marital troubles, and he never mentioned his brother's addiction to alcohol. As might be expected of a close family member—perhaps especially one running for office—he focused on the positive, portraying his brother as upright, elite, and respectable and smoothing over his associations with "working class" minstrelsy and its racism. His conservatism and political aspirations likely informed his portrayal of his family as heroic, brave, and genteel, as well as his choice to emphasize his Scots-Irish heritage (which had strong Democratic associations), ties to founding fathers and American inventors, and—writing in response to the 1890s New Woman—gender conservativism.

Morrison's avoidance of off-putting partisanship and sectionalism also functioned to boost his campaign.[30] Foster, Morrison pointed out, always cared for the "lowly," and he claimed he "founded a new era in melody and ballad" in which "the grotesque and clownish aspect of negro songs was softened, and ridicule began to merge into sympathy." He allowed that his songs may have helped generate a certain degree of sympathy for the enslaved. But he also gently repudiated the alignment of his brother with movements for racial progress, explaining that his brother did not think of himself as an activist. He wrote, "*Unknown to himself*, he opened the way

---

"Democracy Aroused as Pittsburg Never Has Known It to Be," *Pittsburg Post*, August 11, 1896; "Honors for Bryan," *Pittsburg Press*, August 11, 1896; "Honored by Everyone at Every Place," *Pittsburg Post*, August 11, 1896.

[27] See "Foster Pitted against Stone," *Pittsburg Post*, September 6, 1896.
[28] "Pulaski Heard Morrison Foster," *Pittsburg Post*, September 5, 1896.
[29] For parades, see "Great Parade in Allegheny," *Pittsburg Post*, October 18, 1896; and "Silver Cohorts on to Victory," *Pittsburg Post*, October 30, 1896. For campaign literature, see "Delegates Are Off for Erie," *Pittsburg Post*, August 26, 1896.
[30] Christopher Lynch, "From Obscurity to National Icon: Memorializing Stephen C. Foster in the 1890s," *American Nineteenth Century History* 24, no. 3 (2023): 315–37.

to the hearts of the people, which led to actual interest in the black man" (emphasis added).[31] Morrison portrayed his brother as having cared about Black people—a stance that even many steadfast defenders of slavery and White supremacy maintained—but his words were carefully chosen to appeal to many Americans, whether they had supported abolition and racial equality or not. Following the lead of his brother's sentimental minstrel songs, Morrison aimed to maximize his brother's appeal (and his own) to the broadest possible cross section of Americans (and voters in his district)—Whites, Blacks, Northerners, Southerners, Republicans, Democrats, former Confederates, Unionists, and so on. *Sympathy* was the key.

The statue, which was designed by Keenan with input from Morrison and created by sculptor Giuseppe Moretti, made overtures to a similarly diverse cross section of Americans (Figure PII.1). In one sense, it represented how some turn-of-the-century Americans were beginning to view the United States: a union of sections and states representing vast cultural, economic, political, and racial diversity. In Morrison and Keenan's construction, Foster was able to express universally shared emotions because of his great sympathy for everyone living in the nation. In this, his music was positioned as emblematic of the concept of the nation as a "crucible" of different races, ethnicities, and regional peoples, a notion widely discussed following historian Frederick Jackson Turner's landmark lecture *The Significance of the Frontier in American History* at the Columbian Exposition in 1893—the very year Morrison launched his biography and statue projects.[32] The statue portrays the White, urbane Foster as sympathetically transcribing the music of a "lowly" rural black man. The slave caricature doubled as a symbol of the South, allowing the group to depict the reconciliation of the North (Foster) and the South (the caricature). It was a progressive portrayal of Black Americans in that it allowed the Black man to symbolize the South, yet it was also inclusive of Lost Cause proponents in that the man's smiling face nodded toward the myth of the "happy slave" who benefited from the "benevolence" of enslavement. The positioning of the figures with the Black man below Foster also subtly suggests the resurgence of White supremacy at the dawn of the Jim Crow era. The pervasive description in newspapers

---

[31] Morrison Foster, *Biography, Songs and Musical Compositions of Stephen C. Foster* (Percy F. Smith, 1896), 14.

[32] The crucible metaphor was especially prominent in the 1890s. The term "melting pot" would enter widespread use in the United States just eight years after the unveiling of the Foster statue in Pittsburgh because of Israel Zangwill's popular play *The Melting Pot* (MacMillan, 1909).

**Figure PII.1.** Stephen Foster, statue by Giuseppe Moretti. Foster Hall Collection, Center for American Music, University of Pittsburgh Library System.

of the Black man as "at his [Foster's] feet" suggests the statue's hierarchy was not something the creators wanted to go unnoticed.[33] Depicted in the act of writing down the music performed by the enslaved man, Foster is shown to be the visionary poet-composer (or perhaps thief) who brought this inclusive but racially stratified conception of nationhood into being.[34]

Morrison's daughter Evelyn Foster Morneweck would one day admit to later Foster biographer John Tasker Howard that her father "looked at his

---

[33] "Tribute to Foster," *Pittsburgh Commercial Gazette*, May 10, 1899; "Press League Literary Contest No. 3," *Pittsburg Press*, October 29, 1899; "The Stephen C. Foster Monument," *Pittsburg Press*, August 4, 1900; "Story of the Stephen C. Foster Memorial," *Pittsburg Press*, August 5, 1900; "How the Portrait of Foster Was Obtained," *Pittsburg Press*, August 23, 1900; "Pittsburg's Tribute to the Poet of the World," *Pittsburg Press*, September 12, 1900; "Foster Memorial," *Commercial Gazette*, September 13, 1900.

[34] For more on the statue, see Lynch, "From Obscurity to National Icon"; and Kirk Savage, "No Time, No Place: The Existential Crisis of the Public Monument," *Future Anterior: Journal of Historic Preservation History, Theory, & Criticism* 15, no. 2 (Winter 2018): 146–54.

entire family through rose-colored glasses." She added, "As my cousin Mary Crosman used to say, 'All Uncle Mit's crows were swans.' But the beautiful qualities he saw in others, Morrison Foster himself possessed in abundance; he was the soul of honor, and incapable of a mean thought or act. He loved Stephen devotedly, and Stephen returned his affection, as is evident from many letters I have, and from the stories I had from my father himself."[35] Despite his lack of objectivity, Morrison's rosy history of his family exerted a tremendous—albeit gradual—influence.

His construction of Foster with such vaguely defined concepts as "sympathy" transformed him into an empty vessel into which people could place their own hopes and beliefs. Many people, for example, saw him as contributing to the emancipation of enslaved people by depicting them humanely. During the statue project in Pittsburgh, one city resident stated that the composer "did as much if not more toward freeing the southern negro from the bonds of slavery than Mrs. Harriet Beecher Stowe's world-famed novel *Uncle Tom's Cabin*" with his songs that "wielded their softening influences in every portion of the country, preparing the hearts of the people in a measure for the final decision of the martyred president, Abraham Lincoln."[36]

Amid the rise of discourse about Foster's "universally appealing" music, some Black Americans also expressed favorable views of Foster. W. E. B. DuBois was deeply affected by the spirituals that he heard performed by the Fisk Jubilee Singers in Jubilee Hall as a student at Fisk University. Reflecting on his experience in *The Souls of Black Folk*, he wrote,

> When I came to Nashville I saw the great temple builded of these songs towering over the pale city. To me Jubilee Hall seemed ever made of the songs themselves, and its bricks were red with the blood and dust of toil. Out of them rose for me morning, noon, and night, bursts of wonderful melody, full of the voices of my brothers and sisters, full of the voices of the past.[37]

Among the songs he would have heard performed as the music of his "brothers and sisters" were Foster's sentimental minstrel songs, especially "Old Folks at Home." To Du Bois, Foster's songs were evidence of an

---

[35] Evelyn Foster Morneweck to John Tasker Howard, July 8, 1931, FHC, Letters Catalogued, box A-1 (A–H).
[36] "The Composer Did Much Toward Freeing the Negro," *Pittsburg Press*, June 1895[?].
[37] W. E. B. Du Bois, *The Souls of Black Folk: Essays and Sketches* (A. C. McClurg, 1903), 250–51.

important stage in the development of African American music, in which "the songs of white America have been distinctively influenced by the slave songs or have incorporated whole phrases of Negro melody, as 'Swanee River' and 'Old Black Joe.'"[38]

Taking up the topic again a decade later, Du Bois portrayed Foster as an important link between the spirituals of enslaved people and the compositions of later Black composers: "In our day Negro artists like Johnson and Will Marian [sic] Cook have taken up this [Foster's] music and begun a newer and most important development, using the syncopated measure popularly known as 'rag time.'"[39] Du Bois certainly did not believe "Old Folks" and "Old Black Joe" were spirituals or authentic Black folk songs. But he believed their sympathy allowed them to transcend racial divisions, making them universal and aligning them in some ways with the efforts of Black songwriters. Their appeal to Du Bois thus paralleled the appeal in these years of "universal" German classical music to many Black musicians. As Kira Thurman notes, "It was precisely classical music's paradoxical nature that led Black musicians . . . to claim it," adding, though, that "the fact that Black classical musicians in the Caribbean, the United States, and Latin America came to espouse the gospel of musical universalism is, if anything, a testament to German music's hegemonic and expansive reach."[40] Likewise, Du Bois's embrace of the myth of Foster exemplifies the expansive reach of the myth. And Du Bois's favorable view of Foster had a significant influence well into the twentieth century and beyond, contributing to the rise of a prominent strain of Black thought about American cultural history.

Not everyone imagined Foster as a force within the nation's history of racial progress. In fact, some White Americans threw their *racist* hopes and beliefs onto Foster. The vague rhetoric of Keenan and Morrison created space for people who subscribed to the Lost Cause mythologies that portrayed the Civil War as a war to defend states' rights and the "racial harmony" that existed under enslavement, which was portrayed as mutually beneficial and desirable for both Whites and Blacks. The imaginary "happy slave," a symbol of this bygone era of supposed racial harmony under White domination, could be observed in Foster's music. Mildred Rutherford, who oversaw

---

[38] Du Bois, *Souls of Black Folk*, 256.
[39] W. E. B. Du Bois, "The Negro in Literature and Art," *Annals of the American Academy of Political and Social Science* 49 (September 1913): 233–34.
[40] Kira Thurman, *Singing Like Germans: Black Musicians in the Land of Bach, Beethoven, and Brahms* (Cornell University Press, 2021), 7.

educational curriculum for the United Daughters of the Confederacy and was outspoken about her belief in what she referred to as "white supremacy," created propagandistic educational materials for schoolchildren that used Foster's songs as evidence that life under enslavement was good for Black and White people.[41] With these connotations, Foster's songs figured into songbooks celebrating the Confederacy and were adopted by the Ku Klux Klan.[42]

For all the enthusiasm that greeted the Foster myth, many people simply greeted the new narratives about Foster with apathy. In 1895, Keenan schemed to sell commemorative Foster medals for $0.25 and auction off fifteen numbered medals as collectors' items at the Pittsburgh Exposition.[43] Despite weeks of heavy promotion, bids were disappointing.[44] Keenan lamented in the newspaper that "it was hoped ... a good sum might be realized from each [medal], but for some reason the friends of Foster are not taking as heartily to the project as one could wish."[45] Perhaps because of embarrassment, the paper did not publish the results of the contest until five years later, just prior to the statue's unveiling. It turned out that medals 3 through 15 went to people who had already been active in the project. A single bidder took medals 3, 4, and 5, and medals 7 through 15 went to another individual who paid $1 each.[46] As far as unnumbered medals, the *Press* was still pedaling them months after the Exposition closed.[47] At the conclusion of the fundraising campaign, the statue project reached only 60% of its goal. When Keenan formed a committee to accept proposals from sculptors, the *Pittsburgh Commercial Gazette* informed readers that, although the committee had not raised as much as they had hoped, the sculptors who submitted proposals to the committee "declare themselves ready to put up a

---

[41] McWhirter, *Battle Hymns*, 205.

[42] Michael Jacobs, "Co-Opting Christian Chorales: Songs of the Ku Klux Klan," *American Music* 28, no. 3 (Fall 2010): 370.

[43] According to Zachary L. Brodt, "Area businessmen funded the first [Pittsburgh] exposition in 1875 to promote the region as an industrial and commercial powerhouse." Brodt, *From the Steel City to the White City: Western Pennsylvania & the World's Columbian Exposition* (University of Pittsburgh Press, 2023), 17.

[44] The medals were mentioned in the newspaper nearly every day, beginning with "Foster Memorial: A Generous Donation from Heeren Bros. & Co.," *Pittsburg Press*, September 6, 1895.

[45] "Foster Memorial: Souvenir Medal No. 1 is Still Awaiting Bidders," *Pittsburg Press*, September 30, 1895.

[46] "Story of the Stephen C. Foster Memorial."

[47] The medals were still being promoted in April 1896. See "Foster Memorial," *Pittsburg Press*, April 27, 1896.

monument for the amount now in the hands of the committee that will equal many for which a much larger amount of money has been paid."[48]

Some Black Americans actively resisted the new portrayal of Foster. In 1901, the view that Foster occupied an important stage in Black music was rejected by Sylvester Russell, a writer for the Black newspaper the *Indianapolis Freeman*. Attacking an "erroneous report that Stephen C. Foster was the first writer of coon songs," Russell responded, "Mr. Foster extracted 'Old Folks at Home' and 'Kentucky Home' from hearing the slaves sing. ... Slave songs are not coon songs. Coon songs were originated by colored comedians in southern minstrelsy years ago. Ragtime music was discovered in colored piano players who played by ear or sound, a movement recently discerned."[49] Russell was, in fact, not quite correct. "Old Folks" and "My Old Kentucky Home" more strongly resemble Irish ballads by composers like Thomas Moore than actual slave songs, so Foster most likely did not literally "extract" them. But this does nothing to diminish Russell's larger point that Foster was not involved in the creation of slave songs or ragtime. Russell was not willing to let Black music be melted down in the American pot, especially if the result was the ennoblement of a White man as a creator of Black music.

In all, Morrison and Keenan had mixed success in popularizing their construction of Foster. His music began to catch on in songbooks memorializing the Civil War and evangelizing the Lost Cause, and in 1906 readers of *National Magazine* selected more of his songs than those of any other composer to be included in the songbook *Heart Songs Dear to the American People*.[50] But the Foster myth was not quickly accepted by large numbers, and it also failed to boost the political fortunes of Morrison, who lost in a landslide to his Republican opponent in 1896. Overall, in these years the national-universal myth proved its appeal to *enough* people across political, sectional, racial, and ideological divisions that it is understandable how Foster's music *began* to appear to some Americans as emblematic of American democracy. But it would still be decades before the myth was widely accepted.

---

[48] "Tribute to Foster," *Pittsburgh Commercial Gazette*, May 10, 1899.
[49] Sylvester Russell, *Indianapolis Freeman*, March 9, 1901. See also, Dorothy Berry, "The World According to Sylvester Russell: The Career and Legacy of a Black Critic Who Argued for the Elevation of Black Performance," *Lapham's Quarterly*, August 30, 2021, https://www.laphamsquarterly.org/roundtable/world-according-sylvester-russell.
[50] *Heart Songs Dear to the American People* (Chapple, 1909).

# 11
# Reminiscences of Kit Clarke (1893)

### Introduction

*It is unknown why this letter to the editor by Birket "Kit" Clarke (1835–1918; also known as Birchet Clarke) is not in the Foster Hall Collection, but it certainly did not fit into Foster Hall's narrative about the composer. Clarke refers to "Old Folks at Home" as the "most beautiful of all American melodies," but he claims it did not rival "Home Sweet Home" in popularity. To Clarke and his readers in 1893, this statement likely seemed true because Foster was just beginning to re-emerge from obscurity at that time. In fact, Clarke may have been inspired to write this account based on reports of Foster's "My Old Kentucky Home" at the Columbian Exposition in Chicago, or perhaps he heard the song performed in New York in* The South *before the War. His portrayal of "Old Folks" as failing to match "Home Sweet Home," though, would quickly begin to feel untrue. It is a far cry from Keenan's and Morrison's portrayals of Foster about two years later during publicity of the Pittsburgh statue effort. It is their narrative, not Clarke's, that Foster Hall would adopt in the 1930s.*

*Clarke's reminiscences also depart from Foster Hall's narrative by closely associating Foster with minstrelsy. Clarke opens his account with a memory of sitting with Foster and the minstrel Dan Emmett at the Collamore House (Figure 11.1) on the corner of Broadway and Spring Street on June 21, 1863, one day after West Virginia became an official state in the union, separate from Virginia, which had seceded. This anecdote rings true, for Clarke was a theater man himself, a transformative manager and press agent credited with developing "alliterative advertising." He ran publicity for the circuses of Adam Forepaugh and for the magicians Harry Kellar, Robert Heller, Gus Hartz, and Zera Semon, as well as for the Haverly Minstrels, notably their residency in London in the 1880s. (Clarke may have instilled in Houdini an appreciation for Foster's music, whom we will encounter again in Chapter 35. Houdini owned a manuscript of Foster's song "Maggie by My Side," which remains in private hands today.)*

*Formulating Foster*. Christopher Lynch, Oxford University Press. © Oxford University Press 2025.
DOI: 10.1093/9780197811726.003.0012

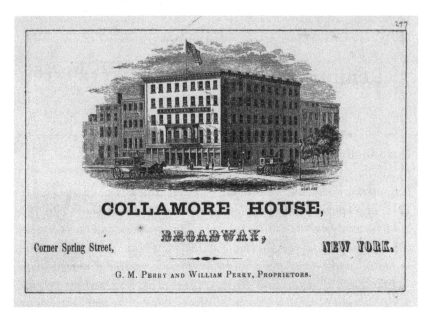

**Figure 11.1.** A lithograph of the Collamore House, New York. Miriam and Ira D. Wallach Division of Art, Prints and Photographs: Print Collection, New York Public Library.

*Clarke also claims he last saw Foster a few weeks prior to his death when the pair attended a performance at a notoriously seedy minstrel theater at 444 Broadway, sometimes referred to as the American Theater. According to historian Timothy J. Gilfoyle, Robert Butler acquired the theater in 1860 and "its immediate popularity rested upon the sale of liquor during performances" and, as Butler advertised, "the engagement of handsome and voluptuous waitresses."[1] Gilfoyle also observes that this part of Broadway comprised the heart of the growing entertainment district, where theaters, saloons, and hotels were mingled with the city's densest concentration of houses of prostitution.[2] The theater at 444 Broadway featured the leading minstrel troupes, and in the 1860s Tony Pastor was a regular prior to opening his own theater in 1866.*

*Other documents further link Foster to the theater. Three songsters—* Wood's Minstrels' Songs, Wood's New Plantation Melodies, *and* George

---

[1] Timothy J. Gilfoyle, *City of Eros: New York City, Prostitution, and the Commercialization of Sex, 1790–1920* (New York: W. W. Norton, 1992), 129.
[2] Gilfoyle, *City of Eros*, 120–21.

Christy & Wood's Melodies—*include numerous songs by Foster and indicate on their title pages that they were performed at 444 Broadway.*[3] *Foster's music was such a fixture at the theater that it formed a touchstone for other performances. The sheet music for "Young Folks at Home," a musical "answer" to "Old Folks at Home," indicates that it was "written & composed expressly for Wood's Minstrels—Minstrel's Hall 444 Broadway."*[4] *Likewise, a song sheet for "The Song of All Songs No. 2," a response to Foster's "The Song of All Songs," indicates that it was "sung by Charles E. Collins, at the American Theatre, 444 Broadway."*[5]

According to a later account by his friend Harry Houdini, Clarke lived with Foster from August to November of 1863. Clarke recalls that he last visited Foster at his room on Hester Street in December 1863. This aligns with Mahon's recollection of giving Foster money for a room at a hotel—which Morrison and Cooper claim was the American House at 15 Bowery—shortly before his death. Mahon must have helped Foster move into the American House shortly after his last encounter with Clarke, perhaps as Foster was trying to recover from what an anonymous friend (probably Cooper) recalled as a "bad burn on his thigh, caused by the overturning of a spirit lamp used to boil water" at a saloon on Hester Street.

## *Brooklyn Daily Eagle*, October 2, 1893.

About the middle of June, 1863, forty counties of the State of Virginia, represented in Convention at Wheeling, repudiated secession and applied for admission to the Union. I do not remember the exact date, but recall the event because, on the following day, Stephen Collins Foster, Daniel Decatur Emmett and myself were seated in what had been the Collamore House, corner of Broadway and Spring street, New York, talking over the subject and war matters in general. Presently we heard music and, stepping to the window, saw a brigade of boys in blue coming down Broadway, journeying to the front, led by a band playing "I wish I was in Dixie."

"Your song," said Foster.

---

[3] *Christy's and White's Ethiopian Melodies* (T. B. Peterson & Brothers, ca. 1850s); *Wood's Minstrels Songs* (Dick & Fitzgerald, ca. 1855), FHC; *Wood's New Plantation Melodies* (Dick & Fitzgerald, ca. 1862), FHC.

[4] Hattie Livingston and Franke Spencer, "Young Folks at Home" (Gould & Berry, 1852), Lester S. Levy Sheet Music Collection, Johns Hopkins Sheridan Libraries & University Museums.

[5] John F. Poole, "The Song of All Songs, No. 2" (Charles Magnus, ca. 1861–67), FHC.

"Yes," replied Emmett.

A regiment passed by, when another band came along playing "The Old Folks at Home."

"Your song," said Emmett.

"Yes," answered Foster.

And there stood I, a beardless young man, between the parents of the most popular songs this country has produced, waiting impatiently to seize my diary and fasten the incident and the words of the moment. I was a dyed-in-the-wool diary fiend at that time, and I am glad of it, for now I find that, like the immortal door plate of *Mr. Toodles*, the old diary is exceedingly handy to have in the house. My recollection of Foster is that of a man about 35 years of age, a little below medium stature, slightly built, with a long, hairless face, most youthful in appearance, brown eyes, high forehead and short brown hair, while the garments he wore had passed well into the sere and yellow leaf of usefulness. But he was a hero in my eyes then, and a far greater one now, as I recall my acquaintances with him and look over a partial list of the beautiful songs he gave the world. "O, Susanna," "Open the [sic] Lattice, Love," "Uncle Ned," "Hard Times Come Again No More," "My Old Kentucky Home," "Massa's in de Cold, Cold Ground," "Old Dog Tray," "Willie We Have Missed You," "Ellen Bayne," "Little Jenny Dow" (his wife), "Jenny's Coming O'er the Green," "Come Where My Love Lies Dreaming," and that simple, touching and most beautiful of all American melodies, "The Old Folks at Home." Foster told me that he hoped and expected "The Old Folks" would rival Payne's "Home, Sweet Home," and that he considered the latter written contrary to the laws of melody.[6] He added that it was a marvel to him how it could ever have achieved such popularity. It may have been Foster's error in localizing his song, giving prominence to the Suwanee River, that affected its success, for he was a poet as well as a composer, and wrote both the words and the music of all his songs, but that "The Old Folks at Home" is a finer, sweeter, more melodious and touching compositions admits of no doubt. Beside, it is original, which can not be claimed for "Home, Sweet Home." More than 400,000 of the "Old Folks at Home" were sold previous to 1862,

---

[6] John Howard Payne wrote the words for "Home Sweet Home," and the song was composed by Henry Rowley Bishop. Clarke's comment about Foster's negative opinion of the song echoes Birdseye's words (see Chapter 3).

one edition attributing its authorship to E. P. Christy, of Christy's minstrels, who paid Foster $350 for this ephemeral honor.[7]

It was minstrelsy which first brought Foster publicity, for when a troupe of serenaders invaded his native city, Pittsburg, he attended the performance, became inspired with "O, Susanna," submitted and had it promptly accepted and produced with immediate and pronounced success. It became the "Ta-ra-ra-Boom-de-ay" of its time, and music publishers began to outbid each other for Foster's compositions. In mentioning "O, Susanna" to me, Foster said he was in his 17th year when it was written, and as he was 38 years of age when he died at Bellevue Hospital, January 13, 1864, the result of a severe fall in a New York theater, the song must have been written in 1843.[8] Negro minstrelsy was, I believe, first produced in this year, and it may have been the inaugural organization that Foster had seen, but of this, of course, I have no knowledge.[9] A few weeks before his death Foster and myself spent an evening together at a variety theater, located, if memory serves me rightly, at 444 Broadway. I think it was called the American and was under the management of a man named Butler.[10] After the performance I went with him to his modest little room on Hester street, near the Bowery, and as he sat upon his bed he sang in a tender voice, but with great pathos, that rare song, "Hard Times Come Again No More." It was the last time I saw Stephen Foster, but I have often thought how very sad it was that the man who was forever singing of home and loved ones had no better place than this to call home and hardly a friend in the great city wherein he constantly sang of "Love, love and only love."

Eighteen years later Dan Emmett came into my employ. I was at that time directing the affairs of a large minstrel company and conceived the idea that a scene representing minstrelsy as first produced would please or at least interest the public. To present this scene I engaged the oldest performers in

---

[7] For more on these inflated sales figures, see Chapter 3, n14. It is unknown why Clarke believed that Christy paid $350 to be listed as the composer of "Old Folks." Other accounts incorrectly state that it was $500 or correctly state it was $15. See Chapter 1, n6.

[8] It is feasible that Foster composed "Oh! Susanna" in 1843, around the time he was performing amateur minstrel shows with his friends in Allegheny. But Clarke's comment that Foster fell in a theater contradicts every other account of Foster's death, which all agree that he fell in his private room.

[9] In 1843 Foster was living in Allegheny, so it is unlikely he saw Emmett's Virginia Minstrels that year because they were performing in New York. He did, however, encounter an early imitator of the Virginia Minstrels in Nelson Kneass and his Sable Harmonists.

[10] Clarke and Foster may have attended the grand variety show at the American Theatre in late December 1863. The show featured J. H. Childers doing "his great musket drill," Tony Pastor singing original comic songs, Charley White in blackface with his troupe the Knights of Ethiopia, and the "fairy drama" "The Lillies of Killarney; or, the Fairy of the Lake."

the business, and they are Archie Hughes, Dave Reed, Sam Sanford and Dan Emmett, all of whom, except Hughes, are still living. Dan Emmett was the originator and founder of what is termed negro minstrelsy in either 1841 or 1843 at the Chatham Theater, New York, at a benefit tendered to Dick Pelham. The idea of appearing upon the stage with faces blackened, giving a performance imitating the antics, the songs and the dialect of the Southern negro was conceived by Emmett, and in its first presentation then appeared William Whitlock, who died in New York in March, 1878, as banjoist; Frank Brower, who died in Philadelphia, in June, 1874, as bones; R. W. Pelham, who died at Liverpool, England, in October, 1876, as tambourine, and Emmett, who is still living, aged about 80 years, as violinist. Meeting with success, the quartet resolved to continue the business, which they did with great prosperity, under the name of "The Virginia Serenaders." It would be utterly impossible to enumerate the various minstrel troupes that have grown from this event, its evolution and expansion into the modern display of silks, satins, velvets, powdered wigs and white faces being only equaled by the great talent and invariably excellent voices found in the minstrel pageant of to-day. When Emmett joined me, I confess I saw but little change in the old man's face, although he was then about 65 years of age.

It was during this engagement that he gave me the particulars of how "Dixie" was written, the memoranda of which I find in the pages of my precious little diary. It is remarkable how many people have claimed the authorship of this song, no less than twenty-seven being on record in my scrap book, and they continue to keep bobbing up. The latest bold adventurer comes to the front in the colums [sic] of that great newspaper, the New York *Sun*, and asserts that once upon a time a man named Dixey owned land and slaves right here in New York, and that the song was written to the eternal glory of this superlatively good Dixey. Ah, indeed! But sometimes if you see it in the *Sun* it ain't so, as in this instance, for instance. "Dixie" was written by Dan Emmett in 1859, while he was a member of Bryant's minstrels, then located at Mechanics' Hall, 472 Broadway, New York. Besides receiving this information from Emmett, Dan Bryant told me the incidents connected with its composition and production, and I think Dave Reed will remember it, for about this time he was a favorite at the Bryant's, his song and dance of "Nancy Fat" being the hit of the day. Mr. Emmett told me that on a Saturday night in November, 1859, Dan Bryant came to him and said: "Joe, can't you get up a walk-around for next week?" At that time the minstrels invariably terminated their performances with a walk-around, in which the entire company appeared, and Emmett wrote nearly all of those produced by Bryant's minstrels. Emmett said he would try, and during the intervening Sunday wrote, "I wish I was in Dixie." Orchestra parts were made that evening, it was thoroughly rehearsed the following morning, produced on Monday night, made an instantaneous hit, and has been popular ever since. Emmett sent the first copy to Billy Newcombe, then a member of Buckley's Serenaders, who paid $5 and the right to use it, and this manuscript is still in existence. It was this copy that has been used by Werling, of New Orleans, in publishing the song under the title of "Dixie's Land," attributing its authorship to a Mr. Peters. Emmett told me that Peters had merely harmonized the music and, he added, "Peters did the job splendidly." A dozen other music dealers stole and published the song, each representing a different author, when Firth, Pond & Co., of New York, to whom alone Emmett had sold the right of publication, called a halt along the entire line. Shortly afterward a convention of music publishers was held at the Fifth Avenue Hotel, and the subject of "Dixie" was introduced and hotly argued. Emmett personally appeared at this meeting and so completely satisfied all that he and he alone was the author of "Dixie" that all the publishers agreed to discontinue its publication and send the plates to Firth, Pond & Co. This they did, but Emmett said he thought that every one printed all the copies they could sell in five years before returning the plates.

The idea of "I Wish I Was in Dixie" was born of Emmett's early experience in the circus business, when all south of Mason and Dixon's line was familiarly known as Dixie. In the autumn, when frost overtook the south-bound circus, the boys would think of the genial sunny South, and as Emmett said, "Many a time I've heard them say, 'I wish I was in Dixie's land now.'" "Dixie" is still an exceedingly popular melody, especially in the Southern portion of our country, and will doubtless remain so for many years. For this reason its author should not be robbed of his honors, and, therefore, I give the facts while they are susceptible of convincing proof by documentary evidence and living witnesses, the latter of whom, in the course of nature, must soon pass away.

# 12

## An Interview with Jane Foster Wiley (1895)

### Introduction

*One of the first people Keenan's newspaper interviewed while promoting the Pittsburgh statue effort was the composer's widow, Jane Foster Wiley (1829–1903). Jane's comments on Foster mostly align with how Morrison wanted his brother portrayed. Although she refers to Foster collaborating with Shiras on one song, she does not substantiate any of the fanciful claims by Shiras's descendants and others that Foster was not the composer or author of many of the songs attributed to him. Her only comment that contradicts the emerging "official" narrative of Foster is her statement that "Mr. Foster was not an accomplished musician." Perhaps out of respect to his brother's widow, Morrison chose not to refute Jane's comments, but just over a week later he did reply publicly to similar comments made by Frank Dumont (see Chapter 13, Introduction).*

*Jane was one of six daughters of Andrew McDowell, a prominent physician in Pittsburgh. The family lived in Pittsburgh on Penn Avenue, across the Allegheny River from Allegheny City, where Foster's family lived in the 1840s. Little is known of the songwriter's early relationship with Jane, but according to Morneweck, the McDowell girls were among the "familiar friends" of the Foster boys.[1] Jane and the composer married on July 22, 1850. Nine months later they welcomed their only child, Marion.*

*Like Morrison's writings on his brother, Jane offers few details of their relationship and makes no mention of their marital troubles. Although the archive seems pretty well scrubbed of documentation of marital troubles, as we have seen when Foster moved to New York and New Jersey in the early 1850s, his sister Henrietta wrote to their brother Morrison that "I last winter felt convinced that she would either have to change her course of conduct*

---

[1] Morneweck, *Chronicles*, vol. 1, 317.

or a separation was inevitable though I never wrote a word of the kind to Stevie."[2] What Henrietta meant by Jane's "course" is unclear. A letter from the composer's brother Dunning to Morrison, in which he expresses his "anxiety" over Foster's "foolish and unaccountable course,"[3] suggests that Jane may not be the only party at fault in the marriage. Whatever was the issue, Jane and Foster eventually reconciled. She joined him in New Jersey, and in 1854 they returned to Allegheny. In the 1860s the family of three moved again to New York, but eventually Jane and Marion left Foster. They resided for a time in Lewistown, Pennsylvania, with one of Jane's sisters; and they eventually moved back to western Pennsylvania, where Jane worked as a telegrapher.

Despite the lack of evidence, many scholars have speculated about the reasons for their separations. Some writers have suggested that they separated because Foster was gay.[4] Others have blamed the clash between the Fosters' conservatism and what they postulate were Jane's family's liberal politics.[5] One of Foster's biographers, John Tasker Howard, privately wrote about family gossip that may shed light on the situation:

> In talking with Mrs. Morneweck I soon learned that there was a sharp division between Foster's direct descendants, his daughter and granddaughter, and his niece and her brother William B. Foster. Apparently this rift dated back to Stephen's lifetime. According to Mrs. Morneweck, Foster's brothers and sisters had disliked his wife Jane intensely. They felt that Jane nagged Stephen constantly so that he became increasingly moody. She did not care for music and hoped that Stephen would give up song-writing after they were married. Later, when I interviewed Foster's granddaughter in Pittsburgh, I found that the feeling between the two branches of the family was mutual, particularly since most of the documents that contained facts about the Foster family were in Mrs. Morneweck's possession, and she knew far more about Stephen Foster than his direct descendants did.[6]

---

[2] Henrietta Thornton to Morrison Foster, June 21, 1853, FHC, C532.
[3] Dunning Foster to Morrison Foster, March 3, 1854, FHC, C539.
[4] This speculation has appeared in fiction, such as Peter Quinn's novel *Banished Children of Eve*, and in non-scholarly nonfiction, such as Lynn Witt, Sherry Thomas, and Eric Marcus, eds., *Out in All Directions: The Almanac of Gay and Lesbian America* (Warner Books, 1995).
[5] Root, "Mythtory," 26; O'Connell, *Life and Songs of Stephen Foster*, 124–26.
[6] Howard, unpublished autobiography, FHC, p. B 57.

*Some members of the family evidently believed that Jane caused Foster to grow depressed.*

Despite their separations, Foster and Jane appear to have loved each other. He wrote numerous romantic songs about characters named Jenny, which was what he called her. And when he passed away, she traveled with Morrison and Henry Foster to New York to retrieve his body. They may have loved each other but had such strong disagreements that they could not live together. They may have separated because of Foster's sexuality, addiction, or spending habits. Or they may have lived apart for other reasons that are perhaps more mundane or practical. Clarity on the matter is unlikely.

After Foster's death, Jane continued to work until about 1869, when she met and married Matthew D. Wiley. They lived in Allegheny until her tragic death, the harrowing details of which appeared in the Pittsburg Press on January 6, 1903:

> Mrs. Wiley had been up less than an hour yesterday and was sitting dozing before her fire. Shortly after 8 o'clock her granddaughter Mrs. Alexander D. Rose [Jessie Welsh Rose], heard Mrs. Wiley screaming and running to her room found the old woman enveloped in flames. Mrs. Rose wrapped a blanket about the burning form of her grandmother and extinguished the flames, but not before the body of the aged woman had been terribly burned. The flames set fire to the room and a silent alarm was sent to engine company No. 10, which responded and put out the blaze. Mrs. Wiley remained unconscious until her death last night.[7]

## Pittsburg Press, May 18, 1895.

In a pleasant home on Montgomery avenue, Allegheny, opposite the park, resides Mrs. Jane D. Wiley, who was the wife of Stephen C. Foster. Several years after Mr. Foster's death she was united in marriage to Mr. M. D. Wiley, and for the past 20 years or more has resided on Montgomery avenue, within a stone's throw of Mr. Foster's old home on Union avenue. Her family consists only of her husband, herself and a granddaughter, Miss Jessie Welsh, whose parents reside in Chicago. Mrs. Wiley is a daughter of Dr. A. N. McDowell,

---

[7] "The Death Record: Mrs. Jane Denny Wiley," *Pittsburg Press*, January 7, 1903.

of this city, who will be remembered by the older residents of Pittsburg as one of the most eminent physicians of the state. A representative of the *Press* called on Mrs. Wiley last evening and found her in the midst of preparations for a journey. She is contemplating a trip to Philadelphia, to visit relatives and friends.

Time has dealt very gently with Mrs. Wiley, and although she is considerably past middle age, she retains much of the brightness and vivacity of her young womanhood. She is a brilliant conversationalist, has a keen sense of humor and is delightfully entertaining. She said she felt very grateful to the *Press* for its efforts to perpetuate the memory of Mr. Foster, and to the public for the interest displayed in the undertaking, and hoped the plans for a memorial in Schenley park would be fully consummated. There had been an effort some time ago, she said, to have a monument to Mr. Foster erected in the Allegheny parks, but she considered Schenley a much more appropriate location.

Mrs. Wiley recalled with pleasure many incidents attending her associations with Mr. Foster, and referred in a feeling manner to his efforts in the field of song composition.

"Our home during Mr. Foster's residence in Allegheny," said she, "was on Union avenue, between Ohio street and what was then called Gay alley, now South Diamond street, I believe. Our nearest neighbor was Mrs. Andrew Robinson, now residing on Cedar avenue, at the corner of Liberty street, who was a great friend of Mr. Foster and greatly admired his genius. She possessed a beautiful soprano voice and to her he referred many of his compositions in manuscript. If she sang them and they met her approval he was satisfied. She also played many of his accompaniments, and his song, 'Open thy Lattice, Love,' was dedicated to her.

"Mr. Foster was a lover of nature and had a fondness for the old commons, now the Allegheny parks. He would stroll through the parks for hours, and I have no doubt caught much of his inspiration through his associations with the trees, the birds and the flowers. Few musicians have been gifted with so fine and sensitive a nature. Mr. Foster was not an accomplished musician, although he played with considerable skill on the flute and guitar. His knowledge of the intricacies of pianoforte music was very limited, and when at the piano, he attempted nothing more than simple chords and harmonies, usually plaintive and in keeping with his thoughts.

"He rebelled at anything that disturbed the tranquility of his mind," continued Mrs. Wiley, and then her countenance brightened and her lips were wreathed in smiles as she recalled how she had once provoked a discord by playing a simple piece of dance music, which reached the ears of Mr. Foster.

"It was a pleasant summer evening," said she, "and having nothing else to occupy my time, I sat down at the piano, and thoughtlessly played a few bars of dance music I had heard somewhere. Just then Mr. Foster entered. 'Oh, don't play that kind of music,' said he, with an injured air; 'people will think it is I.' I stopped right there, and was very careful afterward not to play music of that character.

"'Dimes and Dollars; the Worst of Crimes,' was once a popular song accredited to Mr. Foster, but he really only wrote the music for it. The words were written by Charles P. Shiras, of Allegheny, who was a lifelong friend of Mr. Foster.[8] Another song written and composed by Mr. Foster, but which he never published, was one entitled 'Jennie's Only Seventeen.' I remember well the first stanza:

> "Jennie's coming o'er the green,
> Jennie's only seventeen.
> Fairer form was ne'er seen;
> Jennie's only seventeen.

"I don't know why he never published it," continued Mrs. Wiley. "The melody was beautiful, and I am sure it would have become popular."[9]

Mr. Foster's only child is Mrs. Marion Foster Welsh, who resides in Chicago.[10] She is musically inclined also, and is an accomplished pianist. She has also taught both vocal and instrumental music in Chicago, and has taken a hand at composition. One of her recent compositions is entitled "Beautiful Dreamer Schottische," taken from a quartet of Mr. Foster's entitled, "Beautiful Dreamer."

---

[8] The music for this song has never been found, and the only confirmed musical collaboration between Shiras and Foster is the song "Annie, My Own Love" (1853). Shiras published the text to which Jane refers as "The Popular Credo" in his collection of poetry, *The Redemption of Labor and Other Poems* (W. H. Whitney, 1852).

[9] Jane did not realize that Foster had, in fact, published this song. John Mahon knew it and relates an interesting anecdote about Foster's wife complaining about the line "Jennie's only seventeen," which Foster removed from the published version (see Chapter 5).

[10] Marion preferred to spell her name "Welch."

# 13
# An Interview with Frank Dumont and a Pittsburgh Lady (1895)

### Introduction

*This article, not found in the Foster Hall Collection, includes reminiscences from the minstrel performer Frank Dumont and an anonymous "Pittsburg lady," who link Foster to minstrelsy, critique his musical abilities, and portray him as "moody and reserved." Born in New York, Dumont (1848–1919) began performing in minstrel shows in the early 1860s, when Foster was living in the entertainment district. Later in life, Dumont moved to Philadelphia, where in 1895 he purchased a theater where the Carncross Minstrels performed. He was a student of the history of minstrelsy, collecting articles and programs in a scrapbook and publishing* The Witmark Amateur Minstrel Guide *in 1899.*[1]

*In the following reminiscence, Dumont claims that Foster's musical knowledge was limited and that minstrel composers arranged his songs for him. The* Press *published a letter Morrison wrote in response, in which he retorted that his brother was "an ardent student of composition and harmonies" and "composed his melodies and then himself arranged the accompaniments."*[2] *Morrison would employ similar language in his biography of his brother in 1896 (Figure 13.1).*

---

[1] Frank Dumont (1848–1919) Minstrelsy Scrapbook, 1850–1902, *Historical Society of Pennsylvania*, Collection 3054. Frank Dumont, *The Witmark Amateur Minstrel Guide and Burnt Cork Encyclopedia* (M. Witmark & Sons, 1899).

[2] "Foster Memorial: Popular Melodies That Have Achieved Success," *Pittsburg Press*, May 29, 1895.

*Formulating Foster*. Christopher Lynch, Oxford University Press. © Oxford University Press 2025.
DOI: 10.1093/9780197811726.003.0014

**Figure 13.1.** Frank Dumont. MS Thr 1848, Harvard Theatre Collection, Houghton Library, Harvard University.

## *Pittsburg Press*, May 27, 1895.

The publication in the *Press* several days ago of incidents attending Stephen C. Foster's connection with negro minstrelsy attracted much attention among the members of George Thatcher & Carroll Johnson's minstrel company, which appeared in this city last week. Their manager, Frank Dumont, was especially interested in it, as he was personally acquainted with Mr. Foster for two years during the latter's residence in New York city. Mr. Dumont has won some distinction as a composer, as well as a minstrel manager. The popular song books published by the large New York and Boston music publishing houses contain many of his compositions, which have been sung by minstrel companies all over the United States and Europe. He is heartily in sympathy with the movement to erect a monument to the noted song writer.

"It is true," said Mr. Dumont, "that negro minstrelsy owes much to Stephen C. Foster. His songs helped to make that kind of public entertainment popular. I first met Mr. Foster in New York city, in 1861, when playing there with Arlington & Donniker's minstrels. He visited the theater very often and was a regular contributor to the fund of minstrel songs. He might have become wealthy had he not disposed of his songs so cheaply. I was on the stage in one of the old New York theaters when I became acquainted with Mr. Foster. He came on the stage previous to the entertainment and asked to see the manager. He said he had a new song and wanted him to hear it. He had nothing but the air and the words written on a piece of rough, brown paper. He had a good voice, not strong, but sweet and musical, and we all gathered around him as he sang that song. I do not now recollect what it was, but the manager got it for a paltry sum, which seemed to satisfy Mr. Foster, and the song was afterward sung all over the United States. In this way many of the songs written in the closing years of his life came to public notice.

"Mr. Foster's knowledge of musical composition was very limited, and much of his music was arranged for him by others, he furnishing the melody. Nelson Kneass, once a musician here in Pittsburg, and for several years afterward with E. P. Christy did much to bring Foster's songs before the public, and it is a matter of regret that he took the credit of having composed some of them.[3] Like many other men who have furnished the world something

---

[3] Few of Foster's musical manuscripts survive, making it difficult to assess Dumont's claim that other people wrote the accompaniments to his songs. On the one hand, all but one of the surviving manuscripts in the composer's handwriting almost exactly match the published accompaniment (see Chapter 10, n5), and Foster's friend Mahon testifies that Foster made his own arrangements

worth having, Mr. Foster had to die to become famous. His efforts were not appreciated while he lived, but for many years after he died his songs were all the rage in every large city in Europe and America. Some of his melodies are yet popular and the songs of the present day are thrown in the shade by comparison."

Mr. Dumont made reference to the various minstrel companies that sprang up like mushrooms when Foster's songs came into prominence on the concert stage. Among the companies then on the road were Campbell's, Bryant's, DuPrez & Green, Charles White's Serenaders, Sam Sharpley's, Lloyds', Dumbolton's Serenaders, La Rue's, Skiff & Gaylord's, Ordways' Aeolians, Arlington & Donniker's, Fred Wilson's, Johnny Booker, Carncross & Dixey, E. P. Christy's, Birch & Cotton's, Peel & West's, the Buckley Serenaders, Morris Bros., Pell & Trowbridge, S. S. Sanford, Virginia Serenaders, Eph. Horn's, Rainer Christy's and Rumsey & Newcomb's. Foster's songs were sung by them everywhere, and in those days people went to hear the new melodies, not to witness the antics of the performers.

"J. L. Carncross, proprietor of the Carncross Opera house, in Philadelphia, has done a great deal of late years to revive Stephen C. Foster's songs," continued Mr. Dumont. "Every year he announces and advertises a special night on which nothing but Foster melodies will be sung. The present day stage garb of the minstrel men is discarded for the time being and they array themselves in the checkered shirts and striped trousers in vogue in Foster's time. The more modern scenery gives way to the plantation scenes and Foster's songs are sung with a spirit of enthusiasm that is almost enough to bring the great composer back from the grave. On these occasions the old citizens turn out and the theater is crowded with a class of people that cannot be found within its walls any other night of the year. They go simply to hear the good, old songs that mellowed their hearts in other years, and that when sung now carry them back to the happy days of childhood. I believe if a Foster song night was announced here in Pittsburg you wouldn't be able to find a theater or auditorium large enough to hold all the people who would turn out to hear it."

Some time ago Mr. Dumont arranged a medley of Foster songs, called "Songs of Other Days," in which was incorporated half a dozen of Mr. Foster's most popular melodies. It was sung in this city last year by Dockstader's

---

(see Chapter 5). On the other hand, minstrel bands did not include piano, so it remains plausible that Foster sold some of his melodies and lyrics *without* piano accompaniments directly to minstrel performers in the manner Dumont describes.

minstrels, and was sung every night successively for five weeks, at Carncross' Opera house, Philadelphia, two years ago. Mr. Dumont has in his possession relics of early minstrelsy in the shape of two programs of E. P. Christy's minstrels, in which "O Boys, Carry Me 'Long," "Tilda Horn," "Ellen Bayne," "Few Days I'm Gwine Home" and "Wait for the Wagon," by Foster, are mentioned. These songs were usually sung by Mr. Christy himself.[4]

A substantial addition to the fund for the Stephen C. Foster monument was made this morning by a well-known Pittsburg lady, who writes the *Press* as follows:

> "When I was a child I remember having met Stephen C. Foster at a country hotel where my parents took me to spend the summer. He was always moody and reserved, and with other children, I have been attracted to the door of his room by the melancholy strains of his flute. The impression of his sadness remains after all these years."

---

[4] The only songs in this list that Foster actually composed are "O Boys, Carry Me 'Long" and "Ellen Bayne."

# 14
## Two Interviews with Susan Pentland Robinson (1895)

### Introduction

*When Foster withdrew from Jefferson College after only one week in 1841, he moved with his parents into a house in Allegheny owned by his brother William Jr. There he befriended his neighbors' daughter, Susan Pentland, dedicating his first published song, "Open Thy Lattice Love," to her in 1844. Across Allegheny Commons park lived their good friend Andrew Robinson, whom Susan married in 1849. The Robinsons remained close with the composer. In 1851, he dedicated his "Willie My Brave" to her, and in the 1860s they visited him in New York.*

*The* Pittsburg Press *published two articles with Susan's reminiscences. In both, she tells of a trip she and her husband took with a group of friends, including Foster and Jane, to Mardi Gras in New Orleans in 1851. Her anecdotes were surely intended to show Foster in a humorous light, but they reveal attitudes about gender binarism and female Irish servants considered offensive today. The group of friends understood their high social standing and were not always respectful to those who were different or less fortunate.*

*As far as we know, the trip was the only time Foster traveled to the South as an adult and probably his only trip to the Deep South. The singular occasion made an impression on those who participated, as it was fondly remembered not only by Susan but also by Morrison (see Chapter 24) and Richard Cowan. In a private letter to Morrison written in 1853, Cowan recollected that "Old Folks at Home" and "Wilt Thou Be Gone Love" were "favorites of our party last winter on our trip to New Orleans, and I was vividly reminded of our delightful journey & when we reached the warm latitudes we used to sit on deck to enjoy the moonlight and the sight of the negroes burning the brush and cotton stalks at the plantations."*[1]

---

[1] Richard Cowan to Morrison Foster, February 8, 1853, FHC, D115.

A notice of Susan's death in 1916 claimed that she performed in a quartet with the composer. The notice reads, "When the original Stephen C. Foster Quartet was organized, Miss Pentland was honored with the soprano part. The tenor was 'Billy' Hamilton, at one time superintendent of city parks; the basso was James McBrier, later a successful lumber dealer, and Miss Jane McDowell, who became Mrs. Stephen C. Foster, was the contralto."[2]

## *Pittsburg Press*, June 1, 1895.

The project to erect in Schenley park a memorial to the lamented song writer, Stephen C. Foster, has attracted the attention and interest of many people, but there are perhaps none more heartily in sympathy with the movement than Mrs. Andrew L. Robinson, of Cedar avenue, Allegheny. Mr. Foster never had a better friend than Mrs. Robinson, and there is no doubt that if he were living to-day he would freely admit that much of the success of his more popular songs was due to her kindly interest and encouragement. As children they were almost inseparable, and many of his early songs were dedicated to her.

The writer met Mrs. Robinson last evening at her beautiful home on Cedar avenue, Allegheny, and spent a delightful hour in conversation with her. She still retains much of the brightness and vivacity of her young womanhood, is a brilliant talker, and related many entertaining reminiscences of her acquaintance with Stephen C. Foster.

The older residents of the city will remember Mrs. Robinson as the sweet ballad singer whose frequent appearance in concerts was always a delight to the public. She was, perhaps, better known as a vocalist by her maiden name, Miss Susan E. Pentland. She possessed a beautiful voice, sweet, pure, and full of pathos, and exactly suited for the effective rendition of the plaintive ballads, such as those composed by Stephen C. Foster. Mrs. Robinson became acquainted with Mr. Foster when his parents moved from Lawrenceville to Union avenue, Allegheny. The Foster homestead adjoined that of Mrs. Robinson's parents, and it was only a step from one veranda to the other. Thus the young people were thrown almost constantly into each other's society. Mr. Foster appreciated Susan Pentland's abilities as a

---

[2] "Woman, the Girlhood Muse of Foster, Dies," *Pittsburgh Gazette Times*, February 1, 1916.

performer on the pianoforte and as a vocalist, and invariably sought her aid when perplexed about any technicalities of composition. He had no piano in his own home then, and through the kindness of his friend he was privileged to use her piano whenever he desired. He would take possession of her piano sometimes for hours, and many of the beautiful harmonies of his earlier melodies that have since delighted the whole world were worked out upon that piano. If a composition upon which he had worked for some time did not suit his taste, and he was unable to make the changes necessary to produce the desired harmony, he would immediately call Mrs. Robinson to his aid, and together they would go over the composition, make alterations here and there, until both were thoroughly satisfied with it. New copies were then made, and in due time the manuscript was sent to the publishers.

Mr. Foster's first published song, "Open Thy Lattice, Love," was dedicated to the friend of his youth, Miss Susan Pentland, and to her also many of his later songs were dedicated, among them "Willie, My Brave," "Little Ella," "Maggie by My Side," and "O, Susannah!"[3] She had many of the others, but they have been lost or destroyed. Among other Foster relics she has a flute which he left on her piano when he last visited her home.

Mrs. Robinson relates an amusing incident in connection with Mr. Foster's study of the French language.

"Stephen Foster was remarkably bright," said she, "and whatever he set out to do you may be sure he would accomplish. He was a firm friend of George Shiras,[4] who was a half-brother of the father of the present judge of the supreme court. Both were of a poetical turn of mind, their tastes and inclinations were in the same direction, and they had much in common with each other. Back in the forties there was a Frenchman in Pittsburg who occasionally gave instruction in French to those who desired his services. George proposed to Stephen one day that they take a few lessons. Stephen was delighted with the idea, and together they daily visited the room of the Frenchman. In two weeks' time by close application they had actually mastered the language so well that both could speak and write in French, and communicated with each other almost constantly in that language.[5]

---

[3] Of these songs, only the published versions of "Open Thy Lattice Love" and "Willie My Brave" bear dedications to Susan.

[4] George Shiras was the judge. Susan meant to refer to Foster's friend Charles Shiras.

[5] Susan exaggerated either the speed with which Foster learned French or the extent of his fluency. But Nevin and Morrison confirm that Foster studied the language, and he demonstrated some proficiency when he wrote English words for the French aria "Ah mon fils" by Giacomo Meyerbeer, which was published as "Ah! My Child!"

"Some time after Stephen's marriage to Miss Jane McDowell, of Lawrenceville, a party of us arranged to make a trip to New Orleans by boat and visit the Mardi Gras festival. We invited Stephen and his wife to go along. Stephen was a jovial young man, whose society was largely enjoyed by the young ladies, and it must be admitted he would flirt occasionally. On the boat with us was a charming girl from Pittsburg. Stephen was attracted by her beauty, and occasionally when his wife was not looking would cast admiring glances in her direction. She was somewhat of a linguist, and at the dinner table one day Stephen began conversing with her in French, not thinking there might be others at the table who could understand him. It so happened that Mrs. Foster had been quietly studying French for some time so as to be able to converse with Stephen in that tongue. He did not know this, and was dumbfounded at having his conversation at the table with his pretty vis-à-vis cut short by a severe reprimand from his wife. She had understood every word, and was so highly indignant that Stephen immediately ceased his attentions to the Pittsburg lady and never attempted to flirt again."

### *Pittsburg Press,* June 5, 1895.

Mrs. Andrew L. Robinson, of Allegheny, related an incident in the life of Stephen C. Foster that might have cut short his career and deprived the world of the best display of his genius as a song writer, had it not been for the presence of mind and promptness of a servant.

It was during the time Stephen's brother, Dunning, had charge of several river packets plying between Cincinnati and New Orleans. A party of Pittsburg and Allegheny ladies and gentlemen was formed to visit New Orleans and attend the Mardi Gras festival, and arrangements were made through Dunning Foster for transportation on one of the river packets from Pittsburg through to New Orleans. Among the prominent members of the party were Mr. and Mrs. Robinson and children and Stephen C. Foster and wife. It so happened that Mrs. Robinson's nurse was unable to go, and at the last moment she was compelled to engage the services of another nurse. A stout, masculine looking Irish-woman volunteered to fill the position and was engaged.

Stephen Foster was in the best of spirits during the long river journey and afforded much amusement for the party. He was one of the first to catch a glimpse of the coarse-visaged Irishwoman, serving in the capacity of nurse for Mrs. Robinson's children, and immediately declared he believed the nurse was a man in disguise. He stuck to this declaration so firmly that many of the party began speculating as to whether the nurse was a man or woman. Someone finally mustered up enough courage to ask her to what sex she belonged. She indignantly denied the accusation that she was a man in disguise.

All doubts were dispelled, however, by an incident that occurred shortly before the party reached New Orleans. Mr. Foster was an inveterate smoker, and also addicted to the habit of chewing tobacco. One day a member of the party found him in his stateroom in a semi-unconscious condition, presumably from the effects of excessive use of tobacco. He gave every appearance of having been poisoned, and his mouth and throat were so badly swollen he could not speak. The swelling increased so rapidly he was scarcely able to breath and in imminent danger of death by strangulation.

It was a critical moment, and all the members of the party gathered in the vicinity of Mr. Foster's stateroom, so badly excited that they could not suggest anything that would afford him relief. The big Irish woman was in another part of the boat at the time, looking after the children. She heard of the mishap that had befallen Mr. Foster and ran to his stateroom to see if she could not do something to relieve him. It was then that she displayed her womanly instincts and convinced everybody on board, even Mr. Foster himself, that no man would have had the presence of mind to have done what she did.

At a glance the nurse divined the cause of Mr. Foster's suffering, and like a flash sped down the stairway to the cooking apartment. On the stove she found a kettle of steaming potatoes. She astonished the cook by emptying these edibles into a towel, and then catching up the bundle she rushed back to Mr. Foster's stateroom. Everybody stepped aside as she entered, and she was given complete charge of the case. She held the steaming potatoes close to Mr. Foster's mouth and throat; the swelling quickly subsided, and in the course of a half hour Mr. Foster had so far recovered that he was able to walk about the boat. The nurse was a jewel in his eyes after that incident, and he treated her with the greatest deference. She had saved his life.

# 15

# An Interview with John H. Cassidy (1895)

### Introduction

*John H. Cassidy was born in Ireland in 1834 and moved to the United States in 1849. Pittsburgh directories of the 1880s and 1890s indicate he was a music teacher, and he advertised violin, guitar, and piano lessons in local newspapers. He offered the* Pittsburg Press *the following anecdote about Foster arranging "Come Where My Love Lies Dreaming" for a male quintet performance directed by William A. Lawton for a concert in Pittsburgh in 1854. Perhaps Foster Hall declined to preserve this article because Cassidy's claims cannot be verified. Regardless of the reason for the absence of the article, Cassidy's claims are plausible. Foster and Lawton certainly knew each other. In August of 1856, Lawton joined the Buchanan Glee Club and sang under Foster's musical direction at campaign events for Democrats that fall. And even though a male quintet arrangement by Foster of "Come Where My Love Lies Dreaming" does not survive, Foster was no stranger to these types of arrangements. He made a male quartet arrangement of "I Would Not Die in Springtime," which survives in manuscript (Figure 15.1).*

*Cassidy claims Foster made the arrangement for the quintet's performance in a concert with Nelson Kneass prior to the song's publication in 1855. Kneass performed with Sanford's minstrel troupes in Pittsburgh in the early 1850s,*[1] *so this may very well have happened in one of those performances. It is also possible that Cassidy misremembered the sequence of events and that the performance occurred after the piece's publication in one of Kneass's concerts in Pittsburgh's Masonic Hall in September of 1855, but none of the newspapers reported the involvement of Cassidy's group or the performance of the song in those concerts. It is also possible that the performance occurred at an event advertised in the* Pittsburgh Daily Post *on*

---

[1] On October 14, 1850, the *Pittsburgh Post* reviewed the performance of the New Orleans Opera Troupe, commenting that "the delightful alto singing of Collins, with Swaine, Kneass, and the comical tambourine player, Sanford, is most wonderful."

**Figure 15.1.** "I Would Not Die in Springtime," arranged for male quartet, manuscript. Foster Hall Collection, Center for American Music, University of Pittsburgh Library System.

> *May 28, 1857, as a "charity concert in Allegheny" at Excelsior Hall "under the direction of Mr. W. A. Lawton, the accomplished tenor." Kneass did not participate in that concert, but among other pieces the concert featured "Stephen C. Foster's much admired quartette, 'Come where my Love lies Dreaming.'"*

## *Pittsburg Press,* June 13, 1895.

J. H. Cassidy, a well-known music teacher, for many years in the theatrical business, in conversation with the writer last night, said: "The project is a laudable one and I have no doubt it will be successfully consummated. No American is more worthy of such an expression of esteem from the American people than Stephen C. Foster. I first heard Foster's music back in the fifties. I was quite a boy then, very fond of singing, and was frequently called upon to join in quartets and choral organizations for concerts here and there. Like all young men, we were fond of serenading, and sang many of Foster's songs on such occasions.

"I think the first time I heard Foster's justly celebrated quartet, 'Come Where My Love Lies Dreaming,' was in 1854. That was before it was published and was still in manuscript form. About that time Nelson Kneass was teaching music in this city, and myself and others were asked to participate in a concert given by him in the old Masonic hall, on Fifth avenue. I was then a member of a quintet composed of W. A. Lawton, first tenor; William Silver, alto; myself, second tenor; Samuel Severance, first bass, and John Snodgrass, second bass. Silver sang a falsetto, which was one of the popular features of quintets in those days. We were asked to sing Foster's great quartet, 'Come Where My Love Lies Dreaming,' at Kneass' concert, and had it arranged to suit the quintet. The arrangement was made by Foster himself, as he was then a resident of Allegheny, and he attended the concert and expressed himself as highly pleased at our rendition of the song. He had it published shortly afterward."

# 16

# An Interview with J. William Pope (1895)

---

### Introduction

*Musician and poet J. William Pope (1826–1916) was born in Pittsburgh in the same year as Foster. Widely published in his day, his best-known poem was "Maticia." As a singer, he was on the payroll of every winning presidential campaign from Buchanan to McKinley, rallying crowds with his vocals.*

*In this interview, Pope recalled performing Foster's "Nelly Was a Lady" from manuscript in a minstrel performance in 1849. His story is supported by documentation from Foster's early songwriting career. While he was living in Cincinnati in 1848 and 1849, Foster gave manuscripts of "Lou'siana Belle," "Uncle Ned," and "Oh! Susanna" to minstrels, leading to pirated versions appearing in print. For example, in 1849 the melody of "Uncle Ned" appeared in a medley of tunes celebrating the Whig Zachary Taylor's presidential inauguration called "Old Zack's Inauguration Grand March." Foster, whose family fiercely opposed Taylor,[1] had nothing to do with its publication; and the name erroneously listed on the sheet music as composer was J. C. Beckel.*

*Foster caused similar problems by distributing "Nelly Was a Lady" before it was copyrighted and printed. He mailed a manuscript of the song to Gilead A. Smith in New York and asked him to give it to the minstrel Charles White to perform, but White went on to publish the song with Firth, Pond & Co. under his own name. Foster contacted the publishers to set the matter straight, and the song was reissued and copyrighted again under the correct name. The publishers wrote to Foster to instruct him on how to better protect his and their interests:*

---

[1] Anti-Whig sentiments are expressed in numerous family letters. See William B. Foster Sr. to William B. Foster Jr., May 18, 1834, FHC, C626; Dunning Foster to William B. Foster Jr., October 23, 1841, FHC, C600. Ardent Democrats, William Sr. and Henry Foster were appointed to positions in Washington DC under President John Tyler, a states'-rights Democrat-turned-Whig from Virginia. Although William Sr. worked in the nation's capital only briefly, Henry remained until 1849, when he was fired for partisan reasons after the Whig Zachary Taylor took office. Pittsburgh's Democratic *Morning Post* fumed about the situation on August 13, 1849.

*From your acquaintance with the proprietors or managers of the different bands of "minstrels," & from your known reputation, you can undoubtedly arrange with them to sing them & thus introduce them to the public in that way, but in order to secure the copyright exclusively for our house, it is safe to hand such persons printed copies only, of the piece, for if manuscript copies are issued particularly by the author, the market will be flooded with spurious issues in a short time.*[2]

*Foster quickly wised up. But before Firth, Pond & Co. set him straight, he was in the habit of distributing manuscripts—including the very song Pope claims he performed from manuscript—to minstrels in 1848 and 1849.*

## *Pittsburg Press,* June 23, 1895.

Among the many older citizens of Pittsburg who have been watching with interest the progress of the movement to erect in Schenley park a memorial to the song writer, Stephen C. Foster, is J. William Pope, a musician of some prominence, who was a warm friend of Foster. The publication in [this] column one day last week of Foster's song, "Nelly Was a Lady," brought to Mr. Pope recollections of the first presentation of that song, in which he figured conspicuously.

"In 1849," said Mr. Pope, "I was proprietor and manager of a minstrel company of the old school. We were playing at the historic old Lafayette hall, when one day Stephen Foster brought me the original manuscript for 'Nellie Was a Lady'; also the score. My company gave the song its first rendition in public, at Lafayette hall, and we sang it every night there for three weeks. It was a success from the start, and the people fairly went wild over it.

"I knew Foster well and we were great friends. He showed me the manuscript of many of his melodies before they were sent to the publishers. Foster's ear was correct as to the melody, but he sometimes made amusing mistakes in trying to produce the harmonies. On one occasion I heard him singing a song in one key and playing it on the piano in another. I presume his mind was so wrapped up in the melody he was singing that he paid no attention to the accompaniment. He was certainly a genius for producing melodies.

---

[2] Firth and Pond to Stephen Foster, September 12, 1849, FHC, C916.

His songs have reached the hearts of the masses everywhere and they will endure. I am sure the memorial movement will be successful, and hope some day to see a fine monument of Foster in our favorite park."

Mr. Pope is about 76 years of age and is well-known among the old residents of the city. He retired several years ago from active service in the field of music.

# 17

# An Interview with a "Prosperous Merchant" (1895)

### Introduction

*The* Pittsburg Press *frequently interviewed unnamed associates of Foster. It is clear that when writing his Foster biography in the 1930s, John Tasker Howard had access to the following interview because he quotes it. Foster Hall, though, chose not to preserve the article in the collection, perhaps because it is an anonymous account.*[1]

### *Pittsburg Press*, June 27, 1895.

The movement to erect a memorial in Schenley park to Stephen C. Foster, the writer of melodies, is receiving the hearty sanction of all who have heard and sung his songs, and particularly interest [sic] are the older residents of the city, many of whom knew Foster personally. Among Foster's most intimate friends was a young man, now a prosperous merchant, who came to Pittsburg about the time "Uncle Ned" was published.

"Stephen C. Foster was one of the kindest hearted men I ever knew," said the merchant last night when the subject of the Foster memorial was brought up. "I never saw him angry and I don't believe he had an enemy in the world. He was so good and kind and mild-mannered that he made friends everywhere, and everybody who knew him liked him. He was one of my best friends and we had some very good times together. I greatly admired his genius and it seemed peculiarly appropriate to me that one so gentle and refined should be engaged in furnishing the world with melodies of the heart. He was certainly fitted for that kind of work.

---

[1] Howard, *Stephen Foster*, 255.

"I came to Pittsburgh in 1847, about the time Foster's famous song, 'Uncle Ned,' was published. I made his acquaintance shortly afterward and for years we were boon companions. He showed me the original manuscripts of many of his now popular songs, and often asked me to write some verses for him. I did so under protest on two or three occasions, and he declared I had much talent in that direction if I would only apply myself to it, but I did not agree with him and the result was that my efforts in that direction were confined to less than half a dozen poems, some of which were woven into songs.

"Foster's mind seemed to be full of melodies and I never saw him sit down to a piano that he did not play or sing something he had never heard before. He was continually evolving new songs and new melodies, some of them strange, yet peculiarly sweet and pathetic. Often when we were out spending an evening with friends he would suddenly dart to the piano, unmindful of all about him, and seemingly unconscious of his surroundings, and pick out on the keyboard the notes of some new melody that seemed to be passing through his brain. He would play it over until he had somewhat familiarized himself with the air, then jot the notes down on paper, later on to reproduce it and make up an accompaniment. His friends and acquaintances were never offended at this conduct on his part, as they never went out with him that they did not expect by the close of the evening to hear some new song from his lips. He was a maker of melodies and we all recognized his talents in that direction.

"During the first few months of my residence in Pittsburg I boarded at the Iron City hotel, long since removed, which stood on the south side of Fifth avenue, midway between Wood and Market streets. Foster often went there to see me in the evening, and we would go out together. One night we planned to serenade some young people at the residence of Judge Irwin, on Stockton avenue, Allegheny. About a dozen young men, Foster among the number, met me at the hotel, and we went to the Irwin residence. We sang several popular songs in concert, and Foster rendered two or three of his favorite ballads, 'Old Dog Tray' among the number. Presently we heard a disturbance in the second floor of the house, and noticed a form at one of the windows. A moment later a jar was cautiously lowered to the ground by means of a string. We caught it, examined the contents and found it was filled with pickles. That ended our serenade. We returned to the hotel to discuss the incident. What did the judge's family mean by giving us a bottle of pickles? Did they wish to insult us? We could not understand it. We learned later, however, that the members of the family scoured the kitchen and pantry to find something good to give us, but there wasn't a solitary thing in the house they considered fit for us. Finally they found a jar of pickles and gave that to us in the manner I have described. It appears the judge had a reputation for making the best pickles in this part of the state, and, as we discovered afterward, he could not have paid us a higher compliment. We had preserved the pickles and afterward ate them with a relish."

# 18

# An Interview with Jehu Haworth (1895)

### Introduction

*Jehu Haworth (1804–99) was born in England and settled in Allegheny in 1830, around the same time that the Foster family moved there from Lawrenceville. A consummate businessman, he began making boots and shoes and proceeded to work in the businesses of plumbing, drugs, groceries, and coal. Eventually the Haworths were counted among the region's most prominent families.*

*The following interview with Haworth is not in the Foster Hall Collection, perhaps because curators doubted its veracity. Because he is known to have been in the shoe business in Allegheny during Foster's childhood, his recollections of making shoes for the Foster family and listening to Foster perform in his store ring true. As Haworth admits, however, his memory was "not exactly clear," and his account of Foster performing in a minstrel troupe veers away from plausibility. Haworth could very well have been aware of Foster's amateur troupe that performed his songs in Allegheny, and he may have heard professional groups with international reputations perform Foster's songs. But his claim that he encountered Foster performing in London cannot be true. Foster was not a professional performer and never left the United States.*

### Pittsburg Press, June 28, 1895.

Another contributor yesterday was Jehu Haworth, senior member of the well-known Liberty street mercantile firm of Haworth & Dewhurst. Mr. Haworth is in his 92d year, and remarkably active for one so near the century mark. He called at the *Press* editorial rooms yesterday and gave his personal check for $25 to be applied to the fund. He said he believed the memorial movement would be a grand success and hoped that every Pittsburger would subscribe to the fund.

"Stephen C. Foster was quite a boy when I first met him," said Mr. Haworth. "I liked him from the start, and he often entertained me singing his melodies to a guitar accompaniment. I started in business in Allegheny as a shoe manufacturer, and made shoes for every member of the Foster family. Stephen was a frequent visitor to my shop on Federal street, and it was there I heard many of his melodies before they were sent to the publishers. He played the guitar very well, and I used to invite him to come to the shop in the evenings and sing for me. He was a good boy, always kind and considerate toward all who knew him, and one couldn't help but like him.

"Some time after Stephen took to song writing as a vocation and had composed several songs, which afterward became immensely popular, a minstrel company was formed with Foster as leader, for the purpose of singing his songs in the different cities of the United States. My memory is not exactly clear on this point, but I think Foster traveled with them as manager for a while. They visited several American cities, and finally went to Europe. I visited Europe about that time, and while in London saw advertisements of an American minstrel performance in one of the theaters there. I attended and found many of the performers to be from Pittsburg. One of the company (it occurs to me it was Foster himself) saw me in the audience, and sent a man down to call me to the stage. I went up at the close of the performance and met all the members of the company. They sang nothing but Foster's melodies, and helped to spread their popularity through Europe."

# 19

# An Interview with Marion Foster Welch (1895)

## Introduction

*Foster and Jane's only child, Marion Foster Welch (1851–1935), offered these reminiscences as interest in her father gained momentum during the statue project in Pittsburgh. She married Walter Welsh (1846–1924) in 1874, and she preferred to spell their surname Welch. She and Walter had three children. After the birth of their second child, Marion and Walter moved to Chicago. Their first child, Jessie, however, remained in Pennsylvania, where she was raised by Marion's mother, Jane.*

*In 1914 Marion moved into a house in Pittsburgh located at 3600 Penn Avenue, the site of the White Cottage where Foster had been born in 1826. With her daughter Jessie, Marion served as caretaker of the house, which was owned by the city and open to the public as a museum from 1916 to 1948.*

### *Pittsburg Press*, July 2, 1895.

A Chicago daily journal has taken cognizance of the efforts of the *Press* to arouse interest in a movement to erect a monument to the song writer, Stephen C. Foster, and in its last Sunday edition gave an illustrated sketch of his life, also an interview with the composer's only daughter, Mrs. Marion Foster Welsh, who has been a resident of Chicago for many years. Mrs. Welsh was still a child when her father died, but she has a distant recollection of the latter years of her father's life, particularly of his residence in New York city. The interview with her will be found interesting:

"I was his pet," said Mrs. Welsh, in recounting his recollections. "He took me everywhere with him, and I was the only one who was allowed to invade the sanctity of his 'den,' where he wrote his songs. These hours of song-composing were trying ones to my patients [*sic*], and I fear I frequently made them doubly trying to my father. I could not quite understand how he could suddenly change from my gay, almost childlike companion of the street to the thoughtful, preoccupied, almost stern, man of his study. There he could not bear the slightest noise or interference with his work. He would become so completely absorbed in thought that I think he lost sight of my identity as well as my presence. I would occasionally break in on his preoccupation with the rattle of a toy or some exclamation which would arouse his ire in an instant. I think on such occasions he entirely lost sight of my being his daughter, merely regarding me as the author of noise, the same as he would regard a mouse or a slamming shutter under the same circumstances, something to be gotten rid of at once at all hazards. I soon learned to respect the absorption of his 'composing moods,' and never to interrupt him while they were on.

"We went out a great deal in those days to parties, theaters, etc. At the theaters his love of good music and the execration of [*sic*] had often made it very inconvenient for the rest of us. It was no uncommon thing for him to jump up all of a sudden and bolt right out of the theater if some of the work of the orchestra did not suit him. But altogether our life was very pleasant then and my father's death in 1864 was a severe blow to us all."

Mrs. Welsh inherits much of her father's talent for music. She has three children, Jessie, aged 19, Matthew, 17, and Mabel, 5. All of them have decided musical talent, little Mabel giving especial promise of inheriting her grandfather's great musical talents. Mrs. Welch, though not a composer, writes music readily, and can transfer to paper any melody which catches her fancy almost without effort.

# 20
# Two Interviews with William Hamilton (1895)

**Introduction**

*William "Billy" Hamilton met Foster in the 1850s while working as a steamboat clerk. Billy was one of the first to sign up when Foster cofounded the Buchanan Glee Club in 1856. With the group they sang together at private and public Democratic campaign events in western Pennsylvania, supporting Foster's sister's brother-in-law James Buchanan, who was victorious over the anti-slavery Republican John Fremont in the US presidential race. Foster served as musical director for the Glee Club, and Hamilton assisted him in the selection of instrumental performers (Figure 20.1).*

*In the first of these articles, Hamilton described the partisanship of 1856 as "not altogether as amicable as it might have been." Violence exploded across the country in 1856. With a looming vote in Kansas on whether the territory should be admitted to the union as a free or slave state, free soilers settled in the territory to vote for freedom as pro-slavery border ruffians from neighboring slave states, particularly Missouri, attacked them. As news of the conflicts spread, politically motivated violence arose across the country, including, as Hamilton reveals, in Pittsburgh. On the floor of the US Senate, South Carolina congressman Preston Brooks brutally beat Senator Charles Sumner with a cane after Sumner delivered a speech opposing slavery in Kansas.*

*Hamilton recited the lyrics of an 1856 campaign song he identified as "The White House Chair." Music and lyrics for an 1856 campaign song called "The White House Chair" survive in Foster's handwriting, but they bear no resemblance to the lyrics Hamilton recited. Hamilton appears to have confused the title of the song with another campaign*

# TWO INTERVIEWS WITH WILLIAM HAMILTON (1895) 193

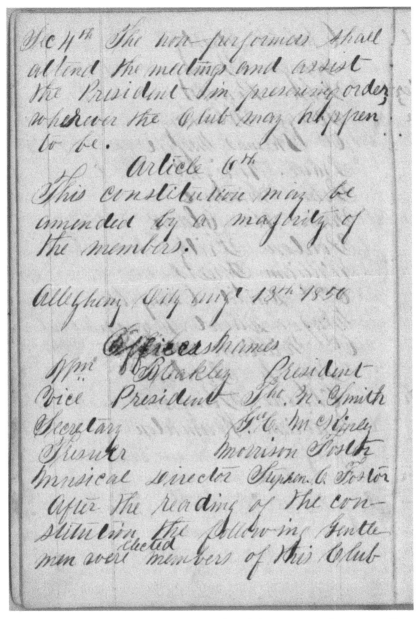

**Figure 20.1.** A page from the Buchanan Glee Club Minute Book. Foster Hall Collection, Center for American Music, University of Pittsburgh Library System.

song. The lyrics Hamilton recited perfectly fit the melody of the 1864 song "Little Mac! Little Mac! You're the Very Man," the sheet music of which indicates it was composed by Stephen C. Foster. Because the lyrics of "Little Mac!" support George McClellan, the Democrat who ran against Lincoln in 1864 (see Appendix C), and Foster died several months before his nomination, Foster could not have written all the words. But the strong poetic resemblance between the lyrics Hamilton recollected from 1856 and the lyrics of "Little Mac" demonstrates that Foster indeed wrote an original version of the song in 1856 and that someone—perhaps Foster's daughter, Marion, who entered the song for copyright in 1864—updated the lyrics for the later election. There is no reason to doubt Marion's indication on the sheet music that her father composed the melody. Perhaps unbeknownst to Marion, Foster returned to the melody while living away from the family in 1862, revising the tune and publishing it as "Sound the Rally," a song that supports Lincoln's aims in the Civil War. But given Marion's indication on the sheet music that her father composed the melody—and given the ease with which the lyrics recited by Hamilton fit the melody of "Little Mac!"—it is most likely that the melody of "Little Mac" was first composed in 1856 for the words Hamilton recited. The 1990 critical edition of Foster's complete works relegates "Little Mac" to a section of "Doubtful Works" because of the reference to the 1864 candidates and because the song's viciously racist lyrics did not fit the then-predominant narrative about Foster's sympathy for the plight of the enslaved. However, thanks to the rediscovery of this interview with Hamilton, the melody can now be added to the list of Foster's authenticated compositions.

In the second article, Hamilton recalled an 1858 trip that Foster, Jane, Marion, and Foster's niece Mary Wick took on Hamilton's steamboat, the Ida May, to Cincinnati. This trip is corroborated in Foster's surviving correspondence. Before departing, he wrote to Morrison that "we will stir [sic] old John McClelland up in Cincinnati, make the children sing and bring in Billy's bass voice," adding that "the trip will be a recreation and variety for me."[1]

---

[1] Stephen Foster to Morrison Foster, November 11, 1858, FHC, A338.

## *Pittsburg Press,* July 11, 1895.

Supt. William Hamilton, of the Allegheny parks, is watching with much interest the progress of the movement to erect in Schenley park a memorial to the songwriter, Stephen C. Foster. He was a warm friend of Foster, and associated with him for many years. He has many interesting reminiscences of the days of Foster's residence in Allegheny and remembers many of the campaign songs as sung by the glee club, of which both Foster and himself were prominent members. In an interview yesterday, Mr. Hamilton said:

"We had some very happy times way back in the '50s, when Foster's father was mayor of Allegheny.[2] I first met Steve, as we called him, in 1855. He was such a genial young man, so kind-hearted and genteel in his manner that I liked him from the start and we became firm friends. Both of us loved music and hardly a week passed that we did not have some concert, musical or serenade on hand. During the summer and fall of the campaign in which Buchanan was elected president of the United States, in 1856, I saw much of Foster, and my recollections of this period are the most vivid, perhaps, on account of the exciting times we had. It was a very hot campaign, as all older citizens will remember. I was a democrat then, as so was Foster, and together we organized a glee club for the purpose of booming the campaign in Allegheny. Among the members of the club were Stephen C. Foster, Morrison Foster, Thomas Smith and myself.[3] There were other vocalists, but their names have escaped my memory. Then we had a body guard of sometimes 50, sometimes 100 men, who joined in the chorus of the songs. We would march through the streets singing campaign songs, and had many an interesting conflict with the whig and political clubs.

"The excitement during that campaign was intense all over the country, and more enthusiasm was shown in Pittsburg and Allegheny, perhaps, than in any other cities of their size in the country. The feeling between the adherents of the different political bodies was not altogether as amicable as it might have been, and the various clubs sometimes met in the streets with disastrous results. The Pittsburg volunteer fire department was an organization much feared in those days, and there were few scraps between

---

[2] William B. Foster Sr. was mayor of Allegheny for two terms, from 1842 to 1844. He would have been the *former* mayor of Allegheny when Hamilton met him.

[3] Thomas Smith is Foster's dedicatee in his vocal quartet arrangement of "I Would Not Die in Spring Time," which survives in manuscript in the Foster Hall Collection. It is possible that Foster made this arrangement for the Buchanan Glee Club to sing. As shown in the organization's minute book, Smith was vice president of the partisan singing club.

political organizations in which the firemen were not interested in some way. Perhaps the most noteworthy incident showing the fighting propensities of the members of the volunteer fire department was one which occurred during the campaign of which I speak. In those days there were no street cars between the old city and East Liberty, or what is now the East End district, and the only way for one to get there was either to walk or take a carriage. We went there several times during the campaign with our glee club and body guard, usually marching out Penn avenue the entire distance.

"On our way home from one of these trips to East Liberty we stopped at a residence this side of the forks of the road, Lawrenceville, to serenade a family with which some of us were acquainted. We sang a Foster song on this occasion, and I had the solo part. Some stranger joined the crowd and persisted in singing the solo part with me, although he was not familiar with it. He annoyed me and I motioned to a member of the body guard to tell him to sing only in the chorus. The guardsman misunderstood me. He thought the fellow had insulted me in some way, and promptly gave him a blow on the left ear, knocking him down. The fellow got up, only to be knocked down again. Directly across the street from the residence we were serenading was the headquarters of one of the largest companies of the Pittsburg volunteer fire department. The firemen saw there had been some difficulty, but waited for no explanations. They joined the crowd and began to strike right and left. In a twinkling our peaceful body of serenaders was transformed into a howling mob. Foster, his brother, myself and other vocalists hastened out of the crowd. We were all too small for our ages and had no business around where any fighting was going on. We always left that to our body guard, and they protected us most effectually in that case. None of us were hurt, and few of the members of the guard suffered, but the firemen were completely routed and driven back into their headquarters. They had tackled the wrong crowd that time.

"Foster wrote both the words and music of many of the campaign songs we sang. One of the best we had was entitled the "Whitehouse Chair." It was a lively air and we sang it well. I have the manuscript some where, but can only recall the words of the first verse and chorus at this moment:

> WHITEHOUSE CHAIR
> Keep it up, keep it up
> All day long;
> All day sing the campaign song.

> Keep it up, keep it up
> Till all turns blue;
> We must beat Fremont and Fillmore, too!
> CHORUS:
> Hurrah! Hurrah! Hurrah!
> Sound the rally for our own candidate;
> Hurrah for Buchanan, of the Keystone state.

"Foster did much to encourage sentimental patriotism," continued Mr. Hamilton. "He wrote many songs of a patriotic character that were sung all over the country during the war, and for years afterward. It is not generally known, but it is nevertheless a fact that the melody of that well-known song, 'John Brown's Body,' was taken from Foster's song, 'Ellen Bayne.'[4] I have manuscripts of many of Foster's songs and also have in my possession a flute he gave me when he left Pittsburg."[5]

Mr. Hamilton said he was satisfied the interest aroused in the Foster memorial movement would be sufficient to insure the erection in Pittsburg's park of a handsome monument to the composer, and he believes the project will be a success in every way.

## *Pittsburg Press*, July 15, 1895.

An interesting incident in connection with Foster's life is related by Supt. William Hamilton, of the Allegheny parks. "I think it was in 1858," said Mr. Hamilton. "I was clerk of the steamer Ida May, plying between this city and Cincinnati, and one day invited Stephen Foster and his wife to take a trip to Cincinnati with me. They accepted my invitation and we had a very enjoyable time. On the way down the river Foster wrote and composed the song, 'Ingomar to Parthenia,'[6] which was afterward published and enjoyed quite a season of popularity in concert circles. He had written some of the melody before, but most of it was composed on that occasion.

---

[4] Mahon claims that Foster himself believed "John Brown's Body" was a reworking of "Ellen Bayne." See Chapter 5.
[5] The flute to which Hamilton refers was donated to the Foster Hall Collection in 1937.
[6] The correct title is "Parthenia to Ingomar," and technically Foster did not "write and compose" this song. The lyrics were written by his friend William Henry McCarthy.

"It is, however, to an incident that occurred in Cincinnati that I have particular reference. During our brief stay there we called on several friends and one evening Foster and I went to the office of the *Commercial Gazette*, on Third Street, to see Cons Miller, river editor of that journal, with whom we were both well acquainted. After a pleasant chat we bade him goodby and started back to the boat to make preparations for our return to Pittsburg. On our way down Broadway we heard music and discovered a party of serenaders in the yard of a residence, directly opposite the home of George K. Schoenberger, a brother of the late John Schoenberger, the iron manufacturer of this city. Serenading was a popular form of amusement for young men in those days, and many serenading parties were formed. We stopped and listened. The melody was strangely familiar.

"'Why, they are singing my song, "Come Where My Love Lies Dreaming,"' exclaimed Foster.

"'It is a bungling effort they are making, too,' I replied. "Let us go over and help them out."

"We had some time to spare, and Foster accepted my proposition. We crossed the street and joined the party. They had not yet finished the song and we chimed in. Naturally they regarded us as intruders, and when the song was finished demanded what right we had to interfere with them in their enjoyment. I asked them if they know the composer of the song they had just sung. They replied that they knew Stephen C. Foster composed the song, but they were not personally acquainted with him. I then introduced Foster, but the young men refused to believe he was the composer of the song, and declared we were impostors.

"The situation began to grow alarming, and we were in danger of having a lively set-to with the young serenaders, when a happy thought struck me. I asked the leader of the party if he knew Cons Miller, of the *Commercial Gazette*. He said he did, and I proposed that we all go over to the *Gazette* office and see Miller. The young men agreed to this, and in a few minutes Miller established our identity in the eyes of the serenaders beyond any question. Nothing was too good for us after that, and although we would have willingly excused ourselves and retired to the steamer, the young men would not hear of it, and we spent the balance of the evening in their company serenading in the residence quarter of the city. We enjoyed the occasion, however, and had many a good laugh over it afterward.

"Foster was a man of more than ordinary literary ability," said Mr. Hamilton. "He was especially fond of magazine reading, and always read carefully all editorial comments in newspapers and magazines. He was a splendid correspondent, and I have preserved numerous letters received from him. I remember the contents of one letter very well, in which he described to me how he and Harry [sic] Kleber had played anvils at the first performance of the anvil chorus from *Il trovatore*, in Masonic hall, which was then the fashionable amusement hall of Pittsburg."[7]

Mr. Hamilton is the possessor of a large portrait of Foster, which is a reproduction of an ambrotype in the possession of Morrison Foster. Only two copies of it were made, and the other is in the possession of John D. Scully, cashier of the First National bank of this city, who was also a warm friend of Foster.[8] Mr. Hamilton some time ago loaned his copy to Sprienterbach, the sculptor, of this city, who desired to make a model bust of Foster. It is still in the sculptor's studio.

---

[7] On January 16, 1857, Foster wrote to Hamilton about declining an invitation from Henry Kleber to perform anvil in a concert performance of the "Anvil Chorus" from the opera *Il trovatore* (FHC, A311).

[8] John D. Scully married Jane Foster's sister Marian McDowell on April 27, 1848.

# 21

# An Interview with an Art Dealer (1895)

## Introduction

*Foster Hall appears to have been inclined not to collect articles with unnamed sources, so it is not surprising that this interview with an unnamed art dealer from New York is not in the Foster Hall Collection. The dealer's assertion that Foster was a capable watercolor painter, moreover, appears to be an elaboration of a more reliable account rather than firsthand knowledge. No evidence from the songwriter's lifetime supports the claim, but the 1864 sketch of his life—likely written by Morrison—that appeared on the day of his funeral in Pittsburgh mentions that "some of the water-color paintings of his youth are still the admiration of his friends." Morrison echoed this comment in his sketch of his brother's life that appeared about one year after this interview, writing, "Stephen also became quite a creditable artist in water colors as an amusement, and some of his pictures are yet preserved with pride by his friends."*

*Interest in Foster as a painter increased following the interview. In September of 1895, two oil paintings purportedly by Foster were displayed at the Pittsburgh Exposition alongside other "relics" from the composer's life. According to the Press, "They cannot be called works of art, but their value lies in the fact that they are the handiwork of one whose fame as a composer is world-wide."[1] The authenticity of these paintings cannot be determined, and no watercolors or oil paintings purportedly by Foster are known to exist today. Based on the characterizations of Foster's artwork by Morrison and the Press, it seems that at the very least this anonymous source greatly exaggerated the songwriter's abilities as an artist and possibly fabricated all the information in this interview.*

---

[1] "Handsome Souvenirs will be Ready by Saturday," *Pittsburg Press*, September 12, 1895.

Formulating Foster. Christopher Lynch, Oxford University Press. © Oxford University Press 2025.
DOI: 10.1093/9780197811726.003.0022

## *Pittsburg Press,* July 31, 1895.

"It is not generally known that Stephen C. Foster, besides being the greatest song writer America has yet produced, was an artist of no mean ability in water colors." This statement was made by a gentleman now a resident of this city, who was an art dealer in New York during the song writer's residence there, and who was personally acquainted with him. "Foster," he said, "paid much attention to art matters and was a frequenter of art galleries. His popularity at that time gave him access to many private collections. As an art critic he was severe, no fault however slight escaping him. I considered him only an admirer of art with no great sympathy for artists, until I chanced to call at his lodgings and catch him at work on a beautiful piece of landscape.

"He was a rapid worker, and it did not take me long to learn that he had a perfect knowledge of what was in his paint box and the ability to transfer it to his paper. How many water colors he painted I am unable to say. I secured several and had no difficulty in disposing of them. Where they are now I am unable to say. If I could learn their whereabouts I would gladly pay my share of any sum necessary to recover them for the art gallery in the Carnegie library, at Schenley park. I would be glad if others would take this matter up after we get through with the memorial.

"I have contributed to the fund, and shall supplement it later on. This is a popular movement and one that is a credit both to the city and to the *Press*, and I am glad to see it moving steadily forward. Pittsburg owes Stephen C. Foster the best memorial that money can buy. There was a song writer in England who wrote of the daring sailors and members of life saving crews located along the coast. His songs were somewhat popular, but none of them had the enormous sale reported for Foster melodies. The English government honored him by naming a life saving station after him, and many smaller boats in English waters bear his name on their bows, but I believe he is the only song writer who has ever been honored by a national government. Foster was as far above him as the brightness of the sun is more brilliant than the moon. It will be remembered that Foster was not a mere ditty writer. He rose above that plane, and is conceded by the musical critics of the world to have been a genius and the originator of the home school of ballads."

# 22
# An Interview with a St. Louis Businessman (1895)

**Introduction**

*This anonymous interview, not found in the Foster Hall Collection, addresses Foster's 1851 trip to New Orleans for Mardi Gras with a group of friends. Susan Pentland Robinson's anecdotes about this trip were published two months earlier, so it is possible that this anonymous businessman fabricated this story after he read her interviews. Or it could be that the Press fabricated this interview altogether. Many of the Press's anonymous interviews are dubious because of the close similarity of their rhetoric to the editorial voice of the newspaper. This interview, for example, is typical of the Press's tone of astonishment at there being no statue of Foster in his hometown. The editors often employed such rhetoric to inspire Pittsburghers to contribute to the statue fund. Ultimately, unless new sources come to light, we cannot know if this article's interesting and new images of Foster on a steamboat are authentic.*

### Pittsburg Press, August 9, 1895.

"What! No monument in Pittsburg to Stephen C. Foster? Why, I'm astonished. Surely the composer of 'Old Folks at Home' and all those delightful songs is deserving of a better fate at the hands of his own people."

These and similar exclamations of surprise were made by a St. Louis businessman who spent yesterday here visiting the large mills and factories that line the rivers. While taking a spin through the East End district on a double-decker he met a *Press* reporter. Inquiries made by the St. Louis man regarding Schenley park brought up the subject of the *Press* memorial movement. The reporter told him that the movement now advocated was the first organized attempt to raise funds for a monument to Foster, and that nothing in the shape of a memorial was now standing excepting a marble slab that rests at the head of his grave in Allegheny cemetery.

"Your people have certainly been remiss in their duty," continued the gentleman, "for if ever a man deserves a monument Stephen C. Foster deserves one. Look what he has done for the common people. He has given them music that has afforded them more pleasure than all the books they ever read. He has given them something to think about. He has pictured out life in its most humble phases and set it in melodies so sweet and plaintive that they have reached the depths of all hearts. Why, sir, I think Stephen C. Foster's songs have done as much good and are deserving of as much reverance [sic] as the good old hymns we sing on Sundays."

"When I first heard of Foster I was quite a boy. I had a good voice and was fond of singing, consequently I always quickly picked up any new air I chanced to hear. I first heard 'Suwanee River' whistled by a charcoal man, who frequently passed our house on his rounds of the city. He had heard it somewhere, doubtless at the theater where it had been sung by some minstrel company. I heard it myself afterward at a concert and soon learned the words. I also heard 'Old Dog Tray,' and used to sing it and other Foster songs to a guitar accompaniment. When I got older I formed a quartet and we used to serenade the girls in our section of the city, singing nothing but Foster songs. Those were good old days and I sometimes wish I could live them all over again."

"I met Foster one time and thought him one of the nicest and most refined men I ever conversed with. He was just a little odd in his manner, but a perfect gentleman, a good conversationalist and quite witty. It was on a steamer on the Ohio, I had been in Cincinnati and took the boat there to go to Cairo. Among the passengers were Foster, his wife and several friends from Pittsburg and vicinity, who were bound for New Orleans to attend the Mardi Gras festival. My first glimpse of him was in the pilot house, where I saw him running the wheel. He was taking lessons from the pilot and seemed to enjoy the experience immensely. I was introduced to him later on and we frequently helped to entertain the passengers during the long evenings, he with the flute, a young lady at the piano, and myself and others forming a vocal quartet. He afterward presented me with copies of many of his songs in sheet music form."

"I hope your memorial movement will be as great a success as it deserves to be, and will expect some day to visit your park and see there a fine monument to my old acquaintance. How nice it would be if the interest and sympathies of the whole nation could be elicited. Then we in St. Louis could take part in the movement, other cities would become interested and a monument fit for kings could be erected. However, you are carrying the movement on in the right manner. It is open to all and should receive the support of all. A popular subscription fund is the best way to get the expression of the general public in an undertaking of this kind. The poor as well as the people of wealth have the same opportunity to contribute."

# 23

# An Interview with a "Prominent Pittsburgher" (1895)

### Introduction

*This anonymous interview is not in the Foster Hall Collection and is heretofore unknown to modern readers. Foster Hall may well have declined to collect it because its source was unnamed, but it nevertheless includes intriguing statements that might fill in a gap in our knowledge of where Foster lived. The anonymous interviewee claims Foster lived in the St. Clair Hotel, which could only have occurred after 1852, for an advertisement appeared that year in* Woodward & Rowlands' Pittsburgh Directory *informing Pittsburghers that the old Exchange Hotel at Penn Avenue and St. Clair Street (also known as Sixth Street) had been transformed into the St. Clair Hotel. The building, "completely remodelled, thoroughly repaired, and newly furnished throughout," was "now open for the accommodation of the public" at "moderate" prices.*

*We can almost always account for where Foster was living from when he returned from New Jersey at the end of 1854 to when he departed again for New York in 1860. Foster, Jane, and Marion lived in his brother William Jr.'s house in Allegheny until William sold it in April of 1857.[1] At that point he and his family lived in hotels and boarding houses around Pittsburgh. His account book shows he made intermittent payments to John Mish, proprietor of the Eagle Hotel on Liberty Street in Pittsburgh, for boarding in 1857 and early 1858. After that his whereabouts are unknown—on May 27, 1858, his niece Lidie Wick even wrote to Morrison to ask if "Uncle Steve" had moved away. Then, in September of 1858, he began boarding with a Mrs. Johnston—probably Mary Johnston's boarding house at 923 Penn Avenue. From February to May of 1859, he paid to board at Mary Miller's boarding house at 73 Liberty Avenue. The* Directory of Pittsburgh

---

[1] William Jr. began advertising his house for sale in August of 1856, and it sold on April 1, 1857.

*Formulating Foster.* Christopher Lynch, Oxford University Press. © Oxford University Press 2025.
DOI: 10.1093/9780197811726.003.0024

& Vicinity for 1859 *gives both his personal and business address as 112–114 Smithfield Street, where he probably lived while Jane and Marion lived with Jane's family and with Henrietta, the songwriter's sister, in Warren, Ohio. Foster, Jane, and Marion lived in Warren from early 1860 until at least August 10, sometime after which they moved to New York. Therefore, if Foster lived at the St. Clair Hotel, it only could have been during the one gap in our knowledge of his living situation between 1854 and his 1860 return to New York: the middle of 1858, when even his niece was unsure of where he was.*

*Foster struggled to write songs in this period, and what he did write failed to match his sales of the early 1850s. Without his family to rely on for loans, and without their understanding leniency with boarding payments, he needed new sources of income. Struggling, Foster turned to his publishers Firth, Pond & Co. for advances and eventually sold them his rights to royalties from all his previous songs for one-time payments. Firth, Pond & Co. were generous, but this move undermined his long-term financial security. On the period immediately after Foster sold his rights away, John Tasker Howard jotted in his notebook from a research trip to Pittsburgh that "Miss Miller could have given J. K. L. [Josiah K. Lilly] a lot of bills that Foster owed her and her mother for board."[2] (Lilly chose not to preserve these bills in the Foster Hall Collection.) I think it is telling that Foster moved his family to New York late in the summer of 1860. His contract with Firth, Pond & Co. expired on August 9 of that year, so the relocation must have had something to do with his desire to negotiate a new contract with them.*

*The following reminiscence helps us understand this difficult period in Foster's life in a new way. Historians have traditionally painted a dark picture of these years, focusing on his artistic drought, depression, intermittent estrangement from his wife and daughter, descent into alcoholism, and financial difficulties—personal struggles that mirror the image often painted of the nation descending into civil war. The person interviewed in this article acknowledges that Foster was "moody and thoughtful" but generally portrayed Foster in good spirits, which, indeed, is the mood that pervades Foster's few surviving letters from 1858 and 1859. He wrote to Morrison optimistically in 1859, for example, that he "sent off a first rate song the other day to Firth, Pond & Co."[3] Perhaps in 1859 and 1860 Foster was showing*

---

[2] John Tasker Howard, "Questions for Pittsburgh for J. K.'s trip to Pitts. in June," notebook, FHC, unprocessed folder labeled "Next Pittsburgh Visit."

[3] Stephen Foster to Morrison Foster, June 13, 1859, FHC, A339.

*renewed confidence as an artist, putting his life and career back together as he emerged from an artistically fallow period. Instead of thinking about his relocation to New York as a move of desperation or a symbol of decline, I suggest we see it as a move inspired by renewed hope—hope that was tragically dashed within a few years* (Figure 23.1).

**Figure 23.1.** A daguerreotype of Stephen C. Foster, which was taken in 1859 and mailed by the composer to his brother Morrison. Foster Hall Collection, Center for American Music, University of Pittsburgh Library System.

## *Pittsburg Press,* August 11, 1895.

"What's this I hear about a memorial to the composer, Stephen C. Foster?" said a prominent Pittsburger yesterday on his return from Europe. A representative of the *Press* had met him at the union station and told him about the memorial.

"The most commendable movement the people of our city ever started," he exclaimed, after listening attentively to a recital of the plan and progress of the undertaking. "No musician ever lived that was more deserving of a monument than Stephen Foster, and I assure you that now I am home and ready for business again I will do all I can to help it along. I remember Foster well and knew him personally. In fact, we had many pleasant hours together. I used to sing a little myself, and was frequently out with Foster at parties here and there, where other young people, myself included, joined in singing some new song of his composition. The good old days; I sometimes wish I could live them over again.

"The first time I met Foster he was staying at the St. Clair hotel, on Sixth street. He lived there, I believe, for some time, and we were much in each other's company. Foster was just a little inclined to be moody and thoughtful. He was very modest, too, I remember, and would never make any reference or talk about his achievements as a composer and writer of songs unless the subject was pressed upon him in such a manner that he could not well avoid it, and then he would drop it as quickly as he got an opportunity. He was not at all conceited, and I have often thought his bearing amid the praise that was almost constantly showered upon him by his friends was something remarkable. It would have turned the head of any other man than Foster. He was always kind, always genial; never wanted for friends, and never had an enemy. Everybody who knew him liked him, and his temperament, tastes and general disposition were such that I could not imagine him writing anything else than the sweet plaintive lines that have made his name famous. True, he wrote some campaign songs, and several humorous negro melodies, but none are of the offensive style that is characteristic of much of the so-called popular music of the present day. The beauty of his songs is that each of them tells a story. Brevity is the soul of wit, they say, and he had that trait down to a greater degree of perfection than any song writer I ever heard of. He always had a good theme and a perfect arrangement for the characters portrayed.

"Where do you suppose I first heard of the Foster memorial? Of course you cannot tell me. It was during my stay in London. A friend of mine, an

Englishman with whom I had some business, remarked one day that he had read in one of the London dailies that a movement was on foot in Pittsburg to erect a monument to Foster, the composer of 'Suwanee River.' 'Do you know,' he said, 'that song is the sweetest I ever heard, and I regard its composer as one of the greatest song-writers I ever heard of. Why, sir, I heard Patti sing that song twice one evening here several years ago. It seemed that the people could not get enough of it. They just simply sat spell-bound. I can almost hear her yet. I have heard Patti many times since then, but I do not believe her voice ever seemed as sweet and plaintive to my ears as on that occasion. It was one of the pleasantest moments of my life and I shall always remember it.' I declare this expression coming as it did so spontaneously and sincerely from the lips of a Briton made me feel like getting on my feet and shouting, 'Bravo, America; bravo, Foster; bravo, Pittsburg, the home and birthplace of the greatest composer of the nineteenth century.'

"I am glad our people have at last awakened to the fact that Foster should be immortalized by the erection of a grand monument. A memorial should have been erected to him years ago, but we will let that pass. The movement is progressing nicely now, and I hope it will not be long until a fund of several thousand dollars will be placed at the disposal of the committee whose duty it will be to select the designs and direct the work of erecting the monument."

# 24
# Morrison Foster's Sketch of His Brother's Life (1896)

## Introduction

*As we have seen, Morrison grew more and more frustrated with his family's lack of control over information about his brother's life and finally took matters into his own hands in 1893. That year, which coincided with "Old Folks at Home" entering the public domain, he began his own biography and collection of his brother's complete works, and he also started working with Keenan to erect the Foster statue in Pittsburgh. His book—of which only the biography is reproduced below—took three years to complete. He responded not only to the reminiscences that had appeared in the previous decades but also to some of the newer comments about his brother that had surfaced during the fundraising campaign for the statue.*

### Morrison Foster. "Stephen C. Foster." Pittsburgh, 1896.

THE great popularity of "Old Folks at Home," "Uncle Ned," "Old Kentucky Home," "Come Where My Love Lies Dreaming," and a hundred and sixty other American songs by the same author, produces a natural desire to know more of his personality and his history. I am prompted to publish this work by the numerous inquiries, increasing yearly, from all parts of the world, received by me, for information in regard to the life and music of my brother, Stephen C. Foster.[1]

---

[1] Morrison preserved dozens of inquiries, which eventually found their way into the Foster Hall Collection by way of Morneweck. Only one is from outside the United States. In the FHC, see Robert P. Nevin to Morrison Foster, July 21, 1865; Karl Merz to Morrison Foster, July 20, 1869; S. Brainard & Sons to Morrison Foster, July 21, 1869; Morrison Foster to Will S. Hays, October 25, 1875; S. Griffith to Morrison Foster, January 2, 1883; S. Reed Johnson to Morrison Foster, July 11, 1883; A. B. Force,

*Formulating Foster*. Christopher Lynch, Oxford University Press. © Oxford University Press 2025.
DOI: 10.1093/9780197811726.003.0025

A stranger meeting him for the first time would have observed nothing striking in his appearance, but an acquaintance and a few moments' observation of and conversation with him would satisfy him that he was in the presence of a man of genius who, however modest in his demeanor, was accustomed to look deep into the thoughts and motives of men.

In person he was slender, in height not over five feet seven inches. His figure was handsome; exceedingly well proportioned. His feet were small, as were his hands, which were soft and delicate. His head was large and well proportioned. The features of his face were regular and striking. His nose was straight, inclined to aquiline; his nostrils full and dilated. His mouth was regular in form and the lips full. His most remarkable feature were his eyes. They were very dark and very large, and lit up with unusual intelligence. His hair was dark, nearly black. The color of his eyes and hair he inherited from his mother, some of whose remote ancestors were Italian, though she was directly of English descent. In conversation he was very interesting, but more suggestive than argumentative. He was an excellent listener, though well informed on every current topic.

His father, William Barclay Foster, was an enterprising, prominent citizen and merchant of Pittsburgh, Pennsylvania, of Scotch-Irish ancestry. Alexander Foster was the first of the family who came to America. He emigrated from Londonderry, Ireland, about the year 1728, and settled in Little Britain Township, Lancaster County, Pa. He had three sons and six daughters. The sons were James (the grandfather of Stephen C. Foster), William, and John. James the eldest son married Ann Barclay and removed to Berkeley County, Virginia. He had three sons, James Barclay, Alexander, and William Barclay; also a number of daughters, all of whom married, and some of whom removed to Kentucky, Tennessee and Ohio. William Barclay Foster was born in Berkeley County, Virginia, September 7th, 1779. Through his mother's family (the Barclays) he was a cousin of Judge John Rowan, of Bardstown, Kentucky, one of the first United States Senators from

---

August 22, 1883; L. F. Jackson to Morrison Foster, January 17, 1884; J. R. Bailey to Morrison Foster, July 25, 1884; Caroline Griffith to Morrison Foster, December 31, 1882; Marcus M. Henry to Morrison Foster, February 6, 1883; F. O. Jones to Morrison Foster, March 8, 1883; Robert McCaslin to Morrison Foster, August 8, 1883; L. F. Jackson to Morrison Foster, January 17, 1884; Edwin R. Parkhurst to Morrison Foster, November 16, 1885; S. Reed Johnson to Morrison Foster, February 12, 1886; J. W. Wiedermeyer to Morrison Foster, March 19, 1886; George Hoyt to Morrison Foster, March 22, 1886; John D. Champlain Jr. of Scribner & Sons to Morrison Foster, January 11, 1888; George H. Welshous to Morrison Foster, November 23, 1891; C. W. Des Islets to Morrison Foster, April 1, 1892; J. W. McCrury to Morrison Foster, August 17, 1892.

Kentucky.[2] James Foster served his country through the Revolutionary war in the Virginia line, and was present at the surrender of Cornwallis at Yorktown.[3] About 1782, he with his family and a number of other Scotch-Irish people removed to Western Pennsylvania and settled near Canonsburg, Washington County, about nineteen miles from Pittsburgh. He was one of the original Trustees of Canonsburg Academy, founded in 1791, the first outpost of learning west of the Allegheny Mountains, and since renowned as Jefferson College.[4]

William Foster, the second son of Alexander, became a distinguished and patriotic minister of the Presbyterian Church, and pastor of the congregations of Octorara and Doe Run. During the Revolution his speeches were so offensive to the British Government that General Howe sent a troop of horsemen to arrest him, but the attempt failed. He died in the neighborhood where he had always lived.

John, the third son of Alexander, emigrated to North Carolina. From thence his descendants removed to Tennessee, where some of them became distinguished at the bar and in the councils of the State.

William Barclay Foster, the father of Stephen, went at the age of sixteen to Pittsburgh and entered into business in the employ of Anthony Beelen and Major Ebenezer Denny, who were engaged in extensive general merchandising. Afterwards he was admitted to partnership with Major Denny, and attended to the active part of the business. It was their custom at that time, the beginning of this century, to load flatboats with the products of the neighboring country, furs, peltries, whiskey, flour, etc., and float them down the Ohio and Mississippi rivers to New Orleans, where the goods were sold for money or exchanged for sugar, coffee, etc. Mr. Foster went on these expeditions about twice a year. Sometimes he returned by land via Natchez, Nashville, Maysville and Wheeling to Pittsburgh, traveling with large parties strongly armed, for the Indians were hostile and dangerous. At other times he took ship and sailed to New York. On one of these voyages the vessel he was on was captured by pirates off the coast of Cuba, but was rescued by a Spanish man-of-war. At New York and Philadelphia he bought goods for the store at Pittsburgh.

---

[2] Foster's precise relation to John Rowan, if any, is uncertain.
[3] Cornwallis's surrender at Yorktown to George Washington on October 19, 1781, marked the end of the last major land battle in the Revolutionary War.
[4] In 1865 Jefferson College merged with Washington College to become Washington & Jefferson College.

These goods were transported across the mountains on the backs of horses in the earlier years of business. Afterwards large wagons were used, drawn by six horses. On each horse (except the one on which the driver sat) a string of bells, attached to a bow above his collar, "discouraged most eloquent music" as the long line of wagons traversed the still forests of the mountains. The wagons were of the pattern used by the farmers east of the mountains, and were called Conestoga wagons.

It was on one of these business trips that he met the lady who became his wife, the mother of Stephen C. Foster, Miss Eliza Clayland Tomlinson. She was at the time visiting her aunt in Philadelphia, Mrs. Oliver Evans, the wife of the great American inventor. Mr. Evans lived on Race street. He built his wonderful amphibious locomotive at the time my mother was there. She related to me how she saw him walk with great pride beside it as it moved out of his yard into the street and down into the river.

The maternal ancestors of my mother, the Claylands, came from England, and settled on the eastern shore of Maryland, in the early days of the colony. Her people were very loyal to the patriot cause, and many of them, Col. James Clayland and others, distinguished themselves in the battles of the Revolution. They were generally accomplished, both men and women, highly educated and refined. It is believed that much of the musical and poetic genius of my brother Stephen was derived from this branch of his family. The ladies were distinguished in Baltimore society for their musical and artistic ability.

Whilst I was burning a lot of old letters in 1855, after the death of our mother and father, the following was rescued from the flames just as its corners were beginning to be scorched. It is a letter from my mother to my father, written while on a visit to her relatives in Maryland:

BALTIMORE, MARCH 11, 1841

DEAR HUSBAND:—I received your letter of the 6th last evening whilst sitting in Mrs. Gwin's parlour, on Charles street, in company with herself and two daughters, one very pretty. Mr. Gwin has been dead for five years, and with all her past beauty, Mrs. Gwin is not looking well. She has one son, a spoiled chap, studying law and not yet admitted to practice. Thomas Tilden has a very handsome appointment in the Post Office Department. John Blake has also received an appointment, but I cannot describe it. I was at his house yesterday. He looks badly, having lost one of his eyes, but he is as merry as ever and would hug and kiss me in the presence of his wife and daughters. Mr. Jacobs, at whose house I had spent the previous evening, was gallanting me. On Monday Miss Tilden (the daughter of Charles Tilden) and myself started to Eutaw street, where Blakes, Beaches, Jacobs', Emorys and a host of Eastern Shore friends and relatives reside. We were invited to Mrs. Beach's, where we spent the night the next day. Mr. Beach is now in bad health. Mrs. Beach is about my size. She has a very pretty daughter who plays and sings charmingly to the piano. Mr. Beach and I had quite a time making out the chronicles of the Clayland family. We were all delving into it like one trying to find perpetual motion.

Robert Wright (Mrs. Beach's son by her first husband, Gustavus Wright, a man of great wealth, formerly of Rio Janeiro) says he will be here this summer; that they must have things in train to identify the descendants of Thomas Clayland and Susannah Seth, for he has made up his mind to go to England and inquire out the story. It seems that Lord Gage came to New York, and learning that Mrs. Kemble was a Miss Seth, told her that there was an ancient West Riding castleated [castellated] estate on the borders of Durham, the lawful heirs to which were somewhere in America. The last rightful owner or occupant was an ancient maiden lady, whose only sister died in Queen Anne County, on the Eastern Shore of Maryland. This sister had fled from her family with William Seth.

It seems by her papers that there was no communication with her family until her father and mother were dead, at which time she wrote that her only daughter, Susanna Seth, has married Thomas Clayland, and begged that her offspring should be thought of when she should be no more. The maiden lady above-mentioned having died, the friend in whose possession these letters are and to whom they were written, sent an agent to inquire after the descendants of Thomas Clayland.

With much affection, your wife,

ELIZA CLAYLAND FOSTER.

My mother was born in January, 1788, in Wilmington, Delaware, where her father, Joseph Tomlinson, was living at that time. My father and she were married at Chambersburg, Penna., where she had relatives, in 1807, by the Rev. David Denny, a Presbyterian minister.

They departed from Chambersburg and crossed the mountains on horseback to their home in Pittsburgh, a distance of nearly three hundred miles.[5]

---

[5] Morrison exaggerates the distance by roughly doubling it.

The following is an extract from the reminiscences of my mother, written for the edification and information of her children:

"The journey was slow and monotonous, and it was not until the fourteenth day that I hailed with delight the dingy town of Pittsburgh, my future home, where every joy and every sorrow of my heart since that bright period have been associated with the joys and sorrows of its people. It was evening when, weary and faint with travel, I was conducted, or, rather, borne, into the hospitable mansion of my husband's partner, the benevolent Major Denny, a dwelling in the centre of the town, where I was received and treated with the most extreme kindness. After resting and changing my apparel, I was shown into an apartment below stairs where blazed in all its brilliancy a coal fire, casting its light upon the face of beauty clothed in innocence in the person of little Nancy Denny, at that time five years old. The well-cleaned grating of the chimney-place, the light that blazed brightly from the fire, the vermillion hearth, the plain, rich furniture, the polished stand with lighted candles in candlesticks resembling burnished gold, made an evening scene that fell gratefully on my pleased sight. Upon a sofa lay the tall and military figure of the Major, a gentleman of the old school, easy and dignified in his bearing, a soldier who had served his country well under Washington at Yorktown, and Harmar, St. Clair and Wayne in the subsequent Indian campaigns."

It must be borne in mind that Pittsburgh, ever since the Revolutionary war, has always been a town of refinement, with a society fit to mingle in the courts of royalty. Before it was safe to live altogether outside of forts, while log dwellings were the homes of the people, while the sound of the pioneer's axe and rifle were familiar every day to the ear, academies and colleges were reared in the midst of the forest. Many officers of the army, with their accomplished families, settled here during and just after the Revolution. Among these were: Col. John Neville, Col. Pressley Neville, Col. William Butler, Col. Richard Butler, Lieut. Col. Stephen Bayard, Major Isaac Craig, Major Ebenezer Denny, Major Edward Butler, Major Alexander Fowler, Major William Anderson, Capt. Abraham Kirkpatrick, Capt. Adamson Tannehill, Capt. Uriah Springer, Capt. George McCully, Capt. Nathaniel Irish, Capt. John Irwin, Capt. Joseph Asheton, Capt. James Gordon Heron, Capt. James O'Hara, afterwards Quartermaster-General; Col. George Morgan, Lieut. Josiah Tannehill, Lieut. William McMillan, Lieut. Gabriel Peterson, James

Foster, Lieut. Ward, Capt. John Wilkins, Surgeon's Mate John Wilkins, Jr., Surgeon's Mate George Stevenson, Surgeon's Mate John McDowell, Quartermast John Ormsby. These, and others who were civilians, brought with them the courtesy and social amenities of the most refined circles in the East, which, in the Colonial times, were an improvement upon those of the nobility of England and France. A number of families had their private carriages and liveried servants. When Louis Philipe [sic] and his brothers, Beaujolai and Montpensier, visited Pittsburgh they expressed surprise at the ease and elegance of their entertainment by the people.[6]

My father was a man of great public spirit and unbounded patriotism. During the War of 1812 he was appointed Quartermaster and Commissary of the US Army. When the Army of the Northwest appealed to the Government for supplies to enable them to continue the contest, the answer was "a mournful echo from the vaults of an exhausted treasury." But my father with his own money and upon his own personal credit procured the necessary supplies. When the British army, which had captured Washington and burned the Capitol, turned their vessels' prows southward for the capture of New Orleans, urgent order came to Pittsburgh to send forward clothing, blankets, guns and ammunition to the relief of Jackson's army. But no money was sent with which to purchase them. Again my father extended his generous hand and himself procured the much needed supplies. He loaded the steamboat Enterprise (the fourth steamboat which ever turned a wheel on the Western rivers) and dispatched her from Pittsburgh on the 15th of December, 1814. She was commanded by Captain Henry M. Shreve, the pioneer boatman. Brave Shreve left Pittsburgh about dark of a winter night, and as the boat rounded to and straightened herself for the voyage, he called to my father on the wharf, "I'll get there before the British or sink this boat." He pushed on through the wilderness, amid the storm and floating ice, and reached New Orleans on the 5th day of January, 1815, three days before the battle which saved Louisiana. Captain Shreve unloaded part of his cargo at the city and ran down the river, passing the British batteries, to Fort Philip, returned again, and was engaged in the battle of the 8th of January, serving at the sixth gun of the American batteries.[7]

---

[6] While exiled from France in the aftermath of the French Revolution, the future king and his brothers toured the United States, visiting Pittsburgh in June of 1797.

[7] The Foster family's lore about the War of 1812 was correct only insofar as William Sr. did use his own money to send supplies on the *Enterprise* to New Orleans. Starting in 1867, Morrison wrote to different federal officials and departments trying to figure out when the steamer departed Pittsburgh and when it arrived in New Orleans. No official ever answered his questions, and he may have

During this time the Government was often indebted to my father as much as fifty thousand dollars. Upon final adjudication of his accounts it became necessary to refer the facts as to certain amounts to a jury. Upon the hearing of the cause in the United States Court at Pittsburgh in 1823, the venerable Judge Walker (father of Hon. Robert J. Walker) in his charge to the jury, used these memorable words:

"Terminate as this cause may, Mr. Foster has established for himself a character for zeal, patriotism, generosity and fidelity which cannot be forgotten, and has placed a laurel on his brow that will never fade."

The jury without leaving the Court returned a verdict in favor of my father. That judgment still stands unpaid on the records of the United States Court at Pittsburgh. In 1814 my father established his residence upon a tract of land belonging to him on the Allegheny river, 2 ½ miles above Pittsburgh. Here he built a beautiful white cottage on Bullitt's Hill, a height commanding a view up and down the river for miles. It was on this same piece of land that George Washington was cast on the night of December 28, 1753, and nearly frozen, when he and his guide, Christopher Gist, were returning from Fort Venango.[8] My father sold thirty acres of this tract to the Government, on which now stands the Unites States Arsenal.[9] He also laid out a town there and called it Lawrenceville in honor of Captain James Lawrence, who was killed while gallantly fighting his ship, the Chesapeake, and whose last words, as he was carried below, were, "Don't give up the ship."

He donated a piece of ground in the town of Lawrenceville to be, as he expressed it, "a burial ground for our soldiers forever," where they might be buried by right, and not by sufferance.[10] At the time this donation was made,

---

invented the rest of his story about Shreve and the *Enterprise* arriving in time to resupply the Army and participate in the battle. In 1994, historian Alfred A. Maass finally conclusively documented that the *Enterprise* departed Pittsburgh on December 21, 1814, and arrived in New Orleans on January 9, 1815, one day *after* the Battle of New Orleans. The *Enterprise* never went to Fort St. Philip. See Alfred A. Maass, "Brownsville's Steamboat Enterprize and Pittsburgh's Supply of General Jackson's Army," *Pittsburgh History* 77, no. 1 (Spring 1994): 22–29.

[8] According to Washington's journal from the trip, after his and Christopher Gist's failed attempt to cross the Allegheny River, they went to John Frazier's trading post on the Monongahela River, not to the land where the Fosters would later live.

[9] The Allegheny Arsenal was operated by the military from 1814 to 1926. It was the site of the Civil War's largest civilian disaster when an explosion killed seventy-eight workers on September 17, 1862, the same day as the Battle of Antietam.

[10] The graves were relocated to Allegheny Cemetery, and the site became home to a branch of the Carnegie Libraries in 1898.

soldiers were passing through Pittsburgh continually, going to or returning from the front of war.[11] Many of them died here, and there was no place to bury them except in a potter's field. My father, being himself the son of an American soldier, determined that this should no longer be the case. A beautiful monument has been erected on this ground. It is of solid granite. The inscription on one side is:

"In honor of the American soldiers who lie buried here."

"We will emulate their patriotism and protect their remains."

On the other side is the inscription:

"This ground was given in 1814 by Col. William B. Foster, the founder of Lawrenceville, as a burial ground for our soldiers."

At the white cottage, overlooking the village of Lawrenceville and the winding Allegheny, the family spent many happy years. Here hospitality and kindness prevailed. Being the only private residence outside of town in that neighborhood where open house was kept, its generous board was free to all comers at all times. Three handsome and accomplished daughters grew up and enlivened the house with music and intellectual enjoyment. The sons, guided by the example and gentle teachings of a Christian mother, and actuated by the manly characteristics of a brave and generous father, were taught to be truthful, honorable and manly.[12] The oldest daughter, Charlotte Susanna, was an accomplished musician and beautiful singer. The others, Ann Eliza and Henrietta, were also good performers and singers, both of them possessed of more than ordinary poetic fancy and literary ability. Charlotte died in Louisville, Kentucky, at the age of nineteen years, while on a visit to her relatives, the Rowans and Barclays. At the time of her death she was engaged to be married to Mr. Prather.[13]

Ann Eliza married the Rev. Dr. Edward Y. Buchanan (brother of President Buchanan), and died in Philadelphia at nearly eighty years of age. Henrietta married Mr. Thomas L. Wick, and after his death Major Thornton, Commissary U. S. A., and died in Germantown (Philadelphia) at the age of seventy years.

It was in such a home and amid such surroundings that Stephen C. Foster was born at the white cottage, Lawrenceville, on the 4th day of July, 1826.

---

[11] Soldiers passed through Pittsburgh as a result of the War of 1812 and the Indian Wars being waged in the Indiana Territory.

[12] The sons of the Foster family were William B. Foster Jr. (ca. 1806–60), Dunning McNair Foster (1821–56), Morrison Foster (1823–1904), and Stephen Collins Foster (1826–64). Two additional boys, William (1814–15) and James (1829–30), died in infancy.

[13] Morrison portrayed all the Foster daughters as fulfilling what he viewed as their societal duty—marriage—but in truth Charlotte was not engaged at the time of her death.

He was the youngest of the family except one (James, who died in infancy). The day was a memorable one for several reasons. Independence had reached its half century. A grand celebration was held in my father's woods back of the house, on General Forbes' old road. The volunteer soldiers from Pittsburgh and the Regulars from the U. S. Arsenal were there. It was a "Bowery dinner," as they called it in those days. At one end of the table sat my father, and at the other, the staunch old editor of the *Pittsburgh Mercury*, Hon. John M. Snowden.

At noon a national salute pealed from the cannon at the Arsenal, and the bands played the national hymn. At that hour my brother Stephen was born. The same day Thomas Jefferson and John Adams died. When Stephen was quite young my father, having served several terms in the Legislature for the purpose of procuring the passage of the bills for the construction of the great Pennsylvania Canal,[14] was appointed the first collector of tolls at Pittsburgh. He removed to Allegheny town, opposite Pittsburgh, where Stephen spent the most of his life.[15] At an early age he was sent to a school founded by the Rev. Joseph Stockton, an old friend of my father, who had known him intimately at Meadville, Pa., and who was largely instrumental in inducing him to come to Allegheny town. Mr. Stockton was pastor of the First Presbyterian church of Allegheny and principal of the Allegheny Academy. This academy was a model institution for the education of youth, and was attended by the sons of nearly all the most prominent citizens of Pittsburgh and Allegheny. Mr. Stockton was a perfect tutor. He was learned, he was firm, he was amiable, and he was thorough and practical. His acquirements were numerous and general. In addition to the classics, he was master of the grammar of the English language, and was also a profound mathematician. He published a work on Arithmetic, which was for a long time the standard in all schools west of the Allegheny mountains, and to-day is unsurpassed by any later work.

Mr. Stockton had with him an assistant who was his equal as a scholar except in knowledge of the classics, Mr. John Kelly, an Irishman, of wonderful accomplishments. He had been a tutor in the family of Sir Rowland Hill, and brought with him letters of introduction from people of the most excellent sort in the refined city of Dublin. Mr. Kelly was a thorough disciplinarian. While he was of genial disposition and out of school played ball and

---

[14] William B. Foster Sr. only served one term in the state legislature.
[15] Morrison declines to mention that the Fosters were evicted from their home when the Bank of the United States foreclosed on it.

prisoner's base with the boys, and excelled in every manly athletic exercise, in school he required rigid attention to business.

Elocution was also taught as a separate branch by Mr. Caldwell, who afterwards became a noted minister of the gospel; and penmanship by Mr. Egerton. It is not to be wondered at that boys who attended this academy became scholars. Many of them were afterwards famous at the bar and in the councils of the nation.

Stephen was not a very methodical student. He early developed erratic symptoms which ill accorded with the discipline of the school room. The first experiment with him was made when he was about five years old. He was sent, along with the rest of us, to an infant school taught by Mrs. Harvey, an elderly lady, and her daughter, Mrs. Morgan. He was called up for his first lesson in the letters of the alphabet. He had not proceeded far in this mystery when his patience gave out, and with a yell like that of a Comanche Indian, he bounded bareheaded into the road, and never stopped running and yelling until he reached home, half a mile away.

He had a faculty of reaching far ahead and grasping the scope of a lesson without apparent effort, which was remarkable and sometimes startling. He preferred to ramble among the woods and upon the hills by the three beautiful rivers of his home with his books and pencil, alone and thoughtful. Here the rustling of the leaves, the twitter of birds, the falling twigs and the rippling waters accorded harmoniously, and fell in grateful melody on his sensitive ear. He was always perfect in his recitations, however, and his shortcomings in discipline were pardoned by my mother and father, who appealed to his tutors for forbearance in his case.

When he was nine years old a Thespian company was formed, composed of boys of neighbor families, Robinsons, Cuddys, Kellys and Fosters.[16] The theatre was fitted up in a carriage house. All were stockholders except Stephen. He was regarded as a star performer, and was guaranteed a certain sum weekly. It was a very small sum, but it was sufficient to mark his superiority over the rest of the company. "Zip Coon," "Long-tailed Blue," "Coal-Black Rose" and "Jim Crow" were the only Ethiopian songs then known. His performance of these was so inimitable and true to nature that, child as he was, he was greeted with uproarious applause, and called back again and again every night the company gave an entertainment, which was three times

---

[16] William "Irish Bill" Robinson was the father of the Foster boys' friend Andrew Robinson. According to the 1850 US census, their teacher John Kelly had two sons—John and James—who were roughly their ages. The 1840 census indicates that James Cuddy had a son around their age as well.

a week.[17] They generally cleared enough to enable the whole party to buy tickets to the old Pittsburgh Theatre on Saturday nights, where they could be seen in the pit listening to the acting of Junius Brutus Booth, Augustus A. Addams, Edwin Forrest, Oxley, Conner, Logan, Proctor, William and John Sefton, Mrs. Drake and Mrs. Duff.

After the death of Mr. Stockton the Academy in Allegheny was continued by Mr. Kelly, and the same thorough system of education was kept up. Lindley Murray was the standard authority on grammar, and the "English Reader" by the same author was used for instruction in reading. Walker's Dictionary was the recognized lexicon. Hutton's Mathematics and the Western Calculator were relied on for arithmetic. These constituted the sources of primary education for the youth of Western Pennsylvania sixty-five years ago. Beyond them the Jefferson College at Canonsburg, Washington College at Washington, Pa., and the Western University at Pittsburgh afforded ample opportunities for treading the higher walks of learning. Education has always been regarded as of the greatest importance among the people of Western Pennsylvania, and nowhere in the world is the English language more generally correctly spoken than in that region.

After several years spent with Mr. Kelly, Stephen was placed under the care of Rev. Nathan Todd, a learned professor, who gave much attention to instruction in Latin and Greek, as well as in the English branches. Under the tutorship of Mr. Todd, Stephen made very satisfactory progress. Mr. Todd was not so rigid a disciplinarian as Mr. Kelly, but Stephen's conduct was always satisfactory. His sense of honor raised him above the meanness of taking advantage of leniency in his tutor. Mr. Todd remarked to my father that "Stephen was the most perfect gentleman he ever had for a pupil."

Stephen was very fond of our oldest brother William, whose business, as Chief Engineer of the Public Works (canals and railroads) of the State of Pennsylvania, kept him from home a great deal. William had a big, affectionate heart, and his little brother had many reasons for gratitude towards him for kind remembrances in the way of frequent presents and other tokens of affection. When he was thirteen years old brother William proposed to take him with him to Towanda in Bradford County, where his headquarters

---

[17] The "Ethiopian songs" listed by Morrison indicate that these young "thespians" modeled themselves on the solo blackface performers who traveled the Ohio River in the 1830s, such as Thomas "Daddy" Rice. At this point, the group of friends was not an amateur minstrel troupe. The term "minstrelsy" was first applied around 1843 to blackface ensemble shows with a semi-circle of performers and a fairly standardized series of acts.

were established at that time, and there being a good school near by (the academy at Athens), he stated that Stephen might go to school there if he wished. With the assent of our parents the offer was accepted. It was winter, and William drove him all the way to Towanda in his own sleigh, drawn by two horses. The distance traveled was over three hundred miles, but the sleighing was good, and, of course, it was a jolly journey for the little boy, especially as brother William was a man of great personal popularity, and had many friends and acquaintances everywhere along the road.[18] Ten years after that time brother William, John Edgar Thomson and Edward Miller were the engineers who built the great Pennsylvania Railroad. At the time of his death William was Vice-President of the company, and Mr. Thompson the President. Here "grateful memory" requires a tribute of affection to good brother William. With a heart as "tender and true" as the Douglas and as brave, he was a dutiful, loving son, and a generous, affectionate brother. He was a Christian firm in his devotion to his Redeemer, and his life's pathway was blazed with the marks of goodness. Always devoted to duty, he put on the harness of industry and usefulness at the age of sixteen years, and wore it continuously to the day of his death. He was honored in many ways by the people of his native State, and now the last survivor of his family is proud to write of him—he was an honor to his State and to his friends.

Long before this time Stephen had displayed some wonderful instances of precocity in musical attainments.

Sister Ann Eliza had a number of musical instruments, among the rest a guitar. When he was two years old he would lay this guitar on the floor and pick out harmonies from its strings. He called it his "ittly pizani" (little piano).

At the age of seven years he accidentally took up a flageolet in the music store of Smith & Mellor, in Pittsburgh, and in a few minutes he had so mastered its stops and sounds that he played Hail Columbia in perfect time and accent. He had never before handled either a flageolet or flute.

It was not long after this that he learned, unaided, to play beautifully on the flute. He had the faculty of bringing those deep resonant tones from the flute which distinguish the natural flutist from the mechanical performer. Later he learned to play remarkably well on the piano. He had but few teachers. Henry Kleber, of Pittsburgh, was one of them.[19] Stephen, however, needed only

---

[18] Morrison greatly exaggerates this distance. It is closer to two hundred miles.
[19] Kleber (1816–97) immigrated to Pittsburgh from Darmstadt in 1831. He was a prominent music teacher, conductor, performer, composer, and merchant in Pittsburgh and Allegheny. See Edward G. Baynham, "Henry Kleber, Early Pittsburgh Musician," *Western Pennsylvania History*

elementary instruction, for his rapid brain and quick perception scorned the slow progress by the beaten path, and he leaped forward to a comprehension of the whole scope of the instrument, by the force of his great musical genius.

But he was not content to rely on inspiration alone for his guidance in music. He studied deeply, and burned much midnight oil over the works of the masters, especially Mozart, Beethoven and Weber. They were his delight, and he struggled for years and sounded the profoundest depths of musical science. The simple melodies which he gave to the public were not the accidental rays from an uncultured brain, but were the result of the most thorough and laborious analyses of harmonies, and when he completed them and launched them on the world, he knew they would strike favorably the ear of the most critical as well as the unlearned in music.

It was while at Athens that he first gave publicity to an effort at composition. He wrote a piece of music for the college commencement, and arranged it for four flutes. He took himself the leading part, and three others of the students the remaining ones. He called it the Tioga Waltz. Its performance was very satisfactory to the audience, and was rewarded with much applause and an encore. It has never previously been published, and is only now reproduced from my memory, where it has lain for fifty years.[20]

After about a year spent at Athens he returned to his home in Allegheny, and afterwards entered Jefferson College at Canonsburg. During this part of his life he studied French and German, and became proficient in both under the instruction of Captain Jean Herbst, a Belgian gentleman, who came to reside in Pittsburgh.[21]

Stephen also became quite a creditable artist in water colors as an amusement, and some of his pictures are yet preserved with pride by his friends.

At sixteen years of age he produced his first published song. It was called "Open Thy Lattice, Love." The music only was his. It was published by George Willig of Baltimore.[22] During these years he was pursuing his studies in practical lines, and had not thought of devoting his time to musical composition and writing of poetry, as afterwards proved to be his destiny.

(September–December 1942): 113-20; and Jean Thomas, "Bullwhips and Bad Reviews: The Colorful Career of Music Man Henry Kleber," *Pittsburgh History* 81, no. 3 (Winter 1998): 108-17.

[20] Morrison remembered the tune and had it transcribed for his book. See Chapter 4, n20.

[21] Morrison declines to mention that Foster was at Jefferson College for only one week, and his wording is misleading. For example, an article appeared in the *Pittsburg Press* on August 19, 1900, titled "Story of Stephen C. Foster's Life," that dutifully summarized Morrison's book but claimed the songwriter studied French and German at the college.

[22] This incorrect publication date for "Open Thy Lattice Love" was a common error. The song actually appeared in 1844, the year Foster turned 18.

In 1845 a club of young men, friends of his, met twice a week at our house to practice songs in harmony under his leadership. They were, J. Cust Blair, Andrew L. Robinson, J. Harvey Davis, Robert P. McDowell, and myself. At that time negro melodies were very popular. After we had sung over and over again all the songs then in favor, he proposed that he would try and make some for us himself. His first effort was called "The Louisiana Belle." A week after this he produced the famous song of "Old Uncle Ned." "Uncle Ned" immediately became known and popular everywhere. Both the words and melody are remarkable. At the time he wrote "His Fingers Were Long Like de Cane in de Brake," he had never seen a canebrake, nor ever been below the mouth of the Ohio river, but the appropriateness of the simile instantly strikes everyone who has traveled down the Mississippi.

The next year Stephen went to Cincinnati at the solicitation of his brother Dunning, who was in business there, and acted as bookkeeper for him. He was a beautiful accountant, and his books kept at that time are models of neatness and accuracy. While in Cincinnati he wrote "Oh, Susanna," a song which soon became famous. There was then in Cincinnati in the music business, W. C. Peters, whom Stephen had known in Pittsburgh, and who had taught music in our family. Stephen had no idea at this time of deriving any emolument from his musical compositions, so he made a present of "Old Uncle Ned" and "Oh, Susanna" to Mr. Peters. The latter made ten thousand dollars out of them, and established a music publishing house which became the largest in the West. The fame of these two songs went around the world, and thousands sang and played them who never heard the name of the author or knew whence they came. In these two songs Stephen showed his intuitive knowledge of negro melody and pathos. He founded a new era in melody and ballad. The grotesque and clownish aspect of negro songs was softened, and ridicule began to merge into sympathy. Unknown to himself, he opened the way to the hearts of the people, which led to actual interest in the black man.[23]

His sympathies were, however, always with the lowly and the poor.[24] Once on a stormy winter night a little girl, sent on an errand, was run over by a

---

[23] This statement demonstrates that Morrison was influenced by Robert Peebles Nevin's *Atlantic* article (see Chapter 4). However, whereas Nevin implies that Foster intentionally set out to generate sympathy for enslaved people, Morrison claims this was not Foster's intention. Nevin chose to omit anything about Foster's conservative politics from his article, which misleadingly strengthens his argument. Morrison is only slightly more open about Foster's connections to the Democratic Party, but based on what we know of Foster's political views, Morrison's portrayal seems more accurate.

[24] Based on the previous sentence, the "however" in this statement suggests that Morrison did not believe his brother's sympathies were with people who were enslaved.

dray and killed. She had her head and face covered by a shawl to keep off the peltings of the storm, and in crossing the street she ran under the horse's feet. Stephen was dressed and about going to an evening party when he learned of the tragedy. He went immediately to the house of the little girl's father, who was a poor working man and a neighbor whom he esteemed. He gave up all thought of going to the party and remained all night with the dead child and her afflicted parents, endeavoring to afford the latter what comfort he could.

It was difficult to get him to go into society at all. He had a great aversion to its shams and glitter, and preferred the realities of his home and the quiet of his study. When he was eighteen years old, a lady who was an old friend of the family, gave a large party, and invited us all, and added, "tell Stephen to bring his flute with him." That settled it so far as he was concerned. He would not go a step. He said, "tell Mrs.—I will send my flute if she desires it." This dislike to being classed as a mere performer characterized him during his whole life, though he was not at all unsocial and willingly sang or played for the enjoyment of himself or others, if the occasions were spontaneous and not set up. He, however, often sang in chorus with others, upon occasions of concerts for charitable purposes, in Pittsburgh.[25]

While he was in Cincinnati, in 1847, he sent to me at my suggestion a song called "Way Down South Whar de Corn Grows," to be entered for a prize at an exhibition in Pittsburgh. The audience gave the applause and the approval to Stephen's song, but the prize, as usual, went to one of the troupe, for a vulgar plagiarism without any music or poetry in it. The next day, whilst I was in the United States Court taking out a copyright for Stephen's song, one of the troupe who had sung it appeared and asked for a copyright in his own name for the very same song. I informed Judge Irwin of the fraud, and the baffled rogue was glad to be allowed to depart unpunished.

Matters of this kind gave Stephen no concern, however. He was always indifferent about money or fame. It was perhaps fortunate for him that he had several older brothers, who, being practical business men, advised him in matters which he would not have realized the importance of.

After his return from Cincinnati in 1848,[26] he devoted himself to the study of music as a science and also perfected his knowledge of languages and other branches of learning. He had found one thing; that he had no taste for

---

[25] Foster is known to have sung with the Buchanan Glee Club and the Philharmonic Society. He may have also sang in the choir at the episcopal church.

[26] Foster returned from Cincinnati in late 1849 or early 1850.

a business life. About this time he wrote the music and words of "Nelly Was a Lady," which was published by Firth, Pond & Co. of New York. Offers began to come to him for his compositions, which were being sung and sought for all over the world.

While, as I said before, he never aspired to greatness as a performer, his voice was a true and pleasing baritone, sonorous and sympathetic. When he sang his own songs, which he did to a perfection no one else could attain, there was a plaintive sweetness in his tone and accent which sometimes drew tears from listeners' eyes.

He would sit at home in the evening at the piano and improvise by the hour beautiful strains and harmonies which he did not preserve, but let them float away like fragrant flowers cast upon the flowing water. Occasionally he would vary his occupation by singing in plaintive tones one of his own or other favorite songs. Of the latter class he much admired the "May Queen" of Tennyson, and the music as composed by Mr. Dempster. His rendering of the verse "Tonight I saw the sun set, he set and left behind," etc., was truly pathetic.[27] At times tears could be seen on his cheeks as he sang this song, so sensitive was his nature to the influence of true poetry combined with music. I usually sat near him on these occasions and listened quietly with profound delight. Sometimes he would whirl round on the piano stool and converse a few moments with me, then resume his improvisations and his singing. Through the long years of the past those pleasing sounds, and the recollection of those "evenings at home," still linger gratefully in my memory.

And yet this sensitive man had the nerve and courage of a lion physically. From earliest childhood he was noted for his courage, coolness and skill in the combats which continually occur among boys of the same town. As he grew up, no odds ever seemed to awe him. He was known as one who must be let alone, and was held in high respect accordingly.

One night as he was returning home from Pittsburgh to Allegheny, he found at the end of the bridge two brutes abusing and beating a drunken man. He of course interfered, and fought them both, rough and tumble all over the street. He managed to pick up a piece of a board in the scramble, with which he beat one almost senseless and chased the other ingloriously from the field. A knife wound on the cheek, received in the encounter, left a scar which went with him to his grave.[28]

---

[27] Foster and Shiras appended their own verses.
[28] Billy Hamilton offers two additional anecdotes about Foster's involvement in conflicts in the street (see Chapter 20).

He had certain favorites among his neighbors and friends whom he preferred to have assist him in singing the choruses of his songs while they were in course of preparation. These he chose because of the excellence of their voices and correct method of singing.

Among them Mrs. Andrew L. Robinson, Mrs. John Mitchell and Miss Jessie Lightner were the most conspicuous. For these reasons, Miss Sophie Marshall, afterwards Mrs. Harry Miller, was a favorite whilst he resided in Cincinnati. He was exceedingly exact in rehearsal, and these ladies understood his methods better than any others.

He always (with very rare exceptions) wrote the words as well as the music of his songs. He said the difficulty of harmonizing sounds with words rendered this necessary, though he would have often gladly dispensed with the writing of the words if he could.

He delighted in playing accompaniments on the flute to the singing and playing on the piano of his sister or one of his lady friends. These little concerts were very delightful and gave the greatest pleasure to the household. As the song went on he would improvise, without the slightest hesitation or difficulty, the most beautiful variations upon its musical theme.

While in Cincinnati he met Miss Sophie Marshall, the grand-daughter of Michael P. Cassilly of that city, a former Pittsburgher, who was an old friend of our family. Miss Marshall possessed a beautiful soprano voice and sang with much sweetness and taste. She was a great favorite in society. For her he wrote, "Stay, Summer Breath," which was among his earliest sentimental productions.

While so many of his best songs are what are called Plantation Melodies, he had no preference for that style of composition. His poetic fancy ran rather to sentimental songs. Many of these gained great popularity and sold in immense numbers—and, indeed, continue to sell largely at the present time—such as "Gentle Annie," "Laura Lee," "Willie, We Have Missed You," "Ellen Bayne," "Old Dog Tray," "Come Where My Love Lies Dreaming," "Ah, May The Red Rose Live Always," etc. Melodies appeared to dance through his brain continually. Often at night he would get out of bed, light a candle and jot down some notes of a melody on a piece of paper, then retire again to bed and to sleep.

Firth, Pond & Co., of New York, were the first to make a regular arrangement with him for publishing his music, paying him a royalty of three cents for each copy printed.

F. D. Benteen, of Baltimore, also made a contract with him of the same nature. Both of these contracts proved mutually satisfactory and profitable to all parties.

He now gave his whole attention to either the study or composition of music. He located himself in a back room at the top of the house, and while in there he locked the door to every one but his mother.

He was very simple in his tastes, and no matter how well his income justified it, he shrank from everything like display. The simplest forms of food satisfied him. Indeed, he never appeared to care what was set before him on the table. If it appeased hunger it was all he cared for. His companions were seldom ever musicians. Outside of his own studies and performances he seemed to prefer to get away from music and musical topics. But he was very fond of the society of cultured people and men of genius in walks entirely different from his own.

In 1850 he was married to Miss Jane Denny McDowell, daughter of Dr. Andrew N. McDowell, one of the leading physicians of Pittsburgh. Dr. McDowell was the grandson of Professor McDowell, who was, in 1799, President of the College at Annapolis, Md.[29] A letter from George Washington, addressed in that year to Prof. McDowell, must be among the last letters written by the great man. In it Washington says:

> "Consequent of a letter I have received from Mr. Stuart I have been induced to confide to your care the young gentleman who will deliver this letter (George Washington Parke Custis). You will find him intelligent, truthful and moral, and I have reason to hope he will live to justify the best expectations of his friends, and to be useful in the councils of his country."

After his marriage, Stephen received very flattering offers from the publishers in New York, and strong inducements to make that city his home. He removed there and had every favorable prospect that a young man could hope for. He was paid a certain sum for every song he might choose to write, besides a royalty on the copies printed.

He went to house-keeping and liked New York very much. But after a year the old fondness for home and mother began to be too strong for him to overcome. One day he suddenly proposed to his wife that they return to Pittsburgh. He brought a dealer to the house, sold out everything in the way

---

[29] John McDowell was president of St. John's College at Annapolis from 1789 to 1806.

of furniture, and within twenty-four hours was on the road to the home of his father in Allegheny. He arrived late at night and was not expected. When he rang the bell his mother was awakened and knew his footsteps on the porch. She arose immediately and went down herself to let him in. As she passed through the hall she called out, "Is that my dear son come back again?" Her voice so affected him that when she opened the door she found him sitting on the little porch-bench weeping like a child.[30]

His love for his mother amounted to adoration. She was to him an angelic creature. There is not one reference to mother in the homely words in which clothed his balance but came direct from his heart and symbolized his own feelings.[31]

Ah, what a mother was that! Handsome, brilliant, and admired, she was the soul of purity, truth and Christian virtue. Her example shone upon her household as a continual light from heaven. No unkind word ever passed between any members of that family, for strife was repelled and anger washed away by the pure stream of love that emanated from her presence. Her precepts were listened to by her children with the reverence due to oracular utterances, and were never unheeded. Whilst she was a devout Christian, she had no method in her teachings, no rules for daily or hourly observance. An unquestioning faith in the Redeemer, and charity in all things, was her rule. She was very fond of entertaining her children with historical facts or recitations from the works of the best authors, which her wonderfully retentive memory enabled her to draw on to any extent. Mother's room was the favorite spot to all the household. It was here that all assembled in the evenings, and, gathering round her chair or couch, would listen with rapt attention to her words of wisdom and instruction.

Her discourses abounded in illustrations of the goodness of God and the necessity for our recognizing the fact that dependence on Him alone constitutes the happiness of mankind. Sometimes she would say, almost abruptly, "And now, my children, kneel down here around me and let us pray to our heavenly Father."

And there on the floor around that blessed mother her children, old and young, threw themselves and listened to her beautiful, touching prayers in their behalf. Rising, her face resumed its sweet, sunny aspect, and everything

---

[30] John Mahon told a different version of this story (see Chapter 5).

[31] Morrison's autobiographical interpretation of Foster's many "mother songs" may well be accurate. But "mother songs" were a popular type of sentimental song, so Foster wrote them not just to express his feelings for his mother but because they were in demand on the marketplace.

went on as though it was the most natural thing in the world to fall down and worship God at any time. Her death, which occurred in January, 1855, created a void in the household which, as beautifully expressed in one of Stephen's songs, "could never be filled."

The following obituary, written by that accomplished lawyer and patriotic soldier, Col. Samuel W. Black, fittingly expresses the general sentiment:

"This respected and beloved lady was buried on Saturday. She died suddenly, without warning, but not unprepared. Being very merciful herself, she trusted faithfully in the mercy of her Redeemer. Mrs. Foster was uncommonly gifted, and endowed with excellent good sense and great refinement. Wisdom and sound judgment accompanied her all her life and sparkled every day with the brightness of extravagant genius. Her intellect is remembered with just admiration, but her life is cherished for her heart's sake. The little children of our two cities will long lament their lost friend. But the especial grief of this affliction is within her own house and home. There the wife who never faltered in the fondest exercise of her duty and devotion has quickened her eager step for the last time. By the bedside of him whom God has stricken, other eyes and hands must perform the ministration of love. The faithful servants that looked upon her as a mother rather than a mistress will sigh for another home like theirs with her. And her children, who have fulfilled by affectionate obedience the first commandment with promise, reciprocating love with love, will tell to one another at the fireside how vacant it looks because she is not there. Sacred to sorrow is the day of her death."

"'She stretched out her hand to the poor; yea, she reached forth her hands to the needy. Her children arise up and call her blessed.'"

Stephen never went away from home to stay, again, as long as his mother and father lived. The latter was an invalid, and was confined to his room for four years before his death, which took place July 27, 1855. Stephen was attentive and devoted to his sick father as long as the latter lived. The sentiment of the poetry in the song of "Massa's in de Cold Ground," expresses his own experience and feelings.[32]

One day in 1851, Stephen came into my office, on the bank of the Monongahela, Pittsburgh, and said to me, "What is a good name of two syllables for a Southern river? I want to use it in this new song of "Old Folks at Home.'" I asked him how Yazoo would do. "Oh," said he, "that has been used before."

---

[32] This statement calls into question Morrison's autobiographical reading of his brother's songs because Foster wrote "Massa's in de Cold Ground" in 1851 and 1852, years before his father's death.

I then suggested Pedee. "Oh, pshaw," he replied, "I won't have that." I then took down an atlas from the top of my desk and opened the map of the United States. We both looked over it and my finger stopped at the "Swanee," a little river in Florida emptying into the Gulf of Mexico. "That's it, that's it exactly," exclaimed he delighted, as he wrote the name down; and the song was finished, commencing, "Way Down Upon de Swanee Ribber." He left the office, as was his custom, abruptly, without saying another word, and I resumed my work.

Just at that time he received a letter from E. P. Christy, of New York, who was conducting very popular Negro Melody Concerts, asking him if he would write a song for Christy which the latter might sing before it was published. Stephen showed me the letter and asked me what he should do. I said to him, "Don't let him do it unless he pays you."

At his request I drew up a form of agreement for Christy to sign, stipulating to pay Stephen five hundred dollars for the privilege he asked.[33] This was forwarded to Christy and return mail brought it back duly signed by the latter. The song sent happened to be the "Old Folks at Home." It was in this manner that Christy's name came to appear on the first edition of the "Old Folks at Home." Stephen sent the manuscript to his publishers, Firth, Pond & Co., who paid him and his heirs the royalty. The publishers furnished Christy an advance copy of the song before publication.

An old friend of ours, Col. Matthew I. Stewart, gave Stephen a handsome setter dog, which for a long time was his constant companion. We lived upon the East Common of Allegheny, a wide open space, now improved into a beautiful park. Stephen often watched this dog with much pleasure, playing with the children on the Common. When he wrote of "Old Dog Tray," he put into verse and song the sentiments elicited by remembrances of this faithful dog.

He was easily disturbed from sleep at night and used every precaution to be as quiet as possible. A strange dog got into one of the back buildings and howled at intervals. Stephen finally could endure it no longer, and sallying forth partly dressed, with a poker in his hand, he pounded the poor dog away from the neighborhood. The family had a good laugh at the author of "Old Dog Tray," the next day.

On another occasion he had bought a small clock, run by springs, and set it on the mantelpiece of his chamber. The thing had a very loud tick, and there was no way of stopping it after it was once wound up. He could not get

---

[33] As we have seen, Christy actually paid Foster $15. It is possible that Morrison is not lying, per se, but is choosing not to tell the whole truth. If he helped Foster write up a contract stipulating a $500 fee, he may have chosen to omit that Christy rejected their terms and agreed to only $15.

to sleep, for the clock, with its monotonous clang, drove slumber away. He wrapped a blanket around it, and shut it up in a bureau drawer. But the dull throbbing sound which reached his ears from that retreat was, as he said, worse than the loud, open, defiant tick from the mantelpiece. He then lit a candle, and took it down to the dining-room cupboard, but still he could hear it faintly. At length, in despair, he carried the ticking monster down to the cellar, in the profoundest depths of which he covered it with a washtub; and then, returning to his room, carefully closed every door behind him, and at last found rest.

When Stephen was a child, my father had a mulatto bound-girl named Olivia Pise, the illegitimate daughter of a West India Frenchman, who taught dancing to the upper circles of Pittsburgh society early in the present century [1800s]. "Lieve," as she was called, was a devout Christian and a member of a church of shouting colored people. The little boy was fond of their singing and boisterous devotions. She was permitted to often take Stephen to church with her. Here he stored up in his mind "many a gem of purest ray serene," drawn from these caves of negro melody. A number of strains heard there, and which, he said to me, were too good to be lost, have been preserved by him, short scraps of which were incorporated in two of his songs, "Hard Times Come Again No More" and "Oh, Boys, Carry Me 'Long."[34]

When he was from ten to thirteen years old, he visited a great deal an old uncle, John Struthers, who had been a surveyor, hunter, and Indian fighter in the first settlement of the country, and who now, past eighty years old, was very fond of Stephen, and always pleased to welcome him to his log house in the Northwest territory. Old Uncle Struthers had dogs and rifles, and himself would lead the hunt at night for 'coons, opossums, and such like nocturnal game.[35] It was tame work to the old pioneer, who had been used to bears, panthers and hostile Indians. These hunts and the stories of adventure told by his aged relative, of course gave great pleasure to Stephen, and kindled the flame of his vivid fancy. One cold day, he was missed from the house, and was hunted for everywhere outside. At last his uncle discovered him sitting up to

---

[34] Morrison's story resembles Birdseye's claims about Black musicians influencing Foster. Although Foster participated in a music industry that stole from Black people their right to self-representation, it has never been determined that he stole any actual melodies. Musicologists have never found the melodic sources of "Hard Times" and "Oh, Boys" to which Morrison alludes. It is possible that Morrison stretched the truth to give the songs a veneer of authenticity.

[35] Morrison might be suggesting that the line in "My Old Kentucky Home" about hunting "no more for the possum and the coon" reflects Foster's personal nostalgia for his childhood days spent with Old Uncle Struthers.

his neck in a pile of chaff, watching the movements of the chickens and other barnyard animals—"just thinking," as he briefly explained. The old gentleman always prophesied that Stephen, who even then displayed great originality and musical talent, would be something famous if he lived to be a man.

At the close of February, 1852, brother Dunning McNair Foster came to Pittsburgh with his steamboat, the James Millingar, to load a cargo for New Orleans. Stephen and his wife, Mr. and Mrs. Andrew L. Robinson, Miss Jessie Lightner, Mrs. William Robinson and her daughter, Miss Mary Ann, embarked with him on a pleasure trip to New Orleans. Miss Louisa Walker and her two brothers joined them at Cincinnati. There was a good deal of musical ability in the party, and they made the trip pleasant, not only for themselves but for the other passengers as well.

On this voyage Stephen observed a good many incidents of Southern life, which he afterwards utilized as points for poetical simile in songs. On the return trip, brother Dunning found it would be more profitable to reship his freight and passengers at Cincinnati and return from there to New Orleans. They were transferred to Captain Charles W. Batchelor's magnificent new boat, the peerless Allegheny, and arrived in Pittsburgh on her. I had met them at Cincinnati, and we were so well treated on the Allegheny that everybody on the boat joined in a complimentary card of thanks to Captain Batchelor. In those days the captains and other officers of the steamboats on the Western rivers regarded the passengers as their guests, and treated them accordingly. These officers necessarily had to be gentlemen, or otherwise they could not continue long in the trade.

Wonderful men were these old-time river commanders. Combinations of shrewd business management, daring seamanship, physical courage, and manners fit for the most refined society. They are nearly all gone now. Before long the landing bell will sound and the gangplank be run out for the last of them to take his place "among the silent sleepers."

During the period between 1853 and 1860 Stephen remained at home, and many of his sentimental songs were written, such as "Willie We Have Missed You," "Gentle Annie," and others.[36]

---

[36] Foster resided in William Jr.'s Allegheny house from 1854 until April 1, 1857, when William sold the house. At that point, Foster struggled to make ends meet, and the family stayed in various boarding houses and hotels, sometimes going their separate ways. Morrison is silent on any hardships his brother endured.

In early 1853, Foster traveled to New York where Richard Storrs Willis, the editor of the *Musical World* and an ally of Firth, Pond & Co., discouraged him from writing minstrel songs because he believed respectable families were less likely to purchase his sheet music. But whereas Foster turned

In 1860 he again received a profitable offer from Firth, Pond & Co., his publishers, and he went to New York, remaining there until his death.[37] In January, 1864, while at the American Hotel, he was taken with an ague and fever.[38] After two or three days he arose, and while washing himself he fainted and fell across the washbasin, which broke and cut a gash in his neck and face. He lay there insensible and bleeding until discovered by the chambermaid who was bringing the towels he had asked for to the room. She called for assistance and he was placed in bed again. On recovering his senses he asked that he be sent to a hospital. Accordingly he was taken to Bellevue Hospital. He was so much weakened by fever and loss of blood that he did not rally. On the 13th of January he died peacefully and quietly. Under request of his family his body was immediately taken to an undertaker's, by direction, of Col. William A. Pond, and placed in an iron coffin.[39] On arrival of his brother, Henry Baldwin Foster, and myself, his remains were taken by us to Pittsburgh, accompanied by his wife. The Pennsylvania Railroad Company carried the party free of charge, and the Adams Express Company declined to receive pay for transporting his body.

On the 20th of January the funeral services were held in Trinity church, the rector, Rev. E. C. Swope, officiating. A special choir, under direction of his old friend, Henry Kleber, sang "Vital Spark of Heavenly Flame" and other beautiful selections. At the gate of the Allegheny Cemetery the funeral cortege was met by a volunteer band of the best musicians of Pittsburgh, who on the march and at the grave performed "Come Where My Love Lies Dreaming," "Old Folks at Home," and other selections of his music. He left one child, a daughter Marion, the wife of Mr. Walter Welsh.

His body lies beside the mother and father he loved so much and near the spot where he was born. His grave is marked by a simple marble tombstone, inscribed on which are the words:

---

away from writing songs that were explicitly about Black characters, he turned to writing songs—such as "Hard Times Come Again No More"—that lent themselves to blackface performance while not offending the sensibilities of "respectable" consumers. Foster returned to overtly racial songs in 1860.

[37] Morrison makes it seem as if Foster went to New York because of a profitable offer from Firth, Pond & Co. But he seems to have traveled to New York because his contract had expired and Firth, Pond & Co. had not yet offered him a new one.

[38] The name of his place of residence was the American House (see Chapter 3, n17).

[39] This contradicts Cooper's account of how Foster's body "had been sent down into the morgue, among the nameless dead," through which Cooper had to search to identify his friend's corpse (see Chapter 37). Morrison's omission makes sense in light of his proclivity for leaving out details that portrayed Foster as anything but high-class, famous, brilliant, gentlemanly, and affable.

## STEPHEN C. FOSTER, OF PITTSBURGH.
Born July 4, 1826;
Died January 13, 1864.

His monument is not grand but it is sufficient. His works will perpetuate his fame and story longer than the chiseled or moulded art of man's hands could do it.[40]

He was named after Stephen Collins, the young son of Thomas Collins, Esq., a leading member of the Pittsburgh bar. Mrs. Collins was a dear friend of my mother, and her only son Stephen had died at the age of twelve years, just before my brother Stephen was born.

In an article contributed to one of the leading magazines of the country, his old friend, Robert P. Nevin, wrote of him:

> "In the true estimate of genius its achievements only approximate the highest standard of excellence as they are representative, or illustrative of important truth. They are only great as they are good. If Mr. Foster's art embodied no higher idea than the vulgar notion of the negro—as a thing of tricks and antics—then it might have proved a tolerable catch-penny affair, and commanded an admiration among boys of various growths, until its novelty wore off. But the art in his hands teemed with a nobler significance. It dealt in its simplicity with universal sympathies and taught us all to feel with the colored man the lowly joys and sorrows it celebrated. May the time be far in the future ere lips will fail to move to its music, or hearts to respond to its influence, and may we who owe him so much, preserve gratefully the memory of the master, STEPHEN COLLINS FOSTER."[41]

---

[40] By including these details of his gravesite, Morrison once again responds to Will S. Hays's incorrect assertion that he did not even have a simple headstone.

[41] By giving Nevin the last word, Morrison strongly embraces Nevin's revision of Frederick Douglass's comments about two of Foster's songs furthering the abolitionist cause. In one sense, Nevin and Morrison do not go so far as Douglass; they assert his music stirred sympathy for the enslaved but not abolitionist sympathies. In another sense, though, they extend Douglass's claims about two of Foster's songs to all his songs. Both shifts were favorable to Foster's memory by helping *all* his music appeal to a wide range of political sensibilities.

Morrison also revised Nevin's words without indicating he did so. In the original passage, Nevin wrote about minstrelsy portraying the Black person as "a man-monkey" and "a funny specimen of superior gorilla." He does not state that Foster's music does not portray Black people in this way but instead asserts it *also* "teemed with a nobler significance." By revising these comments, Morrison further distanced his brother from minstrelsy's "tricks and antics" that he feared "respectable" people disapproved of.

# 25
# An Interview with the "Foster Serenaders" (1900)

**Introduction**

*In this article, which is not found in the Foster Hall Collection, a reporter paraphrased reminiscences shared by unnamed people who had participated in minstrel performances with Foster in the 1830s and '40s. At least some of the testimony came from Patrick F. Kane (1827–1905). Born in Ireland, Kane moved with his family in 1829 to Allegheny, where he resided until he removed to California in 1849. He returned to Allegheny in the 1870s, opening a tobacco store at 232 Third Avenue, where this interview took place.*

*Besides this testimony, no documents link Kane to Foster, but several people mentioned in the article were known associates of the composer. Morrison and Evelyn Foster Morneweck confirm that the Cuddy boys and Robinsons were members of the minstrel troupe. William S. Cuddy was exactly Foster's age, born in Allegheny in 1826. William "Irish Bill" Robinson lived across Allegheny Commons park from the Fosters and was the father of the songwriter's good friend Andrew Robinson. William Robinson was the first mayor of Allegheny City, and he was succeeded by William Foster Sr. In 1849, Andrew Robinson married Foster's neighbor Susan Pentland.*

*In addition to minstrelsy, this article describes the neighborhood boys as engaging in baseball. Although it is unclear if Foster participated—Nevin had stated that he was "not addicted to the active sports or any of the more vigorous habits of boys of his age"—the boys of the neighborhood playing ball is affirmed by Morrison. Describing one of their boyhood teachers, John Kelly, he writes that "he was of genial disposition and out of school played ball and prisoner's base with the boys" (see Chapter 24). John Kelly was the father of two boys—James and John—who were the Foster boys' ages and, Morrison informs us, participated in these blackface shows.*

*Formulating Foster.* Christopher Lynch, Oxford University Press. © Oxford University Press 2025.
DOI: 10.1093/9780197811726.003.0026

*The author of the article gives an incorrect name for the troupe. The Foster Serenaders was a local group that performed to raise money for charities in the 1870s, the decade after Foster's death. If there was a name for the amateur "troupe," it has long been forgotten.*

## *Pittsburg Press,* July 22, 1900.

How many organizations can you enumerate formed 56 years ago, half of whose original membership or more is still in being? The Foster Serenaders, organized in 1844, can still count on their muster roll if it were called at least half of the original membership, though the chief died in early life. This notwithstanding some of the membership participated in two bloody wars. The remaining members are now so widely scattered that they are not likely to celebrate a reunion.

In its primitive days Pittsburg was relatively more important, compared with contiguous territory, than it is to-day with all its multi-millionaires and its hundreds of acres of rolling hills, steel mills, glass houses, blast furnaces and merchant princes, and the Pittsburg boy of half a century ago or more had more incentive for ambition than he has today. There were more fields to conquer then within the limits of Uncle Sam's dominion than there are to-day on the whole planet. Then the great American desert was less known and less exploited than is the Sahara to-day, and no young man of grit then reconciled himself to the idea that he should pass through life a mere clerk or bookkeeper in some commercial house, as the majority are compelled to do at present. Though he might enter some establishment as a sweeper-out or errand boy, he expected to become a partner in due time.

Many of those old time boys have had notable careers that the world knows little about and their vitality is astonishing, many who began active life more than half a century ago still being in harness. Some of them gathered in the store of P. F. Kane, 232 Third avenue, some evenings since. They were in a reminiscent mood and talked of their recollections of the '40's and localities that will some day be marked by tablets or other memorials.

Notable among the institutions of Pittsburg's past were the Stephen C. Foster Serenaders. Though Foster's melodies are sung in every household, few know that the Serenaders were the first local "burnt cork" institution of the city. Strictly speaking, they belonged to Allegheny, but at that time Alleghenians had not got jealous of its people registering as from Pittsburg when they traveled. The Foster Serenaders were composed of aristocrats, as a rule—a sort of troubadour band that sang in front of the houses of the elite and were certain of an invitation to enter and partake of the best cheer. The master spirit of the organization was S. C. Foster. All were loyal to him and sang "Uncle Ned" and other songs which had then but local fame, as he had, as yet found no encouragement from publishing houses.

The first public performance of the "Serenaders" was given in the carriage house of 'Squire William Robinson (Irish Billy), in the rear of his residence, on the corner of Liberty street and Cedar avenue, Allegheny. P. F. Kane, then a lad of 14, was property man, and he states that he had his hands full to secure the essentials for a public performance. No treasurer was needed. Mrs. Cuddy furnished the drop curtain, a green crumb cloth, and the chairs ranged from the wood-bottom kitchen to the most elaborately upholstered seat to be found in the surrounding neighborhood. As the audience consisted of the elite of Pittsburg and "Alleghenytown," there were no reserved seats, and the different kinds of chairs were so mixed that all had to take such accommodation as could be secured by priority. Among the singers were S. C. Foster, his brother, H. Morrison Foster, then dubbed by his democratic associates "Mitt," John Fitzsimmons, now a prominent Pittsburg and Philadelphia property holder, and several others, whose names had faded from the recollection of the gathering. W. S. Cuddy, now paymaster of the Union Pacific railway, rattled the bones and his family, with the Grays, Leeches, Hannas, Curtis, Parks and Breckenridges, leading people at that time, constituted the audience. Mr. Kane says everything was encored, and "Judy Figg," whose real name is refused, divided the honors with the singers. "Judy's" specialty was dancing of the "turnabout-and-wheel-about-Jim-Crow" variety.

At this time the boys played "town-ball," since transformed into baseball. Before the game was emasculated there might be 50 on a side, the more the merrier, and the batter could use a broomstick, wagon spoke or an oar-stem for a bat, just as his fancy dictated. The ball was often of solid rubber, and might be knocked over the entire boundary of what was then "Alleghenytown," now a part of Allegheny. The boys of the rival municipalities then expended a part of their energy in pitched battles, especially on muster days, when Col. Dewsnap was a captain of the militia. These were the days when Pat Murphy and Johnny Triangle were in their prime. Elderly citizens will recollect Johnny's specialty, "Polly put the kettle on." Many of the old-time Pittsburg boys were stage-struck and in the Kane family, in addition to Patrick F., who was a Foster serenader, his brother Michael played for a time in the theater in Baxter's alley, a thoroughfare running east as far as Virgin alley, midway between Market and Wood streets. Fifth avenue was little more than a cowpath in 1844, and Third avenue was then the main street of the city. Henry Kane, a brother of Patrick and Michael, broke away from the democratic faith of the family, and was an abolitionist and a member of the underground railway, and with Charles B. Taylor, a real estate dealer, helped darkies on their way to the polar regions, greatly to the scandal of the Kane family. Henry was a partner in the merchant tailoring firm of Kane & Duffy, 14 St. Clair, now Sixth street. Michael Kane died in California last November. He was one of the Argonauts who went out in 1849. Patrick, a boy of 19, also being one of the company. James Kane was prominent in military circles. He was a veteran of the Mexican war, and after the war was sent to Mexico to get the body of Col. Roberts, of the Second Pennsylvania regiment. Subsequently he joined his brothers in California, and became prominent in mining enterprises.

M. V. B. D.

# 26
# An Interview with Rachel E. Woods (1900)

## Introduction

*Rachel Woods was the middle of the three daughters of the Keller family. The Kellers first resided near the Foster family's cottage in Lawrenceville. The Fosters moved to Allegheny in the early 1830s, and the Kellers eventually moved to Penn Avenue in Pittsburgh; but the families remained close. Foster dedicated "There's a Good Time Coming" to Mary Keller, the youngest of the girls. After she died unexpectedly in late 1846, he wrote "Where Is Thy Spirit Mary?" in her memory, giving a manuscript copy of the song to Rachel, who kept it among her personal possessions. It was brought to public attention and first published in 1895.*

*After Rachel married Harry Woods, Foster dedicated "Farewell Old Cottage" and "Sadly to Mine Heart Appealing" to "Mrs. Harry Woods" in 1851 and 1858, respectively. The first song may have marked the Kellers' move from the arcadian Lawrenceville to Penn Avenue in the city. In 1855, Rachel and Harry moved to the Woods's house in the Hazelwood neighborhood of Pittsburgh. According to Rachel, Foster visited regularly, often with his friend William Henry McCarthy, who wrote the lyrics for his songs "Parthenia to Ingomar," "For Thee, Love, For Thee," and "Linda Has Departed."*

*Rachel also tells us Foster was inspired to write the minstrel song "Nelly Bly" upon meeting a Black "servant" who worked for the Woods family. Since she was the daughter of an enslaved woman, in accordance with Pennsylvania's Gradual Abolition Act she was involuntarily enslaved by the Woods family for the first twenty-eight years of her life. Like many people who were term-enslaved, she probably had few options upon the completion of her twenty-eight-year term and remained in service to the Woods family. Census records reveal that her real name was Nellie Brown. Decades after this article was published, the anecdote about "Nelly Bly" was plagiarized nearly verbatim by Sarepta Kussart in* The Early History of the Fifteenth

*Formulating Foster*. Christopher Lynch, Oxford University Press. © Oxford University Press 2025.
DOI: 10.1093/9780197811726.003.0027

Ward of the City of Pittsburgh *and again by Morneweck in* Chronicles of Stephen Foster's Family.[1]

## *Pittsburg Press*, August 24, 1900.

The unveiling of the Stephen C. Foster memorial erected by the Press Foster fund, at Highland park, Wednesday, September 12, has a deeply personal interest for Mrs. Rachel E. Woods, of Hazelwood. Mrs. Woods was the first to play "Old Folks at Home" upon the pianoforte, at the request of the composer, and the old piano still occupies an honored place in the sitting room of the Woods residence. Mrs. Woods recalls the Pittsburg of Foster's day by telling of the composition of "Nelly Bly," one of Foster's best known lighter pieces. At that time Mr. and Mrs. Woods lived at the corner of Fifth street and Penn avenue, where Horne's store now stands. This was then the fashionable resident part of the town, and Hazelwood was, as Mrs. Woods says, "almost as far as the mountains." Foster was a frequent and delightful visitor to the Woods home and often came in the evenings with his guitar and serenaded the ladies of the household from the front steps.

It was while thus one evening that Nelly Bly, the handsome colored servant of Mrs. Woods, put her head out of the coal cellar door to hear the music and was detected by Foster, who built the song name after her out of the incident.

Later, when the Woods family moved to Tullymet, or the present homestead in Hazelwood, Foster, accompanied by his friend [William Henry] McCarthy, a well-known actor, frequently paid the house a visit. Mrs. Woods' sister, Miss Keller, died suddenly a few days before the day fixed for her marriage, and the unusually sad circumstances led Foster to compose "Where Is Thy Spirit, Mary" and dedicate it to her memory. Mrs. Woods herself was the subject of another melody, "Sadly to Mine Heart Appealing." She was invariably called upon by Mr. Foster to try the compositions before they were made public and, being an excellent pianist, gave the composer many valuable criticisms.

Mrs. Woods remembers the poet as a most agreeable young man, full of excellent spirits and of genial and lovable nature. She gave some of his original scores for the benefit of the *Press* Fund when the movement was begun

---

[1] Sarepta Kussart, *The Early History of the Fifteenth Ward of the City of Pittsburgh* (Suburban Printing, 1925), 36–37. Morneweck, *Chronicles*, vol. 2, 373–74.

three years ago and is much gratified with the design and successful termination of the project. Mr. Foster's work had no more ardent admirers than Mrs. Woods and her two daughters and among the treasured relics of the Pittsburg of ante-bellum days preserved by them none is more honored than Foster's original scores and the piano and guitar which had so often been touched by the composer's hands.

Nelly Bly was the daughter of a slave held by the Woods family and remained with the family long after slavery became a thing of the past. She died many years ago at an advanced age and was always proud of Mr. Foster's melody dedicated in her name.

# 27
# An Interview with the Daughter of a Friend (1900)

**Introduction**

*In the following article, Francis Winons (Mrs. F. C. Winons) states that her father, Thomas Fletcher Grubbs, owned one of Allegheny City's first photography studios and that Foster was a frequent visitor. Grubbs, born in 1841, is listed as a photographer in the 1860 US Census, and an 1862 city directory indicates that he was an artist with a studio in Allegheny. His artistic career appears to have been short-lived because an 1864 directory indicates that his occupation was "grocer." But it is nevertheless plausible that Foster visited his studio before he removed to New York. However, Winons's claim that she was in possession of oil paintings rendered by the songwriter at her father's studio are more farfetched.*

*The article is not in the Foster Hall Collection, but Foster Hall was aware of her claims. John Tasker Howard and Josiah K. Lilly traveled to Pittsburgh in June of 1931. Howard's notebook from the trip includes the following note: "See if Mrs. F. C. Winons of Hazelwood, Penn. has 2 oil landscapes of S. C. F."[1] It is unknown if Howard was able to see the paintings, but the fact that Foster Hall never mentioned them publicly suggests that Foster Hall declined to preserve the article in the collection because he determined there was little merit to Winons's claims.*

---

[1] John Tasker Howard, "Questions for Pittsburgh for J. K.'s trip to Pitts. In June," notebook, FHC, unprocessed folder labeled "Next Pittsburgh Visit." He also took notes on an article in the *Pittsburg Press* dated September 12, 1900: "Mrs. F. C. Winons of Hazelwood has 2 oil landscapes painted by S. C. F. for her father, T. Fletcher Grubb, who was the leading photographer in Allegheny."

*Formulating Foster.* Christopher Lynch, Oxford University Press. © Oxford University Press 2025.
DOI: 10.1093/9780197811726.003.0028

## *Pittsburg Press*, August 30, 1900.

It is not generally known that in addition to his musical genius, Stephen C. Foster also had a talent for painting. Mrs. F. C. Winons, of Chatworth and Berwick avenues, Hazelwood, has two paintings by Foster, which are in an excellent state of preservation, and much prized by their owner.

The pictures were given to Mrs. Winons's father, T. Fletcher Grubbs, at one time a well-known Allegheny photographer, he being, in fact, one of the earliest photographers in that city. Foster was a particular friend of Mr. Grubbs, and was a frequent visitor to his studio. It was on one of these visits that the composer found fault with some paintings on exhibition, and offered to show Mr. Grubbs what he could do with the brush and palette. Mr. Grubbs, not knowing of Foster's skill in this line, had taken the proposition as a joke, and had dismissed it from his memory, when one morning the composer appeared in the studio with these paintings under his arm.

Mrs. Winons kindly consented to the *Press* staff photographer taking the accompanying pictures of the paintings. They are framed in the original heavy gilt moulding, in which they were enclosed when presented to Mr. Grubbs by the artist. Mr. Grubbs had carefully treasured the paintings, which are in oil, all his life, and at his death bequeathed them to his daughter.

# 28
# An Interview with William P. T. Jope (1900)

## Introduction

*This article, not found in the Foster Hall Collection, paraphrases an anecdote offered by William P. T. Jope (1836–1915) about his vocal quartet singing outside the home of Dr. Jonas R. McClintock (1808–79) on an occasion when Foster was present. I have not uncovered much about Jope or his quartet. However, an old photograph reproduced in* Flem's Views of Old Pittsburgh *in 1908 shows Jope and Thomas Armour to be among a Pittsburgh public school's graduating class of 1850.*[1] *Andrew and George Verner were several years younger. They appear in the 1860 US Census as ages 15 and 14, respectively, and living just south of Pittsburgh in Birmingham. The* Directory of Pittsburgh and Allegheny, 1868–69 *indicates that they worked in the family business as glass blowers.*[2]

*Jope's anecdote might appear to be fabricated were it not confirmed by Morrison Foster. Furthermore, existing documentation confirms the article's linking of McClintock to Foster's eldest brother, William B. Foster Jr. McClintock was a Democrat and public servant who founded Pittsburgh's board of health during the 1832 cholera epidemic. He also served three terms as Pittsburgh's mayor (1836–39) and served in the Pennsylvania House of Representatives (1850–54) and State Senate (1854–56). A surviving letter demonstrates that in 1833, at William Jr.'s behest, McClintock attended the wedding of the songwriter's sister Ann Eliza Foster to Edward Buchanan, brother of the future president. McClintock also served as a pallbearer at William Jr.'s funeral in 1859.*

*The article portrays William Jr. and McClintock as having founded Pittsburgh's militia, the Duquesne Grays, in 1831. McClintock was indeed a*

---

[1] *Flem's Views of Old Pittsburgh* (George T. Fleming, 1908), 61.
[2] *Directory of Pittsburgh and Allegheny Cities* (Geo. H. Thurston, 1868), 406.

*Formulating Foster*. Christopher Lynch, Oxford University Press. © Oxford University Press 2025.
DOI: 10.1093/9780197811726.003.0029

*founding officer and served as Captain from 1832 to 1835. But William Jr.'s name does not appear in the militia's own history, published in 1901.*[3]

---

## *Pittsburg Press*, September 8, 1900.

W. P. T. Jope, the grocer at Fifth and South Negley avenues, is very much interested in the Foster memorial movement, and in speaking of the approaching dedication, recalled an incident which is of popular interest at this time. When Mr. Jope was a boy of 19, back in 1856, he and Thomas Armours, now with the Pennsylvania tube works, and Andrew and George Verner, organized a vocal quartet which won much local reputation singing plantation melodies. Among the songs in which they scored their greatest successes were several of Foster's melodies.

One evening when there was a military encampment at the place now known as Point Breeze, the quartet went to a grove of large trees that stood between Penn avenue and the Pennsylvania railroad opposite the residence of Dr. J. R. McClintock, one of the leading physicians of that day with the purpose of serenading Dr. McClintock. While singing one of Foster's songs a man in shirt sleeves and slough hat came out of the house and stood listening to them. When they ended he advanced and told them he had retired but being very fond of music and hearing their singing he had arisen and come down to listen to them. He added that he was always delighted to hear good singing and more especially he felt a personal interest when they sang his own songs. He was Stephen C. Foster. The boys were delighted to have his commendation and ever after had a personal interest in the composer's works. Mr. Jope recalled that they had noticed that Foster's feet looked oddly white in the moonlight and had laughed heartily with the poet when he explained that on arising he had been unable to find his shoes and had tied linen handkerchiefs over his feet to come outdoors.

Hon. Morrison Foster, brother of the composer, when told of this incident, said the encampment then held was that of the Duquesne Greys which had been organized by William Foster, brother of the poet, and Dr. McClintock in 1831. This organization performed splendid service in the Mexican war and was afterwards merged into the Eighteenth regiment.

---

[3] *History of the 18th Regiment Infantry, "Duquesne Greys," Organized 1831* (Eighteenth Regiment Infantry, National Guard of Pennsylvania, 1901).

# 29

# An Interview with Maria Beabout (1900)

## Introduction

*The following interview is extracted from an article not found in the Foster Hall Collection. Published on the day of the statue unveiling, it consists mostly of recycled quotes from previous articles but paraphrases a few pieces of new information, such as Rachel E. Woods's claim that Foster "was more proficient upon the guitar than any other instrument" and Sarah King's (Mrs. Alexander King) recollection that "Foster was a frequent visitor at her home, where his musical talent contributed to many pleasant evenings." It also contained the following reminiscences from Maria Beabout about her experiences in the Philharmonic Society with Foster and Kleber.*

### *Pittsburg Press*, September 12, 1900.

In 1857 Foster was a frequent visitor at the home of the Misses Maria L. and Cornelia A. Saunders on Lacock street. At that time he resided on North avenue, Allegheny. Miss Cornelia Saunders is since dead but her sister Miss Maria L. Saunders, now Mrs. Beabout, living at 1839 Forbes street, is much interested in the dedication today.

Mrs. Beabout, in 1857, belonged to the same philharmonic society as Foster. Her sister Cornelia, David Miller, John Snodgrass, Ed Sherett, Mr. Burgess, Ed Downey and Ben Vandevort were also members. This society took part in many old time concerts in Allegheny in the fifties. Almost every week the poet would call upon the Misses Saunders and ask them to try a new song. Miss Cornelia was a talented pianist, and, while she played, her sister, now Mrs. Beabout, would write the alto for the various pieces. Among the melodies were "Old Dog Tray" and "My Old Kentucky Home, Good Night," to give it its full title in these days. The Misses Saunders took part in the great concert in Allegheny in 1864 given in a big frame hall on the site of the present Carnegie library. Mrs. Beabout recalls that her first vocal teacher

*Formulating Foster.* Christopher Lynch, Oxford University Press. © Oxford University Press 2025.
DOI: 10.1093/9780197811726.003.0030

was Prof. W. H. Slack, ex-supervisor of music in the schools of the western district of Allegheny, a personal friend of Foster, who recently retired after almost half a century of active teaching. Mrs. Beabout sang from the time she was three years old, but her first lesson was taken from Prof. Slack 45 years ago in the old Fourth ward school, Allegheny. The Misses Saunders, during their active musical career, took part in many charitable concerts in Pittsburg and Allegheny.

The late Henry Kleber was also a member of the Philharmonic society, and a firm friend of both Foster and the Misses Saunders. When the Christy minstrels first came here Mrs. Beabout, then 14, so enjoyed the singing of "I Choose to Be a Daisy if I Must Be a Flower" that she joined in the chorus and attracted the attention of Mr. Christy, who afterwards gave her a copy of the song. She has over 2,000 pages of rare old-time music, including "Old Folks at Home," with E. P. Christy's name as author and composer, "My Old Kentucky Home," "Old Dog Tray" and nearly all of Foster's melodies, given to her by the composer.

# 30

# Reminiscences of George C. Cooper (1902)

### Introduction

*George Cooper (1840–1927) met Foster in New York in the early 1860s, when he was a young man still living with his parents. He was close in age to Birdseye, who claimed to have been friends with him. Cooper and Foster collaborated on twenty-three songs in the years when the composer's popularity began to decline, and none of their songs together were initially successful or popular. The continued decline of the composer's stature over the following decades probably explains Cooper's silence about their work together. An accomplished lyricist and composer in his own right, Cooper's most successful song during his lifetime was "Sweet Genevieve" (1869), with music by Henry Tucker. But two years after the Foster statue was erected in Pittsburgh, Foster was beginning to be viewed in a different light. Indeed, in the twentieth century Cooper's previously successful songs were eclipsed by several of the songs he wrote with Foster. It was in the context of this shift that Cooper offered these recollections in* Piano Music Magazine.

*In a 1932 letter to John Wilson Townsend, who frequently corresponded with Foster Hall regarding research and acquisitions, music publisher Edward B. Marks filled in some interesting information about Cooper, which also sheds light on Foster's place in a lineage of popular song composers in New York. He writes:*

> My recollection of Geo. Cooper is very hazy, as I have not seen him since I first went into business about 25 years ago. At that time my associate and myself had a small publishing office under the name of Jos. W. Stern & Co., at 45 East 20th Street—two blocks away T. B. Harms & Co., one of the leading firms of that period had their music publishing offices.

*Formulating Foster.* Christopher Lynch, Oxford University Press. © Oxford University Press 2025.
DOI: 10.1093/9780197811726.003.0031

> Geo. Cooper was employed by Harms as an arranger of music. He also composed melodies, but at the time he was mainly occupied in arranging the piano melodies of other composers.
>
> Another arranger by the name of Mr. Pratt also made his headquarters at Harms. Both of these men were at one time acquaintances of Foster or they may have collaborated with him.
>
> Naturally during the [18]90s, I saw both Cooper and Pratt occasionally at luncheon usually in the Old Continental Hotel at 20th Street and Broadway where I also frequently met Paul Dresser composer of "Banks of Wabash" and "My Gal Sal" etc. At that time Reginald de Koven frequently dined there also. Bill Gray (Wm. B. Gray) composer of "Volunteer Organist," "Church Across the Way" and many other popular songs of the day, also had his offices in the neighborhood and ate his lunch at the Continental. His firm was Spalding and Gray, and among the young song writers who published with him was Geo. M. Cohan."[1]

As Marks's letter demonstrates, it is most directly through Cooper that Foster is connected to the songwriters and publishers who were associated with the popular song industry that coalesced in the 1890s around Manhattan's 28th Street, which came to be known as Tin Pan Alley.

## George C. Cooper, "Stephen C. Foster,"
## *Piano Music Magazine*, May 1902.

Many of those who have sung, or listened to and enjoyed, "Old Folks at Home," "Old Black Joe," "My Old Kentucky Home," and other beautiful songs of Foster's, would like to know something of the personality of the composer and his method of writing. Personal reminiscences of those who have benefited us by their work, whether in song or story, are always interesting, however trivial. This slight sketch is from one who wrote with Foster and was his daily companion for years. A boyish figure, below the medium height, smooth face and dark brown hair and eyes—this will give some idea of his appearance. But to describe the

---

[1] Edward B. Marks to John Wilson Townsend, September 14, 1932, FHC, Letters Catalogued, box A-1 (A–H).

expression of those eyes when their owner was in animated conversation, would be quite as difficult as it would be to depict the varied moods of an April sky.

There was a charming modesty in Foster when anyone alluded to his songs, which would be hard to find in many of the composers and songwriters of to-day. A few moments of conversation with him impressed you with the fact that he was well informed, and moreover, a man of feeling and sentiment.

The writer will never forget his first interview with him. As an embryo verse-scribbler, he bashfully showed Foster a copy of "words" that he, the aforesaid scribbler, fondly hoped might be wedded to immortal melody. The place was the back room of a corner grocery store near the Bowery, in New York City. Foster scanned the words over, and to the intense delight of their perpetrator, drew from a side pocket a rather rumpled sheet of music paper which was immediately spread out and laid upon an upturned cheese box! There was no wooing of the Muse for inspiration. The place and its surroundings were as prosaic as well could be. Moreover it was quite thronged with those who had gathered there for sociability and to quench their thirst; for this grocery store had the usual bar addition in those days. The hum of conversation, and the inquisitive peep over the composer's shoulder of those who wondered what strange writing he was engaged in—nothing disturbed him in the least. The melody was soon dotted down, and the piano accompaniment followed as quickly. When in doubt as to a proper note of said accompaniment, the right hand of the composer would run up and down imaginary piano keys upon the cheese box aforementioned. "Now for a publisher!" exclaimed Foster, as the finishing touches were made to the song, and some sand was gathered from the floor by the manuscript, in the form of a scoop, to hasten the drying of the ink.

In a short time two individuals were walking up Broadway with business on their hands. Wood's Minstrels were then playing in the city; as luck would have it, Wood himself was standing at the door of his house of entertainment. "Hello, Steve!" was his salute, as he eyed the rolled-up manuscript, the sight of which quite often puts the publisher on the defensive now-a-days. "What have you there? Something new?"

Here was an unexpected windfall! It happened that the company was on the stage rehearsing. The leader played over our song. Mr. Wood suggested twenty-five dollars as the honorarium, which was far in advance of what either of us expected, and the deal was closed. On the following Monday—this happened in 1862—"Willie Has Gone to the War," was launched on a confiding public, who little dreamed that its origin was in a grocery store, and its melody dotted down upon an upturned cheese box.

# 31

# Recollections from Classmates at the Athens Academy (1905/1911)

## Introduction

*With interest in Foster growing, members of the Bradford County Historical Society began to investigate the composer's days as a student in the county at Towanda and Athens in 1840 and 1841. The following account is excerpted from a paper read by R. M. Welles at an event of the Bradford County Historical Society on February 11, 1905. The talk, subtitled "Sketch of Stephen Collins Foster, the Musical Genius," was published in the society's journal in 1911. A month after the lecture, another talk that included remembrances of Foster was given at another event by the society. It was published in the journal in 1910, and the full remembrance was published in 1916 (see Chapter 33).*

*The following excerpt amounts to most of the six-page article's original content. The remainder of the sketch is almost entirely quoted or paraphrased from Morrison's biography. Morrison's influence is detected even in these original words. The references to Foster's "genius" and studiousness and his abstaining from sport and not going into society were likely recalled only after reading Morrison's biography.*

## R. M. Welles, "The Old Athens Academy," *Annual* 5 (1911).

It was in January, 1841, that I met Stephen C. Foster at school in Athens. It may be of interest to the reader to have a description of this remarkable musical and poetical writer as I recollect him. He was at the time in his 15th year; his complexion was rather dark; his face and head were apparently of uniform width, neither wide nor narrow, but well proportioned; he had a tall, large head, which was covered with fine nearly black hair, that lay flat

*Formulating Foster*. Christopher Lynch, Oxford University Press. © Oxford University Press 2025.
DOI: 10.1093/9780197811726.003.0032

upon the scalp, and if I recollect correctly his jaws were somewhat square—indicating firmness. This quality was shown in his intense application to study and composition....

John A. Perkins of Fresno, California, had been a prominent member of the Old Academy school—a son of George A. Perkins—writing in 1897, on the occasion of the 100th anniversary or celebration, has this to say about our subject: "Stephen C. Foster, of minstrel fame, was at the academy about this time, and showed some of the genius he displayed in later years. I can see him speaking 'Lord Ullins' Daughter,' as though it was yesterday; at the close he would fold his arms, throw back his head and tragically exclaim, 'My daughter, oh, my daughter!'" Stephen was studious and, according to my recollection, did not join with the boys in their sports. He kept much to his room. I do not remember that he spent any time in society. He was a good penman and made fine ornamental letters. An exhibition was to be held by the school in the old Presbyterian church, April 1, 1841—at that time the only house of worship in Athens. Stephen C. Foster composed and wrote his first piece of music, I think, expressly for the exhibition, and with James H. Forbes and William F. Warner, the three practiced the piece, which Stephen named "Tioga Waltz," and played it upon the stage with their flutes—not "four flutes," as stated by his brother, Morrison Foster. Stephen spent some time in Towanda after leaving Athens. The late Hon. Joseph Powell told me that young Foster played a good deal while here upon the clarionet. From Towanda Stephen Foster returned to his home in Allegheny, near Pittsburg.

## PART III
# REMEMBERING FOSTER AFTER THE NAACP'S 1914 PROTESTS

## Introduction

Published between the 1910s and early 1930s, the last remembrances appeared in a period that witnessed the exponential growth of Foster's music's popularity alongside increasingly outspoken opposition to it. This happened against the backdrop of Foster memory keeping transitioning to what historians refer to as "postmemory," a generational shift as memory passed from those with firsthand knowledge to those who were one or more steps removed from Foster. To scholar Marianne Hirsch, the "generational distance" from what is being remembered makes postmemory "a powerful and very particular form of memory precisely because its connection to its object or source is mediated not through recollection but through an imaginative investment and creation."[1] In this last period of Foster remembrance, accounts by people who knew the composer were published at the same time and in response to portrayals of him by historians, fans, detractors, and children, grandchildren, and friends of people who knew Foster. The agendas behind their interest in Foster's memory inspired different degrees of imaginative remembering and, in many cases, helped solidify the Foster myth.

Despite growing resistance, Foster's place in popular culture and national discourse had never been more secure. Extending from the *Uncle Tom* shows, recitals of opera divas, jubilee performances, and Civil War memorialization, Foster's "big four" sentimental minstrel songs—"Old

---

[1] Marianne Hirsch, *Family Frames: Photography, Narrative, and Postmemory* (Harvard University Press, 1997), 22.

Folks at Home," "My Old Kentucky Home," "Massa's in de Cold Ground," and "Old Black Joe"—were among the most recorded songs of the early recording period.[2] With Antonín Dvořák's approval, orchestral composers increasingly deployed Foster's melodies to invoke the nation,[3] and his music was referenced in popular songs such as Irving Berlin's "Alexander's Ragtime Band" and George Gershwin's "Swanee." As Foster's songs became more known, their melodies became potent sonic references to antebellum America, the South, or the United States in silent film accompaniments and underscoring for the talkies.[4] Led by the Civic Club of Allegheny County, Pittsburghers began singing them in public singalongs, and they quickly became fixtures in singalongs throughout the nation.[5]

Morrison had laid the groundwork in the 1890s for Foster's popular sentimental minstrel songs to be seen not as minstrel songs but as emblems of American patriotism, an idea that many people came to gradually accept over the ensuing decades. James A. Davis has noted that "My Old Kentucky Home," "Old Black Joe," and "Old Folks at Home" were included in a songbook the US government published for soldiers in 1918. Those songs and "Massa's in de Cold Ground" were also included in *The Most Popular Songs of Patriotism* in 1916. Davis correctly concludes that "World War I concretized Foster's wartime songs in the pantheon of patriotic music,"[6] but it is important to specify that at this point it was still only the most famous sentimental minstrel songs that entered that pantheon and that during the war Foster himself received very little mention in the press. Indeed, in the 1910s Foster was primarily discussed only in response to the creation of the Foster Memorial Home in Pittsburgh and debates that followed the NAACP's protests of his music in Boston. The process of establishing Foster as a national icon and all his songs as patriotic was gradual, begun in the 1890s and completed only in the 1930s by Foster Hall.

---

[2] George R. Creegan, "A Discography of the Acoustic Recordings of Stephen Foster's Music," PhD diss., University of Pittsburgh, 1987. See also Creegan, "The Acoustic Recordings of Stephen C. Foster's Music," *ARSC Journal* 33, no. 3 (Fall 2002): 214–28.

[3] Well-known examples of Foster's melodies in classical music include Antonín Dvořák's arrangement of "Old Folks at Home" for soprano, baritone, and orchestra; George Whitefield Chadwick, *Carnival Overture*; Charles Ives, Symphony No. 2; and Aaron Copland, *Lincoln Portrait*.

[4] Kathryn Miller Haines, "Stephen Foster's Music in Motion Pictures and Television," *American Music* 30, no. 3 (Fall 2012): 373–88.

[5] Esther M. Morgan-Ellis, "A Century of Singing Along to Stephen Foster," In *Musical Meaning and Interpretation*, ed. Michael J. Puri, Jason Geary, and Seth Monahan (Oxford University Press, 2025), 118–52.

[6] James A. Davis, "Stephen Foster and Patriotism," In *Foster at 200: A Critical Reappraisal*, ed. Jason Lee Guthrie and Jennie Lightweis-Goff (University of Illinois Press, forthcoming).

In 1912, financially desperate and looking to profit from her father's name, Marion corresponded with Kentucky historian John Wilson Townsend, indicating that she wanted to publish some music: "I have some music I composed and he composed (my father) which I would like to get out very much as I never needed it more than now—but I cannot afford it just now."[7] She was probably looking to sell manuscripts to someone with resources and connections to the publishing industry, but these publications never materialized; in fact, even whether she actually possessed unpublished manuscripts by her father is uncertain. But she did manage to use memory of her father for her own betterment in other ways. In 1913, the *Pittsburgh Post* began a movement to purchase the property on the site of the White Cottage in Lawrenceville, where Foster had been born in 1826.[8] Although Foster's homestead had been replaced with a new building, the site was to be transformed into a "shrine" to the composer and given to the city with the expectation that his descendants would live in the house as caretakers and docents of a small "museum where relics and remembrances of the great composer can be housed."[9]

The *Post* intended to raise money from the public, but one philanthropist, James H. Park, came forward as sole benefactor. Acquiring, repairing, and setting up the site took two and a half years, throughout which the project was promoted using the rhetoric of the myth. As the sentimental songs began to transcend their original meanings, the Foster family helped project the songs' transcendence onto Foster himself. With the Foster family present, on the fiftieth anniversary of the composer's death in 1914 journalist Erasmus Wilson gave a lecture that the *Post* described as "a talk on the life of Foster— his higher life—which lifted him above the sordid things of earth and led him to write his immortal melodies."[10] This rhetoric seems to have aligned with the Foster family's preferred way of discussing the composer. In their correspondence in 1912, Townsend had expressed curiosity to Marion about the "sordid things" of Foster's life, and she responded that she was unwilling to share "all those impertinent points about my father's history."[11] We can

---

[7] Marion Foster Welch to John Wilson Townsend, April 2, 1912, FHC, Letters Catalogued (I–Z), box A-2.

[8] The *Post* launched the effort on March 13, 1913. See "The Stephen C. Foster Homestead," *Pittsburgh Post*, March 13, 1913.

[9] "Birthplace of Famous Composer a Christmas Gift from James H. Park," *Pittsburgh Post*, December 22, 1913, FHC.

[10] "Historical Association," *Pittsburgh Post*, January 21, 1914.

[11] Marion Foster Welch to John Wilson Townsend, April 2, 1912, FHC, Letters Catalogued (I–Z), box A-2.

only guess at the nature of those "impertinent points," but we can be sure that as Marion worked to benefit materially and financially from her father's memory, she chose to leave out details and focus on his music as expressions of "national," "universal," and "immortal" sentiments.

Pittsburgh organist and journalist T. Carl Whitmer helped the project earn national attention. Writing of the effort for a national publication, he made no mention of race but positioned Foster as a folk hero: "The subject [of his songs] was scarcely new; the style certainly and essentially from the eternity of peoples—and surely a folk-song composer is always on the level of 'the people,' and wishes to be nowhere else."[12] The *New York Times* similarly evaded the particularities of his life, stating simply that "his music was American if any music ever was" and asserting—dubiously—that "in the forties and fifties, even in the sixties, of the last century, he was the most popular American composer" and that "so many of his melodies [are] imperishable."[13]

With Foster and his "universal" and "immortal" songs foregrounded in national discourse in 1913 and 1914, the songwriter came to symbolize the need for the American Society of Composers, Authors and Publishers (ASCAP). Founded in 1914 and led by composer Victor Herbert—who had conducted the Pittsburgh Symphony Orchestra, arranged Foster's tunes, and directed an ensemble at the unveiling of the Foster statue in 1900—ASCAP was designed to oversee the licensing of compositions for performance and facilitate the collection of performance fees on behalf of composers in accordance with the 1909 copyright law. Prior to the law's enactment, composers could only collect royalties on the sale of sheet music. ASCAP embraced the story that the "father of American music" and a symbol of democratic inclusivity had died nearly penniless, unable to collect performance fees. The organization continues to tell "the legend behind the law" to this day:

> Stephen Foster was a great songwriter. The creator of more than 200 American ballads including: "My Old Kentucky Home," "Beautiful Dreamer," and "Oh! Susannah" [sic]. And even though Foster's musical legacy is rich in color and tradition, he died with only a few pennies to his name. During Stephen Foster's day, there was no effective way to protect

---

[12] T. Carl Whitmer, "Stephen Foster: An American," *The Musician* 18, no. 12 (December 1913).
[13] "Stephen Foster," *New York Times*, March 18, 1913.

musical compositions and no way to provide songwriting royalties or income.

Almost fifty years after Stephen Foster's death, the American Society of Composers, Authors and Publishers was created by nine illustrious songwriters to uphold the copyright law. John Philip Sousa, Jerome Kern, Irving Berlin, and Victor Herbert were among the first members of ASCAP, now the world's largest performing rights organization. Stephen didn't have ASCAP, but today more than 435,000 beautiful dreamers do.[14]

ASCAP declined to mention how the Civil War upended the music industry in the last three years of his life, during which he drank himself so close to death that his body could not withstand the trauma of a burn on his leg and a fall in his room. But focusing on Foster as a "great composer" whose music is "rich in color and tradition" has helped ASCAP for over one hundred years make use of Foster as a tragic symbol of the perils caused by an industry that lacks legal protections and a national organization to advocate for artists.

The Foster Memorial Home, ASCAP activities, and the fiftieth anniversary of Foster's death inspired the magazine the *Etude* to feature an article about the composer by music critic George P. Upton in a special "All American" issue in November, 1914. Upton summarizes and paraphrases Morrison's *Biography, Songs and Musical Compositions* throughout most of the article, with some additional information—clearly derived from Birdseye's account—of Foster's last years in New York. He characterizes Foster's songs as "sentimental ballads, having the negro life and habits for their subject" and asserts "the melody and words are refined," finding "not a vulgar expression in any of his songs."[15]

Although the terms the Foster family had developed for remembering the composer were echoed across journalism and criticism in these years, they were far from universally agreed upon. The same month as the special issue of the *Etude*, a protest of Foster's music erupted in Boston, where the NAACP worked to ban a songbook containing Foster's songs from the city's schools. At a public meeting hosted by the Boston School Committee, NAACP lawyer Butler R. Wilson objected to schoolchildren singing "songs containing the

---

[14] ASCAP, "ASCAP Keeps You In Tune with the Copyright Law," brochure. See also, Ruth Charles, "ASCAP—A Half Century of Progress," *Bulletin of the Copyright Society of the USA* 11 (1964): 133–43; and Marc Hugunin, "ASCAP, BMI and the Democratization of American Popular Music," *Popular Music and Society* 7, no. 1 (1979): 8–17, especially 11.

[15] George P. Upton, "The Romance of Stephen C. Foster," *Etude*, November 1914: 783–84.

words 'darkey' or 'nigger,' " arguing that "such terms are ... epithets and our children have returned from school heartbroken over the fact that these objectionable songs are sung in school and that the white children have jeered at them as a result." Rev. Montrose William Thornton called the songs "Old Black Joe," "My Old Kentucky Home," and "Massa's in de Cold, Cold Ground" an "insult to the whole colored race." Rev. Samuel A. Brown recounted an incident in which "a teacher asked the only colored boy in the room to sing one of these songs in order that the other children might acquire the right accent," which led to "the other pupils ... jeering him unmercifully." A mother testified that her son "had been jeered at as 'nigger' and 'darkey.' " Following these comments, the committee banned the songbook.[16]

After the NAACP's victory, White newspapers printed counter-assertions about Foster's songs. A Detroit writer retorted that "these compositions ... constitute one of a very few contributions to American cultural development inspired by the African."[17] In a way, this reflects the thinking of W. E. B. Du Bois, who had written passionately in *The Souls of Black Folk* that "the Negro folk-song—the rhythmic cry of the slave—stands to-day not simply as the sole American music, but as the most beautiful expression of human experience born this side the seas."[18] But although Du Bois celebrated their influence on Foster (which in actuality was minimal because of Foster's lack of access to real Black folk music), spirituals themselves represented the pinnacle of American music, not Foster's imitations. To Du Bois, Black spirituals were the *only* uniquely American cultural contribution to the world; music by White composers inspired by spirituals was mere evidence of that contribution. Moreover, throughout many of his writings, but perhaps most poignantly in *Black Reconstruction*, Du Bois celebrated Black institution building following enslavement, including the building of schools, libraries, churches, stores, and industries.[19] In other words, Du Bois emphasized spirituals while actively rejecting the notion that Foster's songs represented "one of a very few contributions" made by his race.

Three responses to the Boston NAACP from the South reveal the influence of Lost Cause propaganda on thinking about Foster. A Memphis

[16] "School Board Heeds Protest," *Boston Globe*, November 13, 1914.
[17] "A Pitiful Misconception," *Boston Evening Transcript*, November 17, 1914. Reprinted from the *Detroit Free Press*.
[18] Du Bois, *Souls of Black Folk*, 251.
[19] Du Bois, *Black Reconstruction in America, 1860–1880: An Essay toward a History of the Part Which Black Folk Played in the Attempt to Reconstruct Democracy in America* (Russell & Russell, 1966).

writer claimed the songs "have been sung for generations by the negroes of the south, who find in them no 'insult,' only true pictures of the sad side of life, set to exquisite melody that seizes the fancy and haunts the imagination."[20] A North Carolinian felt that "it is a pity that the descendants of Uncle Isham and Mammy Jinsey should be ashamed of the tuneful ditties which were dear to the hearts of their ancestors," celebrating his view that the "old songs preserve memories that should not be allowed to perish of the primitive virtues—fidelity, affectionate disposition and cheerful contentment with a narrow dispensation—of a race which, under more benign conditions, is in danger of losing the attributes which were its best endowments."[21] A Kentucky writer objected to banning "My Old Kentucky Home" because "not a negro in all the Southland feels that it is a reproach upon his race, since it tells of a period in Southern history that was picturesque in the extreme, showing the devotion that existed between mistress and slave that has no counterpart in the history of the world."[22] These writers illogically rejected Black protests of the song by claiming that Blacks did not object to the song. They exemplify how sympathy could be put to the service of White supremacy in their belief that Foster's songs were a *sympathetic* tribute to those people who they believed were happy and loyal under the conditions of enslavement. Buying into Lost Cause propaganda, these writers believed Foster's songs accurately reflected what they believed was the harmoniousness of race relations prior to emancipation.

These writers either lied about their knowledge of the diversity of southern Black thought or, perhaps more likely in the age of Jim Crow, were ignorant of Black Americans' ideas about Foster. It is certainly true that the strain of thought that viewed Foster's music positively—eloquently given voice by Du Bois in *The Souls of Black Folk* in 1903—was still prominent in the 1910s. For example, professional singer and jubilee ensemble director George R. Garner Jr. celebrated that "Foster laid bare the heartlife of the Negro[,] and ridicule found no place in his song texts."[23] But, on the other hand, in Kentucky Joseph Cotter took offense to "My Old Kentucky Home" and rewrote the lyrics so that, as historian Emily Bingham puts it, the song

---

[20] "Boston's Latest Folly," *Commercial Appeal, Memphis*, December 4, 1914.
[21] "The Sensitive Boston Negroes," *Winston-Salem Journal*, November 25, 1914.
[22] "The Old Darkey Songs," *Louisville Courier-Journal*, November 20, 1914. Reprinted from the *Bowling Green Messenger*.
[23] George R. Garner Jr., "The Advent of the Negro into American and His Effect in the Production of Music Both of a Popular and More Pretentious Character," *Broad Ax*, September 5, 1914.

"reversed the tide of sentiment from a past of bondage to a future of dignity and prosperity for his race."[24] Cotter suggested changing the lyrics as follows:

> The day trips by with a solace for the heart
> To charm it and give it delight.
> The time has come when the Negro does his part
> To make My Old Kentucky Home alright.
> The time has come when the head will never bow
> Wherever the Negro may go.
> A few more years and he'll show the nation how
> He will thrive where the sugar canes grow.
> A few more years and he'll shift the weary load
> So that it will ever be light
> A few more years and he'll triumph on the road
> And sing, My Old Kentucky Home's alright.

Published in Louisville's Black newspaper, the *Louisville Leader*, Cotter's protest of Foster's lyrics failed to reach a White readership in Jim Crow America.

Each of the White writers responding to the NAACP's Foster songbook protests invoked the notion of universalism in Foster's music to chide the Boston School Committee. The Memphis writer mocked Boston's reputation as the "Hub of the Universe," arguing that the city "had as well stop her ears if she does not wish to hear the tunes, for the rest of us will continue to sing them and love them." To the North Carolinian, the "simple pathos" of Foster's songs "appealed to all grades of taste," and the songs were "world-wide favorites ... sung in every tongue" as "the property of all mankind." The Kentuckian believed that regardless of what happened in Boston Foster's songs would always be sung "throughout the world." Each of these commenters defended Foster's songs not by erasing race from them but by subsuming race into universalism and asserting that the songs *transcended* race.

After 1914, invoking Foster's national and "universal" status became standard among White intellectuals responding to accusations of racism in his music. In the preface to Whittlesey's and Sonneck's *Catalogue of First Editions of Stephen C. Foster* in 1915, Sonneck dismissively writes,

---

[24] Bingham, *My Old Kentucky Home*, 117.

"Misconception or partisanship may succeed in banishing these songs from our public schools, but Stephen C. Foster's place in the history of music in America is too high to be permanently affected by such efforts."[25] A review of the book portrayed Foster's songs as empathetic toward Black people and authentic in their depictions, asserting that "Foster had the good fortune to see in the Negroes of the United States and in their characteristics, as human beings and as melodists, that which he could turn to account as a composer." The reviewer celebrated that "these songs by Foster are still sung by thousands of persons of the Caucasian race" and complained that "the Negroes themselves have in many cases so reacted against anything and everything that reminds them of their race that they chafe whenever one of Foster's ante-bellum characters emerges and, by wholly lifelike art, recalls the 'daddies' and 'mammies' of plantation days."[26]

By the time the Foster Memorial Home opened in Pittsburgh in 1916, the Foster family had long relied on the rhetoric of Foster's "national" and "universal" music to distance the composer from problematic parts of his biography, including his substance abuse, associations with working-class theatrical performers and theatergoers, political partisanship, marital problems, sectionalism during the Civil War, and the racism of minstrelsy. But following the NAACP incident, this rhetoric acquired more urgency at the Memorial Home, shielding the composer against growing complaints of racism. Visitors to the shrine could view objects that supported the national-universal myth, such as a piano that had been owned by Rachel Keller Woods,[27] the letter from W. W. Kingsbury containing his recollections of Foster as a schoolboy (see Chapter 33), portraits and paintings, some of the composer's manuscripts, and one of his flutes that had been donated following the death of Susan Pentland Robinson in early 1916.[28] The stories Marion and Jessie told visitors did nothing to detract from the myth. They talked about the songwriter composing for Rachel and Susan, and they repeated some of the famous anecdotes from Morrison's biography, especially the story of Morrison helping his brother draft the opening line "way down upon the Swanee River" in "Old Folks at Home." Marion, a musician and music teacher, probably played the piano and sang songs from the three

---

[25] Whittlesey and Sonneck, *Catalogue of First Editions*, 3.
[26] "Writer of Familiar Negro Songs," unmarked clipping, FHC.
[27] "Pittsburgh Honors Foster's Memory," clipping dated 1916, FHC.
[28] Several of these items were donated following the death of Susan Pentland Robinson in early 1916. See, "Woman, the Girlhood Muse of Foster, Dies," FHC, 19160016.tif.

bound volumes of Foster's music that had belonged to the composer and had been handed down through the family. A writer who visited the home reported that Foster's songs "may be called America's most lovely folk songs, but any heart from Karachi, India, to Kalamazoo, Mich., who hears these songs knows their meaning and responds to their beauty."[29] Following in Morrison's footsteps, the family at the Memorial Home helped guide visitors to an understanding of Foster's music as embodying national and universal sentiments.

In his biography published in 1920, Harold Vincent Milligan downplayed the NAACP episode by invoking universalism and portraying Foster as inhabiting a plane above the racial politics of his day. He knew better. In his research he had corresponded with Foster's old buddy and songwriting pal George Cooper, who had opined to him that "Foster disliked the [Civil] war as, to my mind, he scorned to see the disruption of the ties that held the negroes to their masters & of which ties he had written so many songs."[30] Although Milligan included many of Cooper's recollections word for word in his book, he chose to omit this quotation. Including these words would have undermined his response to the NAACP protests in Boston. He wrote that the Boston School Committee's decision was "severely criticized throughout the country" and suggested that the NAACP "brought about a discussion of the whole subject of Foster's songs which demonstrated how wide-spread is their popularity and how deep the affection in which they are held." On the basis of Foster's sentimental minstrel songs, he wrote that "these songs are a distinct tribute to the colored race" and that Foster's "song is of that nostalgia of the soul which is inborn and instinctive to all humanity, a homesickness unaffected by time or space."[31] Enshrining the standard language for whitewashing the particulars of Foster's biography in the first book-length biography of the composer, Milligan subsumed race into universalism.

Milligan was far from the only person to embrace whitewashing language about Foster. In 1923 the Kentucky estate known as Federal Hill in Bardstown opened as the "My Old Kentucky Home" museum, drawing thousands of visitors each year with the national-universal myth and new myths unique to Kentucky. Tourism to Bardstown depended on the disingenuous claim that Foster had written the song on the premises of Federal Hill. The claim,

---

[29] "Stephen C. Foster Home Is Visited," *The Index*, July 29, 1916, FHC.
[30] George Cooper to Harold Vincent Milligan, July 2, 1917, FHC, C929.
[31] Harold Vincent Milligan, *Stephen C. Foster: A Biography of America's Folk-Song Composer* (G. Schirmer, 1920), 116.

percolating in Kentucky lore for decades, rested on distant memories of the Foster family's connections to the Rowan family who owned the estate. Although the last Foster family member documented in Bardstown was the composer's older sister Charlotte in 1829—when the composer was barely two years old—amateur historian Young E. Allison was content building a tourist attraction on the idea that it was possible that Foster had visited the site. As Bingham writes, "The true north to Young Allison's compass that directed so much of his decision making was that no place in Kentucky had a *better* claim to the songwriter."[32] In 1921, he led the "propaganda" to solicit donations from Kentuckians to purchase the property from its owner, Madge Rowan Frost. Allison knew there was no proof that Foster had visited the site, but for the sake of honoring Foster and generating tourism revenue for Kentucky he publicly refuted the naysayers by stating that "the only thing clearly true is that he wrote it at Federal Hill."[33]

Needing to distance Foster and the Rowan family from racism, Allison informed an inquiring historian, E. Jay Wohlgemuth, that the songwriter "cared nothing for the minstrels, as such ... only wrote *for* them"[34] and that Federal Hill had practiced enslavement of a benevolent kind.[35] Benjamin Labree, curator of Federal Hill from 1923 to 1931, established many of the myths associated with the estate. Visitors viewed the desk where Foster had supposedly written "My Old Kentucky Home" and gazed out the window where he had allegedly sympathetically observed enslaved people working on the land while writing "Massa's in de Cold Ground."[36] Labree hired Bemis Allen, a Black man, to play the part of a freed man claiming to have lived at Federal Hill since Foster's day. Playing into the myth of loyal slaves and benevolent masters, Allen told visitors that he was the son of "Old Black Joe" and played "My Old Kentucky Home" on the harmonica.[37]

Looking to portray Foster and the Rowan family as sympathetic and benevolent toward the people they enslaved, Labree took steps to humanize Federal Hill's enslaved people. It was probably Labree who placed unmarked stone markers in the ground to create the appearance of a slave cemetery on

---

[32] Bingham, *My Old Kentucky Home*, 110.
[33] [Young E. Allison], "Foster and Kentucky," *Louisville Times*, October 1, 1921; quoted in Bingham, *My Old Kentucky Home*, 113.
[34] Young E. Allison to E. Jay Wohlgemuth, August 6, 1918, folder 5, Otto A. Rothert Collection on Young Ewing Allison, Filson Historical Society, Louisville Kentucky; quoted in Bingham, *My Old Kentucky Home*, 107.
[35] [Allison], "Foster and Kentucky," quoted in Bingham, *My Old Kentucky Home*, 113.
[36] Howard, *Stephen Foster*, 172–73.
[37] Bingham, *My Old Kentucky Home*, 125–26.

the land behind the Rowans' home. In 2010, archaeologists were unable to identify any actual graves at the site, concluding that "it appears that in fact this cemetery was created by a park employee to acknowledge the enslaved African Americans who lived, worked, and died at My Old Kentucky Home."[38] As historian Gerald L. Smith notes, "In his zeal to promote the Home for tourist attraction, [Labree] was likely the 'park employee' who had created the slave cemetery."[39] The "zeal" of Labree, Allison, and their allies paid off. "My Old Kentucky Home" became a powerful symbol of the state that drove economic activity. During Labree's eight-year leadership, the performance of "My Old Kentucky Home" at the Kentucky Derby became an annual tradition that remains in place today, state leaders made "My Old Kentucky Home" the state song, and over 300,000 tourists visited Federal Hill.[40]

The Foster family knew that stories being told at Bardstown were "pure bunk," as the composer's granddaughter Jessie Welsh Rose put it in a private letter to Josiah K. Lilly. She believed that Foster had probably visited Federal Hill in his youth (probably because of two letters by William Foster Sr. to William Foster Jr. that mention a trip a young Foster took with his mother and sister Henrietta to Augusta, Kentucky, in 1833[41]), but she did not believe he visited the estate once he was married. "My Old Kentucky Home," she knew, "was certainly... not written in Kentucky." She wrote,

> My grandmother [Jane] loved to talk of trips she had taken and places she had been. She never mentioned Kentucky or "Old Kentucky Home." She took many a trip down the Ohio River in one of Dunning Foster's steamboats with her husband and I think their wedding trip was a trip of this kind—of this I am not positive—but there is not one bit of evidence anywhere to the effect that Foster ever saw Kentucky but once. These boat trips ended at Cincinnati—they came back the next day.

---

[38] Philip B. Mink II, "An Electrical Resistance Survey and Subsequent Evaluation of the 'Slave Cemetery' at My Old Kentucky Home State Park, Nelson County, Kentucky," Kentucky Archaeological Survey jointly by University of Kentucky Heritage Council, Kentucky Archaeological Survey Report no. 188, OSA Registration no. FY10-6499, 2010, 2; quoted in Gerald L. Smith, Introduction to *Slavery and Freedom in the Bluegrass State: Revisiting My Old Kentucky Home* (University of Kentucky Press, 2023), 23.

[39] Smith, Introduction, 23.

[40] LaBree Logbooks, Benjamin L. LaBree Papers, Filson Historical Society, Louisville, Kentucky; cited in Bingham, *My Old Kentucky Home*, 120.

[41] William B. Foster to William B. Foster Jr., June 1, 1833, FHC, C619; and William B. Foster Sr. to William B. Foster Jr., July 4, 1833, FHC, C620.

Lilly had recently purchased Foster's manuscript book in which he drafted many of his lyrics. Rose pointed him to it for proof that the song was written in Pittsburgh after he married Jane and was done traveling down the river: "It was written in 1851 or 2—just as you see the date in the manuscript book."[42]

In the same letter to Lilly, Jessie also denounced as "another myth" Federal Hill's claims that "an old colored man"—Bemis Allen—was "a grandson of the original 'Old Black Joe.'" The family knew the song was actually inspired by Jane's "father's coachman, or rather buggy-driver" in Pittsburgh.[43] Jessie debunked another myth about one of Federal Hill's pianos. In 1926, Queen Marie of Romania visited Bardstown and was told, according to Jessie, by a "silver tongued orator" that "this is the very piano upon which Stephen C. Foster wrote 'Old Kentucky Home.'" This so impressed the queen that she had a photograph taken in front of it, but Jessie knew the story to be false because her friend Lorena Lanahan Lott had recently purchased the piano for the home. Jessie supposed that the photograph went on to solidify the myth: "Devil only knows where that picture has gone in its travels by this time. So you see how these things start and grow little by little."[44]

Jessie and other family members were unwilling to publicly renounce the Federal Hill myths. She wrote to Lilly, "I was once asked if I would be willing to check upon statements constantly being made there—but Mr. Lilly—I would not dream of doing this." She was conflict-averse, describing herself as "peace-loving by disposition." And she also claimed to "understand that in making these wild statements no real harm is meant—they are merely trying to make the place interesting and 'put it over' to the public as it were."[45] Although she intended her words to be private, her letter found its way into the Foster Hall Collection. Perhaps unintentionally, then, Jessie put it into the record that the Foster family tolerated mythologizing in the name of winning favor with the public.

Not wanting to be outdone by Bardstown, Pittsburghers also looked to capitalize on the Foster mania. The same year Federal Hill opened, the Civic Club of Allegheny County began leading annual commemorations of the composer, including a graveside ceremony and concerts on the anniversary of his death, which came to be known locally as Stephen Foster Day. In the fall

---

[42] Jessie Welsh Rose to Josiah K. Lilly, July 7, 1931, FHC, Letters Catalogued (I–Z), box A-2.
[43] Jessie Welsh Rose to Josiah K. Lilly, July 7, 1931, FHC, Letters Catalogued (I–Z), box A-2.
[44] Jessie Welsh Rose to Josiah K. Lilly, July 7, 1931, FHC, Letters Catalogued (I–Z), box A-2. Howard summarized this anecdote in *Stephen Foster*, 173.
[45] Jessie Welsh Rose to Josiah K. Lilly, July 7, 1931, FHC, Letters Catalogued (I–Z), box A-2.

of 1927, the Tuesday Musical Club—a women's club that sponsored musical performances—began to raise money to build the Stephen Foster Memorial, the building where the Foster Hall Collection would reside from 1937 until 2023. The project was envisioned by club president Birdelle Earhart, who claimed to have been inspired by a lecture on Foster in 1925 by Harold Vincent Milligan. For years the Tuesday Musical Club had explored ways to acquire its own facilities suitable for their performances, office needs, and social affairs; but it was the Foster Memorial idea that finally gained traction. The idea received the enthusiastic approval of the club's members, and soon the chancellor of the University of Pittsburgh agreed to have the building constructed on the university's grounds. Early fundraising was successful, but the project stalled when the stock market crashed in 1929. Dire for more than a year, the project's outlook suddenly changed when an Indianapolis-based Foster fanatic and billionaire—Josiah K. Lilly—learned of the memorial plans and decided the facility would also make a fitting home for his growing collection of "Fosteriana." It would ultimately be his financial assistance that enabled the completion of the building and its opening in 1937, three years after the last reminiscences of the composer were published.

It was thus in this Jim Crow context, amid the transition to postmemory, the continuing tradition of jubilee singing, the insinuation of Foster's popular sentimental minstrel songs into displays of patriotism, and growing protests of racism in Foster's music that the final memories of the composer were recorded. Memory keepers contested, celebrated, and denounced each other while appropriating Foster's memory for various political, economic, institutional, legal, and personal ends. Accounts of Foster's life responded to each other as well as to other commentators participating in this memory work, often reflecting their present-day concerns as much as historical fact.

# 32
# Reminiscences of Susan McFarland Parkhurst (1916)

### Introduction

*When Susan McFarland Parkhurst (1836–1918) met Foster, she worked for the New York publisher Horace Waters, who published many of the songwriter's last compositions. Parkhurst was a composer in her own right, earning modest recognition for the temperance song "Father's a Drunkard and Mother Is Dead," which appeared in 1866.*

*How well Parkhurst knew Foster is difficult to assess. Her account of his death is generally accurate, but it contains details that are contradicted by other sources, raising suspicions that she borrowed (and misstated and embellished) facts from Birdseye, Morrison, or other sources. Her self-serving tendencies also raise questions about her account. She emphasizes her own charitability, claims to have arranged Foster's songs for him, asserts that she helped Waters publish Foster's last composition, and portrays herself as having possessed conspicuously accurate foresight about how Foster would be remembered in the twentieth century. Embracing the myth of Foster, she practically confers sainthood upon him and attributes moral uprightness to his songs.*

*Harold Vincent Milligan was already at work on his Foster biography when Parkhurst's article appeared. He wrote to her for clarification about her claim that "When Old Friends Were Here" was his last song. The earliest known edition of the song made no such claim; instead, Waters issued "She Was All the World to Me" with a cover that indicated it was "the last song of the late Stephen C. Foster who died January 13th, 1864." Adding to the confusion, Waters's advertisements in the spring of 1864 stated that "'When Old Friends Were Here,' and 'She Was All the World to Me' . . . are his last composition [sic],"[1] and Waters also issued an edition of the two songs together, with a cover that read "the last two songs of the late Stephen C. Foster, who died January 13th, 1864."*

---

[1] "New Music," *Brooklyn Daily Eagle*, April 9, 1864.

*In her response to Milligan, Parkhurst explained that Foster "gave me his last two sketches the day he did his last work." These sketches were still in her possession, and she gave them to Milligan. It is unknown what happened to them after that. She added that of the two songs he gave her "we never knew which was really the last song in his mind, but decided 'She was all the world to me' would not be as taking as 'When Old Friends Were Here.'"*[2]

---

## Mrs. E. A. Parkhurst Duer, "Personal Recollections of the Last Days of Foster." *Etude*, September 1916.

This is a story filled with human interest written by a lady who in her youth was known as a successful composer and who, when a young woman, took a friendly interest in Stephen Foster. She now wishes to tell the readers of THE ETUDE that Foster was not altogether dissolute as many people have supposed.

A half century has passed, since all that was mortal of Stephen Collins Foster, was laid away to a peaceful rest. He left to the world a legacy of song, more precious, more enduring, than silver or gold; a legacy that has cheered the hearts of the sorrowing, lifted the burdens from weary souls, and blessed alike the palace and the hovel. A few sketches of the early life of Mr. Foster have appeared from time to time, but it is noticeable that no mention has ever been made of the last years of his life upon the earth, of the cause or manner of his death. It is only recorded that he died in a hospital, was taken to his birthplace, near Pittsburgh, Pa., and buried with honors. All that this writer knows of Stephen Foster's early days was heard from his own lips, when his troubled existence was drawing to its close. He told of the wrongs he had suffered, of the temptations thrown around him during his years of prosperity and popularity until all he possessed was gone. With a broken heart, crushed spirit, health destroyed, nerves shattered, he broke away from old associations, and secluded himself, hoping to regain his health, and position in the world. Nobly he struggled to conquer his foe, the "wine cup," by which means, evil companions had sought his ruin. I suppose it was then the

---

[2] Mrs. E. A. Parkhurst [Susan McFarland Parkhurst] to Harold Vincent Milligan, October 1, 1916, FHC, C964.

curtain dropped between Stephen Foster and his historians. Like a star that falls in the darkness of night and disappears, this brilliant man was lost to public view. I have been asked to raise the curtain upon the last scenes of Mr. Foster's life.

They are sad pictures, but the brief pathetic story may serve a purpose at this time, when there seems to be a general revival of Stephen Foster's memory and his wonderful songs, throughout our nation.

When this unhappy man began to fight his own great battle, he was followed by misjudgment, and even after his death it was supposed by many that drink was the cause. It is hoped that this simple story will remove all such belief, if it yet exists in a human heart.

## An Interesting Meeting

I do not recall the length of time that elapsed, between the days of Mr. Foster's prosperity and the time that he came under my observation. I shall never forget the day I met him. I was engaged in a large music publishing house on Broadway, New York City, leading a very busy life, although but twenty-one years of age.[3] Every day I met teachers and composers, and was ever hoping that Stephen Foster would appear. I had heard that he was living in New York but had never known anything about his life; yet his songs had created within me a feeling of reverence for the man, and I longed to see him. One day I was speaking with the clerks, when the door opened, and a poorly dressed, very dejected looking man came in, and leaned against the counter near the door, I noticed he looked ill and weak. No one spoke to him. A clerk laughed and said:

"Steve looks down and out."

Then they all laughed, and the poor man saw them laughing at him. I said to myself, "who can Steve be?" It seemed to me, my heart stood still. I asked, "who is that man?"

"Stephen Foster," the clerk replied. "He is only a vagabond, don't go near him."

"Yes, I will go near him, that man needs a friend," was my reply.

---

[3] Parkhurst Duer worked for the publisher Horace Waters. She would have turned 24 in 1860, not 21, when Foster moved to New York.

I was terribly shocked. Forcing back the tears, I waited for that lump in the throat which prevents speech, to clear away. I walked over to him, put out my hand, and asked, "Is this Mr. Foster?"

He took my hand and replied: "Yes, the wreck of Stephen Collins Foster."

"Oh, no," I answered, "not a wreck, but whatever you call yourself, I feel it an honor to take by the hand, the author of *Old Folks at Home*, I am glad to know you." As I spoke, the tears came to his eyes, and he said: "Pardon my tears, young lady, you have spoken the first kind words I have heard in a long time. God bless you." I gave him both hands, saying:

"They will not be the last." I asked him to sit at my desk awhile, and get acquainted. (He seemed pleased, but apologized for his appearance. He was assured it was not his dress, but Mr. Foster I wanted to see.) I judged him to be about forty-five years of age, but the lines of care upon his face, and the stamp of disease, gave him that appearance.[4] We had a long conversation. (I told him of the effect his music has upon me, since my childhood, and how I had longed to know him.) He opened his heart to me, and gave me an insight of his true character, which greatly increased my admiration, but which cannot be repeated in a writing of this length. Stephen Foster was a man of culture and refinement; a purity of thought breathed through every line of his songs. A good old Christian minister once said to me:

"The songs of Stephen Foster could be sung in a prayer meeting, and do lots of good."

## A Friend in Need

When this first visit was ended, Mr. Foster thanked me for my interest in him, and said it had done him a world of good to have some one to talk with. He had no one to call a friend. I asked him to let me be a friend, and perhaps in my humble way, I might be of service to him. I said if he would bring me his manuscript songs that he had not been able to write out, I would do the work for him at his dictation. He was very grateful, and from that time until he

---

[4] Foster was 37 years old when he died in 1864.

died I was permitted to be his helper. Out of respect for my efforts to aid Mr. Foster, all the men in the store treated him kindly. He was made welcome, and no one laughed at him. They were convinced he was no vagabond, and no drunkard. He was poor; disease brought poverty; he had been unable to write, and soon his personal appearance caused him to be misjudged.[5] No hand was stretched out to rescue him in a great Christian community. I dared not question him concerning his comforts in life, or how he existed, but I was confident he needed help; yet how to aid without humiliating him was a study.

## Composed on Wrapping Paper

When he brought me his rude sketches, written on wrapping paper, picked up in a grocery store, and he told me he wrote them while sitting upon a box or barrel, I knew he had no home. I asked him if he had a room; he said:

"No,—I do not write much, as I have no material or conveniences." He then told me that he slept in the cellar room of a little house, owned by an old couple, down in Elizabeth Street in the "Five Points," who knew who he was, and charged him nothing.[6] He said he was comfortable, so I suppose he had a bed. Then I told him that unless he had the right kind of food, he could not be restored to health, and a kind manager of a nearby restaurant had arranged to provide him with a hearty dinner every day, and he need not pay for anything until he was able to do business, and a friend had sent him some medicine which he must take. He looked at me a moment and that fervent "God bless you," paid for all the planning. It was an easy matter to provide other necessary comforts, to be paid for when he recovered his health. We who were near him had no hope of his recovery, but the few comforts provided lessened the suffering of a dying man. This messenger of song, God had given to the world, was not appreciated, and when overtaken by misfortune, was treated as other great souls were in the past, left to die, forsaken by a nation he had blessed by his living.

---

[5] That he had been unable to write appears to be confirmed in the letter he wrote informing George Birdseye that he would arrange a melody as soon as his hand healed.
[6] This contradicts the accounts of Birdseye, Mahon, Morrison, and Cooper, which suggest Foster was living at the American House at 15 Bowery at the time of his death. See Chapter 3, n17.

## Foster's Last Song

One day Mr. Foster came to my desk with the sketch of a song entitled *When old friends were here*. He remarked it might be his last song, and that would be the end of "Foster." Like an inspiration came an impression to my mind, yet in a joking way I said:

"Mr. Foster, I am not a prophet, but I tell you now, that fifty years hence monuments will be erected to Stephen Collins Foster all over this nation. You will be called the author of 'American Folk Song,' and your songs will live forever.["]

He laughed at the idea, but to-day the monuments are appearing, and during the past few years there has been a Foster revival throughout the United States. As Mr. Foster prepared to leave the store, it was growing dark, and as he appeared weaker than usual, I offered to go with him to the street, as I helped him into the stage, he said very earnestly "you are my only friend," and as the door closed he waved his hand, and the last words I heard were "God bless you." I am sure they were his last words on earth. The echo of that fervent prayer will linger near, while life remains.

The next day he did not call for his song, but the evening paper appeared with a great headline, "Stephen C. Foster, dead."[7] "At eleven o'clock last night"—the paper stated—a policeman heard groans, in the cellar of a house he was passing, and upon entering found a man bleeding to death, from a gash in the throat. He had evidently risen from his bed for some water, and had fallen over a broken pitcher. He was taken to Bellevue Hospital in an unconscious condition, and passed away at one o'clock. He was identified by a manuscript in his pocket with his name upon it. Relatives in Pennsylvania claimed the remains. Nothing more concerning his death was published.

## A Pretentious Funeral

There were glowing accounts of a great funeral at his birthplace, with flowers and bands of music playing his famous songs, and a fine monument stands over his grave. The honors were due and I was glad, but, I thought, "A rose to the living, is more than wreaths to the dead." There was a time before

---

[7] Parkhurst Duer's timeline is not correct. Hospital records reveal Foster was admitted on January 10, 1864, and died on January 13. George Cooper wrote to Morrison Foster on January 12. On January 14, he sent Morrison a telegram informing him Foster was dead.

I met Stephen Foster, when he could have been restored to health, and to usefulness.

After Mr. Foster's death, I was silent, as I believed silence would be pleasing to him, but after the years had passed and I heard of the movement to revive his memory, and historians knew nothing about his last days, it seemed a necessity as well as a matter of justice to tell the sad story, that probably no one else living at this time could do. Silence now is harmful, as it might cause misjudgment and injustice.

It has been a difficult task to prepare the above sketch, as there were but two principal actors. The writer was one, and was compelled to appear unpleasingly prominent. I should be sorry to be regarded as boasting of any kindness shown to one in need of a friend. In my heart there dwells only the one deep feeling of gratitude that I was permitted to be the messenger of good tidings to a very weary soul, and given the power to remove any false impressions from the minds of the old or the young, concerning the life and character of Stephen Foster. His last song, finished the day he died, was published by Horace Waters.

My association with Mr. Foster is one of the saddest, sweetest memories of my life. He sometimes seemed to me like one great song, melodies poured forth from his soul continuously, no matter what his physical or mental condition might be, they would be dotted down as if he heard them in the air. He was a wonderful man, with a nature far too sensitive to battle with the world in which he dwelt.

The young generation growing up around us, should be taught to revere the author of American Folk Song, and to pay the homage due. The mists have cleared away that shadowed his early life. His great soul dwells in the sunlight of immortality, and his memory should be sacredly cherished in every heart and home.

# 33
# A "Letter" by W. W. Kingsbury (1905/1916)

**Introduction**

*Around 1840, Foster went to live with his brother William Jr. in Towanda, Pennsylvania, where he attended school. The following year he attended the Athens Academy and boarded in a nearby town. William Wallace Kingsbury (1828–92) lived his entire life in Towanda and attended school with Foster. According to the article, Kingsbury was also friends with William C. Bogart (1802–93), whose daughter Harriet Charlotte Bogart Thompson (1854–1927) discovered the letter reproduced in the following article among his possessions. Kingsbury had apparently written the letter in 1889 and intended to send it to Jane Foster Wiley.*

*Kingsbury's words, however, were not unknown when they appeared in the newspaper. In 1905 his brother Adolphus H. Kingsbury quoted the account in a paper he read to the Bradford County Historical Society. He referred to it not as a letter but as an account titled "Simple Tribute to a Cherished Friend."[1] The paper was published in 1910 in the society's journal. The Foster Hall Collection does not include the letter or newspaper article, but it does include the journal article, which Morneweck quoted in* Chronicles of Stephen Foster's Family.[2]

---

[1] A. H. Kingsbury, "The Old Towanda Academy: History and Reminiscences—Paper by A. H. Kingsbury before the Bradford County Historical Society, March 25, 1905," *Annual* 4 (1910): 15–22.
[2] Morneweck, *Chronicles*, vol. 1, 188–89.

*Formulating Foster*. Christopher Lynch, Oxford University Press. © Oxford University Press 2025.
DOI: 10.1093/9780197811726.003.0034

## "Old Letter Is Found Praising S. C. Foster,"
*Pittsburgh Sun*, September 11, 1916.

Another remembrance of Stephen C. Foster has been added to the permanent collection in the Foster homestead in Penn avenue and Thirty-sixth street by a letter received yesterday by *The Sun*. The letter is a tribute to the composer, written in 1889 but evidently never sent to his widow. It was discovered in an old trunk by Mrs. H. G. Thompson of Grove City while searching among her father's possessions. The letter was written by W. W. Kingsbury of Towanda, a boyhood friend of the composer and also of Mrs. Thompson's father. Mr. Kingsbury died several years ago.

The letter chronicles boyhood days with the composer and is couched in the formal language of the gentleman of the antebellum period. The writer, "most sincerely, your obedient servant," says:

"Well do I remember the inimitable Stephen C. Foster. He was my especial friend and champion. Being older than myself and considerably larger he used to defend me in my boyhood antagonisms with belligerent schoolmates. We often played truant together, rambling by the shady streams or gathering wild strawberries in the meadows and pastures removed from the sound of the old academy bell.

"One mutual luxury in which we jointly indulged in those excursions without leave was in going barefoot and wading pools of running water that meandered through Mercer's farm, and down Mix's run in the village of my nativity. Foster wore a fine quality of hose and I remember how it shocked me to see him cast them away when soiled by perspiration or muddy water.

"His was a nature generous to a fault with a soul attuned to harmony. His love of music was an all-absorbing passion, and his execution on the flute was the very genius of melody, and gave rise to those flights of inspired pathos which have charmed the ear of the English-speaking world with their excellence from cabin to palace.

"Genial, well-remembered friend! How proud I have been in the thought that it was my good fortune to have been the boyhood comrade of a character commanding such world-wide fame as you have established in the hearts of a song-loving people.

"If, as I firmly believe, we are permitted to prosecute the avocations of this life to an advanced state of perfection as we cross to the Shining Shore, I expect to hear your divine invocations, both vocal and instrumental, mellifluently ringing through the corridors of a domain pre-eminently 'fairer than this.'"

The letter of Mr. Kingsbury was sent to *The Sun* for delivery to the Foster descendants. The letter will be placed in the display case in the memorial room, according to Mrs. A. D. Rose, a granddaughter, now living in the homestead.

## 34

# An Interview with B. D. M. Eaton (ca. 1916)

### Introduction

*This clipping is in the Foster Hall Collection and labeled 1916. The article asserts that B. D. M. Eaton was the nephew of Daniel L. Eaton, who was the editor of the* Pittsburgh Commercial Gazette. *In the 1850s B. D. M. Eaton moved from Pittsburgh to St. Louis, where he worked for newspapers and started the* Home Journal, *which later became the* Hotel Reporter. *Among other things, he reported on guests checking in and out of St. Louis hotels, particularly people who worked in the theater.*

### Unidentified Clipping, Foster Hall Collection.

B. D. M. Eaton, now of St. Louis, but formerly a Pittsburgh newspaper man, and whose uncle, Daniel L. Eaton, was at one time associate editor of the *Commercial Gazette*, has long been a writer on stage topics and in some interesting articles that he has recently written he refers at some length to the subject of stage inheritances through blood and family ties.[1] Mr. Eaton, by the way, writes interestingly of his former residence in this city 60 years ago, when he wrote for the old *Gazette*. Of this period, he writes:

> In 1853 I lived on Beaver street, opposite Capt. Koontz's residence, and from his bedroom window he could look down on the penitentiary to the south and up on the Presbyterian College, which looked as if the congregation had cut into the top of a hill to locate its university and wanted to be protected from the right and left environments.

[1] In 1889, *Rowell's American Newspaper Directory* (Rowell, 1889) lists B. D. M. Eaton as editor of the *St. Louis Daily Hotel Reporter*.

This was before the railroad company had purchased the buildings on the side of the canal that connected with the canal that crossed the Allegheny River to Pittsburgh proper.

My favorite Sunday trip was to visit Stephen C. Foster to hear him play and sing. He had just composed the *Old Kentucky Home*—had just returned from the South—and had just purchased a new piano, and lived in a handsome cottage in Lawrenceville.[2]

---

[2] Foster published "My Old Kentucky Home" in 1853, and about two years earlier he had gone on a trip to the South. However, he lived in New York until the end of 1854, when he moved back to Allegheny to live with his family in his brother's house. It is possible that Eaton heard him sing in this home in Allegheny.

# 35

# Harry Houdini's Take on Kit Clarke's Memories of Foster (1916)

### Introduction

*After the publication of Susan Parkhurst's article, the magician Harry Houdini wrote to the* Etude *to dispute some of her claims. Houdini did not know Foster firsthand, but, as we have seen, he was friends with Foster's friend Kit Clarke. He claimed to be relaying information from Clarke in his article, but very little of the information he provided seems accurate. As a friend of Clarke's, Houdini probably misremembered stories Clarke had told him about Foster and fused them with information he had read elsewhere.*

### *Etude*, November 1916.

DEAR SIR:—I have read with interest the various articles regarding Stephen Collins Foster appearing in the September ETUDE. It may interest you to know that in my search for data to enlarge my collection of literature pertaining to the drama, minstrelsy and stage magic I am in a position to shed further light upon Foster's last days. This information is secured from Mr. Brikett [sic] Clarke, a newspaper man and press agent well known in his day. Mr. Clarke and Stephen Foster shared the same room during the months of August, September, October and November, 1863—in fact, practically up to the time of Foster's removal to Bellevue Hospital. They lived on the south side of Hester Street. Next door to them was a grocery store on the corner, facing Hester Street on one side and Elizabeth Street on the other.

Mr. Clarke is now seventy-six years of age but, apart from deafness, his mind and senses are keen and bright. He assures me that Foster did not have to live in a cellar, but had full use of the room they shared together. His account of Foster's death is as follows: Shortly after New Year's Day, 1864, Clarke had an appointment with Foster to see the Woods' Minstrels on Broadway, opposite the St. Nicholas Hotel. Foster not showing up, Clarke went to the entertainment alone. On his return to his room he found a letter awaiting him, delivered shortly before his arrival, telling him to come immediately to the American Hotel, as Foster was hurt.[1] He hurried there, and found the composer in an unconscious condition. It appears that Foster had slipped, and in falling struck his head against the stove, fracturing his skull over the right temple. Clarke carried Foster to a four-wheeler, and then took him to the Bellevue Hospital.[2] He then rushed out to send a wire to Dr. MacDowell [sic], Foster's father-in-law. In doing so he neglected to inform the hospital authorities that Foster was the composer and author, and this is the reason Foster was described on the hospital books as a "laborer," as reported in the ETUDE by Dr. G. O. Hanlon, General Medical Superintendent of Bellevue. Clarke realized that Foster had been seriously injured, and though he knew that Foster and his wife had been separated for some time, he thought that a telegram to Dr. MacDowell, who was a well-known physician in Pittsburgh—then a much smaller place than it is to-day—would result in Mrs. Foster being informed.

Clarke visited the sick man in the hospital two and three times a day, until, on the morning of the thirteenth of January, he arrived to find that poor Foster has passed away. Nothing being known of Foster, and no one appearing to claim the body, it was taken to the morgue. Clarke also went to the morgue, and while standing there Mrs. Foster appeared, having come too late to see her husband alive. She was dressed in black. Looking at the body, she fell down upon her knees. Clarke did the same, their prayers and tears intermingling. Subsequently Mrs. Foster had the body removed to Pittsburgh, where it now rests.

Mr. Clarke knows positively that Christie paid Foster the sum of $500 to have his name printed on the Pond edition of *Old Folks at Home*, as he desired to have the honor of being known as the composer of that deathless folk-song. On receiving the money Foster searched for and found his great boon companion, George Cooper, a young newspaper man and writer of

---

[1] The name of Foster's place of residence was the American House (see Chapter 3, n17).
[2] In a letter to Harold Vincent Milligan dated March 24, 1917, Houdini wrote, "Mr. Clarke was the man who took him [Foster] in his arms and carried him into the carriage, which took Foster to the Hospital" (FHC, C962). This is almost certainly untrue, however, for in his own reminiscence Clarke stated that the last time he saw Foster was weeks before his death (see Chapter 11).

verse, who hailed from Strawberry Plain, N. J. They went to Pfaff's that night, where Clarke subsequently joined them.

Mr. Brikett [sic] Clarke also related a unique experience in connection with Stephen Foster which is not without interest. It happened about the middle of June, 1863. Clarke cannot recall the exact date, but it was at the time of the Wheeling Convention, in which forty counties of Virginia repudiated secession and applied for admission to the Union. The day following this event he was seated with Stephen Foster and Daniel Decatur Emmett at the old Collamore House, corner of Spring and Broadway, New York, talking over war topics in general, when they saw through the window a brigade of boys on their way to the front. They were led by a band playing *I Wish I Were In Dixie*.

"That is your song," said Foster.

"Yes," admitted Emmett.

Presently another regiment went by, and the band was playing *The Old Folks At Home*.

Clarke, young as he was, appreciated the fact of knowing two authors who he felt were destined to be remembered long after both he and they were dead. Being in the habit of keeping a diary, he made an elaborate entry of the event.

Trusting you will see fit to give space to this letter in your publication, I beg to remain,

Sincerely yours<br>
Harry Houdini

# 36

# Reminiscences of John W. Robinson (1920)

## Introduction

*While writing his biography, Harold Vincent Milligan corresponded with John W. Robinson, son of Susan Pentland and Andrew Robinson. John faintly recalled visiting Foster in New York with his parents when he was a boy. Unfortunately, Robinson's original letter is lost, and we are left only with Milligan's summary.*

### Harold Vincent Milligan. *Stephen Collins Foster.*

During the early part of his life in New York, Stephen received a visit from his former sweetheart, Susan Pentland, to whom he had dedicated his first published song, "Open Thy Lattice, Love." She was now Mrs. Robinson, and her son, John W. Robinson of Pittsburgh, remembers the trip to New York with his parents and the meeting with Stephen Foster. The exact date is uncertain, but Mr. Robinson believes that it was just before the outbreak of the war, probably late in 1860, or early in 1861. They stopped at the St. Nicholas Hotel, on Broadway, near Spring Street, and the street, jammed with busses, made a deep impression on the small boy. He remembers that his father hunted up Stephen and brough him to dinner at the hotel and that they had a merry time. After dinner they all went to Laura Keen's Theatre. Mr. Robinson is under the impression that Stephen was making a living as a music teacher. He remembers him as bright and entertaining, and in his recollection of the event there is no hint of the misery and destitution that afterward overtook Stephen.

# 37

# More Reminiscences from George C. Cooper (1920)

## Introduction

*Although Milligan incorporated into his biography much of the information he gleaned from his interviews and correspondence with Cooper, it is also apparent that Milligan had Birdseye's account in hand when writing about the period of Foster's life when he knew Cooper, for much of the phrasing is identical or similar. Cooper, however, reviewed the text and signed off in the end, confirming Milligan's portrayal of his remembrances of Foster and corroborating several of Birdseye's claims.*

Not all of Cooper's reminiscences made it into Milligan's book, though. In one case this was due to Cooper's wishes. Privately, for example, Cooper informed Milligan that he had personally given clothing to a destitute Foster, but he asked him not to publish about it. He wrote, "This seems to me (although true) just a little like bragging of a kindness done." It is unknown why other anecdotes are excluded. For example, Cooper also revealed privately that Foster "liked to ride up and down Broadway in the old time omnibuses; their rattling stirred up melodies in his head, so he declared!" He also relayed that "Foster liked to execute a few chords on a tinkly, rickety, yellow hollowed out [illegible] piano" and that "he always said he preferred such a one to a brand new Steinway!"[1]

Some of Milligan's other omissions reveal that he was reluctant to cast any shadows over his subject. As we have already seen, he chose to omit Cooper's recollection that Foster opposed abolition. He also declined to include what Cooper had told him about the origins of the song "Jenny June." Cooper explained that the song was originally the drinking song "When the Bowl Goes Round" but that the words "were changed at my suggestions as not likely to suit the general public." Cooper speculated that Foster probably

---

[1] George Cooper to Harold Vincent Milligan, July 2, 1917, FHC, C929.

gave the original drinking song to the publisher Daly without him knowing, suggesting that Daly's was a "<u>clearing house</u> for rejected manuscripts, and I've no doubt Foster left this as security for a slight loan." Milligan chose to leave out this information about Foster's drinking song and financial desperation, opting instead to only briefly acknowledge and romanticize Foster's alcoholism. He wrote,

> "Drunken" he may have been in these last sad days; "dissolute" he never was. The least sympathetic of his memorialists give him credit for the purity of his soul and the manner of his life. He impressed all who met him with the delicacy and sensibility of his nature. A more robust character, a stronger will, might have taken a firmer grip on life and shaken off the benumbing influence of the weakness that ruined his career, but on the other hand probably such a temperament could not have produced "Swanee River." Sensitive, introspective, given to brooding rather than to action, Stephen paid the penalty of his temperament; the world is richer for his weakness.[2]

Milligan's biography was not immediately influential, but his choices about what to include would eventually play a central role in cementing the Foster myth.

## Harold Vincent Milligan, *Stephen Collins Foster.*

One of the most interesting events connected with the writing of this biography was the discovery that George Cooper, the friend who notified Morrison Foster of his brother's illness and death, is still living; Mr. Cooper is able to furnish some accurate and first-hand information with regard to Stephen's last days, and to dispose of many of the legends and faulty reminiscences which have flourished of late years. His collaboration with Stephen Foster was the beginning of a long and very successful career as a writer of song lyrics, a career that brought him into intimate contact with the course of American musical composition during the past fifty years. His name appears on the list of first editions of Foster's songs, published by the

---

[2] Harold Vincent Milligan, *Stephen Collins Foster: A Biography of America's Folk-Song Composer* (G. Schirmer, 1920), 99–100.

Library of Congress, as the author of the words of eighteen of the songs.[3] One of them is erroneously attributed to "Henry" Cooper, due to a typographical error on the title-page of the first edition....

George Cooper tells of meeting Stephen Foster in the back-room of a disreputable grocery on the corner of Hester and Christie Streets. According to the custom of that time, the front of the shop was devoted to the sale of groceries, but back of a partition was a small room which was used as a saloon, and here Stephen spent much of his time. Mr. Cooper describes him as a man utterly careless of his appearance, having apparently lost the incentive power of self-respect. He lived at 15 Bowery, in a cheap lodging-house where he paid 25 cents a night.[4] He told Mr. Cooper that he had had a regular income of $1,500.00 a year from his songs, and Mr. Cooper is under the impression that, although in destitution himself, he was at this time supporting his wife and daughter in Pittsburgh. He was very fond of the poetry of Edgar Allan Poe, and recited long extracts from it with thrilling effect.

Young Mr. Cooper was something of a poet, and the two formed a partnership. The first of the songs of which Cooper wrote the words was published in 1863 and in less than a year they wrote and published eighteen [sic]. These songs they sold for whatever they could get for them, which was never much. The song "Willie Has Gone to the War" was written one morning, and after it was finished, Stephen rolled it up and tucking it under his arm, said, "Well, where shall we put this one?" Cooper says that he remembers it was a cold, raw, winter day, snow falling drearily, and the pavements covered with slush. Stephen's shoes had holes in them and he had no overcoat, but he seemed oblivious to discomfort and misery. As the author and composer proceeded up Broadway, they passed Wood's Music Hall, and the proprietor, standing in the lobby, hailed them as they passed with the question, "What have you got there, Steve?" The song was sold then and there, Wood paying $10 cash, $15 more to be paid at the box-office that evening.

Stephen called Cooper "the left wing of the song factory," and most of their songs were written and sold in very much the same manner as "Willie Has Gone to the War." They sold all of their songs for cash, receiving no royalties on any of them. This was not important to Cooper, who was a youth of about twenty, living at home with his parents, and song-writing was something of a pastime for him, but to Stephen, entirely dependent upon his songs for

---

[3] A total of twenty-three songs resulted from the Cooper–Foster collaboration.
[4] The American House was located at 15 Bowery (see Chapter 3, n17).

livelihood, it meant destitution. His clothes were poor and sadly worn, a fact to which he seemed totally indifferent. Cooper says that on several occasions friends gave him clothes, but usually Stephen appeared again after a few days in his ragged suit and glazed cap. This cap seems to have been an outstanding feature of his appearance in these last days, as it is mentioned by several biographers.

This sorry picture of Stephen's disreputable appearance is somewhat belied by the ambrotype of Stephen and George Cooper, taken in 1863, only a few months before his death. True, his good clothes may have been assumed for that occasion only, but the picture is hardly that of a man in the last stages of alcoholism. Unfortunately the ambrotype is not a good one, and both the faces are blurred, but the likeness of Stephen is distinct enough to give the lie to those of his biographers who describe his face as that of Silenus.

Although he drank constantly, Cooper says that Stephen was never intoxicated. He was indifferent to food, often making a meal of apples or turnips from the grocery shop, peeling them with a large pocket-knife. The "rum" he drank was concocted by the barkeeper from French spirits and brown sugar, and was kept in a keg.

He wrote with great facility and without the aid of a piano. If no music-paper was handy, he would take whatever paper he could find, and, ruling the lines on it, proceed without hesitation to write. He seemed never at a loss for a melody, and the simple accompaniment caused him no trouble. These first drafts were taken out and sold to a publisher or theatre manager, practically without correction. To this habit is evidently due the "brown wrapping paper" legend, as Cooper says that he would use brown wrapping paper if he couldn't find anything else.

George Cooper enlisted in the 22nd New York Regiment in 1862, and was at the front during a large part of this year. He was with the same regiment in 1863, serving in the Gettysburg campaign, returning to New York upon the disbanding of the regiment on July 24th, 1863. From this time until Stephen's death, a few months later, they continued their collaboration. Cooper's story of Stephen's death, which is undoubtedly the true one, is as follows:

"Early one winter morning I received a message saying that my friend had met with an accident; I dressed hurriedly and went to 15 Bowery, the old lodging-house where Stephen lived, and found him lying on the floor in the hall, blood oozing from a cut in his throat and with a bad bruise on his forehead. Steve never wore any night-clothes and he lay there on the floor, naked, and suffering horribly. He had wonderful big brown eyes and they looked up at me with an appeal I can never forget. He whispered, 'I'm done for,' and begged for a drink, but before I could get it for him, the doctor who had been sent for arrived and forbade it. He started to sew up the gash in Steve's throat, and I was horrified to observe that he was using black thread. "Haven't you any white thread," I asked, and he said no, he had picked up the first thing he could find. I decided the doctor was not much good and I went down stairs and got Steve a big drink of rum, which I gave him and which seemed to help him a lot. We put his clothes on him and took him to the hospital. In addition to the cut on his throat and the bruise on his forehead, he was suffering from a bad burn on his thigh, caused by the overturning of a spirit lamp used to boil water. This had happened several days before, and he had said nothing about it, nor done anything for it. All the time we were caring for him, he seemed terribly weak and his eyelids kept fluttering. I shall never forget it.

"I went back again to the hospital to see him, and he said nothing had been done for him, and he couldn't eat the food they brought him. When I went back again the next day they said 'Your friend is dead.' His body had been sent down into the morgue, among the nameless dead. I went down to look for it. There was an old man sitting there, smoking a pipe. I told him what I wanted and he said "Go look for him." I went around peering into the coffins until I found Steve's body. It was taken care of by Winterbottom, the undertaker, in Broome Street, and removed from Bellevue. The next day his brother Morrison, and Steve's widow, arrived. They stayed at the St. Nicholas Hotel. When Mrs. Foster entered the room where Steve's body was lying, she fell on her knees before it, and remained for a long time."

# 38
# An Interview with Marion Foster Welch (1924)

### Introduction

*By the time of the sixtieth anniversary of Foster's death in 1924, the Foster Memorial Home on Penn Ave. in Pittsburgh had been open for eight years with Marion and Jessie acting as caretakers. The previous summer, Federal Hill in Bardstown had opened as a museum. In the days leading up to the death anniversary, Marion offered the following reminiscences in an interview with the* Pittsburgh Gazette Times.

### *Pittsburgh Gazette Times*, **January 10, 1924.**

Memories of her father, Stephen C. Foster, in the happy years when he lived in Pittsburgh and she as a child played at his knees, came back clearly yesterday across the span of years to his only daughter, Mrs. Marion Foster Welsh, aged 72, in the Foster Memorial Home, 3600 Penn avenue.[1]

Bright-eyed and with gleaming face she told of the many kindnesses which she and her mother received from him in spite of the difficulties which he was finding at the time in marketing his compositions. She told of how often she and her mother were taken to the theaters to hear good music even though the cost must have meant sacrifice to the father.

"He had so much trouble with the publishers," said Mrs. Welsh. "In spite of what he wrote it was all he could do to earn a living. That is what finally drove him to New York in an effort to sell his music, but I knew later that he found it just as hard there, and there are trunks containing some of his original

---

[1] Marion preferred to spell her name "Welch."

*Formulating Foster*. Christopher Lynch, Oxford University Press. © Oxford University Press 2025.
DOI: 10.1093/9780197811726.003.0039

manuscripts that he left in a rooming house in New York that would be very valuable today.[2]

"I was born in a house on Union avenue, Pittsburgh," she said, "and from the time I was just a little girl my father took much interest in my dancing. He would take me to a dancing academy taught by Prof. Cowper on Liberty avenue, and there was a taffy shop near and as a reward he would often stop and buy me candy. Oh, I think those were the happiest days of my life.

"Father never had much opportunity to work on his compositions, as I remember it. For a while we lived in a house on Seventh avenue and then we had a third floor room where he could go off by himself and play. I remember once when he took another little girl and myself to the theater. In the middle of the performance he told us he would leave and come back for us later. I found out that it was something in the music that displeased him. After that I noticed him do the same thing on other occasions."

Her face saddened when she spoke of his death. "I was only 11 years old when he died," she said, "and in the years since then how they have changed his music. The music that you hear played in the theaters now ascribed to him is not really his. Notes are changed and added. This is so even in many of the song books and I don't think it is right when it is credited to him. I have the first editions of all of his work here."

"Yes I play sometimes too," she said, "and I have composed music but never with any great success with the publishers. It is very hard. I guess it's the way of the world."

She spoke of the controversy as to the correct location of the old Foster homestead where her father was born. "All the records that I have been able to find," she said, "show that this was the spot where the old home stood. It was the only house in this district at the time, and the fields sloped from the house to the Allegheny River."

---

[2] Mahon refers to Foster as having had a trunk in his room filled with his papers (see Chapter 5). It is unknown what happened to his trunk after his death, but presumably Morrison took it back to Pennsylvania. Marion may have been suspicious that more manuscripts were in New York because of the way Foster's manuscript book of lyrics was returned to the family around the year 1890. In a letter to Josiah Kirby Lilly dated October 15, 1934, Alexander D. Rose explains that Jane received the book in the mail with an explanatory letter from Mattie Stewart de Witt, dated January 2, 1890. Rose sent the letter to Lilly, but it is now lost. He writes: "This lady the writer was the daughter of Mrs. Stewart who kept the boarding house at which Stephen, Jane and Marion lived. She has also enclosed her picture with the letter." Apparently the book was overlooked by Morrison when gathering up the belongings of his brother after his death—or perhaps Mrs. Stewart the landlady thought it might be a good memento to keep herself. At any rate, some twenty-six years after Foster's death her daughter sent the book to his widow.

Mrs. Welsh has two daughters, Mrs. Alexander Rose of Pittsburgh, and Mrs. Mabel Reed of New York. There are three children in the Rose family, Stephen, Dallas and Dorothy Rose. The children in the Reed family are Virginia and Marshall Reed.

# 39

# An Interview with Marion Foster Welch (1929)

**Introduction**

*In 1929, the American Society of Composers, Authors, and Publishers (ASCAP) invited Marion to a party in her honor at the Ritz-Carlton Hotel in New York. While preparing for the trip, she informed a Pittsburgh newspaper that "some of the time I remember best are the parties which father, mother and I attended at the homes of the Dennys, Schenleys and other old Pittsburgh families." She added, "I used to dance at them. I was quite a dancer, you know, and father was very proud of me."[1] She elaborated slightly in the following interview, frustratingly written as it may be, which took place at the ASCAP party.*

## *Kansas City Star*, April 11, 1929.

If counted in money, Mrs. Marion Foster Welch has little to show for the songs her father wrote, but she computes her wealth in memories and thrills she experiences when she hears them played. Recently Mrs. Welch came from Pittsburgh, her home, to New York City to be the guest at a banquet given in her honor and in the commemoration of her father. In an interview in the *New York World* she told of her recollections of her father and why she is not discontented at not having received royalties from her father's melodies, which are among the most popular in this country.

Lively as a cricket at 77, eyes twinkling, small hands quick to jab punctuation into the running flow of her speech, Mrs. Marion Foster Welch sits in a stiff-backed hotel room chair and smiles at her visitors, her black taffeta

---

[1] "Stephen Foster's Daughter Planning Trip to New York," *Pittsburgh Press*, March 24, 1929.

crinkling as she leans forward, tense with the excitement which is her life and has been her life.

Stephen Collins Foster created a lot of happiness for America when he wrote "My Old Kentucky Home" and "Way Down Upon the Swanee River," the first of America's folk songs. A little old lady, his only daughter breathes that happiness as she spirals words into a jumble of reminiscences of her father, her mother, herself when she was "dressed like a fairy, dancing on my tip-toes on the best plush carpets of Pittsburgh."

A pretty girl in a yellow silk dress gurgles with laughter as her grandmother tells of the olden days when Marion Foster and Jennie, her mother, and Stephen, her father, went miles by horse and buggy to parties "at a judge's house way out in Ohio." She came all the way from Pittsburgh to New York, where she shares the Stephen C. Foster home with her daughter, Jessie Rose, Jessie's two boys, and Matthew, that incorrigible bachelor of 52, her oldest child, for—a party!

## Came for a Party

And that was some party, too, that party the American Society for Composers, Authors and Publishers had Thursday night at the Ritz.

"And what do you s'pose? When I came in they all clapped me and wanted me to make a speech before I got a chance to sit down."

The little hands stabbed the air to make it all clear. And the visitors thought perhaps, the people who say this only daughter of an American genius is unfortunate, that with copyrights what they should be, she would have millions from her father's songs—the visitors thought, perhaps, this little lady was very far from unfortunate. They said so. She agreed. She has her memories of the man who lived "for nothing but to make us happy."

All the sorrow which Stephen Foster's strange humors generated, his death in Bellevue, a pauper estranged from his family—that is no longer alive in the mind of the girl who wrote her own "Beautiful Dreamer" at the age of eight, who danced on the best plush of Pittsburgh and was to have been a great actress had Stephen Foster had his way with "ma."

## Remembers Her Father

Her life, the past she remembers, is tinkling tunes that still dance in the evening when she sits by the piano; is a strong fine man, Bill Welch [sic], now twenty years gone to his reward; is the memories of parties with the man whose life, clipped short at 38,[2] yet overfilled with sorrow, must have held moments of intense happiness. For the father the little lady in taffeta with the red rose, "which I forgot to put in water," gallant above trim lace, remembers, was a gay flare of a person, who even now is "just full of music."

Off come the tortoise shell spectacles for a picture. Then Mrs. Rose, who came up to New York with her mother, is ready to guide her over to Brooklyn to see another daughter, Mrs. Mabel Foster Reed, the mother of the girl in yellow silk, Virginia. Virginia's mother has supper waiting. The visitors go out past the gold braid to a street corner. An old man is working hard to make notes come from a flute. Stephen Foster's "Way Down Upon the Swanee River" swings bravely into Madison avenue as the calloused fingers labor on. "All he thought of was ma and me—and our happiness."

---

[2] Foster was 37 at the time of his death.

# 40
# Family Memories Relayed by the Grandson of Thomas "Daddy" Rice (1931)

### Introduction

*Dean J. Rice, the grandson of the blackface performer Thomas "Daddy" Rice, claimed Foster wrote the songs "Long Ago Day" and "This Rose Will Remind You" for his grandfather. Although his grandfather never performed them, the manuscripts supposedly remained in the family's possession, and Dean J. Rice transcribed them before losing the originals. He supposedly forgot about them until he rediscovered them while conducting research on his grandfather in 1930. At that point he began to pursue the publication of the songs and arranged for a performance of "Long Ago Day" to be broadcast in Salt Lake City on April 5, 1931, sung by baritone Shipley Burton and accompanied by Frank W. Asper, the first Tabernacle organist.[1] Lilly likely learned about "Long Ago Day" through the press coverage in Pittsburgh of the song's rediscovery.[2] He reached out to Rice on March 24, 1931, and ultimately helped have the songs published and recorded in the* Foster Hall Recordings.[3]

*The authenticity of the songs and Dean J. Rice's story about them are questionable. Pointing to stylistic departures from Foster's typical songwriting, musicologists Deane L. Root and Steven Saunders classify them as "doubtful works" in their critical edition of Foster's music.[4] Additionally, some details in Dean J. Rice's story about the songs shifted slightly throughout a series of letters he sent to Lilly, which suggests, perhaps, that he strained to remember the details.*

---

[1] Dean J. Rice to Josiah K. Lilly, April 5, 1931, FHC, unprocessed folder labeled "Rice, Dean J. 1931."
[2] William R. Mitchell, "May Add Additional Songs to Foster List," *Pittsburgh Press*, April 27, 1930.
[3] Lilly's original letter is lost, but Rice refers to it in his reply dated March 27, 1931.
[4] Saunders and Root, *Music of Stephen Foster*, vol. 2, 472–76.

*Formulating Foster*. Christopher Lynch, Oxford University Press. © Oxford University Press 2025.
DOI: 10.1093/9780197811726.003.0041

*Dean J. Rice's initial response to Lilly's inquiry, dated March 27, 1931, is his longest and most thorough account of the songs and their provenance. It is reproduced below with annotations detailing contradictions and elaborations found in subsequent correspondence dated April 4 and April 5, 1931, as well as the official "statement" on the songs' provenance that Dean J. Rice wrote to be included in the new sheet music.*

*An excerpt from another letter, dated April 14, 1931, is also reproduced below. Following the broadcast of "Long Ago Day," a radio listener directed Dean J. Rice to Nevin's article about his grandfather and Foster, prompting him to write to Lilly to respond to several of Nevin's assertions.*

## Dean J. Rice to Josiah Kirby Lilly, March 27, 1931.

Dear Sir:

I have your letter, March 24, respecting the Stephen C. Foster song "Goin Down De Road." Of necessity I shall have to reply at some length. My grandfather was Thomas D. Rice (1808–1860). See Amer. Encyclopaedia, Winter's "Wallet of Time," Hornblow's "American Stage," etc. Mr. Rice was the first actor to make negro minstrelsy popular here and in England, with his character and song "Jim Crow"; he was also the author of the songs "Lucy Long" and "Sich a Getting Upstairs" and others—all of a light type and so arranged as to give him opportunity to dance. Mr. Rice was not a musician and his songs were all re-drest [sic] by a musician friend who published in either Pittsburg or Cincinnati.

The foregoing and following information came to me from my father, now dead, Thomas C. G. Rice (1842–1892). My father had known Foster personally in New York City in the early sixties and both had attended the Bowery Theatre in that city. It seems that Foster as a very young man had brought some of his songs to T. D. Rice but Rice refused them. In those days Rice was very popular in Louisville, Pittsburgh, Washington and Cincinnati. Foster told my father that his idea of writing negro songs first came to him after seeing T. D. Rice in "Jim Crow." The Christy Bros. minstrels were next approached by Foster and this organization used his compositions. The Christy Bros. refined negro minstrelsy, where heretofore, Rice and his imitators had presented the grotesque plantation negro. Mr. Rice quick to see symptoms of public change of sentiment, set out to write less farcical delineations and at this period Foster came to him with two songs, "Goin

Down De Road" and "This Will Remind You."[5] The first was Foster's own work words and air, the second was only Foster's by reason of its air—the words were by a G. Mellen a newspaper poet I believe whose poem had struck Foster's fancy.[6] Mr. Rice bought both songs readily to incorporate into his proposed new offering. Foster told my father that he by terms of the sale had to teach Rice the songs and secured a guitar and taught Rice the cords [sic] of accompaniment with much difficulty and with great amusement.[7] Mr. Rice objected to the title "Goin Down De Road" so it was at Rice's request renamed "Long-Ago Day." Rice was dissuaded by managers from attempting to change his type of performance—so he abandoned his new work which included the negro song. It was his intention to use "Long Ago Day" however until his friend and advisor a Mr. O'Connor pointed out that its sentiment was anti-slavery and that his audiences in the South where he was popular might take offence—so he or no one else ever used the song.[8] As for the dual composition, it was so unsuited to anything Rice portrayed—it was

---

[5] In his "statement," Dean J. Rice stated that this meeting of his grandfather and Foster was "in 1851 and in Cincinnati."

[6] This letter suggests that Foster himself chose the poem, but in a subsequent letter dated April 4, 1931, Rice claimed, "The words were in my grandfather's possession first, of this I feel certain." In his official "statement" of provenance, Rice asserted that at their meeting in 1851 Foster presented only "Long Ago Day," after which Thomas Rice requested that Foster "compose an air to some verses written by a G. Mellen (or Mellon) which Rice treasured for their sentiment, so the song 'The Rose Will Remind You' came to be."

[7] On April 4, 1931, Rice wrote to Lilly that "'The Rose Will Remind You' was only Foster's by reason of the air he wrote for it and that this air had to be written expressly to suit the range of T. D. Rice's range of voice." On April 5, 1931, he elaborated to Lilly: "Foster made no accompaniment for the songs. Mr. Rice knew music chiefly by 'ear.' Foster used a guitar while working on the song with Rice and Foster's comment made long after to my father was that he had a difficult time instructing Rice on the simple chords of the instrument." "It is certain that Rice would have turned the mss. over to his orchestra leader had he used the songs. This particular leader followed Rice in all his engagements as Rice's erratic songs and dances together with his improvised verses called for a musician who was familiar with Rice's eccentricities in art."

[8] According to Dean J. Rice's "statement," this explanation for why the songs were never performed came from "Foster's account of the songs related to Thos. C. G. Rice, the minstrel's son, after his father's death." On April 5, 1931, Rice informed Lilly that the manager who had misgivings about "anti-slavery" sentiments in the song was his grandfather's "personal friend" and that his name was "Mr. Connor (or O'Connor)." Considering how abolitionists harnessed sentimentality to humanize enslaved people and recruit supporters into the abolitionist movement, it is understandable that this friend of Thomas Rice would have reservations about the song.
   However, in the "statement," Dean J. Rice stated that Foster found the feared Southern reaction "hard to imagine and ... resented the criticism." This reaction makes sense. Because Foster harnessed sentimentality to sidestep sectionalism and partisanship, he would have believed that the lyrics would be well received in both the North and South by people for and against enslavement. According to the "statement," "It was [Foster's] desire to repossess ['Long Ago Day'] after T. D. Rice's death and have it published but an embarrassment in Rice's estate at the time prevented this. Rice had reserved the song 'The Rose Will Remind You' for a production he was not destined to complete, so it likewise found oblivion."
   Rice also explained on April 5 that he believes his grandfather did not intend to perform "This Rose Will Remind You" himself but to pass it on to someone in his troupe. He wrote, "'This Will

not considered. My father brought together other mss. and souvenirs from New York City in 1869 to Omaha the guitar and the two songs.

Some years later while living in Evanston, Wyoming my father gave into the hands of a Mr. Archbald Forbes, a man who had known his father, the old lithographs (published Pittsburgh) stage acts, and mss. of T. D. Rice to be delivered to my father's sister a Mrs. Elizabeth Fogarty in New York. Mr. Forbes made copies of all he took and left these with my father. The songs of Foster I copied from these copies.[9] I do not know whether the mss. taken East by Forbes were the original from Foster's pen or copies made by T. D. Rice. Altho I am sixty years old I never bothered to look over the old papers preserved by my father until last April 1930, when a cousin whom I didn't know existed wrote to me for some information concerning my grandfather. My father was the only son of T. D. Rice. I am his last male representative. While I know all about the songs from my father, I shared his lack of interest in them as far as to their author but last May I showed them to a friend who enthused over them and from him the local paper took the matter up. I have had dozens of letters from all over the country concerning them. I have answered very few of them. I really would like them published to rebuke the trash of this present day. I submitted them to one publisher at the suggestion of a friend, and this concern replied that they were too "old fashioned" for this day—that Foster only wrote two good songs in his day and that they even would not pass muster today. Now I am determined that the one "Long Ago Day" shall be known. I have recently made it a point to inform myself on songs for the sole purpose of knowing "what's what." If the present day songs are music or decent even I am mistaken. My father T. C. G. Rice said of Foster repeatedly that he was a man of the highest type, refined, kindly and above all sober and <u>not given to liquor</u> and America's greatest composer in that the Old Folks at Home was America's greatest song.

My father was not a musician but he said that he was often amused to see Foster suffer at the musical attempts of the Bowery artists. I have had to impose this long letter on you under the circumstances. As I have stated I was too young at the time Mr. Forbes took the Rice papers East with him to know

---

Remind You' could it seems to me, never have been in Mr. Rice's mind to use, it seems so foreign to his presentations. There were actors who assisted him in his productions, and he wrote his own and many of them, who sang sentimental songs. I think it was his intention to so use this song."

[9] On April 5, 1931, Rice testified that "the copies are reliable and exact." On April 4, 1931, Rice wrote that he accompanied himself on guitar in a performance of "Long Ago Day" at his school when "I was about 12 years of age," after which he put both songs away and forgot about them.

whether the copies he took where [*sic*] Foster's notes or Rice's—that was about 1879 I should judge. My father's sister Elizabeth Fogarty is dead and if she had children I do not know. A cousin by the name of Sanborn wrote to me a year ago for family information, which I gave, but in turn for that I asked for concerning my aunts, he has made no reply. I am sending you the words of the two songs. I would send you also the airs were it not for the fact that a motion picture company has offered $300.00 for the songs and I may not do any better with the publishers who have written to me concerning them.[10] Certainly some of the publishers names would discredit the songs. I have ignored such firms. If I had the copies Mr. Forbes took with him I would be only too glad to send them to you without price.

As for the picture concern, if I find as I have been warned that they want the songs to embellish some crazy story pertaining to the South and my grandfather and Foster, I will refuse to sell to them.

Yours most respectfully<br>
Dean Joseph Rice<br>
657 West 1st South

## Excerpt from a Letter by Dean J. Rice to Josiah Kirby Lilly, April 14, 1931.

Since the "broadcast" of the song "Long Ago Day" I feel certain that the song is going to meet with wide appreciation. I have had to decline many requests for its repetition, at least for the present. Together with the letters and cards recently received all complimentary of the song, was a card which might be of interest to you. It referred me to the *Atlantic Monthly* of November 1867 Page 608. At the library I found the reference to be an article on S. C. Foster, prefaced by several pages covering the history of the song "Jim Crow" and its author my grandfather. The article is good but not accurate in some ways. My grandfather did not retire until 1857—some of his greatest American triumphs were achieved after the accident the writer mentions. The reference to Foster's weakness for drink and also his hot temper altho personally

---

[10] In 1931 Rice published "Long Ago Day" with Shapiro, Bernstein & Co., who issued the song as "a 'new' Stephen C. Foster song" with a new text by Jack Lawrence and title "My Story of Love." Lilly helped Rice publish the two songs that year with the original words and accompaniments that were more historically accurate (J. Fischer & Bro., 1931). Lilly also included them in the *Foster Hall Reproductions* and had both songs recorded in the *Foster Hall Recordings*.

vouched for by the writer (a Mr. Nevin) is contrary to my father's (Thomas C. G. Rice) version of his close acquaintance with Foster. My father was vehement on the point that Foster was not over indulgent in drink. An article published years ago intimated this and I vividly remember my father's anger at the time. He told of the long walks and talks he had with Foster—of Foster's sudden silence when a theme for a new song came to his mind—of his innumerable half completed verses—written, rewritten and destroyed. Half my father knew of his own father's triumphs in the West—Pittsburg, Cincinnati, Louisville, came from Foster's lips. My father was then a very young man, keen and observant and in the memories he carried from those early 60[s] in New York, Foster's was among the dearest—a refined quiet, sympathetic, unworldly man just the type who would have found his qualities counterparted in my father. It was these characteristics which Foster admired in T. D. Rice, the minstrel and dwelt on them to my father. Foster's first attempts at writing <u>farcical</u> negro songs was inspired by hearing Rice's "Jim Crow." Foster was then nothing more than a boy. Mr. Rice played for two years in Pittsburg. As late as 1850 the rivertowns like Cincinnati for instance more than rivaled New York City in business volume and amusements flourished in proportion.

# 41
# An Interview with Katherine Schoenberger Mygatt and Martha Stough (1934)

## Introduction

*Foster's sister Henrietta lived in Warren, Ohio. In the late 1850s, as Foster struggled to produce music and earn money, Jane and Marion lived there for extended periods. The composer joined them in early 1860 and stayed until at least August of that year, when the family moved to New York. The composer never returned to Pennsylvania or Ohio.*

*The following reminiscences of Foster's time in Warren were offered by Katherine Schoenberger Mygatt (1855–1936) and her sister Martha Stough (1862–1942). Their father, Edward Schoenberger, owned the Gaskill House, which he ran with his wife, Catherine Paltzgraff Schoenberger. While in Warren, Foster lived in the Gaskill House when not staying with his sister. Recorded almost seventy-four years after they knew Foster, Mygatt's reminiscences are typical of distant recollections of early childhood in that she offers general memories of Fosters' presence and appearance with few details. Because Stough was born two years after Foster stayed in Warren, her memories of Foster are disingenuous or false. Eight days after this interview was published, a second interview appeared in another Youngstown newspaper in which Mygatt and Stough offered the same anecdotes, nearly verbatim.[1] Slight differences between the interviews are noted in the footnotes.*

*The following article is not in the Foster Hall Collection, but Evelyn Foster Morneweck had access to it and references it in* Chronicles of Stephen Foster's Family.[2] *Interestingly, a photograph of the second article is found*

---

[1] "Picture of Foster's Wife Found in Attic, Nets $200," *Youngstown Vindicator*, February 11, 1934.
[2] Morneweck, *Chronicles*, vol. 2, 522–23.

*Formulating Foster*. Christopher Lynch, Oxford University Press. © Oxford University Press 2025.
DOI: 10.1093/9780197811726.003.0042

in *Foster Hall's* records, but it was not cataloged or officially added to the collection. Paperclipped to the article is a note in Fletcher Hodges's handwriting dated June 9, 1936, explaining why Foster Hall declined to purchase a book of Byron's poetry that Stough claimed had been left behind in Warren: "Mr. Lilly, after inspecting the book of Byron poems, decided that the signature did not seem to be Stephen's own, and accordingly the book was returned to Mr. Richards. Our offer for $150.00 was to hold good only if the signature was definitely Stephen's."[3] Foster Hall probably did not retain either article in the collection because they found Mygatt's and Stough's statements dubious.

## Esther Hamilton. "Sells Foster Picture from Attic for $200: Struthers Man's Discovery Revives Interest in Composer Who Wrote Songs at Warren." *Youngstown Telegram*, February 3, 1934.

Jules Richards, Struthers safety and service director, is $200 richer today because of America's revived interest in Stephen Foster, who wrote "My Old Kentucky Home" and other songs.

Mr. Richards sold a picture given his grandmother by Mrs. Stephen Foster when she and her husband were living at the Gaskill house in Warren.

The picture of Mrs. Foster and two friends, is used to illustrate John Tasker Howard's biography of "Stephen Foster: America's Troubadour."

It is one of 29 illustrations and in the foreword to the book author Howard acknowledges his gratitude to Mr. Richards for his aid in assembling the material.

### Found in Attic

The picture is of Mr. Foster's wife and two girls, believed to be Wick women. It was given Mrs. Edward Schoenberger, grandmother of Mr. Richards when she left Warren with her husband.

---

[3] "Picture of Foster's Wife Found in Attic, Nets $200," *Youngstown Vindicator*, February 11, 1934, unprocessed article in Foster Hall papers, with note dated June 9, 1936.

For many years it was carried around by members of the Schoenberger family, finally turning up in the Richards attic, where it was identified and authenticated by Mr. Richards thru two aunts, Mrs. Martha Stough, 3411 Hillman, and Mrs. C. G. Mygatt, 429 S. Tod, Warren, both of whom knew Foster when he stayed at the hotel run by their parents in Warren.

Mr. Richards also has a copy of Byron's poems with Mr. Foster's signature in the front.

Mrs. Mygatt recalled today the time when Stephen Foster and his wife and daughter stayed at her father's hotel.

## Foster Liked To Sing

"Mr. Foster," she said, "would sit in the big public parlor on the second floor in the evening and play and sing. I recall that a Frank Leroy, a photographer of Warren of that time used to be in the company. The Civil War officers always stopped at our hotel and they used to sing, too."[4]

"I remember Marion Foster, the daughter of Mrs. Stephen Foster. We used to go up to the big ballroom and play 'dolls' and have a grand time together. She was a beautiful dancer and her father would stand in the doorway and applaud when Marion danced and kept time with castanets.

"Mrs. Foster never left her room and Marion always took her meals up to her. Now and then my mother would talk to her but mother was a very busy woman and the hotel kept her busy all the time. She did not have much time for idle conversation."[5]

---

[4] In the February 11 article, Mygatt stated that the officers "would join in the music," suggesting that they sang with Foster. But Foster was present in Warren only in 1860, departing months before the outbreak of the Civil War. Mygatt may be conflating later memories with her memories of Foster, or, if there were officers present at the Gaskill House when the composer was there, they would not have technically been Civil War officers at that time.

[5] This intriguing statement might suggest tension between the composer and his wife—but it is wise not to read too much into Mygatt's words, given that she was five years old when she knew the composer and these memories were recorded almost three-quarters of a century later.

## Watched Sally Tod

Mrs. Mygatt recalled today standing with Marion Foster and watching with awe while Sally Tod daughter of the governor, swept down the grand staircase attired in the height of the fashion of that period.[6]

It is her belief that, "Oh, Willie, I Have Missed You," was written while Mr. Foster lived at the Gaskill House and that it was written for William Birchard, son of Judge Birchard who served in the Civil War.[7]

"Under the Willow She Is Sleeping," is another song that Mrs. Mygatt believes was written in Warren, also, "Come Where My Love Lies Dreaming."[8]

"He always wore a high silk hat," says Mrs. Mygatt, "and was gentle and kind to us. I thought he was a very handsome man."

Mrs. Stough, some years younger than Mrs. Mygatt, also recalls the Fosters when they lived at her father's hotel.

She remembers particularly the day they left, when the stagecoach pulled up and Mrs. Foster swept into it followed by her daughter and husband. "He lifted his high hat and waved goodbye," she says, "and I know we all felt very badly."[9]

---

[6] Mygatt's timeline is incorrect because David Tod was governor from 1862 to 1864. It is possible that the Fosters and Tods were at the Gaskill House together when Foster was there in 1860, but Tod would not have been governor yet. As governor, Tod was a forceful Union Democrat allied with the prosecution of the Civil War by Republican Abraham Lincoln. It is interesting to consider that shortly before the war Foster may have been in the orbit of people like Tod, who would become War Democrats. At this time, Foster was also close to his sister Henrietta, who also lived in Warren but opposed Tod's 1864 re-election bid, favoring the anti-war Democrat Clement Vallandigham. Henrietta took a campaign melody Foster had written for Buchanan in 1856 and wrote pro-Vallandigham lyrics for it. In a different campaign song from 1856, Foster mocked "Ohio yankees of Western Reserve/Who live upon cheese, ginger cakes and preserve," which differentiated people such as Tod—whose families migrated to the Western Reserve (Ohio prior to statehood) from Connecticut—from "rugged" pioneers. But during the Civil War Foster seems to have shifted his positions, writing wartime songs that suggest views more in alignment with Tod than Henrietta—pro-war but still anti-abolition.

[7] In the February 11 article, Mygatt expressed some doubt about this claim, prefacing it with "if my memory serves me right." Foster's "Willie We Have Missed You" was published in 1854, so he could not have composed it at the Gaskill House. Also, Foster wrote four "Willie" songs throughout his career: "Willie My Brave" (1851), "Willie We Have Missed You" (1854), "Our Willie Dear Is Dying" (1861), and "Willie Has Gone to the War" (1863). "Willie" was a generic name used in many songs; the name most likely did not refer to anyone Foster knew.

[8] "Under the Willow She's Sleeping" was published in 1861, so it is possible that it was written and composed in 1860 at the Gaskill House. "Come Where My Love Lies Dreaming" was published in 1855. As one of Foster's most popular songs, it is quite possible Foster performed it in the parlor at the Gaskill House in 1860, but it is unlikely that he composed it there earlier.

[9] The February 11 article states that Stough "vividly recalls" the day the Fosters left, but it is impossible because she was born after his residency there.

The Fosters left behind them a small trunk in which was but two articles, a book of Byron's poems now in Mr. Richards' possession and a red silk ruffled dress that had belonged to Marion.

Mrs. Stough told today of trying on the dress and feeling very grand in it, "with its black ribbon trimming."

## At Warren in 1862

Just exactly how long Mr. Foster stayed in Warren with his family is not known, but he was there along about 1862 and remained for several months.[10]

Stephen Foster's sister, Henrietta, was married to Thomas Wick in 1842. In 1847 she married Jesse Thornton and moved to Warren.

It is believed that Mr. Foster went to Warren because his sister was living there.

Youngstown again come into the picture of Foster's life when Mr. Howard shows in his biography that about 1846 Mr. Foster's parents boarded in Youngstown with a Mr. Richards, and his aunt was married to a John Struthers, of Poland.

A copy of the picture that came out of the Richards attic in addition to being carried in the book is also being shown at Foster Hall, Indianapolis, where J. K. Lilly has a large collection of Fosteriana.

## Promised Not To Play

In Mr. Howard's book he reveals how Foster, then 14, wrote to his older brother who wanted to send him away to school in 1840, "I will promise not to pay any attention to my music until after 8 o'clock in the evening."

The brother thought the boy was wasting his time in writing songs, the boy who later wrote the immortal "Swanee River," "Oh, Suzanna," "Old Black Joe," and others.

"Oh, Suzanna," it is revealed in "American Troubadour," was sold for $100 and Foster thought the sum a fortune. It later became the marching song of

---

[10] Foster's correspondence reveals that he was in Warren, Ohio, in 1860. He moved to New York later that year and never returned. Howard is clear about this in his biography, but the author of this article appears to have not wanted to portray Mygatt and Stough as disingenuous.

the "Forty Niners." He received nearly $2,000 royalties on "Suwanee River." He earned about $15,091 in the 11 years when he was producing his greatest songs and he lived a portion of that time in Warren.

## Never Lived in South

Most of America at that time whistled and sang his songs as today. Altho many of the songs have a southern flavor, Foster never lived in the south and Mr. Howard explains how Mr. Foster got much of his southern dialect from a bound black boy and girl in his boyhood home.[11]

In 1860 Mr. Howard says Mr. Foster went to New York and left his wife. He had taken to drinking heavily, and lived in the Bowery. One of the songs he wrote at that time, "Old Black Joe," still survives.

The book is full of references to Pittsburgh, Youngstown, Cincinnati, the place where Foster lived and occasionally worked.

The daughter with whom Mrs. Mygatt and Mrs. Stough played as children at their father's hotel now lives in Pittsburgh.

---

[11] This probably refers to Thomas Hunter, a boy bound to the Foster family in infancy because his father died and his mother was incapable of caring for him. He was White.

# 42
# Jessie Welsh Rose Relays Her Grandmother's Memories (1926/1934)

## Introduction

*Foster's granddaughter, Jessie Welsh Rose (1875–1959), was Marion's daughter but lived with Jane in Allegheny after Marion and her husband, Walter Welsh, moved to Chicago. Born more than eleven years after Foster's death, she never knew her grandfather. The memories she offered in this article are purportedly Jane's and were told to her before Jane passed away.*

*Jane had passed away in 1903, twenty-three years before Jessie published the first version of the following article in the* Louisville Courier-Journal. *That version appeared one week after Foster's one hundredth birthday and three years after Federal Hill had begun espousing its Foster mythology not far from Louisville. After the creation of the Foster Hall Collection, Jessie revised the article for the* Foster Hall Bulletin *in 1934.*[1] *Even though Jessie presents the anecdotes in the article as stories her grandmother told her, her accounts are clearly also informed by legends, her uncle Morrison's biography, and new research.*

*The following article reproduces Jessie's revised text from 1934. Major differences from the original version are pointed out in the annotations, revealing that her story changed over time and when writing for a different audience. Writing for Kentuckians before the existence of Foster Hall, she more openly embraced the Lost Cause and mythology of Federal Hill that incorrectly linked Foster to the site. When writing for the* Foster Hall Bulletin, *she more fully embraced the rhetoric of the national-universal myth.*

---

[1] Jessie Welsh Rose, "His Widows Memories of Foster's Life Are Recalled by Granddaughter," *Louisville Courier-Journal*, July 11, 1926.

## Jessie Welsh Rose. "My Grandmother's Memories." *Foster Hall Bulletin* 10 (May 1934): 9–14.

In trying to recall to mind a few of my grandmother's memories of her husband Stephen C. Foster, I perhaps should say first of all that I was a grandmother's girl.

Any person who has been raised by a fond and indulgent grandmother knows what that means. From the age of two years she lovingly cared for me. I was married in her home on Montgomery Avenue, Allegheny, (now Pittsburgh, [North Side]), afterward becoming the housekeeper myself. She lived with me until her death, at the age of seventy-two.[2] I knew my grandmother.[3] Buoyant and sunny in disposition, she was attractive and lovable and full of joy of living to the last day of her life.[4]

She was very original in her ways and had a large and meaningful vocabulary of strange and unusual words. I remember the "condign punishment" she promised any particular delinquent who happened to become too "brashy" and the "eye servant" we occasionally acquired. Almost daily she used the same effective procedure at my morning rising time. She would come tripping into my room singing a little ditty at the foot of my bed, meanwhile beating a sharp tattoo with her fingers on the bedstead. Sometimes she admonished me with "Get up! Get up! The Sun is up! The birds are up! And You should be up!" and then she sang her little song with great emphasis and rapidity:

> "Ma-hay! Ma-hay! Ma-hoe! Ma-hum!
> Marum Stick! Bummy Diddle!
> Nip-Cat! Soap-Bag!
> Sing-Song Polly!
> Wont you Kymeo!"

---

[2] Jane Foster burned to death in their home in 1903. Jessie extinguished the flames but could not save her grandmother. In the revised version of the article, she cut a line about her grandmother's last words: "My name was the last she ever spoke, as she reached for my hand, just before lapsing into unconsciousness, 'I just want Jessie and the doctor now.'"

[3] In the original, Jessie followed this sentence with "And may I not say just a few words about this dear wondrous person, of whom the world has heard so little."

[4] In the original she followed this statement with "she was in truth a very mate for Stephen C. Foster" and asked "a generous world to never place upon the shoulders of his wife the failing of the latter days of the poet, when he was no longer his own master."

The verses seemed endless, but grandma knew them all. Only two of them remain with me to-day. There was

> "Mrs. Mouse lived in a house
> with a Sing Song Catchee-Catchee-Kymeo.
> Mr. Frog lived in a well, and, etc., etc.,"

I sometimes fancy that if in some beautiful "Isle of Somewhere" I should hear that gay tattoo again, I will know it for my clear call, and that it is Sunrise again.[5]

Grandmother was the daughter of Dr. A. N. McDowell, a distinguished physician of Pittsburgh, the granddaughter of Dr. Nathan P. McDowell, also of Pittsburgh, and in turn the great-granddaughter of Prof. McDowell, who was, in 1799, the first President of Annapolis Naval Academy. A letter from George Washington addressed in that year to Prof. McDowell, is among the last letters written by our first President. The letter concerned the entrance of Martha Washington's son to the Naval Academy at Annapolis.[6]

Dr. A. N. McDowell had in all six daughters—no sons. My grandmother, Jane Denny McDowell being the second daughter of the family. Miss Jane McDowell was a renowned beauty in her girlhood, having that very rare shade of hair—auburn—with eyes almost matching. Foster told her that he fell in love with her hair first. She had a vivacious optimistic mind, never dulled by troubles or care, amiable almost to a fault, and chatty in disposition.

In the last years of her life, when she had much leisure, her mind seemed to hark back to her girlhood days and early married life, and she talked almost daily to me of my grandfather as often as I would listen. It was like a shower of gold that she was letting fall upon me, but with the heedlessness of youth I tossed much of it away, allowing many of these precious memories of hers to roll into the limbo of forgotten things. Now that she has gone far beyond my ken, and life has brought me a truer appreciation of its real value, how much I would give to sit by her side again and have her tell me of "Old Kentucky Home," "Swanee River," "Old Black Joe," "Under the Willows She's Sleeping" and "Where Is Thy Spirit, Mary?"

It seemed as though many of the songs had a little story connected with their writing—something suggesting the theme. Old Black Joe for instance

---

[5] Jessie added this entire section on Jane's strange and unusual words in 1934.
[6] Jessie added this sentence in 1934, and she was incorrect. John McDowell was president of St. John's College at Annapolis from 1789 to 1806.

was a very real person and drove Dr. McDowell's buggy for many years. In the evenings he "pottered", as grandma expressed it, around the house and felt all dressed up in an old blue coat with brass buttons on the tails—the coat only doing duty when Joe "buttled" in the house.

He loved "his family" dearly[7] and when the beaux of the period brought their stiff starched bouquets to the McDowell girls, five of them then living, no one was more intensely pleased than Joe. Grandma recalled him shuffling down the hall carrying a bouquet behind his back, his countenance shining with delight, and calling in a pleased voice "Miss Jinny! Miss Jinny! Come see what I have for you!" When dusk came Joe lit the candles and lamps—laid the logs in the fire place, and waited upon the door. All through the sweetheart days Joe watched Foster come and go. The two became great friends.[8] "Some day I am going to put you in a song, Joe," Foster told him, and felt in his heart that it was a promise. The old man was gone when the day of fulfillment came, but today and perhaps always Old Black Joe lives again.

There is one remembrance that came to me at this writing and that is how inseparably the song *Old Black Joe* was associated in my grandmother's mind with her own life and family.[9] It was the one song we couldn't sing in Grandma's hearing during her last years. It brought back days of unforgettable happiness among those she had loved and lost, and left her always in tears.

Don't sing "Old Black Joe" was understood among us.

Foster was never the "melancholy Dane" some biographers delight to picture him. On the contrary he was of a friendly, social disposition—very companionable, a splendid listener, although himself well informed. Raised in an atmosphere of culture and wealth, his family moved in the pleasure loving circles of old aristocratic Pittsburgh society.

Morrison Foster in his biography of his brother, speaks of the elegance and culture of old Pittsburgh social circles, even in the early days closely following the Revolution, of the Academies and Colleges reared in the midst of the forest; of the surprise expressed by Louis Phillippe and his brothers Beaujolois [sic] and Montpensier at the ease and elegance of their

---

[7] Jessie added this line about Joe loving the family in 1934.
[8] Jessie added the line about them becoming great friends in 1934. Her original portrayed Joe in a more minstrel-like manner: "All through the sweetheart days Joe watched Foster come and go, presenting to 'Miss Jenny' with much shuffling of feet and many broad grins his and other admirers' bouquets, so stiff and starch in their tin foil and embroidered paper frills."
[9] Jessie added this entire paragraph in 1934.

entertainment by the people of Pittsburgh.[10] Popular in his youth, loved by all his friends for his magnetic personality as well as his genius, naturally he had many carefree boon companions.

When he and my grandmother in their early married life lived across the river in Old Allegheny City (now Pittsburgh, [North Side]), one of those lifelong friends lived next door on Union Avenue. He and Stephen were both members of a small company of musicians, each playing the banjo or guitar, who met frequently for rehearsal. One summer evening the rehearsal seemed to prolong itself into unseemly proportions. When they were assisting each other home in the wee small hours of the morning, they passed the old Allegheny market house. Feeling the necessity for a peace offering of some kind for their respective and presumably unconciliatory wives, they argued the matter pro and con on the market house corner, finally deciding that a live goose would be about the right thing. The farmers in those days drove into market at night, ready for the morning trade. Well the first intimation that my grandmother had of the whereabouts of her convivial spouse, was the uproar made by the terrified goose, when he arrived at the front door with it clutched tightly to his breast. "Oh! Jenny," he called, "see the nice goose I have for you." The fate of the bird is not recorded, but my grandmother's comment at the time ran something to the effect that it would be a matter of fine discrimination to know "tother from which."

Foster, although mild and gentle of disposition, was known to his family and friends to be the possessor of an iron will, when he chose to exercise it. His very proposal of marriage to his wife was typical of this.

At the same time Foster was courting her, she had another very attentive admirer, Richard Cowan. Mr. Cowan was a lawyer, wealthy, handsome and distinguished in appearance. Mr. Foster suffered somewhat from the contrast, as he was small in stature, and, although his features were regular and pleasing, he was not of the type which women call handsome. The two of them continued each to pay court. One evening owing to some miscalculation on Miss Jane's part, both called at Dr. McDowell's home at the same hour. Steve came first. When Richard was ushered in by Old Black Joe, Steve promptly turned his back upon the pair, took up a book and read the evening through (Grandma always delighted to tell this story). At ten-thirty (10:30) calling hours were over in those good old days and Richard, punctilious in

---

[10] Jessie probably got this information about the dukes of Montpensier and Beaujolais from Morrison's sketch of his brother's life (see Chapter 24).

all things, arose wrapping his military broadcloth cape about him elegantly, he bid the forbidding back of Stephen a low sweeping "Good Evening Sire." No answer from Stephen. Jane accompanied Richard to the door, feeling in her heart that a crisis of some kind was impending. She often laughingly said that when she came back into the room that night, she scarcely knew where her sympathies lay; whether they had departed with Richard, or were present with Stephen. At any rate she had small time for speculation—Steve had arisen, was standing by the table pale and stern as she came in. "And now, Miss Jane, I *want* your answer! Is it yes? or is it no?" And grandma, nineteen in years and unused to quick decisions, made one then and never regretted it.

Jane and Stephen were married in 1850 in the home of her parents, Dr. and Mrs. Alexander [*sic*] N. McDowell.[11] The rector of Trinity Episcopal church, Dr. Lyman officiating. The McDowell home was a brick—typical of the good homes of the period and was located on lower Penn Avenue, Pittsburgh, then a residential section. The house still stood in my childhood, and I recall when shopping with Grandma at Joseph Horne's store, located directly across the street from the site of the McDowell home, how she usually stood just a few seconds glancing at the old house in contemplative reverie.

There is in existence to-day a most interesting letter written by Grandma's sister Agnes, describing the wedding—how pale Stephen was during the ceremony—how Agnes was bridesmaid, and Morrison groomsman.[12]

It tells of the brides cake, three kinds of wine served and ice cream. How beautifully Jane's dresses fit her—how the house was serenaded after the wedding by a party of "plebeians" whose music was "horrible." My grandparents never had but one child, my mother, Marion Scully Foster, named for grandma's older sister Mrs. Marion Scully. Grandmother and Mrs. Scully resembled one another closely in appearance. Quite often Grandma was addressed as "Mrs. Scully" by trades people. As her sister Marion was quite handsome, and always charmingly gowned, Grandma thought it rather complimentary.

My mother inherited much from her father's musical temperament, and much of his nervous high strung energy. Musical composition of a simple nature comes easily to her, and after an entire life almost obsessed with music practice and music teaching, she still finds untold pleasure and solace in her large collection of fine sheet music, Tchaikowsky being her great favorite.

---

[11] Jessie added this and the following three paragraphs in 1934. Jane's father's name was Andrew N. McDowell.

[12] Agnes McDowell to John D. Scully, undated (FHC, D104).

"Open Thy Lattice, Love," was written at the early age of sixteen years, dedicated and manuscript afterward presented to Miss Susan Pentland, later Mrs. Andrew L. Robinson of Allegheny.[13]

The Pentlands, Robinsons and Fosters were friends of many years standing. The music of this song was his, as he had not yet begun to clothe his music in words. He always said that he would have preferred not to have written his own words, but he was unable to find words of others or poems to fit his music. Perhaps this was fortunate, as his own words were poems in themselves and many of them could live independently of the music.

I am sometimes asked if I knew Susan Pentland to whom the song "Open Thy Lattice Love" was dedicated.[14] Oh! yes indeed I knew Susan. She was afterward Mrs. Andrew L. Robinson and lived but a short distance away from my childhood home on Montgomery Avenue, facing beautiful East Park (as it was in those days of old Allegheny City). Just a few blocks around the corner and across the park on Cedar Ave., Mrs. Robinson lived in one of the many imposing and substantial homes, then making the old city of Allegheny such a delightful residential district. The house was a large center hall brick with attractive grounds and high wrought iron fence of elaborate design. Next door to Mrs. Robinson in a house of similar construction her husband's sister Miss Mary Ann Robinson lived for many years.

Grandmother and Mrs. Robinson had been friends since childhood. Grandma called her "Sis Pentland" and I in my childish way thought the names were one—"Suspentland," and was quite a large girl before I learned the name was not "Suspentland." Often I went hand in hand with Grandma down the park to "Suspentlands." I wish I knew now and could recount their conversations. I do remember that they sighed contentedly at times and shook their heads in reminiscence, but alas, my most vivid memory seems to center around the cookie jar that so abstracted my attention upon these informal and delightful occasions.

It was at the early age of two that the family of Foster first noticed his precocity in music. His sister, Ann Eliza, had a number of musical instruments, among them a guitar. While scarcely more than a baby he would be noticed to lay the guitar down on the floor and lying down beside it, pick out harmonies on its strings, calling it his "Ittly pisano."

---

[13] "Open Thy Lattice Love" was often incorrectly stated to have been published in 1842. It appeared in 1844, the year Foster turned 18. The similarity to Morrison's phrasing suggests that Morrison was Jessie's source for this incorrect information (see Chapter 24).

[14] Jessie added this and the following paragraph in 1934.

At the age of seven years in the old music store of Smith and Mellor, Pittsburgh, Pa., he accidentally picked up a flageolet and in a few minutes had mastered its stops and sounds, playing "Hail, Columbia."

He had certain favorites among his old neighbors and friends whom he preferred to have assist him by singing his songs while they were in course of preparation, choosing them, of course, because of their fine voices and the correctness of their technique. Among them was Mrs. Andrew Robinson, before mentioned, Mrs. John Mitchell, and the first wife of his brother Morrison, Jessie Lightner Foster.

The daughter of Mrs. Mitchell told me of the writing of "Old Dog Tray." They were neighbors at the time, and Foster had dropped in as was his custom, to go over some of his writings with her mother. He played over a few bars of "Old Dog Tray" and jotted them down on paper. He left in a little while and she did not see him again for three months, as he had been called to New York on business with his publishers. When he returned and came in again with more music, Mrs. Mitchell said to him, "What about that song you wrote when last here?" "Oh, I don't know, I didn't think much of it." "But it was very pretty, I saved it. I have it here in the table drawer. Try it again." He sat down at the piano and tried it over. Mrs. Mitchell with sympathetic understanding, slipped out of the room. Returning some time later she knew by the high color of his cheeks and the burning intensity of his eyes, that the song was made.

"Listen," he said, and turning again to the piano, he played and sang the music and words almost exactly as they stand to-day. "The morn of life has passed and evening comes at last." The name was quite accidental, but Morrison Foster says he undoubtedly had in mind a beautiful setter dog given him by a friend of the family Colonel Matthew I Stewart.

This dog was his constant companion for several years in his youth. He owned another dog later in life—a homeless hound he picked up in the street. He named this dog "Calamity" on account of the mournful quality of his howl when registering dissatisfaction. "Calamity" never became historical and probably ended his canine days in obscurity, unheralded and unsung.[15] Being of a highly sensitive nature with ready sympathy for humanity and for all dumb animals, he never could pass a homeless kitten or starving dog without offering help—many of them he brought to his home.

---

[15] Jessie added this sentence in 1934.

One small incident of this very acute sensitiveness, I recall my grandmother saying, occurred shortly after their removal to New York to be near his publishers. They had not yet gone to housekeeping, and were boarding in one of the numerous old brownstone front houses so common in New York in the fifties.

In this particular boarding house the star boarder for a number of years had been a tall, gaunt Episcopal minister, very courteous, gentle and humble in his mien. He occupied the end seat at the table and did the carving. So thoughtful and generous to others was this kindly man, that after he had bountifully helped the rest at the table, it generally fell to his lot to enjoy the neck of the fowl or a tough end of steak. After this had gone on for several weeks, so enraged was my grandfather at the penuriousness of the boarding house mistress, who, by cutting corners so closely, allowed this sort of thing to continue, that he suggested a new boarding house be found, where they would not have to witness the daily sacrifice of this too gallant gentleman.

They afterward spent a very happy year or so boarding in the comfortable home of Mrs. [Louisa] Stewart, who set a very bountiful table and served delicious sea food.[16] Grandma often watched her prepare lobsters, thereby hoping to become proficient herself in administering the boiling-water plunge, but she never did acquire the art. "She felt too sorry for the poor things." Grandma always spoke of Mrs. Stewart with affection and occasionally received a letter from her.[17]

In the latter days of his life, when he had become quite careless in his garb, and indifferent to the world's opinion, his brother Morrison often tried to inject new ambition into his world weary heart. "Steve," he said one day, "why do you go around looking so careless and unkempt? If I went about like that I would be afraid of being insulted." Raising his head and looking wearily at his brother, he replied, "Mitty (a pet name) don't worry so about me. No gentleman will insult me, and no other can."[18]

---

[16] Jessie added this paragraph in 1934.

[17] None of these letters survive, and Jessie appears to be exaggerating the relationship that existed between her mother and Louisa Stewart. The only letter Jane is known to have received from her was mailed in 1890, and it came not from Mrs. Stewart but from her daughter, who mailed Jane her husband's sketchbook. That letter was sent to Foster Hall, but it cannot be located in the collection today, suggesting Hodges may have discarded it.

[18] In the earlier version of the article, Jessie indicated that "'Gentleman'... was a term my grandfather seldom used, thinking it overworked—but he did so once meaningly."

After moving to New York, they were at once drawn into musical circles. People entertained musically to a large extent in those days. There were balls, singing clubs, minstrels, concerts, etc., with invitations often to the Fosters.[19]

Grandma loved to recall these happy times, and one outstanding memory was the great New Year's ball held at one of the New York hotels, when upon the morning of the event she found her costume still unfinished.[20] There were myriads of spangles yet to be sewed on. My grandfather was not a patient man, but the occasion was pressing, so he clumsily tried to help with the spangles. Grandma could see he was mentally consigning these spangles to the "Nether Regions," but he valiantly carried on, and between them the gown, a fairy princess dress of tarltan and spangles, was made ready.[21]

It was to be a masked ball. Grandma, dressed as a fairy queen, but grandfather would not reveal to her his costume. All evening at the ball grandma hunted him but could not find him. Being young and a good dancer, she had no lack of partners, but her husband was missing.

At midnight they unmasked, when down from the stage came Foster. He had been playing first violin in the orchestra. With the aid of false whiskers and "plumpers" (grandmother called them) he had been entirely unrecognizable.[22]

Stephen C. Foster was brilliant of mind and polished of manner. He was kind, sympathetic and charitable, sometimes presenting a proud exterior to a world that wounded him upon occasions unnecessarily.[23]

He received but little return in terms of money.[24] In the things of the spirit perhaps he lived satisfactorily and abundantly.

---

[19] Jessie cut a lengthy description of her grandfather's alcoholism that followed this paragraph. The original reads: "Wine flowed freely, like water. This is where Stephen C. Foster met the crushing defeat of his life. He was highly strung, temperamental, frail of physique. He sank rapidly where a physically stronger man might have survived. He suffered much and died for his fault. No other stigma of any kind has ever attached itself to his name. Cannot an understanding world allow this one human failing to lie buried and forgotten? There seems to be such a growing tendency on the part of some biographers to play this failing up theatrically, that there is almost danger of its becoming the dominant act in the history of his life, eclipsing entirely his many noble qualities."

[20] In the original, Jessie prefaced this anecdote with "although impatient and highly nervous as most people are who do creative work, yet his love for his beautiful wife was so great."

[21] In the earlier version, Jessie said that Foster was "inwardly cursing as grandma could see the needles which pricked his fingers."

[22] In the original, Jessie adds at the end of this anecdote that "as long as he lived he studied intensely the works of the great music masters bringing to his own music a thorough understanding of harmony, so that his songs appealed to musicians, as well as the unlearned in music."

[23] Jessie cut some of her earlier hyperbole from this paragraph. She had initially written that Foster was "highly educated" and "could have written the words of his music in seven languages if he had so chosen."

[24] In the original, Jessie had written that "he gave his music to the world freely."

At the time that he wrote "Old Uncle Ned" and "Oh! Susanna" there was an old music teacher who had taught in his family, W. C. Peters, also in the music publishing business in Cincinnati, Ohio. Foster gave the manuscripts of these two songs to Mr. Peters who realized Ten Thousand Dollars ($10,000.00) in the sale of them and established the well known music publishing house of Peters. Foster never made a penny on them.

In 1847 at a minstrel competition in Pittsburgh, Morrison Foster entered for the prize a song by Stephen called "Way Down South Whar de Corn Grows."[25] The audience selected this song for the prize, voicing their approval by applause; but the prize went to a member of the troupe for a vulgar song afterwards proved to be a plagiarism.

He cared little for name or fame, however, and was wont to exclaim, "Oh! It's all 'hocus-pocus'" when pressed for his reaction to the plaudits of the world.[26]

He played almost any musical instrument—both by ear and by note. For purposes of composition, however, he found a piano more convenient to his use. A cousin quite recently told me of the circumstances of my grandfather's acquisition of at least one piano during his life time.[27] For the time being he was without a piano of his own. Goaded by his intense desire to compose, he would arrive at his brother Henry's home at any hour of the day or night, filled with a burning purpose to write some new music. Henry's distracted wife finally presented him with the piano, more to get rid of her nocturnal and importunate visitor than because she really wanted to part with the piano.

He composed almost constantly—anywhere—when visiting, on the street, at the theatre or even shopping at the nearby grocery. Several years ago a New York newspaper reporter implored my assistance in locating a grocery store in New York City, which has come down by tradition as a place of the writing of some of Foster's songs on the store's brown wrapping paper.[28]

Foster's brother, Dunning McNair Foster, owned and operated several steamboats on the Ohio and Mississippi Rivers upon which Stephen and his wife, Morrison and his wife, and Mr. and Mrs. Andrew L. Robinson (the

---

[25] In the original, Jessie indicates that she takes this anecdote from Morrison's biography, and she quotes him. In this version she chose to paraphrase her uncle with attribution, giving the appearance that this story was also a family memory relayed to her by her grandmother.

[26] The original read, "He cared nothing for name or fame, or money, but much for love, family and friends."

[27] This anecdote is not found in the original.

[28] This anecdote was told by Birdseye (see Chapter 3) and Cooper (see Chapter 30).

latter the Susan Pentland of "Open Thy Lattice Love") together with other friends, occasionally went upon pleasure jaunts, sometimes going as far as New Orleans and back.[29] Of all the pleasurable trips my grandparents ever enjoyed I believe Grandma recalled most vividly these river excursions. She found her steamboats hard to translate into terms of modern steamboat language. Their steamboats were different! They were very luxurious, the top deck being fitted up like a beautiful garden with flower, fountains and a band of music to play the moonlight. These were days of great romance. They had much fun at embarking, their friends coming down to see the boat leave loaded with gifts and floral offerings; for it was considered quite a trip to New Orleans and anything might happen! Tears were shed at the departure.

Upon these trips Foster saw the slaves at work in the cotton fields. At Bardstown, Ky., he had a cousin, Judge John Rowan, whose beautiful estate was called Federal Hill. Judge Rowan was the owner of many slaves and if Foster visited him when young, as tradition relates, it is easy to-day to understand his great interest in the colored man and his songs of plantation life.[30]

These were the scenes of the inspiration of "Old Kentucky Home," "Swanee River," "Massa's in the Cold, Cold Ground" and others. It was just after his father's death in 1855 that he composed the latter.[31]

"Where Is Thy Spirit, Mary?" was composed after the death of a very early sweetheart, Mary Keller. I have been told by a relative that Foster visiting the grave after many years and finding it still unmarked, caused to be erected the very unusual and artistic headstone marking her grave in Allegheny Cemetery.

In attempting to write down these few recollections of my grandmother—most of them never before recorded—but culled from her conversation through many years of close association, I am not trying, of course, to give

---

[29] Jessie added this paragraph in 1934.
[30] Jessie significantly tempered her embrace of Federal Hill's Lost Cause mythology in this version. Writing for Kentuckians in 1926, she wrote, "It was during a visit to his cousin Judge John Rowan at Federal Hill, near Bardstown, Ky., that Foster first saw the slaves in happy surroundings, kindly and considerately treated—saw them at their best. It was here that he got his great inspiration for his master melodies, 'Old Kentucky Home,' 'Swanee River,' 'Massa's in the Cold, Cold Ground,' and others." The museum at Federal Hill, which had opened in 1923, had been spinning tales that Foster visited John Rowan and was inspired by his benevolence toward his enslaved people and the harmonious interracial lifestyle at the estate.
[31] It is surprising that this error got past Foster Hall staff. William Foster died in 1855, but "Massa's in de Cold Ground" was published in 1852. Jessie's mistake probably reflects the influence of Morrison's misleading comment that the song exhibits Foster's feelings about his father's death in 1855.

any biographical sketch of my grandfather. The story of his life—is it not written for all eternity in the pages of his compositions?[32]

Who, among the discerning cannot read between the lines of "A Dream of My Mother and My Home," "Ah, May the Red Rose Live Always," "Beautiful Dreamer," "Come Where My Love Lies Dreaming," "Give the Stranger Happy Cheer," "Gentle Annie," "Hard Times Come Again No More." Many songs tell of the touching love he bore his highly accomplished mother—"Kiss Me Dear Mother," "Farewell Sweet Mother."

Love for his winsome wife is seen in "Jenny's Coming O'er the Green," "Jenny June," "Jeanie with the Light Brown Hair."

Who cannot read the pathos in "Comrades, Fill No Glass for Me," "I Cannot Sing Tonight," "Mine Is the Mourning Heart," and "None Shall Weep a Tear for Me."

There was a lighter strain, too. Who could not laugh at the sheer foolishness of "If You've Only Got a Moustache," "There Are Plenty of Fish in the Sea," "Don't Bet Your Money on the Shanghai," and "Mr. and Mrs. Brown." And then the many hymns written in the last years of his life, do they not speak for him of his soul's abiding faith in God? "Suffer Little Children to Come Unto Me," "Tears Bring Thoughts of Heaven," "There Is a Land of Love," "We'll All Meet Our Savior." A few years ago at the grave in Allegheny Cemetery we read as being the most appropriate poem we could find for the occasion, his song:

> I would not die in springtime,
> When all is bright around
> And fair young flowers are peeping,
> From out the silent ground.
> When life is in the water
> And joy upon the shore;
> For winter, gloomy winter
> Then reign o'er us no more.
> But let me die in winter
> When night hangs dark above,
> And cold the snow is lying

---

[32] In the original, Jessie did not invoke the eternal when describing them. Instead she explained that she did not write a biography because that "has been beautifully done by her brother, Hon Morrison Foster, in his Book of Biography and Song, also by others." Of course, understanding Foster's life through his songs was precisely what Morrison wanted.

On bosoms that we love.
O! May the wind at midnight
That bloweth from the sea
Chant mildly, softly, sweetly
A requiem for me.

The funeral of Foster was an unforgettable one, full of pathos; several bands participated, leading the funeral cortege playing the Foster melodies as they marched.[33] Behind the hearse many of his fellow musicians of Pittsburgh fell in line on foot. As the funeral party entered the cemetery the strains of "Old Black Joe," "Massa's in the Cold, Cold Ground," gave way to "Come Where My Love Lies Dreaming," and so this beautiful song of Foster's became the last dirge at his funeral.

Yes, Stephen C. Foster was his own best biographer. The spirit that was his stands forth revealed in all his writings. He gave to the world abundantly. Very little of the bread which he cast upon the waters seemed to return to him in any tangible form, but in the outpourings of his soul in song, his name and fame may safely rest throughout all ages.

---

[33] Jessie added these last two paragraphs in 1934.

# 43
# Concluding Essay

## After Archival Amnesty: Toward a New View of Stephen C. Foster

The oral histories show that the national-universal myth of Foster depended on forgetting and remembering certain facts and anecdotes after Foster's death. As a result of forgetting his sectional compositions (e.g., "We Are Coming Father Abraam"), partisan compositions (e.g., "The White House Chair"), and explicitly racist compositions (e.g., "Oh! Susanna"), coupled with the continued rebranding of some of his humanizing sentimental minstrel songs (e.g., "Old Folks at Home") in performances by opera divas and Black jubilee ensembles, by the 1890s Morrison's construction of his brother as an embodiment of the nation's post–Civil War sectional, class, and racial diversity—largely constructed around the notion of the sentimental songs' universal appeal, particularly in songs that express nostalgia for "home"—began to take hold. As Morrison promoted his version of his brother in his book and statue, most of the oral histories about Foster were published by his partner in the statue effort, Thomas Keenan Jr., editor of the *Pittsburg Press*. All the interviews except William Hamilton's were silent on Foster's partisan, conservative politics, and few anecdotes about the composer's personal life circulated. The proliferation of stories, however, about his love for his home and family, and his kindness and respect toward all people regardless of their race or background, created an image of the composer as sympathetic toward all people of the nation in his own life and in his craft. Keenan and the interviewees probably chose to focus on the aspects of Foster's personality and career that united rather than divided people to support the effort toward public memorialization. They likely did not intend to support Morrison's deliberate erasure of aspects of Foster's life.

After Morrison's death the Foster family continued to tell his version of Foster's story at the Stephen Foster Memorial Home starting in the 1910s. As Foster's minstrel depictions of African Americans were very publicly contested by the NAACP, the myth took on a new character as it was

*Formulating Foster*. Christopher Lynch, Oxford University Press. © Oxford University Press 2025.
DOI: 10.1093/9780197811726.003.0044

primarily deployed to distance Foster from the racism of minstrelsy. This required not only continued emphasis on universalism but also forgetting the composer's participation in amateur minstrel shows, as recalled in the earlier accounts from P. F. Kane's store, as well as forgetting Foster's career-long personal and professional relationships with minstrel performers, as recalled by Samuel Sanford, Frank Dumont, Kit Clarke, John H. Cassidy, and George Cooper. In 1920, Foster's first biographer, Milligan, further distanced Foster from racism when he chose to omit Cooper's testimony about the composer opposing emancipation. Federal Hill next embraced—and embellished—the myth when the "plantation" in Bardstown became a museum in 1923, portraying Foster as sympathetic and Kentucky slavery as benevolent.

These efforts had wide reach but limited impact. Bardstown was a tourist destination, never a center of scholarship. The Foster family gained national headlines but exerted for the most part only a local influence. And Milligan's biography was not exactly a bestseller. In 1933, he informed Lilly that the book had typically sold only "25 or 30 copies" each year since its publication.[1] Collectively, then, these efforts only minimally advanced the myth of Foster, exerting small or local influences while falling far short of transforming popular opinion. In other words, by the early 1930s the myth had been defined but needed a national champion.

Eager to take on that role, Lilly worked closely with the Foster family to select and curate items for the collection. In surveying the remembrances, we have already seen some of Foster Hall's choices about what to preserve and discard. They declined to preserve most anonymous accounts, as well as accounts that they deemed spurious, such as the accounts claiming the composer painted oil paintings and the interview with Mygatt and Stough. Their choices to cite some sources in their own writings but discard them from the collection exude their hubris. Whereas today conscientious archivists might keep all these materials while noting their subjective doubts about their veracity, Foster Hall acted as the arbiters of truth, often erasing certain information from the collection altogether and keeping only what they wanted. In many of the omissions we have already encountered—such as the remembrances by Kane, Sanford, Dumont, and Clarke—Foster Hall distanced the composer from minstrelsy and racism.

It is possible that these omissions were no more than simple oversights, but, as the first part of this concluding essay documents, there is an

---

[1] Harold Vincent Milligan to Josiah K. Lilly, October 26, 1933, Josiah K. Lilly Correspondence.

abundance of evidence that Lilly and Foster Hall declined to collect materials that countered the myth and that when items that told a different story found their way into the collection, they deployed strategies of archival organization and description that concealed them. Lilly also employed the power of narrative, self-publishing and widely distributing an immense body of literature about Foster, in which Foster Hall shied away from addressing Foster's racism and the racist thinking of his day more generally. Their methods proved effective. They convinced bureaucrats, military officers, university presidents, historians, musicologists, and many, many everyday Americans of the myth's veracity.

The second half of this essay examines the impact of the manipulated archive, focusing on how its gaps and silences have encouraged different writers to fill in the blanks in creative ways. Given the collection's many holes, it is not surprising that fragments and transmutations of the myth survive in recent scholarship, nor is it surprising that other scholars fill in the silences with new postulations diametrically opposed to the myth. In these writings, Foster tends to be portrayed as either a detestable racist or a laudable social justice activist. How do we move beyond this impasse? Ultimately, I suggest, the remembrances point toward a consensus view that reconciles scholars' seemingly intractable differences.

## Constructing the Foster Hall Collection

Archival theorist Tonia Sutherland identifies a tendency in archives to grant their creators and subjects what she calls "archival amnesty," which she defines as an "intentional turn away from the suffering of human beings, [a] turn away from justice and toward maintaining the status quo."[2] Working closely with the Foster family, Lilly and Foster Hall granted Foster archival amnesty by turning away from the racism of his music, his White supremacist views, and what they viewed as his "weaknesses." With varying degrees of intentionality, they highlighted items that supported the myth and suppressed items that countered it. The evidence of their bias is both direct and indirect—that is, it is composed of both what *is* in the collection and what we can surmise is *not*. Although arriving at conclusions based on the

---

[2] Tonia Sutherland, "Archival Amnesty: In Search of Black American Transitional and Restorative Justice," *Journal of Critical Library and Information Services* 1, no. 2 (2017): 7.

absence of evidence can be a fraught approach, historian Marisa J. Fuentes notes that, in cases in which archives reproduce oppressive values and the violence of the past by objectifying and erasing people who were historically subjugated, "productively mining archival silences and pausing at the corruptive nature of this material" can yield important insights into the forces that shaped historical records and knowledge of the past.[3] Pausing at the silences in the Foster Hall Collection exposes how the collection was corrupted by the national-universal myth.

In a promotional pamphlet published by Foster Hall in 1933, Lilly portrayed himself as the savior of Foster's memory. He identified his inspiration as a quiet evening at home with his family in January 1931, when he was early in his retirement as president of Lilly Pharmaceuticals and searching for a new hobby. He painted a romantic scene:

> An elderly man, with children and grandchildren gathered about, sits before a newly acquired Orthophonic Victrola. One after another, recent reproductions of Foster's songs by Nathaniel Shilkret's Orchestra and the Victor Singers are rendered. What a flood of memories pour through the mind and heart of him of three score years and ten! "The past rises before me like a dream," filled with *Old Black Joe, My Old Kentucky Home, Jeanie with the Light Brown Hair, Beautiful Dreamer*, and others of Foster's songs. Truth compels it to be recorded that silent tears were in evidence and deepest emotions stirred.[4]

According to Lilly, on this fateful evening a simple, tear-filled "chance remark ... brought into being a comprehensive collection of data and material pertaining to the life and work of America's greatest composer of beautiful melodies." When he asked his son where he could secure first editions of Foster's songs, his son connected him with a rare book dealer from whom "several hundred early editions of Foster's songs were secured, *among them nearly one hundred first editions!*" Through "extensive inquiry" Lilly learned that "a comprehensive collection of Fosteriana did not exist." He vowed "then and there ... that this vacancy in American historical records should be filled." As his work was nearing completion in 1933, he asserted that *he*

---

[3] Fuentes, *Dispossessed Lives*, 5.
[4] Josiah K. Lilly, *Fosteriana at Foster Hall* (Josiah K. Lilly, 1933). The recording was Nat Shilkret and the Victor Salon Group, *Stephen Foster Melodies*, 78 rpm shellac, Victrola 9246, 1928.

rectified the "very meagre ... records of [Foster's] life and character" and that *he* fixed "how incompletely his songs had been collected and credited to him."[5]

John Tasker Howard further illuminates Lilly's motivations. According to Howard, prior to collecting Foster materials Lilly had been looking to gather items related to a "founding father," especially Benjamin Franklin, as a retirement hobby, but "he learned that many institutions had done the same and that any collection he might assemble would merely duplicate another."[6] This suggests that Lilly came to his Foster project with the goal of building an archive that enshrined a founding father. Since no archive of Foster's music existed, it seems that Lilly saw the composer as a figure he could establish as a *cultural* founding father. This attitude appears to have influenced his collecting choices. He probably initially believed he was gathering all the facts of the composer's life, but his attitudes and preconceptions would ultimately cause him to gather *certain* facts of the composer's life, namely those that helped him elevate Foster to founding-father status.

At first he found only affirmation of his attitudes and project goals. Within days of settling on Foster as a collecting focus, he had read Milligan's biography and written to the author. On January 10, 1931, he wrote,

> Possibly in the course of the year I shall want to get together and publish a catalogue, illustrating first editions and other interesting data. Expert assistance will be secured to do this in the proper manner and make it a credit to Foster and his work. It has occurred to me that possibly you might be willing to furnish me with five hundred copies of your Biography of Foster that could be bound the same as the catalogue. They would be for presentation purposes exclusively, to be placed in the Library of Congress, other libraries, and in the hands of individuals who would appreciate them.[7]

Lilly was in touch with Morneweck in the early days of 1931 as well, so he quickly learned that Milligan's biography was lacking crucial details and anecdotes and decided that his idea of producing a catalogue to supplement

---

[5] Josiah Kirby Lilly to John G. Bowman, December 1934, Box 11, Folder 320, "Pittsburgh, University of, 1934," Josiah K. Lilly Correspondence, Center for American Music, University of Pittsburgh Library System.

[6] John Tasker Howard, untitled and unpublished autobiography, Center for American Music, University of Pittsburgh Library System, B25.

[7] Josiah K. Lilly to Harold Vincent Milligan, January 10, 1931, Josiah K. Lilly Correspondence, 1931–1944, box 1, folder 37.

it was insufficient.[8] Nevertheless, his early letters with Milligan demonstrate how important Milligan's version of Foster was to Lilly.

Lilly probably could not have realized at this stage that Milligan's portrayal of Foster as "America's folk-song composer" and a composer of "universal" music was based on Milligan's choices about what evidence to present and conceal, nor could he have known how much Morneweck had manipulated the biography. Howard later confessed that "there were certain phases of Foster's character that [Morneweck] did not want publicized and she kept from Milligan everything that would throw light on Stephen's weaknesses."[9] Although Howard never clarified the details that she kept from Milligan, it is clear that he came to believe that she spruced up Foster's portrayal in Milligan's biography. Unable to grasp this in 1931, Lilly must have read Milligan's book as authoritative confirmation of his belief that Foster was a founding father and national symbol. Lilly certainly read the passage about the NAACP protests in Boston's schools in 1914 and believed Milligan's retort because it resonated with his own beliefs about Foster's music as "universal." I see no evidence that Lilly *intended* to take a side in an ongoing discussion of racism in Foster's music, but that is precisely the outcome of his choice to position Milligan's biography as the intellectual foundation of his work.

Lilly also quickly found further affirmation of his belief in Foster's music as a positive, uplifting, and unifying force in Morrison's biography. Unaware of the political context of the book's creation, and initially unaware of the contradictory accounts to which Morrison's biography responded, Lilly simply assumed the book was accurate because it came from Foster's closest brother. One of his first actions was to rush out a new edition of the biography in 1932. He uncritically wrote in the volume's prefatory remarks that "the world owes much to Morrison Foster" because "he rescued from possible oblivion many songs and compositions of his brother" and "accompanied them with this intimate and affectionate story."[10]

There is no question, then, that in *the earliest stages of his work* Lilly's interest in founding fathers, his personal affection for Foster's songs, and the affirmation he found in two highly biased sources—the context of which he was largely ignorant at that time—caused him to build a collection that proved his a priori assumption of the validity of the national-universal myth. He had

---

[8] The earliest correspondence between Lilly and Morneweck I have found is a letter from Morneweck dated January 9, 1931, Josiah K. Lilly Correspondence, 1931–1944, box 1, folder 40.
[9] Howard, untitled and unpublished autobiography, B58.
[10] Morrison Foster, *My Brother Stephen* (Josiah K. Lilly, 1932).

financial resources that most professional historians could only dream of. But, untrained as a historian or archivist, and as a dilettante with an agenda to leave behind a positive legacy on more than just pharmaceuticals, he failed to question his assumptions. Instead, his collecting procedures produced confirmation bias.

Despite his initial intentions, it was not long before Lilly knowingly made several compromises that risked the integrity of his work. He needed the Foster family, and the Fosters needed him. Most of the documents from Foster's life were in Michigan in the possession of the composer's niece, Morrison's daughter Evelyn Foster Morneweck, who had inherited them from her father. Some also resided with Marion, Jessie, and Jessie's husband Alexander D. Rose at the Foster Memorial Home in Pittsburgh. Howard characterizes Lilly's relationships with the Fosters as mutually beneficial— "Members of the Foster family were helpful in supplying rare items, and to them J. K. [Lilly] proved a gold-mine"[11]—but he fails to disclose the power dynamics at play in these relationships.

Owned by the city of Pittsburgh, the Foster Memorial Home had fallen into disrepair; and Marion, Jessie, and Alexander, residing there as caretakers, were desperately poor. A report made for city officials dated May 31, 1930, describes the Memorial Home as barren and inadequate, having a display case "resembling the kind used in meat shops" that "does not even lock," an unattractive display of a poorly rendered crayon drawing of Foster on an easel, and a "terrible drawing of Stephen's brother" William Jr. The report continues, "The paper on the room is unattractive, the woodwork needs painting and a large mirror over the mantelpiece reflects the bareness and ugliness of this apartment to a startling degree. The hallway also is in bad repair and so far as carpets, painting and papering are concerned this entrance way and the main room together with other things mentioned in the specifications indicate the type of place this is."[12] On numerous occasions, the Fosters and their supporters petitioned officials for financial assistance, which was never sufficiently provided.

Lilly never supported the Foster Memorial Home, but he was willing to pay the Fosters residing there generously for their treasures. On one occasion, Alexander forwarded Lilly an old letter to Jane Foster Wiley from the daughter of Louisa Stewart, with whom Foster boarded in New York,

---

[11] Howard, unpublished autobiography, B26.
[12] Report dated May 31, 1930, Foster Hall Curatorial Correspondence, folder labeled "Foster Memorial Home."

along with a picture of Louisa. Rose wrote, "If you think this letter and picture of Stephen's boarding house keeper is of any value, you might send me a check for enough money to get a winter overcoat."[13] Lilly responded one week later: "You have been very courteous and very helpful in many ways in bringing to Foster Hall valuable material and it occurs to us that we have not been sufficiently appreciative in a substantive way. In order to set our minds at rest in this connection, will you be good enough to accept the check herewith enclosed with our very best wishes?" He enclosed a check for $100.[14] Over the course of a couple of years, Lilly purchased from them Foster's manuscript sketchbook of lyrics, for which Lilly's sons paid $25,000[15] ($561,952.78 as of this writing, using the Consumer Price Index to adjust for inflation); the composer's three bound volumes of music that had been passed down to Marion; the family Bible; and a diary that belonged to Jane.

Lilly used the Fosters' dire situation to get what he wanted, but so did the Fosters. In exchange for their items, Lilly not only paid generously but also granted them considerable curatorial control. In fact, he hired Morneweck to select and arrange items for the Foster Hall Collection and write a book about the materials, giving her the power to frame the archive for posterity. She provided Foster Hall with chronologies, genealogical information, and transcriptions of documents (sometimes only excerpts) from her personal collection, much of which she gradually donated to Foster Hall. Her work culminated in the two-volume *Chronicles of Stephen Foster's Family*, published in 1944.[16]

Needing the support of the Fosters, Lilly was complicit when Morneweck censored Howard. Performing work for hire and not protected by tenure or academic freedom, Howard had little choice but to comply with his patron's wishes. In an unpublished whistleblower account of Foster Hall's practices that he bequeathed to his daughter—who donated it to the Foster Hall Collection in the 1990s—Howard praised Morneweck because she "did cooperate fully in almost everything I needed to know," but he also pointed out that she "did hold out on me in several important matters" by withholding documents, suppressing information, and censoring his words. He was suspicious of Morneweck, describing her as "a quiet, rather repressed, lady,

---

[13] Alexander D. Rose to Josiah Kirby Lilly, October 15, 1934, FHC, unprocessed folder labeled "Jessie Welsh Rose."
[14] Foster Hall to Alexander D. Rose, October 22, 1934, FHC, unprocessed folder labeled "Jessie Welsh Rose."
[15] Howard, unpublished autobiography, B27.
[16] Morneweck, *Chronicles*.

whose conversation never seemed to tell all she might have in mind." In their private correspondence, she was particularly concerned about concealing anecdotes and facts that had the potential to embarrass descendants of the Fosters and their associates, including herself and current "business friends of my brother." She asked him to "delete all names whose printing might cause any unhappiness—for it would, I know, make these people feel just as I would feel myself under like circumstances."[17]

Howard discloses that Morneweck withheld letters by Jane Foster that would have shed light on her marriage and her husband's death. He writes,

> The talks I had with Mrs. Morneweck were most informative, but they were exasperating and frustrating, too. She told me that Stephen's sisters blamed his wife for the events that caused his tragic end, and she admitted that she had three letters written by Jane during Stephen's last years in New York that explained the situation. Then she refused to let me see the letters.[18]

Morneweck wanted this information suppressed, and she appears to have gotten what she wanted. Howard had access to three letters by Jane from this period that found their way into the Foster Hall Collection but never the three that Morneweck kept in her possession.

The three letters in the collection are instructive but incomplete. On September 30, 1861, Jane informed Morrison she had left her husband in New York and had been "spending a couple months" in Lewistown, Pennsylvania, but because she was "now beginning to feel very uneasy about 'Steve' and he has not at present the money to send me," she requested that Morrison send her $10. She wrote, "I wish to go back to him immediately and indeed it is very necessary that I should be with him." Apparently Foster and Jane had been relying on family money for some time. As Jane explained, "I have asked John Scully [her sister's husband] for money so often that I do not like to impose upon his generosity and kindness anymore."[19] Morrison sent her the money along with a message for her to deliver to his brother (now lost), and Jane replied on October 5, thanking him and informing him that Marion was doing well in school.[20] On June 30, 1862, Jane wrote to Morrison again from Lewistown thanking him for another five dollars. She told him

---

[17] Evelyn Foster Morneweck to John Tasker Howard, August 10, 1933, FHC, D159a.
[18] Howard, unpublished autobiography, B57.
[19] Jane Foster to Morrison Foster, September 30, 1861, FHC, C578.
[20] Jane Foster to Morrison Foster, October 5, 1861, FHC C579.

that she "left Steve in New York" where he "publishes once in a long while with Pond." She also wrote, "The clothing you sent him [Foster] he was very much obliged to you and told me that he would write and thank you."[21] If Foster ever wrote that note, it is now lost.

In her book, Morneweck provides information that came from additional sources, probably including the three letters she never let Howard see. For example, she writes in *Chronicles*:

> Stephen's faithful efforts to throw off the habit that was threatening to ruin him kept his wife in a continual state of alternating hope and despair. Many dollars that she greatly needed for herself and the little girl, she conscientiously paid out for various "cures" to which Stephen submitted himself. And for months at a time, Stephen would be himself again, and his wife and loving sisters and brothers offered up prayers of gratitude and thankfulness.

The letters Howard had access to and that are in the collection today make no mention of his wife paying for cures or his siblings expressing gratitude. Similarly, Morneweck related more information about the composer's family's worries about him in New York, information she presumably acquired from documents that are not in the Foster Hall Collection and were denied to Howard. She writes,

> Stephen's frequent financial emergencies were not the chief cause of anxiety to his family; but his growing dependence on alcohol, the carelessness of his appearance, and the precarious state of his health filled them all with dread for the future. Not only was he their adored youngest brother, but he had been their mother's darling, and there was not one of his brothers and sisters but had a feeling of personal responsibility for his welfare. Ann Eliza's anxiety was so great that on one occasion she sent Edward to New York for the express purpose of bringing his Uncle Stephen to her home in Philadelphia. Edward was instructed to take no refusal—he was to insist that his uncle return with him. Edward was received by a sober, cheerful and perfectly poised Stephen, who expressed great pleasure at his nephew's visit, and so completely assumed the superior role that the younger man did not dare reveal the real purpose of his coming. "There

---

[21] Jane Foster to Morrison Foster, June 30, 1862, FHC, C580.

was no way that I could broach the matter," Edward reported to his mother, "without seeming very presumptuous."[22]

What did Morneweck want to hide from the public about Foster's last years that these sources divulged?

The letter that Alexander mailed to Lilly in exchange for money for a coat is also curiously missing from the Foster Hall Collection but described—at least partially—in Morneweck's book. Morneweck explains that the letter was from Mattie Stewart de Witt to Jane and dated January 2, 1890. The writer of the letter was the daughter of Louisa Stewart, with whom the composer, Jane, and Marion boarded in New York. The portion of the letter that Morneweck reproduces in her book reveals that the letter contained reminiscences about Foster. Morneweck writes,

> In New York, Stephen and his family found a pleasant home at the boardinghouse of Mrs. Louisa Stewart, on Greene Street.... Mrs. Stewart proved a kind and sympathetic friend. Her daughters, Rushanna and Mattie (who became Mrs. de Witt), grew very fond of Jane and Marion, and the latter's "funny little ways." When Stephen first came to New York, the relations between himself and his publisher were strained, possibly on account of Stephen's failure to deliver the songs he had promised. On January 1, 1860, his accounts show that he was overdrawn $1,479.95 at his publishers. It is also quite likely that Firth, Pond objected to Stephen's attempts to make contracts with other publishers before he had fulfilled his agreements with them. That there was tension between them is evident from a letter written many years afterwards by Mattie Stewart de Witt to Jane, dated January 2, 1890—"Mr. Foster brought the manuscript [of "Under the Willow She's Sleeping"] to us wet [?] from the printer, and he told ma—'that he could not try it at Mr. Pond's,' so used our piano. Mr. Pond was not fair to Mr. Foster. I remember that very well." Although "Under the Willow" was copyrighted by Firth, Pond on May 3, 1860, it might not have been published until Stephen and Jane went to Mrs. Stewart's. Mrs. Mygatt, whom we have quoted before, was of the belief that "Under the Willow She's Sleeping" was written in Warren while Stephen

[22] Morneweck, *Chronicles*, vol. 2, 541–42.

was at the Gaskill House. This seems quite likely as Stephen was in Warren in April, 1860.[23]

This letter clearly possessed valuable information. Morneweck's knowledge of Jane and Marion's relationship with the Stewart daughters could only have come from it, and it would be informative to read de Witt's own words about their relationship. The letter's apparent removal from the Foster Hall Collection raises suspicions about Morneweck's framing of it. She culls information from it to portray the composer in a happy living situation and make inferences about the chronology of his professional activities. But one wonders what other information was in the letter. Was there content that Morneweck did not want known, perhaps about Foster's marriage, addiction, or racial views?

Howard reveals that Lilly and Hodges were complicit with Morneweck's secret-keeping and archival manipulation. In his research he noticed discrepancies about the birth year of Foster's oldest brother, William B. Foster Jr. The family Bible lists his birthday in 1814, but Morneweck had written that he was born around 1808.[24] When he asked Lilly and Hodges about the matter, he learned the truth:

> In late January of 1933, I told Mr. Lilly and Mr. Hodges of my confusion. Mr. Lilly said he could explain the discrepancy in dates and proceeded to tell me the following story: When the two oldest children of the family, Charlotte and Ann Eliza were little girls, their mother looked out of the window one afternoon and saw an older boy talking to them. She did not interrupt them for they started playing together and apparently were enjoying themselves. When it was time for the girls' supper Mrs. Foster went to the door and told the boy that the girls must come in now, but that if he would go home now he was welcome to come back tomorrow and play with the girls again.
>
> The boy replied that his own mother had brought him here and told him that this was to be his home. Mrs. Foster took him aside and asked him what he meant. He said that his mother had said that from now on he was to live with his father. When Mrs. Foster asked him who his father was, the boy answered: "Mother says it's Colonel Billy Foster." The boy was immediately taken inside for supper with the girls. He was given a bed in the

---

[23] Morneweck, *Chronicles*, vol. 2, 533–34.
[24] Howard, unpublished autobiography, B39.

guest room, the girls were sent to bed, and their mother waited alone for her husband's return. Whatever was said between them was not known. All the girls remembered was that the boy was at breakfast the next morning and [they] were told that he was to be their older brother. He was given the name of William B. Foster, Jr., that of the child born in 1814 who had died in infancy.[25]

Howard felt that this was "a most beautiful story" that "must be in my book." He recalls that "Mr. Lilly agreed with me but said that we must have the consent of Mrs. Morneweck, on whom we were all dependent for the bulk of our information about the Foster family."[26]

Howard goes on to lament, though, that he failed to secure Morneweck's "consent to write about brother William's real origin." He explains her reaction and the compromise they reached:

> She was annoyed to learn that I knew about it, and said that it must remain a family secret. I pleaded with her, pointing out that the episode was a tribute to her grandmother's womanliness. I also remarked that Brother William had left no descendants who would be embarrassed by the story. She replied that her own brother bore the name of William B. Foster....
>
> We argued for several hours. Mr. Lilly was present during most of our talk, and although he had nothing to say for a long while he became increasingly restive. Finally, when my arguments were exhausted and I had accomplished nothing, he said quietly: "John is right, Mrs. Morneweck, he cannot ignore the discrepancy in dates. I can understand too why you are unwilling to have the story told. Why not settle the matter this way: John can say in his book that Brother William was actually a relative of William B. Foster, senior, and was adopted by the family and given the name of a child who had died in infancy." In agreeing to this compromise I felt that I was guilty of a gross understatement. Yet it certainly was true that he was a relative of his father's.[27]

If it were not for Howard's unpublished account—and his daughter's willingness to donate it to the Foster Hall Collection—we would know nothing of William Jr.'s real origins.

---

[25] Howard, unpublished autobiography, B40.
[26] Howard, unpublished autobiography, B41.
[27] Howard, unpublished autobiography, B57–B58.

But sadly, because of the Foster family's secrecy and Lilly's complicity, we know nothing of William Jr.'s real mother. Could Morneweck really have been so upset that 125 years earlier her grandfather, a man who died more than thirty years before she was born, had a son out of wedlock? Or was there more? In the early 1800s it was common in Pennsylvania for White men to rape women they enslaved.[28] We also know that the Fosters were at least adjacent to this practice because one of the women they enslaved, Olivia Pise, was the daughter of the White Henry Pius and a woman he enslaved. Could William Jr.'s mother have been a woman who was enslaved? In the absence of evidence, it must be added to the range of plausible scenarios. Since Morneweck and Lilly conspired to ensure that nothing of William Jr.'s mother could ever be known, and since William Jr. has no direct descendants for DNA testing, the race of William Jr. and his mother's identity will probably forever remain open questions. If William Jr. had "passed" as White his whole life, he would have been illegally elected as a Pennsylvania Canal Commissioner and he would have risen to positions of power, such as vice president of the Pennsylvania Railroad, which Black people were restricted from obtaining. Perhaps this would have been embarrassing to the Fosters and their business associates. On the other hand, although the sexual violence perpetrated upon William Jr.'s mother would be despicable, the family's treatment of William Jr. might have provided the only real evidence that the Fosters were in some cases concerned about the struggles that Black people faced and were at least occasionally willing to take extreme and risky measures to help them.

A few illuminating items linking the family to enslavement did find their way into the collection, and close comparison of them with Morneweck's *Chronicles* suggests that Morneweck likely suppressed other slavery-related items. Gradual abolition in Pennsylvania largely culminated during Foster's boyhood in the 1830s, because the wording and implementation of Pennsylvania's Gradual Abolition Act of 1781 stipulated that children of enslaved mothers were to be enslaved for the first twenty-eight years of their lives. A letter from 1834 by William Foster Sr. indicates that "Mrs. Collins made your ma a present of an excellent coloured girl a few days ago, who has upwards of three years to serve,"[29] suggesting that this woman was

---

[28] Cory James Young, "For Life or Otherwise: Abolition and Slavery in South Central Pennsylvania, 1780–1847" (PhD diss., Georgetown University, 2021), 173–84.

[29] William Foster Sr. to William Foster Jr., July 14, 1834, FHC, C628.

twenty-five and the Fosters enslaved her until she turned twenty-eight. Tellingly, William does not identify this person by name, but Morneweck—born in 1887, fifty years after the person labored for the family—reveals her name was Kitty. Morneweck also obfuscates the fact that she was enslaved for a term, referring to her only as a "bound servant" and dubiously asserting that "bound children fared as well as the children of the house."[30] She clearly did not want readers to know that the Fosters enslaved Kitty, and the fact that she somehow knew her name suggests that she most likely possessed and suppressed other slavery-related documents. In *Chronicles* she cleverly covered her tracks. She did not have to cite items that she never donated to the collection because she rarely provided citations for any archival materials at all.

Morneweck thus did not write her book in a way that would help later researchers discover materials in the collection, and Foster Hall seems to have been complicit when items such as William Sr.'s letter about Kitty slipped in. The staff created an extensive card catalog, arranged and written to accommodate much more detail than a typical catalog. The catalog represents most people with whom the Fosters corresponded or interacted, describing their relationship to the family, relevant items in the collection, and secondary sources for further reading. For example, the cards about Foster's friend William Hamilton in the "General Index" describe each letter in the collection that mentions Hamilton as well as the composer's flute, which he gifted to Hamilton in 1857 and was donated to Foster Hall in 1935 (Figure C.1).[31] The card catalog, though, does not contain cards describing records related to Kitty or Olivia Pise. Similarly, several pieces of William Sr.'s correspondence are cataloged, and the card for a letter addressed to him by his wife Eliza on February 24, 1841, contains a summary of the letter typical of the catalog:

> Foster, Eliza C[layland]. Pittsburgh, Pa. To William B. Foster, Jr. Towanda, Pennsylvania. Approves of his plan to marry Miss Overton; personal mention of Dunning [Foster] and Morrison [Foster]; a reference to William B. Foster. A typewritten copy. 2 pp. (A portion of this letter has been destroyed.)[32]

---

[30] Morneweck, *Chronicles*, vol. 1, 103.
[31] "Hamilton, William," General Index, Card Catalog, FHC.
[32] William B. Foster, February 24, 1841, General Index, Card Catalog, FHC.

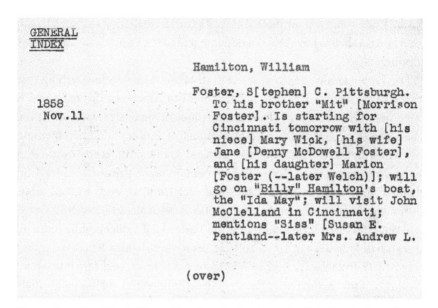

**Figure C.1.** Card for William Hamilton in the Foster Hall Collection's card catalog. Foster Hall Collection, Center for American Music, University of Pittsburgh Library System.

Curiously, Foster Hall did not catalog William Sr.'s letter about Kitty or Eliza's writing about Olivia Pise in her memoir.[33] Without tools to guide researchers to these materials, Foster Hall forced researchers to read every document in the collection of more than ten thousand items to find them, essentially rendering them invisible for decades.

Other curious gaps in the Foster Hall Collection point to a general avoidance of issues of race and racism. Foster Hall employed a clippings service that collected thousands of newspaper and magazine articles about the composer, from his time to the 1960s. The vast number of articles gives the first impression that the clippings files are exhaustive. But close examination reveals that there is not a single article from the Black press and that the reminiscences by Kane, Sanford, Dumont, and Clarke—all of which link Foster to minstrelsy throughout the entirety of his career—are also missing. Most conspicuous, though, is the absence of a single article about the 1914 NAACP activism regarding the Boston Public Schools. Later activism by the

---

[33] Olivia is mentioned twice in Eliza Foster's memoire: "Sketches and Incidents," FHC, C386, pp. 139 and 141.

NAACP and other organizations, as well as racist retaliation to that activism (more on this below), are also not documented in the Foster Hall Collection's clippings files.

The Foster family clearly worked to distance Foster from anything that might have suggested he was not a symbol of American diversity, which raises questions about other curious omissions in the Foster Hall Collection. The collection contains two transcriptions of Foster's mother's memoir, "Sketches and Incidents," but the original manuscript is lost. Morrison made the transcriptions, both of which contain many gaps where Morrison claimed the original manuscript had deteriorated and was illegible. Curiously, the surviving pages have recollections of all of Eliza's children except one—Stephen Foster. Similarly, the Foster Hall Collection includes all known letters by Foster. He must have been a prodigious letter writer, but only twenty-five mostly anodyne letters survive. They reveal very little about the kinds of things the Foster family actively suppressed, including his marriage and sexuality, addiction and mental health struggles, views on slavery and racism, and political opinions.

Working closely together, Lilly and Morneweck generated large amounts of correspondence that might have illuminated such collection gaps. Lilly eventually donated his correspondence related to his Foster work to the University of Pittsburgh along with the Foster Hall Collection. According to the Guide to the Josiah K. Lilly Correspondence, 1931–1944, the correspondence between Lilly and Morneweck "grew to several hundred pieces a year," and although "many items are factual in nature ... some letters are filled with rumors, gossip and speculation." Unfortunately for historians, the finding aid adds that Hodges "weeded these files ... feeling that certain letters shouldn't be made available to the public."[34] These letters would be of great interest to historians today because they would illuminate the attitudes that shaped Lilly's and Morneweck's work and relationship. This correspondence likely contained information or speculation about the "phases of Foster's character" that the family and Foster Hall kept secret, but Hodges's destructive actions made it impossible for researchers to investigate.

With their sights set on glorifying Foster, Foster Hall failed to collect items that told a different story and suppressed items that slipped into the collection. But it is unclear how aware of their actions they were. Their belief in the

---

[34] Guide to the Josiah K. Lilly Correspondence, 1931–1944, description of Box 1, Folder 40, Center for American Music, University of Pittsburgh Library System, https://digital.library.pitt.edu/islandora/object/pitt%3AUS-PPiU-camjklcorr2016/viewer.

national-universal myth might have blinded them to evidence to the contrary and made them susceptible to the Foster family's machinations. With Lilly committed to permanently linking his name to a "founding father," and with Morneweck's focus on enshrining and profiting from her uncle's accomplishments, they seem to have found common ground over the myth of Foster as an American icon whose sympathy for the nation's inhabitants enabled him to compose the first songs that embodied the nation's democratic ideals. Lilly could not afford to offend Morneweck, and Morneweck did not want to damage the family's public image or upset family business partners. Their shared approach, therefore, came to resemble the motto Lilly immortalized on a bronze plaque at the entrance to Foster Hall in Indiana:

FOSTER HALL
Dedicated to Harmony
Let No Discordant Note Enter Here

Morneweck and Foster Hall believed—or needed to believe—that Foster represented sympathy, inclusion, and democracy, so they refused entry to any archival object that suggested otherwise. Their actions created a collection with what historian Ann Laura Stoler describes as an "archival grain" made by the directions in which their attentions "were trained and selectively cast."[35] To this day, the grain of the Foster Hall Collection continues to point researchers in specific directions at the expense of others.

## The Narratives and Rituals of Foster Hall

With the approaching publication of Howard's biography on January 8, 1934, Howard and the staff of Foster Hall deliberated over the final form of the book. Howard wanted to call it "Dear Friends and Gentle Hearts," a phrase found scribbled in Foster's hand on a scrap of paper in the songwriter's wallet at the time of his death. As an apparent germ of a new song lyric, the phrase symbolized a musical life cut short and fittingly encapsulated Foster's life and career.[36] But the publisher, Crowell, expressed concern that the title did not adequately communicate to consumers the book's subject and

---

[35] Stoler, *Along the Archival Grain*, 1.
[36] Foster's Last Message, 1863–1864, FHC, A322.

would hurt sales. Lilly agreed, writing to Howard that the Foster Hall team "was unanimous that your publishers were probably right in not wanting a title about which your readers would not know of at first" and suggested the title "Stephen Foster—American Troubadour." Lilly did not want to subtitle it something like "America's Beloved Composer" or "America's Immortal Composer" because "the words *beloved* and *immortal* seem to have been worn out." He felt justified in "American Troubadour" because Foster "was really the first American successor to the ancient troubadours."[37] "Troubadour" thus suggested to Lilly immortality in its evocation of the "ancient" without sounding cliché, and Lilly felt it captured Foster's originality as, in his view, there had not been an American troubadour before him. As always, Howard deferred to his patron. After conferring further with Crowell, he reported to Lilly that they agreed on "Stephen Foster, America's Troubadour."[38] Replacing "American" with the possessive "America's" connoted more strongly that Foster's music spoke to the world on behalf of America. A few days later, Lilly affirmed that "everyone here approves of *Stephen Foster America's Troubadour.*"[39]

This anecdote reveals Foster Hall's meticulous attention to detail in its quest to reach the highest number of people with the message that Foster was a national symbol and composer of eternal music, which in turn caused them to both support and control Howard. In the end, just like the archive, Howard's biography contains great detail about Foster's movements, family, social life, business dealings, and finances, with little detail about minstrelsy or his love life, alcoholism, and political opinions. It chronicles in scrupulous detail when and where the composer wrote his music, but there is hardly any analysis or contextualization of the music and lyrics. Howard unearths a great deal about the facts of Foster's life but only superficially portrays the music as simply "a nationalistic expression." The book set the tone for Foster Hall's activities throughout the rest of 1934 and beyond.

Strongly influenced by Morneweck, Foster Hall set its gaze precisely on what Morrison had hoped—Foster's music—and never delved deeper into contextualization and analysis than Howard. Howard, in fact, was explicit about this approach. He wrote, "Why try to analyze his tunes, so lovely in

---

[37] Josiah K. Lilly to John Tasker Howard, October 20, 1933; and Josiah K. Lilly to John Tasker Howard, October 23, 1933, Josiah K. Lilly Correspondence, box 6, folder 191C.
[38] John Tasker Howard to Josiah K. Lilly, October 23, 1933, Josiah K. Lilly Correspondence, box 6, folder 191C.
[39] Lilly to Howard, October 27, 1933, Josiah K. Lilly Correspondence, box 6, folder 191C.

their simplicity? Classifying their intervals may well be left to scholars.... He was a good enough musician to harmonize his songs as they should be harmonized—quite simply. What more can we ask of a man who has touched our hearts?"[40] Foster's songs, in other words, were presented at face value with little investigation of their technical features or meanings. Later in 1934, the Foster Hall Collection neared completion, and Lilly reissued first editions of all of Foster's compositions in facsimile, creating the first complete-works edition ever to be compiled for an American composer. Lilly sent the *Foster Hall Reproductions*, as they were called, to one thousand libraries at no charge.[41] The *Reproductions* placed Foster in company with European "masters," such as Mozart, Beethoven, and Schubert—figuratively, in the sense that the compositions of these Europeans had been issued in complete-works editions in the previous century, and literally, in the sense that the Library of Congress assigns all these works the call number M3, which means they are placed next to each other in most US libraries.

Devoid of contextual information except for basic bibliographic data, the *Reproductions* were also shaped by the ideals of German Romanticism that situated German music as autonomous and universal, that is, as *above* worldly concerns such as commercialism and politics. Noting that "universal" music "has a strong German accent," historian Kira Thurman observes that "the compositions of Mozart or Beethoven in particular have earned a reputation for universality because of their supposed ability to transcend national boundaries as they transport listeners to another realm." Thurman observes that these ideas, which first emerged in nineteenth-century German music criticism and historiography, linked notions of the universal to the German nationalist project: "By próposing that universal music was serious, pure, and soulful and by positioning German music as the only true expression of these universal values, German aesthetes, nationalists, and even politicians transformed a universalist message into a nationalist idea. Simultaneously belonging to all and also authentically German, the Austro-German musical canon paradoxically tied the universal to the nation like no other."[42] Taking Foster's songs out of context and focusing on them as autonomous objects

---

[40] John Tasker Howard, *Our American Music* (Crowell, 1931), 201.
[41] Foster Hall Reproductions: Songs, Compositions, and Arrangements by Stephen Collins Foster, 1826–1864 (Josiah Kirby Lilly, 1933).
[42] Thurman, *Singing Like Germans*, 6. See also Richard Taruskin, *Music in the Nineteenth Century*, Oxford History of Western Music (Oxford University Press, 2010), 422; and Susan McClary, "Narrative Agendas in Absolute Music," in *Musicology and Difference: Gender and Sexuality in Music Scholarship*, ed. Ruth A. Solie (University of California Press, 1995), 327.

helped Lilly establish Foster as an American counterpart to Austro-German musicians such as Mozart and Beethoven.

Employing musicological methods largely developed in Germany, Foster Hall embraced a common and reductive nineteenth- and early twentieth-century musicological approach to biography that employed a composer's most popular music as a lens into their world and inner self. At the expense of Foster's other songs and other evidence of his character, Foster Hall emphasized the ambiguous sentimental minstrel songs to construct Foster as an interracially sensitive composer who embodied American ideals of tolerance and democracy. Lilly knew this construction overly relied on only a subset of his songs. He knew there were objections to his music along racial lines (thus undermining claims of universality), and he knew that not all of Foster's songs were universally appealing. He admitted this in 1931 when writing to Dean J. Rice, who had expressed concerns about what he perceived as the low quality of one of the Foster songs that he believed to possess in manuscript. Lilly conceded that "it may be said that all [Foster's] two-hundred-and-fifty songs and compositions will not survive the musical gymnastics of the ages," but he emphasized that the universal songs would withstand the test of time, writing, "It is quite certain that those Foster songs which have universal appeal will be preserved, generation after generation."[43] Fully aware that not all of Foster's songs were universally appealing, Lilly built a public image of Foster upon only those songs he could—or, because of their controversial nature, needed to—present as universal.

Foster Hall interpreted Foster's life through his decontextualized music and characterized his songs as universal in arrangements, songbooks, and songsters that it created and disseminated around the globe. Characteristically, in a songbook for schoolchildren, it introduced the songs as "simple and lovable" and asserted that "they belong to the whole world; for all hearts are alike in feeling tenderness, merriment, joy, sympathy, and love of home, and must have some beautiful way of expressing these feelings, such as we find in song."[44] Howard made his own arrangements of Foster's songs in *A Program of Stephen Foster Songs*, which Lilly sent (again free of charge) to performers and radio stations across the United States to encourage radio

---

[43] Josiah K. Lilly to Dean J. Rice, November 24, 1931, FHC, unprocessed folder labeled "Dean J. Rice."
[44] Stephen Foster, *Songs of Stephen Foster Prepared for Schools and General Use*, ed. and arr. Will Earhart and Edward B. Birge (Josiah K. Lilly, 1934), 4.

performances. Leaning into the notion that the songs told us all we need to know about Foster himself, Howard wrote in the introduction that the songs "form an autobiography, for Stephen Foster himself is apparent in his music and verse." Following Jessie Welsh Rose's 1926 reminiscence, he provided two "classifications" of Foster's songs that each exhibit "a phase of his temperament." He writes,

> First come the laughing, buoyant songs—Oh! Susanna, Camptown races, The Glendy Burk. Here we find the Stephen Foster who liked the minstrel shows, who loved company and the serenading parties with friends in Pittsburgh and Allegheny. Then come the homesick songs—probably the greatest of all his works because they speak of the emotion that was strongest in his own nature—his love for his own home. Foster was never happy when he was away from Pittsburgh, from the surroundings of his youth and the companions of his early manhood.[45]

Howard's descriptions erase the racism of Foster's minstrel songs, and by leaving out war songs like "We Are Coming Father Abraam," his song choices erase Foster's sectionalism. In their broad generalities, Howard's categories present something to which most people can relate—playing into the notion of universalism—while telling us next to nothing about Foster's real character.

Howard also cites Foster's songs that express nostalgia and homesickness as evidence of the factors that led to his alcoholism and early death. Based solely on these songs, he concludes, "It is altogether apparent that the tragedy of his last years in New York was brought about largely by a nostalgia that weakened his resistance to the habits that proved his undoing."[46] Howard probably knew that—as Morneweck would reveal in her book—Ann Eliza and Morrison had both unsuccessfully attempted to convince the composer to move back home. As much as we might want to believe that Foster expressed his own homesickness in his songs, this was probably not the case. His "homesick" songs may contain kernels of what he felt being away from his family and hometown, but he most likely wrote them because homesick

---

[45] Foster, *A Program of Stephen Foster Songs*, ed. and arr. John Tasker Howard (J. Fischer & Bro., 1934), v–vi.
[46] Foster, *Program*, vi.

songs had been immensely popular since Henry Rowley Bishop's "Home Sweet Home" became a hit in the 1820s. By decontextualizing Foster's songs and paying little attention to his contemporaries or their song subjects, Foster Hall concealed that Foster deployed basic genre conventions, making everything he wrote and composed appear as if it flowed directly from his soul.

Naturally, Lilly's efforts to establish Foster as a universal composer extended beyond the United States. In 1933, he sent the *Foster Hall Bulletin*—which contained information about his collecting activities—to the Pan American Union in Washington DC. In subsequent correspondence, Franklin Adams informed Lilly that the Pan American Union sponsored concerts in the nation's capital to bring "the music of Latin America to the attention of the people of the United States." He proposed a quid pro quo of international cultural diplomacy in which Lilly would commission Luis Guzman, a native Colombian and member of the US Marine Band, to create instrumental arrangements of Foster's melodies that would be performed in a concert produced by the Pan American Union and made available to Latin American bands.[47] Lilly accepted the proposal and commissioned band, orchestral, and choral arrangements from Guzman. He seems to have hoped that Foster Hall's rhetoric of universalism would be well suited for the scores' international target audience. The preface to the scores only obliquely refers to race and highlights Foster's sentimental minstrel songs, stating that Foster's fame "rests principally on his four greatest songs, 'Old Folks at Home' . . . 'My Old Kentucky Home,' 'Massa's in de Cold Ground' and 'Old Black Joe.'" It then pivots to the universal: "The simplicity and sincerity of Foster's songs have endeared them to the hearts of people, not only in his native land, but in other countries also."[48] But despite Foster Hall's appeal to universalism, it does not appear that it received many South American requests for the scores. In 2023 I removed hundreds of unpurchased copies from the basement of the Stephen Foster Memorial, where they had been stashed, sealed in their original packaging, for more than eighty years.

As these scores were being published and distributed throughout 1934, Lilly was in regular contact with John G. Bowman, chancellor of the University of Pittsburgh, about the donation of the collection to the university's Stephen Foster Memorial, which Bowman was helping raise the

---

[47] Franklin Adams to Josiah K. Lilly, August 16, 1933, FHC, Letters Catalogued (A–H), box A-1; and Franklin Adams to Josiah K. Lilly, August 28, 1933, FHC, Letters Catalogued (A–H), box A-1.

[48] Stephen Foster, *Stephen Foster Melodies*, arranged for orchestra by Luis Guzman (Foster Hall, 1938); also arranged for chorus by Luis Guzman (Foster Hall, 1941).

money to construct. The memorial fit into Bowman's efforts to transform the struggling university into a world-class research university, an endeavor that revolved around building a campus skyscraper that, according to Bowman, "would express by means of the art of architecture the response of Pittsburgh's creative soul to the material world and to the world of the immaterial."[49] The Foster Memorial would be designed by the same architect and artists as the Cathedral and would be situated in its shadow on a fourteen-acre plot of land newly acquired to realize Bowman's vision. By the end of 1934, Lilly and Bowman had finalized Lilly's donation, the university's trustees had signed off, and Bowman was in touch with *The Atlantic* about placing an article on Foster and the Foster Hall Collection in the magazine.[50]

Written by Bowman himself, the article, which appeared in July 1935, not only embraced but extended Foster Hall's rhetoric. Bowman reduced Foster to a caricature by interpreting his whole character through only one of his sentimental minstrel songs, and he never mentioned race, sectionalism, or political partisanship at all. To Bowman, Foster drew on his experience of Pittsburgh's growth from a pioneer town to an industrial center in songs about home that "steadied the hope of the pioneers" as they pushed the frontier farther west. He described Foster as "a home boy, through and through" and wrote that "Old Folks at Home"

> is Foster himself. In it he expressed the depth of his heart; he let himself go in imagination, and, wandering far, made a discovery. For a brief moment in a distant somewhere he sang what he found. Sang... he did not argue or plead. He did not question or speak as a prophet. Coldly stated, he found that a man could be happy in a hut. The idea was not new. It was even commonplace; the folk of the [Ohio River] valley had long ago had faith in the hut theory and were now in a mood to doubt it. But coldly stating Foster's discovery in this way does not tell what he found. He gave to the old idea so much sincerity and beauty of expression that the idea rose above its former meaning. In effect his discovery was new. In as true a sense as Columbus sighted new land off San Salvador, Foster on a far journey came upon new

---

[49] Bowman, *Unofficial Notes* (T. and F. Bowman, 1963), 38.
[50] The process through which Lilly donated the collection to the University of Pittsburgh is documented in his correspondence with John G. Bowman in Box 11, Folder 320, "Pittsburgh, University of, 1934," Josiah K. Lilly Correspondence, Center for American Music, University of Pittsburgh Library System.

faith in human nature. He went to the materials of his own experience, simplified them and enriched them, and gave them words and melody and soul.[51]

To Bowman, Foster was a "discoverer," comparable to Columbus because he rediscovered and breathed new life into old ideas of home, supporting the nation's growth in songs that encouraged Whites who were embracing their "manifest destiny" to colonize the West. Bowman based his version of Foster on his interpretation of a minstrel song, and he erased divisiveness from the song altogether.

Foster Hall's influence grew when it attained the imprimatur of the University of Pittsburgh. Lilly had his sights trained on securing Foster's election to the Hall of Fame of Great Americans at New York University, an induction process that occurred only once every five years. He had been unsuccessful in lobbying the electors in both 1930 and 1935, but in 1940, after the collection moved to Pittsburgh, Foster Hall succeeded. As curator of the collection, Hodges personally wrote to each of the Hall of Fame's electors, which included university presidents and prominent intellectuals. He also wrote to correspondents of Foster Hall, including Howard, to ask them to join him in lobbying the electors. In his letters, Hodges explicitly built an image of Foster on "Old Folks at Home," "My Old Kentucky Home," "Massa's in de Cold Ground," and "Old Black Joe," which he claimed were "known, loved, and sung, not only in his native country, but in all parts of the world." Also mentioning "Jeanie With the Light Brown Hair" and "Come Where My Love Lies Dreaming," he asserted that these songs "describe a definite period in our country's growth,"[52] noting also that "Oh! Susanna" "played a large part in our Western development" as "a marching song by the Forty-Niners." Employing the standard rhetoric, he declined to mention race, sectionalism, or political partisanship, invoking only the universal and national. He kept a close tally of where the vote stood (Figure C.2). Electors who had expressed ambivalence or did not reply received follow-up letters.

A press release from the Hall of Fame dated November 15, 1940, indicates that on the previous day Foster was "named on 86 of the 108 ballots," becoming "the only successful candidate in a field of 141 nominated by

---

[51] John G. Bowman, "A Singer to Pioneers," *The Atlantic*, June 1935.
[52] Fletcher Hodges Jr. to Roy Chapman Andrews, April 25, 1940, Fletcher Hodges Correspondence, Folder 138, Hall of Fame Fletcher Hodges Jr., Center for American Music, University of Pittsburgh Library System.

CONCLUDING ESSAY 347

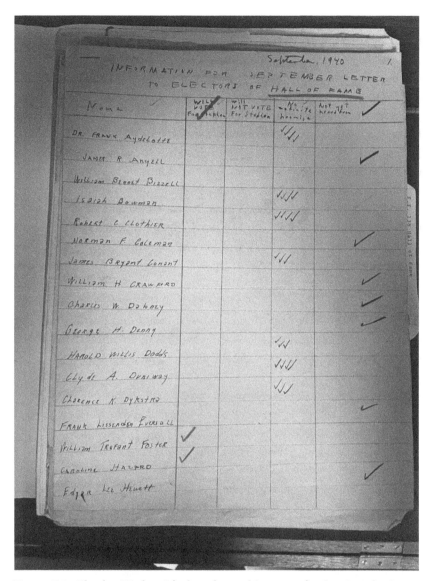

**Figure C.2.** Fletcher Hodges Jr.'s chart for tracking votes for the 1940 election of Foster to the Hall of Fame of Great Americans. Foster Hall Collection, Center for American Music, University of Pittsburgh Library System.

members of the public earlier this year."[53] At the induction ceremony the following spring, Lilly unveiled a bronze bust by sculptor Walter Hancock and a slate of distinguished speakers invoked nationalism and universalism.[54] Howard claimed that Foster "gave us kindliness and peace" and that the electors "have reminded us of what the spirit of America really is" by celebrating songs that "express the true soul of our great nation."[55] Howard Hanson, a renowned composer and dean of the Eastman School of Music (whose words were read by Sigmund Spaeth because Hanson was ill on the day of the ceremony), claimed that Foster's music "bears upon itself the stamp of the American soul."[56] When presenting the bust, Lilly stated that Foster's "simple lyrics and divine melodies, so native and genuine, appeal to the finest emotions of the *human* heart" (emphasis added).[57] Alongside performances by the New York University Glee Club, Foster's music was presented in the "universal" style of classical music by operatic soprano Rose Bampton and violinist Albert Spalding.

When the United States entered the Second World War later that year, Foster Hall leapt at the opportunity to insert Foster into wartime patriotic discourse, distributing a songbook and songsters to members of the armed services free of charge. Introducing the songbook, they wrote,

> The songs of Stephen Foster have become the heritage, not only of his native America, but of the world. Who has not heard and loved *Old Folks at Home, My Old Kentucky Home, Massa's in de Cold Ground* and *Old Black Joe*? Who can not sing them? These "old favorites" were intended to portray one race of people, one section of our country, one period in our history, yet through his genius Foster succeeded in creating songs which have

---

[53] New York University Bureau of Public Information, "Stephen Collins Foster Elected to Hall of Fame on N.Y.U. Campus," Press Release, November 15, 1940, Foster Hall Curatorial Correspondence, Folder 142, "Hall of Fame Press Releases, Articles," Center for American Music, University of Pittsburgh Library System.

[54] The bust was a gift of Josiah Kirby Lilly, Stephen J. Wigmore, Mrs. Agnetta F. Kerns, Mr. and Mrs. Fletcher Hodges Jr., and Judson Cole. See Theodore Morello, ed., *The Hall of Fame of Great Americans at New York University* (New York University Press, 1962), 141.

[55] John Tasker Howard, "Address of John Tasker Howard, Biography, at the Unveiling of the Bust of Stephen Collins Foster in the Hall of Fame," Foster Hall Curatorial Correspondence, folder 143, "Hall of Fame Speeches," Center for American Music, University of Pittsburgh Library System.

[56] Howard Hanson, "Address to be Delivered in Connection with the Unveiling of the Bust of Stephen Collins Foster in the Hall of Fame," Foster Hall Curatorial Correspondence, folder 143, "Hall of Fame Speeches," Center for American Music, University of Pittsburgh Library System.

[57] Josiah Kirby Lilly, "Dear Friends and Gentle Hearts," Foster Hall Curatorial Correspondence, folder 143, "Hall of Fame Speeches," Center for American Music, University of Pittsburgh Library System.

leaped the boundaries of space and time and express universal thoughts and emotions.[58]

Foster Hall conveyed a clear and consistent message: Foster's music portrayed Black people in the South but transcends race and sectionalism. In the context of the Second World War, when nationalism was associated with Nazism and genocide, the purported "universalism" of Foster's music resonated with the "American" democratic ideals that the members of the Armed Forces were fighting to defend. Foster Hall printed and distributed the armed services songbook for decades. On the centenary of Foster's death in 1964, Hodges wrote that "from 1942 to the present, there have been eleven printings of this edition, consisting of approximately 750,000 copies."[59]

Also in 1941, Stephen Wigmore encouraged Foster Hall to raise money for a memorial to the composer in Washington DC and began contributing money toward the effort.[60] Hodges solicited and collected contributions for the remainder of the decade, and on May 24, 1949, he wrote to the Commission of Fine Arts to propose a plaque by Walter Hancock on federal land in the nation's capital. He earned the support of the commission when he addressed them in person on June 20, and by the end of the year Representative Harry J. Davenport of Pittsburgh and Senator Edward Martin of Pennsylvania signed on. With their assistance, on September 9, 1950, an act of Congress approved the memorial.

It would take more than two years for the bust to be unveiled, but in the meantime Stephen Foster Day, which had been a local Pittsburgh celebration up to that time, was transformed into a federal day of observance. On October 15, 1951, the House Judiciary Committee recognized Foster as "the father of American folk music" and "a national expression of democracy through his clear and simple embodiment of American tradition" before recommending the passage of the law by the full Congress, which was quickly achieved.[61] Soon thereafter President Truman designated January 13

---

[58] Stephen Foster, *Songs of Stephen Foster Prepared especially for the Armed Forces by the Staff of the Foster Hall Collection of the University of Pittsburgh* (University of Pittsburgh Press, 1944).

[59] Fletcher Hodges Jr., "Finder of Many Melodies," *Palimpsest* 45, no. 1 (January 1964): 29.

[60] The initial donations are documented in two letters: Stephen Wigmore to Fletcher Hodges, June 20, 1941; and Fletcher Hodges Jr. to Stephen Wigmore, June 23, 1941, Foster Hall Curatorial Correspondence, folder 294, "Wigmore, S. F.," Center for American Music, University of Pittsburgh Library System.

[61] House of Representatives, 82nd Congress, Rep. No. 1185, Stephen Foster Memorial Day, October 15, 1951.

as Stephen Foster Day.[62] Hancock's bust of Foster, which was finally unveiled at the Library of Congress on the eve of Stephen Foster Day in 1953, bears the inscription "he made the Swanee River and My Old Kentucky Home imperishable symbols of our nation." Of course, Foster did not really make those songs symbols of the nation. That work was begun by Morrison and carried through by Lilly, who leveraged his influence and fortune to enlist the support of the University of Pittsburgh, New York University, the US military, US Congress, the president, and the Library of Congress in enshrining the Foster myth.

Educating the world about Foster's "greatness" as a national-universal figure continued to be the mission of Foster Hall through Fletcher Hodges's retirement in 1982 and beyond. A report Hodges prepared for the Lilly Endowments in 1980 stated that "Stephen Foster holds a unique place in the history of American music and American culture." The report celebrated him as "more than a Pittsburgh composer" because "he is one of the great American composers" and asserted that "as a creator of folk songs, which are known and loved throughout the civilized world, he is an international figure." Foster Hall, therefore, was "involved in Foster work on a local, a national, and an international scale."[63]

History shows that Foster Hall's framing of Foster was not completely incorrect. It was rooted in the fact that he had consciously written some songs that managed—in one interpretation of them—to transcend race, section, and political divisions and spread to far locations across globe. Even his racialized songs had always carried non-racial meanings to many listeners and performers. And Foster's music had transcended its original contexts and meanings, taking on new meanings in particular to Black audiences and performers. But Foster Hall erred in following Morrison's lead in exaggerating Foster's music's "universalism" and using a small subset of pieces—his sentimental minstrel songs—to define what they portrayed as the essence of Foster's inclusive nature and convince many people that Foster and his music embodied American democracy.

Their actions had great consequences. Not only had Howard felt remorse about the compromises he was forced to accept but, as his daughter told later

---

[62] President Harry S. Truman, Proclamation 2957, Stephen Foster Memorial Day, in *Code of Federal Regulations, Title 3—The President, 1949-1953* (US Government Publishing Office, 2019), 143.

[63] Report on the Stephen Foster Memorial Building by Fletcher Hodges Jr., Manager, Stephen Foster Memorial, June 30, 1980, FHC, unprocessed papers.

Foster biographer Ken Emerson, his work on the biography "had driven him to a nervous breakdown."[64] More generally, their embrace and amplification of national-universal rhetoric to position Foster as a symbol of democracy was decidedly undemocratic because it silenced and marginalized oppositional voices. The growing chorus touting the national-universal myth drowned out naysayers, many of whom were already hidden away behind Jim Crow's walls. Those walls began to crumble in the mid-1950s, but historians attempting to unearth richer, more complete stories about Foster were still forced to contend with the grain of the Foster Hall Collection.

## The Consequences of Archival Amnesty: Memory of Foster since 1954

Historian Hayden White has lamented that the theoretical separation of history and historical fiction has resulted in a historical method that "refuses the *possible*" by retaining only the narrative structures of novels "while depriving [history] of both the techniques and imaginative resources of invention and representation that were henceforth exiled into the domain of 'fiction.'"[65] Most historians today carefully weigh evidence, while historical fiction writers take more latitude to create a *sense* of the real, the way things *could* have been, or the way things *felt*. It is generally assumed that good historical fiction writers are well versed in history but rely on their imaginations, while good history is grounded in verifiable evidence rather than the imaginative. But, as White implies, history also relies on the imaginative, particularly when the archival record contains gaps and erasures. By building an archive limited to evidence that supported their construction of Foster as a national icon, the Foster family and Foster Hall created many opportunities for other imaginative constructions of Foster.

In fact, for nearly one hundred years, historians have followed the leads of writers of historical fiction and non-scholarly non-fiction who have filled in the sparse historical record in ways that sometimes align Foster with anachronistic political concerns. I contend that the problem with these narratives is not that they are overly imaginative but that they are not imaginative

---

[64] Ken Emerson, "Stephen Foster and American Popular Culture," *American Music* 30, no. 3 (Fall 2012): 398.

[65] Hayden White, "Introduction: Historical Fiction, Fictional History, and Historical Reality," *Rethinking History* 9, no. 2/3 (June/September 2005): 149–50. Emphasis in original.

enough. They expose a danger of rigid adherence to the narrative structures of fiction: historians hamper their imaginations by giving in to fiction's demand that characters be developed as singular, unified, whole individuals in unified, character-driven stories that too often fail to represent the full range of possibilities of Foster's self. This is particularly evident in the three areas of speculation that have been continually debated by scholars throughout the twentieth and twenty-first centuries: Foster's sexuality, death, and views on racial politics.

## Foster's Sexuality

The scrutiny of Foster's sexuality in recent decades probably stems from the gaps in Howard's biography. When writing about Foster's romantic life and marriage, Howard is either uncharacteristically unclear or deliberately suggestive, choosing words and phrases that have suggested to many readers that he may have known something about which he could not write openly in the age of the closet. On Foster's marriage to Jane, he wrote,

> Although he was thoroughly masculine, it is doubtful that the love for woman, as a physical, male emotion, was in any way a dominant passion of his existence. He loved his home, his songs show that, but to Foster home meant his parents, his brothers and sisters, and the surroundings of his youth. His wife and the daughter that was born the year after marriage were included in that home, but I do not believe that they were by any means the first and only consideration of Stephen.[66]

What did Howard mean by this? A very literal reading of his words would conclude Foster was heterosexual. But the words about Foster's only daughter being born the year of their wedding might be taken to suggest that Foster and his wife had sex only once, and Howard's suggestion that Foster's wife was not his first and only consideration could be read as implying that Foster was queer. With Morneweck and Lilly micromanaging his work, was Howard only able to hint at Foster's queerness? Howard's final word on the subject offers no more clarity: "It is not to be doubted that Stephen

---

[66] Howard, *Stephen Foster*, 161.

loved Jane—at least as much as his temperament would allow of such an attachment."[67]

If Howard was trying to convince his readers of Foster's heterosexuality, he failed. In 1994 novelist Peter Quinn portrayed the composer as gay in the popular novel *Banished Children of Eve*. Quinn's Foster, estranged from Jane in New York in the last years of his life, is filled with regret but does not miss his wife. At one point, he recalls scenes of discontent in their marital bed:

> What had he said? *I'm sorry, Jane.* His mouth was so dry his tongue felt as if it were made of cotton. He fell asleep. He tried many times after that. Usually after drinking heavily. A few times successfully. They made a daughter. But he came to their bed much as he had gone to milk the cow his father kept behind their house in Pittsburgh. Something to be avoided, if possible. A cloud that hung over you, a duty, a chore, another impediment to happiness. *Stephen*, Jane said, *what is it you want? Name it.* He had no answer. At least none he could speak.[68]

Quinn's Foster, isolated in New York, regrets his time with Jane but never misses her. His sexual fulfillment, Quinn implies, is found only with men.

Quinn's compelling story appeared amid a societal awakening that witnessed individuals and public figures publicly "coming out" about their queerness, signaling a new age of sexual openness. The year after the novel's publication, *Out in All Directions: The Almanac of Gay and Lesbian America* appeared with the stated mission of contributing to a popular effort "to show the world, both gay and nongay, the depth and breadth of the people, the history, and the communities that have been created by gay men and lesbians." The non-fiction but decidedly non-scholarly almanac features a list titled "A Few American Gay Composers" that included a brief entry on Foster: "Stephen Collins Foster (1826–1861 [sic]), self-taught composer of popular American songs 'Old Folks at Home,' 'My Old Kentucky Home,' 'I Dream of Jeannie (with the Light Brown Hair)' [sic], 'Oh, Suzanna' [sic], 'Old Black Joe,' and a number of Civil War songs."[69] Supposedly as evidence of Foster's queerness, a "Did You Know" box on the same page states: "In a move that killed his popularity, Civil War–era composer Stephen Foster

---

[67] Howard, *Stephen Foster*, 163.
[68] Peter Quinn, *Banished Children of Eve* (Empire State Imprints, 2021), 41–42.
[69] Witt et al., *Out in All Directions*, chap. 1.

('I Dream of Jeannie' [sic]) left his wife to live with handsome fellow composer George Cooper ('Sweet Genevieve'). Eventually impoverished in the Bowery, then the site of several gay taverns, he died in the Bellevue Hospital charity ward." The statement elaborates Quinn's novelistic portrayal of Foster's relationship with Cooper, suggesting that his declining popularity and early death resulted from social stigmas associated with homosexuality. Foster appears in another list in the book titled "Claiming our own—Famous Names," suggesting that Foster's gayness needed to be "reclaimed" from the patriarchal forces that had erased it.

This view of Foster's sexuality lives on in more recent historical fiction. In the 2013 homoerotic Civil War–era novel *Where My Love Lies Dreaming*, author Christopher Hawthorne Moss includes an appendix called "Historical Note" in which he writes that Foster, who is referred to regularly in the book, "was what we would now call gay."[70] In the novel, Foster's music appears as a leitmotif punctuating romantic encounters between Johnny and Frankie on steamboats traveling the Mississippi River. In a dramatic scene in which Johnny questions if it is possible for two men to be in love, Frankie invokes Foster and his music:

> That song you sing to me, the one by Stephen Foster, "Come Where My Love Lies Dreaming'? Did you think it was about a woman? No. He wrote the music for lyrics written about him by his lover, the poet, George Cooper. I know them both. If a song like that is not about love then I. . . ." His voice faltered. He slowly turned to look at Johnny. "I had hoped that someday you would feel the same about me."[71]

Moss takes great liberties with facts. Not only did Cooper not write the words of "Come Where My Love Lies Dreaming" but Foster wrote them himself at least five years before he met Cooper.

The entirely imaginative portrayals of Foster's sexuality by Quinn and Moss and in the *Almanac* inspired scholars to question past heteronormative assumptions and re-examine the evidence of Foster's romantic life. In his 1997 biography, Ken Emerson expresses skepticism that Foster was heterosexual or homosexual. He points to Foster's multiple long-term separations from Jane and the birth of their daughter exactly nine months after their

---

[70] Christopher Hawthorne Moss, *Where My Love Lies Dreaming* (Dreamspinner Press, 2013), 333.
[71] Moss, *Where My Love Lies Dreaming*, 138.

wedding, suggesting like Howard that Foster and his wife had sex only once. Looking for further evidence in Foster's songs, he speculates that Foster may have been asexual: "Maybe it was just coincidence that they had only one child, born nine months after their wedding, but it's striking how infrequently sexual sparks fly in Stephen's letters and music. If Jane wasn't his 'type,' no one else seemed to be, either."[72] Whereas Emerson finds it "striking how infrequently sexual sparks fly in Stephen's letters," I find it striking how few of Foster's letters were preserved. Arriving at many conclusions beyond the specific content of the surviving letters based on such a small sampling—especially a sampling that is known to have been manipulated—is, in my opinion, not particularly fruitful. What is probably more fruitful is acknowledging the possibility that sexuality, particularly historically oppressed queerness, *could* have been suppressed in the Foster Hall Collection.

By conceding to the narratological demand that Foster be characterized in a singular manner, Emerson may have blinded himself to the sexual sparks that can, in fact, fly in Foster's music. That Foster did not write overtly sexual songs was probably another manifestation of his desire to write songs that appealed to as many consumers as possible. Rather than write openly about sex, Foster nods toward promiscuity in his lyrics in "Angelina Baker," for example, in which the title character "likes de boys as far as she can see dem," and in "Way Down in Ca-i-ro," in which the singer begins "Oh! ladies dont you blush when I come out to play;/I only mean to please you all, and den I'd guine away." Sexual suggestiveness is not limited to his minstrel songs. In the serenade "Beautiful Dreamer," the singer addresses a woman as she sleeps in her room:

> Beautiful dreamer, wake unto me,
> Starlight and dewdrops are waiting for thee;
> Sounds of the rude world heard in the day,
> Lull'd by the moonlight have all pass'd away!
> Beautiful dreamer, queen of my song,
> List while I woo thee with soft melody;
> Gone are the cares of life's busy throng,
> Beautiful dreamer, awake unto me!

---

[72] Emerson, *Doo-Dah!*, 202.

Is the singer serenading her from outside the home, as some of the reminiscences reveal Foster did? Or is he singing to her in the intimate and private setting of her bedroom? If the latter, what does the man hope to do with the woman when she awakes?

Quinn grasped the implicit sexuality in Foster's serenade texts. In *Banished Children of Eve*, he has Jane sing Foster's "Open Thy Lattice Love" while trying to entice Foster to bed:

> When he opened the door to the room, she was in bed with the quilt pulled up to her neck. *Close the door*, she said. She pushed down the quilt and knelt on the bed. She was naked. She cupped her breasts in her hands so that the nipples stuck out between her fingers. "Come to bed, my love," she said. She lay back on the bed, her legs open wide. In almost a whisper she sang, "Open thy lattice, love, listen to me! While the moon's in the sky and the breeze on the sea!"[73]

As Quinn realized, Foster filled his music with sexual possibilities.

Sexuality is also an inherent possibility in piano music for four hands. According to Thomas Christensen, "Piano duet performances are arguably a doubly eroticized activity, for not only are there twenty fingers touching the keys, two bodies are coming into contact with each other—hands crossing over and interlocking; legs, hips, elbows, and shoulders rubbing and bumping into each other."[74] In "The Soirée Polka"—the one four-hand arrangement probably made by Foster—the composer takes advantage of the genre's physical intimacy, writing music in which the players' hands are often just two—and sometimes just one—note apart, necessitating that the two players' arms, hands, and buttocks bump and grind as the duo plays beside one another at the keyboard.

Adrian Daub points out that four-handed piano music's sexual "connotations weren't clear, uniform, or predictable" and that the communication between the players "could assume any number of guises, suggest all manner of relationships, or oscillate unsettlingly between different kinds

---

[73] Quinn, *Banished Children of Eve*, 41.
[74] Thomas Christensen, "Four-Hand Piano Transcription and Geographies of Nineteenth-Century Musical Reception," *Journal of the American Musicological Society* 52, no. 2 (Summer 1999): 293.

of relationship."[75] As Philip Brett puts it, "Like all relationships this most intimate of musical ones can run the gamut of human possibilities, even with the same couple, and in ways that affect the music. Parent–child, teacher–student, pursued–pursuer, even adult–adult, all these can enrich the texture of a musical partnership."[76] Among those relationship possibilities, of course, are same-sex possibilities. It was easy for Moss to imagine Johnny singing "Come Where My Love Lies Dreaming" to his male lover Frankie, and it is just as easy for historians to imagine Foster and another man flirtatiously soirée polka-ing together at the keyboard. Foster's four-hand piano arrangement is imbued not so much with sexuality as with *suggestiveness* that opens up the possibility of hetero and queer interpretations.

Writing ten years after Emerson in *The Gay & Lesbian Theatrical Legacy*, Stephen Berwind offers a balanced take of the limited evidence related to Foster's sexuality: "Given the limitations of our knowledge resulting from partial erasure of the record, any current definitive identification of the sexuality of Stephen must remain speculative."[77] I appreciate Berwind's healthy skepticism of claims about Foster's homosexuality, but neither he nor Emerson thoroughly considers the manipulation of the archive and Howard's biography. In my opinion, the most compelling evidence that Foster was queer is Howard's unusually vague wording about the composer's sexuality. It is plausible that he was trying to slip something by his censor.

Of course, I wish I could find concrete evidence of Foster's romantic life. The remembrances, even those neglected by Foster Hall, only heighten suspicion. Birdseye writes that Foster "not only sang his wife's praises, but always spoke of her in the fondest terms; yet why they thus lived separated he never mentioned, avoiding the subject whenever it was approached" (see Chapter 3). And when recollecting about the condition in which he found Foster after he suffered his accident that would prove fatal, Cooper wrote, "Steve never wore any night-clothes and he lay there on the floor, naked, and suffering horribly" (see Chapter 37). How did Cooper know that Foster never wore any clothes to bed? Did Foster sleep nude when he shared a room with Kit Clarke?

---

[75] Adrian Daub, *Four-Handed Monsters: Four-Handed Piano Playing and Nineteenth-Century Culture* (Oxford University Press, 2014), 90.
[76] Philip Brett, "Piano Four-Hands: Schubert and the Performance of Gay Male Desire," *19th-Century Music* 21 (1997): 154.
[77] Stephen Berwind, "Foster, Stephen (Collins)," *The Gay & Lesbian Theatrical Legacy: A Biographical Dictionary of Major Figures in American Stage History in the Pre-Stonewall Era* (University of Michigan Press, 2006), 171.

Historical fiction writers have filled in the archival gaps about Foster's marriage and separations by fleshing out stories about his queerness. That this fiction compellingly created a sense of the possible, of the way it may have *really* felt to be gay in Foster's day, is attested by the inclusion of Foster in the *Almanac* and the serious consideration that subsequent scholars continue to give to Foster's sexuality. I recently detected the strong influence of Quinn, for example, in the comments I received from an anonymous peer reviewer on an article I submitted to a journal. The reviewer encouraged me to "extend more of an understanding shoulder" to the composer because "it must not have been easy being Stephen Foster, a creative, sensitive, alcoholic, perhaps/probably gay man living during the years of build-up to the Civil War, often alone and impoverished, even ostracized from his family."[78] But whereas fiction writers must make choices to create a sense of the real in the worlds they construct, scholars err when they concede to the narratological urge to *choose* a singular characterization of Foster, closing off viable possibilities. Scholars would be wise to drop the constraints of narrative structures and go further into the imaginative than their counterparts in fiction by embracing the range of possibilities, arrived at by careful consideration of the evidence and the patriarchal forces that shaped the archive. Although I believe that the sexual suggestiveness in Foster's music undermines Emerson's claim that the composer was asexual, I have found no strong evidence to suggest that Foster was either heterosexual or queer. By assuming heteronormativity or rushing to characterize Foster in a singular way, scholars overlook evidence—scant as it may be—that suggests a range of possibilities.

## Foster's Death

The remembrances in the Foster Hall Collection portray Foster in the days leading to his death as weakened by illness and a burn on his leg, suggesting that Foster succumbed to injuries suffered during an accidental fall in his room. Most historians have accepted the accounts' general contours, even as they differ in their details. Henry Foster claimed that Foster "cut his head badly," while Morrison claimed that his fall resulted in a "gash to his neck and face." George Cooper wrote that he suffered a "cut in his throat and . . . a bad bruise on his forehead." In a private letter to a person outside of the family,

---

[78] Anonymous peer reviewer to the author, April 8, 2021.

Henry does not inform the recipient of what it was that his brother hit when he fell, but when writing to his sister he informs her he struck "the chamber." Morrison, on the other hand, writing for the public, says his brother struck a "washbasin." Cooper does not indicate that Foster fell at all. Instead he intimates that he "received a message saying that my friend had met with an accident."

For a long time, I have agreed with the consensus and felt that these discrepancies reveal something very interesting: when writing to family members, Henry admitted that the composer fell and hit the chamber, referring to the pot Foster used for urination and defecation in his room; but when writing to someone outside the family, he omitted that detail. I strongly suspected that these discrepancies exposed the family's desire to keep private that Foster died because he struck his head and/or neck on his chamber pot. As historian Drew Gilpin Faust points out, "The concept of the Good Death was central to mid-nineteenth-century America, as it had long been at the core of Christian practice." The art of dying a good death stipulated that a dying individual exhibit magnanimity, bidding farewell to loved ones while fading away in their home. Gilpin Faust writes, "The *hors mori*, the hour of death, had therefore to be witnessed, scrutinized, interpreted, narrated—not to mention carefully prepared for by any sinner who sought to be worthy of salvation."[79] Foster's family idealized this manner of dying. When the composer's older sister Charlotte grew ill and died while visiting the Barclay family in Kentucky in 1829, Atkinson Hill Rowan conveyed the details of her death in a letter to her sister Ann Eliza, assuring the Foster family of her dignified passing. He described how while lying in bed in her final hours she spoke with friends, sang a song, prayed, asked a friend to give a ring from her finger to her sister Ann Eliza, conveyed "messages of an affecting character to her father, mother, yourself [Ann Eliza] and sisters and brothers," and conversed "until within twenty minutes of her death." He assured the family that "never never have I seen anyone die so easy."[80] Morrison carefully preserved this letter, as did his daughter; and it is now preserved in the Foster Hall Collection.

For many individuals and families, the Civil War disrupted the possibility of a good death. Gilpin Faust notes that "the sudden and all but unnoticed

---

[79] Drew Gilpin Faust, *This Republic of Suffering: Death and the American Civil War* (Vintage Books, 2008), Kindle, chap. 1.
[80] A. Hill Rowan to Ann Eliza Foster, November 19, 1829, FHC, C451.

end of the soldier slain in the disorder of battle, the unattended deaths of unidentified diseased and wounded men denied these consolations."[81] Although Foster did not die on the battlefield, he died poverty- and disease-stricken at least in part as a result of the war's disruptions to his livelihood. The grief felt by his survivors must have closely resembled the experiences of families of fallen soldiers who found themselves grieving not just loss but the denial of what was viewed as a proper, Christian manner of dying. Foster's lonely, probably drunken death-by-potty in a dingey hotel was especially undignified. So, depending on whom they were addressing, I surmise, his family and friends omitted or tweaked details of his passing.

Historian JoAnne O'Connell suggests that discrepancies between accounts point to a coverup of suicide, a suggestion I long thought amounts to an unethical stretch beyond any reasonable reading of the evidence. But my stance somewhat softened when I discovered the 1889 anonymous reminiscence, not found in the Foster Hall Collection. I believe this account is most likely fraudulent, but I cannot deny that I find its characterization of Foster's death as a suicide to be tantalizing, particularly when viewed in light of the other reminiscences referring to Foster as "moody" (see Chapters 9, 13, and 23), "melancholy" (see Chapters 4 and 9), "sensitive" (see Chapters 3, 4, 12, 24, 32, and 42), and "at times being melancholy, then again cheerful and vivacious" (see Chapter 9). Furthermore, the composer's mother is known to have suffered at least one long bout of depression following the deaths of her children James and Charlotte and the bank's foreclosure on the family home. In 1832 she wrote to her son William Jr. that "the only time I have had a pen in my hand ... for two years or more" was when she wrote "one letter to Ann Eliza." She described herself as in a "weak and tremulous state" and lamented that "the sources of my earthly joys, and all my gone by hopes are nothing but a dream."[82] We should resist the urge to conclusively connect these dots without more evidence. But there is enough evidence to suggest that it is *possible* that Foster lived with depression or bipolar disorder, a condition that he may have shared with his mother, and that he died by suicide.

In their efforts to build Foster into a national icon, the Foster family certainly wanted to portray his death to the public as more in alignment with the ideals of the good death than it really was. Evidence supports speculation about a range of possibilities of what they covered up, from small details

---

[81] Gilpin Faust, *This Republic of Suffering*, Kindle, chap. 1.
[82] Eliza Foster to William Foster Jr., May 14, 1832, FHC A306.

(i.e., whether he struck a washbasin or chamber pot) to the cause of death (i.e., an accident or suicide). Like his sexuality, there is a range of plausible explanations for Foster's death.

## Foster's Views on Race

Lilly, Howard, and Hodges, three of the most influential keepers of Foster's memory in the 1930s and 1940s, were aware of Foster's views on racial politics from the items that slipped into the Foster Hall Collection. They collected letters that revealed the family's loyalty to the slavery-aligned Democratic Party,[83] family writings that expressed their romantic views of enslavement,[84] Morrison's account books detailing his work in the cotton industry,[85] the campaign songs in Foster's handwriting that express anti-abolitionist opinions,[86] the Buchanan Glee Club minute book that detailed Foster's extensive political involvement in the 1856 Democratic campaigns in Pittsburgh,[87] and the letter from George Cooper to Harold Vincent Milligan in which Cooper stated his belief that Foster "scorned to see the disruption of the ties that held the negroes to their masters & of which ties he had written so many songs."[88]

They knew what all of this meant. Eliciting no objections from Foster's family, Howard wrote that "the Fosters were ardent Democrats and hated the Abolitionists,"[89] and Hodges concluded that "Foster had no use for either the Abolition movement or abolitionists." Hodges continued, "In my opinion, Stephen Foster shared the viewpoint of many other sincere and patriotic Americans—slavery was, perhaps, an evil but the preservation of the Union was

---

[83] See William B. Foster Sr. to William Foster Jr., December 1, 1840, FHC, C697; Dunning Foster to William Foster Jr., October 23, 1841, FHC, C600; William Foster Jr. to Morrison Foster, September 22, 1843, FHC, C496; and Henry Foster to Morrison Foster, March 12, 1853, FHC, C533.

[84] Eliza Foster, "Sketches and Incidents," FHC, C386, 139 and 141; Eliza Foster to Henrietta Foster, April 9, 1842, FHC, A304; and Henry Foster to William B. Foster Jr., March 25, 1842, FHC, C514.

[85] Morrison Foster's Pocket Ledger for Pollard McCormick, 1842–1846, FHC, D323; Morrison Foster's Ledger/Diary, 1847–1849, FHC, D324; Morrison Foster's Ledger/Diary, 1849–1853, FHC, D325; Morrison Foster's Check Ledger, 1853–1857, FHC, D326; Morrison Foster's Ledger/Diary, 1852–1853, FHC, D327; Morrison Foster's Ledger/Diary, 1855, FHC, D328; and Morrison Foster's Ledger/Diary, 1844–1847, D408.

[86] "Hurrah for the Bigler Boys," in Stephen Foster's Sketchbook of Lyrics, A298; "The Abolition Show," March 11, 1857, FHC, A331; and Copyright submission of "The White House Chair," September 3, 1885, FHC, D316.

[87] Buchanan Glee Club Minute Book, FHC, A229.

[88] George C. Cooper to Harold Vincent Milligan, July 2, 1917, FHC, C929.

[89] Howard, Stephen Foster, 82, 177.

of more importance than the abolition of slavery."[90] Morneweck herself wrote, "All of Stephen's melancholy Negro songs reveal that he was decidedly fatalistic about the institution of slavery."[91] To Howard, Hodges, and Morneweck, Foster may or may not have preferred the institution of slavery; but he was at least resigned to it. They were certain of one thing: he opposed abolition.

But their honesty about Foster's views on slavery was tucked away in an obscure periodical and only quickly mentioned in passing in their monographs. Like Milligan, who had chosen to exclude Cooper's recollection of Foster's opposition to abolition from his biography, they chose not to dwell on what the evidence tells us about Foster and his music. They opted instead to expend most of their energy on creating archival descriptions and literature on Foster's sympathy and universal appeal, almost none of which mentioned Foster's political or racial views. In Hodges's sketch of Foster's life, he mentions Foster's activities in the 1856 elections on behalf of Democrats but does not address the politics at all.[92] By not erasing altogether but almost always avoiding Foster's politics and associations with minstrelsy, the Democratic Party, and enslavement, they distanced the composer from racism and encouraged the creation of new fictions. Eventually, as the racial landscape shifted in the United States in the era of desegregation, these new fictions found their way into scholarship.

While Hodges, Howard, and Morneweck were at the peak of their influence, the influence of W. E. B. Du Bois's thinking about Foster continued to resonate with many Black people. John Rosamund Johnson, for example, celebrated in 1937 that "it was undoubtedly the influence of Negro idioms in the musical mind of Stephen Foster that produced his best-loved songs."[93] And on May 20, 1942, W. C. Handy, known as the "father of the blues," visited the Stephen Foster Memorial to learn more about the composer, whom he viewed favorably (Figure C.3). He had reflected in his autobiography, which was published the year before his visit, that "it is my belief that 'Old Kentucky Home' and 'Old Black Joe' touched the heart of Lincoln, and thus helped to make this book possible."[94] Combined with Foster Hall's evasiveness on political issues, a powerful interracial coalition of pro-Foster commentary dominated public discussions of the composer in Jim Crow America.

[90] Fletcher Hodges Jr., "Stephen Collins Foster, Democrat," *Lincoln Herald* 47, no. 2 (June 1945): 9.
[91] Morneweck, *Chronicles*, vol. 2, 409.
[92] Fletcher Hodges Jr., *The Swanee River: A Biography of Stephen C. Foster* (Stephen Foster Memorial Association, 1958).
[93] John Rosamund Johnson, *Rolling Along in Song: A Chronological Survey of American Negro Music* (Viking, 1937), 27.
[94] W. C. Handy, *Father of the Blues: An Autobiography* (Macmillan, 1941), 112.

**Figure C.3.** W. C. Handy's signed photograph for Fletcher Hodges. Foster Hall Collection, Center for American Music, University of Pittsburgh Library System.

But the NAACP incident in Boston exposed a strong current of resistance to Foster's music and opposition to minstrelsy that was also running through Black thought. Just as Douglass had a century before, in 1956 Margaret Just Butcher described Foster's music as a double-edged sword for African Americans in a book inspired by notes and writings that Alain Locke left unfinished at the time of his death. Acknowledging that "Foster's ballads did more to crystallize the romance of the plantation tradition than all the Southern colonels and novelists put together," Butcher/Locke claim that "it is indeed an ironic tribute to Negro idioms that they inspired a popular balladry that reinforced and helped perpetuate the very system that kept Negroes enslaved."[95] Butcher/Locke recognize the view that the songs were

[95] Margaret Just Butcher, *The Negro in American Culture, Based on Materials Left by Alain Locke* (Knopf, 1972), 114.

a tribute to their race—that they were sympathetic, if you will—but that they had also reinforced the justifications for slavery and oppression.

When Butcher's book appeared in the mid-1950s, Foster's songs had once again become entangled with the NAACP's activism. In July of 1957, with the civil rights movement gaining momentum and the United States gradually beginning to desegregate, NBC and CBS jointly agreed to the NAACP's request that they broadcast songs only in versions that revised offensive lyrics and terms such as the N-word, "darkey," "Old Black Joe," and "mammy." The backlash was swift. Failing to embrace the spirit of integration, Hodges called such censorship "a terribly foolish thing" and said that "those who might object to certain words don't have to listen to the songs."[96] The governor of Florida, LeRoy Collins, retorted, "There may be a lot of things going out over the air that we could get along better without, but let's not put the whammy on mammy."[97] In Kentucky, state representative Frank Chelf introduced legislation that banned revised versions of Foster's songs, eventually causing NBC and CBS to relent and accept a compromise in which they lifted their ban on offensive lyrics in official state songs. "My Old Kentucky Home" and "Old Folks at Home," then, would continue to be performed with the word "darkey."

Aware of the NAACP's well-publicized opposition to "Old Black Joe," Whites opposed to integration quickly transformed the song into a racial taunt. Later that year, when the first Black family moved into Levittown, Pennsylvania, White residents harassed them by singing the song at their house from the sidewalk.[98] In 1960, when the student body at Indiana University, Bloomington, elected a Black student president, protests erupted where a fifteen-foot-tall cross was burned, crowds chanted "the South will rise again," and demonstrators sang "Old Black Joe."[99] During a civil rights demonstration in Maryland, White terrorists tried to silence the voices of Black peaceful protesters. According to reporting in the *New York Times*, "As they [Black demonstrators] sang freedom songs and prayed, whites standing nearby began jeering and singing 'Old Black Joe.'" The White

[96] "Foster Songs Censored by 2 Networks," *Pittsburgh Press*, July 19, 1957.
[97] "Censors' Scissors Snip at Foster Lyrics," *Tampa Bay Times*, July 19, 1957.
[98] William G. Weart, "Home Is Guarded in Levittown, Pa.," *New York Times*, September 25, 1957; "Racist Group Would Drive Myers Out of Levittown," *York Gazette and Daily*, October 1, 1957; "Myers Injunction Case Under Way," *Levittown Times*, December 9, 1957; "Housewife Tells of Myers Incident," *Levittown Times*, December 10, 1957.
[99] "Cross Burned at Indiana U. after Vote," *Baltimore Sun*, April 9, 1960.

terrorists tried to attack the protesters, only to be repelled by police.[100] "Old Black Joe" became so polarizing that in 1963 a writer for the *York Dispatch* in Pennsylvania—not far from Levittown—quipped that "you've been around some time now if you can remember when ... you could sing 'Old Black Joe' without being denounced as a segregationist."[101] Amid these controversies, schools began dropping Foster's music from curriculum, including Foster Hall's *Songs of Stephen Foster Prepared for Schools and General Use*, use of which declined until the last printing of the book in 1978.[102]

In 1957 a fictional outdoor musical called *The Stephen Foster Story* received its world premiere at My Old Kentucky Home State Park, where the Federal Hill museum is located in Bardstown, Kentucky. Written by Paul Green, *The Stephen Foster Story* presents Foster as a well-to-do composer who frequently visited Bardstown, despite the complete absence of documentation that he ever set foot there. The Foster of the play struggles with alcoholism but ultimately conquers his vice, proves his good intentions, and wins the girl—his wife, Jane. The show portrays him attempting to sympathetically tell real stories about real people, White and Black, only to have performers such as the minstrel Edwin P. Christy distort his music into racist caricatures against his wishes.

The Foster of the play shares many warm scenes with his family's "servant" Olivia. In real life, as we have seen, the Fosters enslaved Olivia for the first twenty-eight years of her life. Olivia's name disappears in family documents after 1828, when the composer was about two. The musical smooths over these details, portraying Olivia as a beloved family maid and close confidant to Foster into his young adulthood in order to romanticize Foster's relationships with Black people. Foster, as an idealistic young adult, tells Olivia that he wants to "write songs, make music, help others to make music—write about it all, write about the way I feel, about the friends I love and the places—about the woods there and the people in the town—home and mother and father and wood, about you and [old black] Joe—and about, Jeanie—all!" Drawing on Morrison's reminiscence (see Chapter 24), the character then says to Olivia, "I ought to write a song about you ... telling of all I owe to you ... how you taught me old Negro hymns and songs and stories and took me to Negro church meetings when I was a boy." The play

---

[100] Marjorie Hunter, "Riot Averted as Whites March in Cambridge, Md.," *New York Times*, June 14, 1963.
[101] Hal Boyle, "Reporter's Whatnot," *York Dispatch*, January 10, 1963.
[102] Foster, *Songs of Stephen Foster*.

embraces the myth of Foster, portraying him as a color-blind composer who wanted to write songs celebrating the whole American melting pot.

In one of the climactic scenes, we see minstrel troupe leader Edwin P. Christy perform Foster's songs in a dehumanizing minstrel show. A disgusted Foster interrupts the performance, yelling, "That's no way to sing my song.... This song was written about people—humble and good people—and it was not made for a mocking piece of entertainment for silly souls." The fictional message is clear: Foster intended his music to dignify Black people, and his intended meanings were distorted by evil performers such as Christy. Of course, this is utter nonsense. As we have seen, Foster once wrote to Christy to beg him to let him "unite with you."[103] But the reasons for the play's historical distortions are plainly evident. The positive and uplifting *Stephen Foster Story* continues to entertain thousands of visitors from around the world every summer, fitting neatly within Bardstown's tourist industry.[104]

The highly public discrepancies between portrayals of Foster and his music in the 1950s inspired scholars to reassess the composer and ponder the accuracy of competing views of him. Most White scholars ultimately protected Foster by highlighting evidence that supported the characterization of him in *The Stephen Foster Story*, constructing a new version of Foster that was "safe" for a desegregated society. Interrogating this body of literature, Jennie Lightweis-Goff points out that in the 1970s scholars not only began portraying Foster's music as representing the nation's musical emergence but also portrayed Foster himself as representative of the nation's racial progress in the Civil War era. She writes, "For Foster, the narrative has been nationalized by the imposition of a fundamental cultural myth—the American exceptionalist conception of racial progress and progressive revelation—onto his personal story—a putative conversion narrative."[105] According to the conversion narrative, Foster experienced some kind of progressive awakening, softening his views on race relations and moving away from the harshest racism of minstrelsy and his family's conservative politics.

Scholars painted his conversion in a range of ways. On the less audacious side, they characterized him as conscientiously crossing racial boundaries

---

[103] Stephen Foster to Edwin P. Christy, February 23, 1850, FHC, C917.

[104] See Bingham, *My Old Kentucky Home*, 104–32; and Bingham, "'Let's Buy It!': Tourism and the My Old Kentucky Home Campaign in Jim Crow Kentucky," *Ohio Valley History* 19, no. 3 (Fall 2019): 27–56.

[105] Jennie Lightweis-Goff, "'Long Time I Trabble on de Way': Stephen Foster's Conversion Narrative," *Journal of Popular Music Studies* 20, no. 2 (June 2008): 151.

or displaying sympathy for the plight of the enslaved.[106] In more extreme characterizations, they painted him as harboring "liberal views,"[107] embarking on a mission to portray Black people with dignity,[108] as a "fellow traveler" with abolitionists,[109] or as an abolitionist himself.[110] Regardless of the degree of the conversion, these White scholars collectively created a dominant narrative within Foster scholarship that imagined Foster moving toward racial progressivism at precisely the moment the nation experienced the revolutionary conversion to emancipation. These scholars, in other words, found a way in the era of integration to preserve the structure of the Foster myth—the belief that Foster symbolized the nation's story—by linking his personal life to the nation's racial progress.

Time and again, these scholars drew on the Foster Hall Collection, especially what Morrison had hoped memory keepers would draw on—Foster's music—to construct their revisionist versions of the myth. Charles Hamm charted changes in Foster's compositions over time, noting the shift of Foster's minstrel songs from overtly derogatory to sentimental in the early 1850s and Foster's abandonment of overtly racial songs in early 1853. Connecting these developments to the publication of the abolitionist novel *Uncle Tom's Cabin*, he concluded that "there is evidence that events of the early 1850s had a profound effect on him."[111] Building on Hamm's observations, Deane L. Root noted that sheet music for Foster's minstrel songs tended not to feature derogatory caricatures on the covers and that Foster "gradually dropped from these songs the use of terms that could be deemed offensive" and "softened the dialect."[112]

---

[106] Scott Gac, *Singing for Freedom: The Hutchinson Family Singers and the Nineteenth-Century Culture of Antebellum Reform* (Yale University Press, 2007); Crawford, *America's Musical Life*, 214–17.

[107] Lee Glazer and Susan Key, "Carry Me Back: Nostalgia for the Old South in Nineteenth-Century Popular Culture," *Journal of American Studies* 30, no. 1 (April 1996): 9.

[108] Saunders and Root, *Music of Stephen C. Foster*, xiv; and Root, "Mythtory," 29–34.

[109] Susan Key, "Sound and Sentimentality: Nostalgia in the Songs of Stephen Foster," *American Music* 13, no. 2 (Summer 1995): 155–56; Alex Lubet and Steven Lubet, "The Complicated Legacy of 'My Old Kentucky Home,'" *Smithsonian Magazine*, September 3, 2020; and Root, "Music and Community," 45–46.

[110] Shaftel, "Singing a New Song," 16. In 2012, Dale Cockrell did not exactly claim that Foster was an abolitionist but very misleadingly chose his words characterizing Foster and his music: "If, as [Abraham] Lincoln suggested, Uncle Tom's Cabin was the cause of the Civil War, it was Stephen Foster who got everyone singing, in chorus, a strongly voiced refrain of support for that cause." Cockrell, "Of Soundscapes and Blackface: From Fools to Foster," in *Burnt Cork: Traditions and Legacies of Blackface Minstrelsy*, ed. Stephen Johnson (University of Massachusetts Press, 2012), 68.

[111] Hamm, *Yesterdays*, 215.

[112] Root, "'Mythtory,'" 31–34.

Hamm's and Root's work, grounded in strong historical methodologies, remains an important foundation for our current understanding of Foster's music. Even as subsequent research has enriched our knowledge and pulled us away from some of their conclusions, their observations remain invaluable to our understanding of *one* of Foster's music's functions in his day—its ability to resonate with the worldviews of people with racially progressive views. But not all scholars of the conversion narrative have matched their rigor. Musicologist Matthew Shaftel was so convinced that Foster's songs revealed his racially progressive views that he failed to investigate the context and historical meanings of songs before citing them as evidence in support of his claims. He writes,

> In 1847 Shiras started an abolitionist journal, the *Albatross*. While the journal only lasted a few months, Shiras remained an anti-slavery activist until his death from consumption in 1854. It seems likely that the poet had long preached to Foster about the injustices of slavery, but the new law may have helped him to secure Foster's sympathies. This is corroborated by a reactivation of their friendship at that time including collaborations on a song entitled "Annie My Own Love" and a play, "The Invisible Prince," in 1853. A short time after Shiras's death, Foster wrote music for a show commonly called "The Abolition Show," indicating that by then Shiras's influence had had the desired effect.[113]

None of this supports Shaftel's conclusion. "Annie My Own Love" is an apolitical love song. Eleven years before Shaftel published his article, Emerson had already debunked the false assertion that Foster and Shiras collaborated on *The Invisible Prince*, pointing out that Foster lived in New York during the play's only run, which occurred in Pittsburgh.[114] And had Shaftel studied the readily available score and lyrics for "The Abolition Show" (published in the complete edition of Foster's works in 1990) he would have realized that (1) it was a song, not a show, and (2) it was anti-abolition.[115] Foster wrote "The Abolition Show" as a Democratic campaign song that mocked abolitionists and Republicans.

---

[113] Shaftel, "Singing a New Song," 16.
[114] Emerson, *Doo-Dah!*, 205.
[115] "The Abolition Show," in Saunders and Root, *Music of Stephen C. Foster*, vol. 2, 12–13.

In her 2016 biography of Foster, JoAnne O'Connell adheres to the conversion narrative, claiming that "Foster came into his own when he began writing sympathetic minstrel songs that offered cryptic messages of compassion." For O'Connell, Foster's silence about his supposed racial progressivism is easily explained away. She writes, "Foster never had to say anything himself, because his songs did and they had far greater reach than his personal voice. He had learned to keep his opinions to himself and let his inner voice be expressed through his songs."[116] Like Shaftel, she also exaggerates Foster's professional relationship with Shiras. In O'Connell's overly imaginative version of events, after Foster and Shiras coproduced the play *The Invisible Prince* (which they did not do), Foster remained at the theater for the next production, which happened to be the Pittsburgh premiere of *Uncle Tom's Cabin* featuring interpolations of "Old Folks at Home," "My Old Kentucky Home," "Massa's in de Cold Ground," and "Lilly Dale." She writes, "Stephen was kept busy during rehearsals ensuring that his songs were performed with the right amount of pathos, knowing full well that they would now be associated with the antislavery cause."[117] Beyond the mere interpolations of the songs into the Pittsburgh premiere of *Uncle Tom's Cabin*—which were also interpolated into theatrical shows all over the country without Foster's presence or approval—there is no evidence this happened. Once again, as Emerson points out, Foster was in New York at this time, not Pittsburgh.[118]

Although Morrison wanted to ground Foster's memory in his music in order to construct a national image of his brother, musical meaning is slippery, and Foster's music's openness can lead to very different narratives than the ones created by Morrison and the scholars of the conversion narrative. Recently Foster's music has been analyzed in studies that make claims that are diametrically opposed to the conversion narrative, portraying him not as an interracially sympathetic "fellow traveler" with anti-slavery activists but as a racist who set out to romanticize the South. From her examination of Foster's songs, historian Karen Cox concludes that Foster was "the most famous" of the Northern composers who first wrote "nostalgic songs with southern themes . . . that emphasized an idyllic and monolithic South" for "northern audiences [who] shared the composers' nostalgia for the South and sentimentalized its race relations." Cox argues that Foster and his peers

[116] O'Connell, *Life and Songs*, 158.
[117] O'Connell, *Life and Songs*, 165–66.
[118] Emerson, *Doo-Dah!*, 200.

created a fantasy that established a mythology about "masters" and "happy slaves" in a "preindustrial South" that served Confederate and, later, Lost Cause propaganda.[119] Like the original and revised versions of the myth, and just as Morrison wanted, Cox bases her claims on her analyses of Foster's songs. As suggested by the seemingly unbridgeable chasm between her interpretation and the conversion narrative, music is often a terrible source of information about its composer's worldview.

As they would in their interpretations of Foster's sexuality and death, historians would be wise to embrace a range of possibilities for Foster's political views. But evidence does not support the range of interpretations among scholars who embrace the conversion narrative, which suggest Foster possessed relatively progressive views somewhere between sympathy for people who were enslaved to support for abolition or equal rights. The plausible range of Foster's views is considerably rightward from the conversion narrative. Foster was an anti-abolition Democrat throughout his life. But how would he have voted if he lived in Kansas in 1856? Would he have voted to make Kansas a free state? Or a slave state? We cannot answer this question based on the available evidence. He personally harbored conservative, anti-abolitionist views somewhere on the spectrum between supporting "states' rights"—that is, the White supremacist and misogynist belief that the White male voters of each state should decide the issue of slavery—and full pro-slavery views.

## Listening with New Ears

Public historian Joshua Dubbert writes that "since so much of the existing evidence related to [Foster] is second-hand or hearsay, the more one examines his life and work the more he seems to disappear."[120] Due to the extensiveness of archival manipulations, this may be truer of Foster than many biographical subjects, but it is a natural outcome of all serious biographical research. According to Jolanta T. Pekacz, critics of biography argue that "lives do not have a neat trajectory" and "personalities and 'selves' often are fragmented

---

[119] Karen Cox, *Dreaming of Dixie: How the South Was Created in American Popular Culture* (University of North Carolina Press, 2011), 10–13.

[120] Joshua Dubbert, "Stephen Foster at Home in the 19th Century," master's thesis, Bowling Green State University, 2022.

and shifting rather than unitary and coherent, defying any biographical aspiration to identify the 'real' person."[121] The more one studies any individual, the more familiar become their internal contradictions, paradoxical behaviors, and changes over time.

Because of archival manipulations, Foster will always remain somewhat out of focus. But, because no individual can be easily reduced to a simple formula, in some ways this is probably closer to his true self than any existing, reductive biography. When we scrutinize what the family and Foster Hall bequeathed to posterity, and when we subject memory, postmemory, myth, counternarrative, and fiction to comparative and critical study, we end up with ranges of possibilities that delineate the parameters of Foster's worldviews, living situations, and aesthetic choices. Like all humans, he must have lived within such ranges, adjusting his behaviors and views in different contexts and over time. For this reason, I find that Austin surpasses other Foster scholars in his description of the mutability of the composer's opinions in different contexts. Austin writes,

> Foster was inevitably involved in controversy about [*Uncle Tom's Cabin*], and his attitude probably vacillated.... If Foster discussed *Uncle Tom* in the Shiras household, he could identify himself to some degree with the young George Shelby, son of Tom's first master, who, when his father dies, proceeds to free all his slaves, offers them wages to continue working for him, and urges them to emulate Uncle Tom.... If Foster read and pondered alone, he identified himself more fully with St. Clare, who confesses that he is "a dreamy, neutral spectator of the struggles, agonies, and wrongs of man, when he should have been a worker."[122]

As I wrote in the introduction, with Foster there are no simple narratives.

The remembrances and other evidence show decisively that Foster maintained close personal and professional relationships with minstrel performers and the working-class minstrel theater at the same time that his family always maintained relationships with elite businessmen and politicians and that he remained a conservative Democrat opposed to abolition but had professional and personal relationships that crossed party lines and eschewed politics altogether. He must have projected a range of

---

[121] Pekacz, "Memory, History and Meaning," 45.
[122] Austin, *"Susanna," "Jeanie," and "The Old Folks at Home,"* 227.

images in different professional and personal contexts. Perhaps if politics came up when Foster ran into Nevin in a saloon, the composer expressed sympathy with the enslaved to avoid antagonizing Nevin's Republican values without compromising his own anti-abolition stance. When he rubbed shoulders with abolitionists at a bar in New York, maybe he talked up the Union. Perhaps when the topic of politics came up when corresponding with his pro-slavery family members Morrison and Henrietta, Foster more unequivocally expressed White supremacist, anti-abolition stances. Perhaps because of this they destroyed these letters.

We see *something* of the ranges of Foster's views, opinions, and projected images in the diversity of his music: love songs, nostalgic songs, homesick songs, mother songs, war songs, patriotic songs, comic minstrel songs, serenades, comic songs, battle songs, campaign songs, and much more. But Foster scholarship, and musical biography more generally, has been plagued by an obsession with music as superficially autobiographical, so much so that by claiming that music is not always a good source of information about its creator I risk being ostracized within the field of musicology. But it is crucial that Foster's family and Foster Hall cynically put Foster's music to their own uses precisely because they knew that music was of limited value as a biographical source. They knew that they could distance Foster from some of his own views by relying so heavily on his music.

They specifically constructed a misleading image of Foster as a symbol of the nation and democracy upon his most ambiguous songs, which also happened to be his most successful: the sentimental minstrel songs, especially "Old Folks at Home," "My Old Kentucky Home," "Massa's in de Cold Ground," and "Old Black Joe." In the introduction to this volume, I laid out the circumstantial evidence that suggests that Foster was intentionally vague in these songs. We know Foster wrote them to transcend class, gender, performance settings, social codes of etiquette, partisan politics, and sectionalism, which to a degree allowed them to also transcend racial divisions. In the remembrances, we encounter direct evidence of his intentions: John Mahon testifies that Foster told him and his wife that he was deliberately ambiguous in "Under the Willow She's Sleeping."

According to Mahon, Foster informed him that one day his daughter Marion went missing, and finally after a long search he found her sleeping beneath a willow tree. Mahon's wife was surprised at the literalism of the song, having assumed the song metaphorically referred to a girl who had died. Foster's publishers apparently thought so too, adorning an early edition of the song with a lithographic rendering of a grave under a tree (Figure C.4). But when Mahon's wife remarked, "Well, I think, Mr. Foster, it was a strange thing for you to write that song as if it were a lament for a dead child," the songwriter replied, "I then for the first time realized the extraordinary beauty of my little darling, and thought what a horror it would be to me if I had found her dead instead of asleep. But in the line 'There's where my darling lies dreaming' I show my feelings. The words are poetical, and may be understood either of death or of sleep, or of both."

This eyewitness testimony contains Foster's deepest—albeit brief—surviving meditation on the poetics of his commercial songs. In "Under the Willow She's Sleeping" listeners may cry tears of sadness because they believe the girl is dead, they may cry tears of joy because they believe the sleeping girl is so delicate and beautiful, or they may think of the girl in both ways. In this anecdote, Foster tells us that he deliberately opened up the meaning of the song to allow listeners to hear it however they pleased.

Extending this intentional opening up to the majority of Foster's commercial songs allows us to understand the composer's relationship to the varied interpretations of these songs that persist to this day. Foster started his compositional process with something personal—his experience of finding his daughter under a tree, opinions about relations between "masters" and "slaves," courting young women in Pittsburgh parlors, relationships with enslaved or formerly enslaved people such as Nellie Brown and Joe, several relocations that removed him from family, loss of friends and family members, notions of the union of states, experience of industrialization, evenings spent serenading friends, love for a dog, estrangement from his wife and family, loss of his childhood home, experience of gradual abolition—and then opened up the meanings, increasing their appeal and allowing them to sell across political, social, and, to an extent, racial divisions. His ability to craft songs that spoke to people in whatever ways they wanted is the root of both his brilliance and the controversies surrounding him.

It is clear, then, that Foster chose not to write commercial songs that overtly expressed his personal political opinions. Instead, he chose to write ambiguous songs that split the difference between his and opposing views. In a sense, the music was designed to be *inclusive* of a broad swath of ideologies. In his songs about enslavement, he sidestepped violent anti- or pro-slavery debates by writing songs that were sympathetic to enslaved people, allowing the songs to appeal to consumers who were anti- or pro-slavery. His inclusivity in these songs accommodated everything from views many of us today

**Figure C.4.** "Under the Willow She's Sleeping," cover. Foster Hall Collection, Center for American Music, University of Pittsburgh Library System.

find abhorrent (pro-slavery) to views we celebrate (equality), as well as everything in-between and adjacent.

Focusing on Foster's vague and ambiguous songs and forgetting his racism, partisanship, and sectionalism in support of the national-universal myth have advanced all sorts of different agendas. It helped Robert Peebles Nevin pivot his career to Republican journalism by publishing in the progressive *Atlantic*, it helped multiple generations of the Foster family benefit politically and financially, it justified the rejection of the NAACP's critiques, it helped justify the existence of ASCAP, it allowed prominent citizens in Kentucky to encourage tourism to Bardstown, it enabled Lilly to associate himself with a "cultural founding father," it helped the Tuesday Musical Club raise the money for their long-desired new facilities, it helped Chancellor John Bowman establish the University of Pittsburgh as an important center of humanistic research. But, as expressed in the reminiscences and as Joshua McCarter Simpson, Frederick Douglass, and Margaret Just Butcher/Alain Locke grasped, even the few songs around which this construction of Foster was formed always conveyed messages that were in opposition to tolerance and democracy, from Foster's day to ours.

For a brief time in the early 1850s, Foster was one of the most successful composers among White artists in large part because he chose not to take sides in his commercial music during this turbulent and virulently racist moment. Foster did not personally support the racial "progress" of his era, but he was neither the monster nor hero he is made out to have been. He was not the musical equivalent of pro-slavery politician John C. Calhoun, nor was he the musical equivalent of the pro-equality politician Thaddeus Stevens. He was a conservative opposed to the Civil War era's progressive reforms who was willing to write some songs that allowed for conservative and non-conservative interpretations and applications of them. The notion of him as the "father of American music" may be exaggerated, oversimplified, and narrowminded in its conception of America. But Foster's knack for ambiguity—that is, his skill at *not* simply expressing his own perspectives in his songs—was for a brief time unsurpassed in realizing the music industry's goal of generating mass appeal. Thus, Foster's stature as an important figure at a critical moment in the development of the US music industry remains undiminished, even as we take a more sober look at his life and music by dispensing with the view of him as a symbol of post–Civil War America and accepting that his music was not immediately present throughout the entire nation or viewed as uniquely national.

Shedding the myth not only does no harm to Foster's stature but also allows us to more fully appreciate his accomplishments, regardless of whether we individually choose to celebrate or denounce them. Foster's ability to "unite with" figures such as the minstrel Edwin P. Christy in exploiting what was quickly becoming one of the primary paradigms of American popular culture, a kind of perspective openness that remains pervasive in all forms of popular culture, allowed him to be mythologized as a national symbol of post–Civil War democracy after his death. But the myth requires a myopic view of Foster's real life that blurs his real achievement. Did Stephen Foster write his most famous commercial songs to be progressive or conservative? Genteel or unrefined? Pro-South or anti-Confederate? Working class or middle class? Racist or anti-racist? Sexual or asexual? Yes. He wrote them to appeal to the vast majority of White consumers in the evolving markets open to him throughout his career. If he is a symbol of anything national, it is of the rapidly expanded geographical reach and narrowly delimited social inclusivity of antebellum American capitalism.

# Appendices

*William Hamilton's remembrances of Foster (see Chapter 20) illuminate a longstanding mystery about a possible Foster song: "Little Mac! Little Mac! You're the Very Man!" As printed on the cover of the first edition, Foster's daughter Marion deposited the song for copyright in 1864 in Philadelphia and credited her father as composer. Given the song's reference to the Republican and Democratic presidential and vice presidential candidates, all of whom were nominated months after Foster's death, it has long been believed that Foster could not have written the song. However, since Hamilton recited lyrics for a campaign song from 1856 that overlap with the lyrics and perfectly fit the melody of "Little Mac," we can now say with confidence that Foster wrote the melody in 1856 with the lyrics that Hamilton recited (Appendix A). The composer returned to the melody in 1862, tweaking the tune, writing lyrics in support of the Union, and publishing it as "Better Times Are Coming." In 1863, his sister Henrietta wrote new lyrics for the melody that opposed Lincoln (Appendix B). Finally, Marion adapted the song once again for the 1864 election in support of Lincoln's opponent, George McClellan (Appendix C). It is unknown how much of the text of "Little Mac" was written by Marion. Some of it may have been adapted from lyrics her father penned in 1856 that are now lost because Hamilton happened not to recite them in the interview.*

## A: Stephen Foster's Music and Words for a Campaign Song for Buchanan (1856)

# Hurrah for Buchanan of the Keystone State

Stephen C. Foster

APPENDICES 379

## B: Henrietta Foster Thornton's Text for "Sound the Rally" (1862)

Democratic freemen of the Buckeye State,
Hasten to the rescue before it is too late;
Look out for your liberties—hesitate no more,
Up, up, and be doing, boys, "The wolf is at the door."
CHORUS: Hurrah! Hurrah! Hurrah!
Sound the rally for Vallandigham and Pugh!
Hurrah for the Union and the Constitution too!

The Dictator Lincoln has put us under ban,
He has exiled Vallandigham for speaking like a man;
He scoffs at the people's right, we are no longer free,
Unless we stop the despot who strikes at liberty.
CHORUS

Then rally to the ballot box—rally every man,
Our country cries aloud to us, to save her while we can.
Though martial law be threatened, the people to defy,
We will march up like freemen, and cast our votes or die!
CHORUS

Three cheers for our candidates, Vallandigham and Pugh—
The Old Flag, the Union, and the Constitution, too.
With hearts right, our cause just, our watchword "Liberty,"
We wait for October, when Ohio shall be free!
CHORUS

## C: Words for "Little Mac! Little Mac! You're the Very Man" (1864)

Little Mac, little Mac you're the very man,
Go down to Washington as soon as you can.
Lincoln's got to get away and make room for you,
We must beat Lincoln and Johnson too.
CHORUS: Hurrah, Hurrah, Hurrah!
Sound the rally thro' the whole United States,
Little Mac and Pendleton are our candidates.

Democrats, Democrats, do it up brown
Lincoln and his Niggerheads wont go down.
Greeley and Sumner and all that crew,
We must beat Lincoln and Johnson too.
CHORUS

Abraham the Joker soon will DISKIVER
We'll send him on a gun boat up Salt River,
Scotch caps and military cloaks wont do,
We must beat Lincoln and Johnson too.
CHORUS

Southern men come again, Little Mac's a trump,
He'll restore the Union with a hop, skip and jump,
With nigger proclamations full in view,
We must beat Lincoln and Johnson too.
CHORUS

# Bibliography

## Archival Sources

Foster Hall Collection. Center for American Music, University of Pittsburgh Library System.
Foster Hall Curatorial Correspondence. Center for American Music, University of Pittsburgh Library System.
Josiah K. Lilly Correspondence, 1931–1944. Center for American Music, University of Pittsburgh Library System.
Stephen Foster Memorial Building Blueprints and Plans. Center for American Music, University of Pittsburgh Library System.
*Youngstown Telegram*, microfilm. Youngstown Historical Center of Industry and Labor, Youngstown, Ohio.

## Online Archives

Ancestry.com
Harvard Theatre Collection of Blackface Minstrelsy. Harvard University. https://hollisarchives.lib.harvard.edu/repositories/24/resources/11997.
Illinois Digital Newspaper Collections. https://idnc.library.illinois.edu/.
Lester Levy Sheet Music Collection. Johns Hopkins University. https://levysheetmusic.mse.jhu.edu/.
New York Public Library Digital Collections. https://digitalcollections.nypl.org/.
Newspapers.com
University of Pittsburgh Library System Digital Collections. https://digital.library.pitt.edu.

## Published Sources

"Another Author of 'Old Folks at Home.'" *New York Clipper*, May 12, 1877.
Asim, Jabari. *The N Word: Who Can Say It, Who Shouldn't, and Why*. Houghton Mifflin, 2007.
Austin, William W. *"Susanna," "Jeanie," and "The Old Folks at Home": The Songs of Stephen C. Foster from His Time to Ours*. 2nd ed. University of Illinois Press, 1987.
Bailey, Candace. "Binder's Volumes as Musical Commonplace Books: The Transmission of Cultural Codes in the Antebellum South." *Journal of the Society for American Music* 10, no. 4 (2016): 446–69.
Bailey, Candace. "Music and Black Gentility in the Antebellum and Civil War South." *Journal of the American Musicological Society* 74, no. 3 (Fall 2021): 600–10.
Bailey, Candace. "Opera, Lieder, or Stephen Foster? Popular Song in the Antebellum US South." In *Popular Song in the 19th Century*, edited by Derek B. Scott. Brepols, 2022.
Bailey, Candace. "'Remember Those Beautiful Songs': Preserving Antebellum Cultural Practices through Music Collection during the Civil War." *American Music* 38, no. 3 (Fall 2020): 263–302.

Bailey, Candace. *Unbinding Gentility: Women Making Music in the Nineteenth-Century South.* University of Illinois Press, 2021.
Bair, Geraldine Morris. "Beautiful Dreamers: The Founding of the Stephen Foster Memorial in Pittsburgh, Pennsylvania, 1927–1937, the Working-in, and the Aftermath." Manuscript, 1997. Digital Collections, University of Pittsburgh Library System.
Baptist, Edward E. *The Half Has Never Been Told: Slavery and the Making of American Capitalism.* Basic Books, 2014.
Bateson, Catherine V. *Irish American Civil War Songs.* Louisiana State University Press, 2022.
Baynham, Edward G. "Henry Kleber, Early Pittsburgh Musician." *Western Pennsylvania History* (September–December 1942): 113–20.
Beckert, Sven, and Seth Rockman, eds. *Slavery's Capitalism: A New History of American Economic Development.* University of Pennsylvania Press, 2016.
Bedell, Rebecca. *Moved to Tears: Rethinking the Art of the Sentimental in the United States.* Princeton University Press, 2018.
Beiner, Guy. "Troubles with Remembering; or, the Seven Sins of Memory Studies," *Dublin Review of Books*, November 2017. Accessed September 1, 2023. https://drb.ie/articles/troubles-with-remembering-or-the-seven-sins-of-memory-studies/.
Berry, Dorothy. "The World According to Sylvester Russell: The Career and Legacy of a Black Critic Who Argued for the Elevation of Black Performance," *Lapham's Quarterly*, August 30, 2021, https://www.laphamsquarterly.org/roundtable/world-according-sylvester-russell.
Berwind, Stephen. "Foster, Stephen (Collins)." In *The Gay & Lesbian Theatrical Legacy: A Biographical Dictionary of Major Figures in American Stage History in the Pre-Stonewall Era*, edited by Billy J. Harbin, Kimberley Bell Marra, and Robert A. Shanke. University of Michigan Press, 2006.
Bingham, Emily. "'Let's Buy It!': Tourism and the My Old Kentucky Home Campaign in Jim Crow Kentucky." *Ohio Valley History* 19, no. 3 (Fall 2019): 27–56.
Bingham, Emily. *My Old Kentucky Home: The Astonishing Life and Reckoning of an Iconic American Song.* Alfred A. Knopf, 2022.
Birdsall, S. H. Birdsall. *The Latest Songs for the Grand Army and for the Sons of Veterans.* L. Kimball & Co., 1884.
"Birthplace of Famous Composer a Christmas Gift from James H. Park." *Pittsburgh Post*, December 22, 1913.
Bonds, Mark Evan. *The Beethoven Syndrome: Hearing Music as Autobiography.* Oxford University Press, 2020.
Bowman, John G. "A Singer to Pioneers." *The Atlantic*, June 1935.
Bowman, John G. *Unofficial Notes.* T. and F. Bowman, 1963.
Brett, Philip. "Piano Four-Hands: Schubert and the Performance of Gay Male Desire." *19th-Century Music* 21 (1997): 149–76.
Brodt, Zachary L. *From the Steel City to the White City: Western Pennsylvania & the World's Columbian Exposition.* University of Pittsburgh Press, 2023.
Brooke, John L. *"There Is a North": Fugitive Slaves, Political Crisis, and Cultural Transformation in the Coming of the Civil War.* Amherst: University of Massachusetts Press, 2019.
Butcher, Margaret Just. *The Negro in American Culture, Based on Materials Left by Alain Locke.* Knopf, 1972.
*A Catalogue of the Law School of the University at Cambridge for the Academical year 1864–65.* Sever and Francis, 1865.
*Catalogue of the Officers and Students of Columbia College, 1864–65.* D. Van Nostrand, 1864.
Charles, Ruth. "ASCAP—A Half Century of Progress." *Bulletin of the Copyright Society of the USA* 11 (1964): 133–43.
Christensen, Thomas. "Four-Hand Piano Transcription and Geographies of Nineteenth-Century Musical Reception." *Journal of the American Musicological Society* 52, no. 2 (Summer 1999): 255–98.

Christy, David. *Cotton Is King; Or, the Culture of Cotton, and Its Relation to the Agriculture, Manufactures and Commerce*. Moore, Wilstach, Keys & Co., 1855.
*Christy's and White's Ethiopian Melodies*. T. B. Peterson & Brothers, ca. 1850s.
Chybowski, Julia J. "Blackface Minstrelsy and the Reception of Elizabeth Taylor Greenfield." *Journal of the Society for American Music* 15, no. 3 (August 2021): 305–20.
Cockrell, Dale. *Demons of Disorder: Early Blackface Minstrels and Their World*. Cambridge University Press, 1997.
Cockrell, Dale. "Nineteenth-Century Popular Music." In *The Cambridge History of American Music*, edited by David Nicholls. Cambridge University Press, 1998.
Cockrell, Dale. "Of Soundscapes and Blackface: From Fools to Foster." In *Burnt Cork: Traditions and Legacies of Blackface Minstrelsy*, edited by Stephen Johnson. University of Massachusetts Press, 2012.
*Code of Federal Regulations, Title 3—The President, 1949–1953*. US Government Publishing Office, 2019.
Cox, Karen. *Dreaming of Dixie: How the South Was Created in American Popular Culture*. University of North Carolina Press, 2011.
Crawford, Richard. *America's Musical Life: A History*. Norton, 2001.
Creegan, George R. "The Acoustic Recordings of Stephen C. Foster's Music," *ARSC Journal* 33, no. 3 (Fall 2002): 214–28.
Creegan, George R. "A Discography of the Acoustic Recordings of Stephen Foster's Music." PhD diss., University of Pittsburgh, 1987.
Daub, Adrian. *Four-Handed Monsters: Four-Handed Piano Playing and Nineteenth-Century Culture*. Oxford University Press, 2014.
Davis, James A. "Stephen Foster and Patriotism." In *Foster at 200: A Critical Reappraisal*, edited by Jason Lee Guthrie and Jennie Lightweis-Goff. University of Illinois Press, forthcoming.
"The Death Record: Mrs. Jane Denny Wiley." *Pittsburg Press*, January 7, 1903.
Delany, Martin. *Blake; or the Huts of America*. Corrected ed. Edited by Jerome McGann. Harvard University Press, 2017.
Derrida, Jacques. "Archive Fever: A Freudian Impression," *Diacritics* 25, no. 2 (Summer 1995): 9–63.
*Directory of Pittsburgh and Allegheny Cities*. Geo. H. Thurston, 1868.
*Directory of Pittsburgh & Vicinity for 1859*. George H. Thurston, 1859.
Douglass, Frederick. *Frederick Douglass: Selected Speeches and Writings*. Edited by Philip S. Foner. Lawrence Hill Book, 2000.
Douglass, Frederick. "The Hutchinson Family." *North Star*, October 27, 1848.
Douglass, Frederick. *My Bondage and My Freedom*. Miller, Orton & Mulligan, 1855.
Dubbert, Joshua. "Stephen Foster at Home in the 19th Century." Master's thesis, Bowling Green State University, 2022.
Du Bois, W. E. B. *Black Reconstruction in America, 1860–1880: An Essay toward a History of the Part Which Black Folk Played in the Attempt to Reconstruct Democracy in America*. Russell & Russell, 1966.
Du Bois, W. E. B. "The Negro in Literature and Art." *Annals of the American Academy of Political and Social Science* 49 (September 1913): 233–37.
Du Bois, W. E. B. *The Souls of Black Folk: Essays and Sketches*. A. C. McClurg, 1903.
Dumont, Frank. *The Witmark Amateur Minstrel Guide and Burnt Cork Encyclopedia*. M. Witmark & Sons, 1899.
Dunson, Stephanie. "The Minstrel in the Parlor: Nineteenth-Century Sheet Music and the Domestication of Blackface Minstrelsy," *ATQ* 16, no. 4 (December 2002): 241–56.
Dunson, Stephanie. "The Minstrel in the Parlor: Nineteenth-Century Sheet Music and the Domestication of Blackface Minstrelsy." PhD diss., University of Massachusetts Amherst, 2004.
Dvořák, Antonín. "Music in America." *Harper's New Monthly Magazine*, February 1895, 429–34.

Elliker, Calvin. "The Collector and Reception History: The Case of Josiah Kirby Lilly." In *Music Publishing and Collecting: Essays in Honor of Donald W. Krummel*, edited by David Hunter. Graduate School of Library and Information Science, University of Illinois at Urbana-Champaign, 1994.

Emerson, Ken. *Doo-Dah!: Stephen Foster and the Rise of American Popular Culture*. Simon & Schuster, 1997.

Emerson, Ken. "Stephen Foster and American Popular Culture." *American Music* 30, no. 3 (Fall 2012): 397–404.

Ewell, Philip. *On Music Theory and Making Music More Welcoming for Everyone*. University of Michigan Press, 2023.

Fauser, Annegret. *Sounds of War: Music in the United States during World War II*. Oxford University Press, 2013.

Feagin, Joe. *The White Racial Frame: Centuries of Racial Framing and Counter-Framing*. Routledge, 2013.

Finson, Jon W. *The Voices That Are Gone: Themes in 19th-Century Popular Songs*. Oxford University Press, 1994.

*Flem's Views of Old Pittsburgh*. George T. Fleming, 1908.

Foner, Eric. *The Fiery Trial: Abraham Lincoln and American Slavery*. Norton, 2010.

Foner, Eric, and Joshua Brown. *Forever Free: The Story of Emancipation and Reconstruction*. Vintage Books, 2006.

*Foster Hall: A Reminder of the Life and Work of Stephen Collins Foster, 1826–1864*. Josiah Kirby Lilly, 1935.

*Foster Hall Reproductions: Songs, Compositions, and Arrangements by Stephen Collins Foster 1826–1864*. Josiah Kirby Lilly, 1933.

Foster, Morrison. *Biography, Songs and Musical Compositions of Stephen C. Foster*. Percy F. Smith, 1896.

Foster, Morrison. *My Brother Stephen*. Josiah K. Lilly, 1932.

Foster, Stephen. *Massa's in the Cold, Cold Ground*. Illustrated by Charles Copeland. Ticknor & Co., 1889.

Foster, Stephen. *My Old Kentucky Home*. Illustrated by Charles Copeland. Ticknor & Co., 1889.

Foster, Stephen. *Nelly Was a Lady*. Illustrated by Charles Copeland. Ticknor & Co., 1889.

Foster, Stephen. *A Program of Stephen Foster Songs*, edited and arranged by John Tasker Howard. J. Fischer & Bro., 1934.

Foster, Stephen. *Songs of Stephen Foster Prepared Especially for the Armed Forces by the Staff of the Foster Hall Collection of the University of Pittsburgh*. University of Pittsburgh Press, 1944.

Foster, Stephen. *Songs of Stephen Foster Prepared for Schools and General Use*. Edited and arranged by Will Earhart and Edward B. Birge. Josiah K. Lilly, 1934.

Foster, Stephen. *Stephen Foster Melodies*. Arranged for chorus by Luis Guzman. Foster Hall, 1941.

Foster, Stephen. *Stephen Foster Melodies*. Arranged for orchestra by Luis Guzman. Foster Hall, 1938.

Foster, Stephen. *The Swanee River* [Old Folks at Home]. Illustrated by Charles Copeland. Ticknor & Co., 1889.

Frazier, Petra Meyer. "American Women's Roles in Domestic Music Making as Revealed in Parlor Song Collections: 1820–1870." PhD diss., University of Colorado, 1999.

Frick, John W. *Uncle Tom's Cabin on the American Stage and Screen*. Palgrave Macmillan, 2012.

Fuentes, Marisa J. *Dispossessed Lives: Enslaved Women, Violence, and the Archive*. University of Pennsylvania Press, 2016.

Gac, Scott. *Singing for Freedom: The Hutchinson Family Singers and the Nineteenth-Century Culture of Antebellum Reform*. Yale University Press, 2007.

Gilfoyle, Timothy J. *City of Eros: New York City, Prostitution, and the Commercialization of Sex, 1790–1920*. W. W. Norton, 1992.

Gilpin Faust, Drew. *This Republic of Suffering: Death and the American Civil War.* Vintage Books, 2008.

Glazer, Lee, and Susan Key. "Carry Me Back: Nostalgia for the Old South in Nineteenth-Century Popular Culture." *Journal of American Studies* 30, no. 1 (April 1996): 1–24.

Goodman, Glenda. "Transatlantic Contrafacta, Musical Formats, and the Creation of Political Culture in Revolutionary America." *Journal of the Society for American Music* 11, no. 4 (November 2017): 392–419.

*Gopsill's Philadelphia City Directory, 1885.* James Gopsill's Sons, 1885.

Graham, Sandra. "The Fisk Jubilee Singers and the Concert Spiritual: The Beginnings of an American Tradition." PhD diss., New York University, 2001.

Graham, Sandra. *Spirituals and the Birth of a Black Entertainment Industry.* University of Illinois Press, 2018.

Grier, Katherine C. *Culture and Comfort: Parlor Making and Middle Class Ideology, 1850–1930.* Smithsonian Institution Press, 1988.

Guthrie, Jason Lee. "America's First Unprofessional Songwriter: Stephen Foster and the Ritual Economy of Copyright in Early American Popular Music." *Journal of the Music & Entertainment Industry Educators Association* 19, no. 1 (2019): 37–72.

Haines, Kathryn Miller. "Stephen Foster's Music in Motion Pictures and Television." *American Music* 30, no. 3 (Fall 2012): 373–88.

Hallowell, Anna Davis. *James and Lucretia Mott: Life and Letters.* Houghton, Mifflin and Co., 1884.

Hamm, Charles. *Yesterdays: Popular Song in America.* Norton, 1979.

Handy, W. C. *Father of the Blues: An Autobiography.* Macmillan, 1941.

Harris, Verne. *Ghosts of Archive: Deconstructive Intersectionality and Praxis.* Routledge, 2021.

Hartman, Saidiya V. *Scenes of Subjection: Terror, Slavery, and Self-Making in Nineteenth-Century America.* Oxford University Press, 1997.

*Heart Songs Dear to the American People.* Chapple, 1909.

Helgert, Lars. "Herrman S. Saroni: Paths to Success as a Composer in New York, 1844–52." *American Music* 40, no. 2 (Summer 2022): 141–79.

Hirsch, Marianne. *Family Frames: Photography, Narrative, and Postmemory.* Harvard University Press, 1997.

*History of the 18th Regiment Infantry, "Duquesne Greys," Organized 1831.* Eighteenth Regiment Infantry, National Guard of Pennsylvania, 1901.

Hodges, Fletcher, Jr. "Finder of Many Melodies." *Palimpsest* 45, no. 1 (January 1964): 19–32.

Hodges, Fletcher, Jr. "Stephen Collins Foster, Democrat." *Lincoln Herald* 47, no. 2 (June 1945): 2–30.

Hodges, Fletcher, Jr. *The Swanee River: A Biography of Stephen C. Foster.* Stephen Foster Memorial Association, 1958.

Hoover, Cynthia Adams, and Edwin M. Good. "Piano." Grove Music Online, Oxford Music Online, January 31, 2014. Accessed November 24, 2021. https://doi.org/10.1093/gmo/9781561592630.article.A2257895.

House of Representatives, 82nd Cong., Rep. No. 1185, Stephen Foster Memorial Day, October 15, 1951.

Howard, John Tasker. *Our American Music.* Crowell, 1931.

Howard, John Tasker. *Stephen Foster, America's Troubadour.* Apollo ed. Thomas Y. Crowell, 1964.

Hugunin, Marc. "ASCAP, BMI and the Democratization of American Popular Music." *Popular Music and Society* 7, no. 1 (1979): 8–17.

Jacobs, Michael. "Co-Opting Christian Chorales: Songs of the Ku Klux Klan." *American Music* 28, no. 3 (Fall 2010): 368–77.

Jenkinson, Hilary. *A Manual of Archive Administration.* Clarendon Press, 1922.

Johnson, John Rosamund. *Rolling Along in Song: A Chronological Survey of American Negro Music.* Viking, 1937.

Johnson, Rossiter. *Campfire and Battlefield: A History of the Conflicts and Campaigns of the Great Civil War in the United States.* Bryan, Taylor & Company, 1894.

Johnston, William Graham. *Life and Reminiscences from Birth to Manhood of Wm. G. Johnston.* Knickerbocker Press, 1901.

Key, Susan. "Sound and Sentimentality: Nostalgia in the Songs of Stephen Foster." *American Music* 13, no. 2 (Summer 1995): 145–66.

Kingsbury, A. H. "The Old Towanda Academy: History and Reminiscences—Paper by A. H. Kingsbury before the Bradford County Historical Society, March 25, 1905." *Annual* 4 (1910): 15–22.

Knittel, K. M. "The Construction of Beethoven." In *The Cambridge History of Nineteenth-Century Music*, edited by Jim Samson. Cambridge University Press, 2001.

Koza, Julia Eklund. "Music and the Feminine Sphere: Images of Women as Musicians in *Godey's Lady's Book*, 1830–1877." *Musical Quarterly* 75, no. 2 (Summer 1991): 103–29.

Kussart, Sarepta. *The Early History of the Fifteenth Ward of the City of Pittsburgh.* Suburban Printing, 1925.

Kyner, James Henry. *Odes, Hymns and Songs of the GAR.* H. Gibson, 1880.

Lhamon, W. T., Jr. "Turning around Jim Crow." In *Burnt Cork: Traditions and Legacies of Blackface Minstrelsy*, edited by Stephen Johnson. University of Massachusetts Press, 2012.

Lightweis-Goff, Jennie. "'Long Time I Trabble on de Way': Stephen Foster's Conversion Narrative." *Journal of Popular Music Studies* 20, no. 2 (June 2008): 150–65.

Lilly, Josiah K. *Fosteriana at Foster Hall.* Josiah K. Lilly, 1933.

"Literary Items." *Boston Evening Transcript*, September 22, 1886.

Lobel, Cindy R. "'Out to Eat': The Emergence and Evolution of the Restaurant in Nineteenth-Century New York City." *Winterthur Portfolio* 44, nos. 2–3 (Summer–Autumn 2010): 193–220.

Lott, Eric. *Love & Theft: Blackface Minstrelsy & the American Working Class.* 20th Anniversary ed. Oxford University Press, 2013.

Lubet, Alex, and Steven Lubet. "The Complicated Legacy of 'My Old Kentucky Home.'" *Smithsonian Magazine*, September 3, 2020.

Lynch, Christopher. "Die Zauberflöte at the Metropolitan Opera House in 1941: The Mozart Revival, Broadway, and Exile." *Musical Quarterly* 100, no. 1 (Spring 2017): 33–84.

Lynch, Christopher. "From Obscurity to National Icon: Memorializing Stephen C. Foster in the 1890s." *American Nineteenth Century History* 24, no. 3 (2023): 315–37.

Lynch, Christopher. "The Metropolitan Opera House and the 'War of Ideologies': The Politics of Opera Publicity in Wartime." In *Music in World War II: Coping with Wartime in Europe and the United States*, edited by Pamela M. Potter, Christina L. Baade, and Roberta Montemorra Marvin. Indiana University Press, 2020.

Lynch, Christopher. "Stephen Foster and the Slavery Question." *American Music* 40, no. 1 (2022): 1–38.

Maass, Alfred A. "Brownsville's Steamboat *Enterprize* and Pittsburgh's Supply of General Jackson's Army." *Pittsburgh History* 77, no. 1 (Spring 1994): 22–29.

McClary, Susan. "Narrative Agendas in Absolute Music." In *Musicology and Difference: Gender and Sexuality in Music Scholarship*, edited by Ruth A. Solie. University of California Press, 1995.

McInnis, Maurie D. *Slaves Waiting for Sale: Abolitionist Art and the American Slave Trade.* University of Chicago Press, 2011.

McWhirter, Christian. *Battle Hymns: The Power and Popularity of Music in the Civil War.* University of North Carolina Press, 2013.

Meer, Sarah. *Uncle Tom Mania: Slavery, Minstrelsy & Transatlantic Culture in the 1850s.* University of Georgia Press, 2005.

Meyer, David R. *The Roots of American Industrialization.* Johns Hopkins University Press, 2003.

Milligan, Harold Vincent. *Stephen Collins Foster: A Biography of America's Folk-Song Composer*. G. Schirmer, 1920.
Morello, Theodore, ed. *The Hall of Fame of Great Americans at New York University*. New York University Press, 1962.
Morgan-Ellis, Esther M. "A Century of Singing along to Stephen Foster." In *Musical Meaning and Interpretation*, edited by Michael J. Puri, Jason Geary, and Seth Monahan. Oxford University Press, 2025.
Morneweck, Evelyn Foster. *Chronicles of Stephen Foster's Family*. 2 vols. University of Pittsburgh Press, 1944.
Morrison, Matthew D. "Blacksound." In *The Oxford Handbook of Western Music and Philosophy*, edited by Tomás McAuley, Nanette Nielsen, Jerrold Levinson, and Ariana Phillips-Hutton. Oxford University Press, 2020.
Moss, Christopher Hawthorne. *Where My Love Lies Dreaming*. Dreamspinner Press, 2013.
Nat Shilkret and the Victor Salon Group. *Stephen Foster Melodies*. 78 rpm shellac. Victrola 9246, 1928.
Neely, Mark E. *Lincoln and the Democrats*. Cambridge University Press, 2018.
Nevin, Robert Peebles. "Stephen C. Foster and Negro Minstrelsy." *Atlantic Monthly*, November 1867, 608–16.
Nora, Pierre. "Between Memory and History: Les Lieux de Mémoire," *Representations* 26 (Spring 1989): 7–24.
Norris, Renee. *Opera Parody Songs of Blackface Minstrels*. A-R Editions (forthcoming).
Norris, Renee Lapp. "Opera and the Mainstreaming of Blackface Minstrelsy." *Journal of the Society for American Music* 1, no. 3 (August 2007): 341–65.O'Connell, JoAnne. *The Life and Songs of Stephen Foster*. Rowman & Littlefield, 2016.
"Old Folks at Home." *New York Clipper*, May 26, 1877.
*The Old Songs: A Collection of National Airs, Hymns of Patriotism, and Camp-Fire Melodies Compiled for the St. Paul Grand Army of the Republic*. McGill Printing Co, 1986.
"Old-Time Minstrelsy: An Interview with the Veteran Sam. S. Sanford." *Washington National Republican*, September 11, 1874.
*Our War Songs North and South*. S. Brainards' Sons, 1887.
Pekacz, Jolanta T. "Deconstructing a 'National Composer': Chopin and Polish Exiles in Paris, 1831–1849." *19th-Century Music* 24, no. 2 (Autumn 2000): 161–72.
Pekacz, Jolanta T. "Memory, History and Meaning: Musical Biography and Its Discontents." *Journal of Musicological Research* 23, no. 1 (2004): 39–80.
Pickering, Michael. *Blackface Minstrelsy in Britain*. Ashgate, 2008.
Preston, Katherine K. "Music in the McKissick Parlor." In *Emily's Songbook: Music in 1850s Albany*, edited by Mark Slobin, James Kimball, Katherine K. Preston, and Deane Root. A-R Editions, 2011.
Quinn, Peter. *Banished Children of Eve*. Empire State Imprints, 2021.
*Quinquennial Catalogue of the Officers and Graduates of Harvard University 1636–1905*. Harvard University, 1905.
Riis, Thomas. "The Music and Musicians in Nineteenth-Century Productions of *Uncle Tom's Cabin*." *American Music* 4, no. 3 (Autumn 1986): 268–86.
Riis, Thomas, ed. *Uncle Tom's Cabin (1852) by George L. Aiken and George C. Howard*. Garland, 1994.
Roppolo, Joseph P. "Uncle Tom in New Orleans: Three Lost Plays." *New England Quarterly* 27, no. 2 (June 1954): 213–26.
Root, Deane L. "Foster, Stephen C(ollins)." Grove Music Online, Oxford Music Online. 2013. Accessed June 20, 2023. https://doi.org/10.1093/gmo/9781561592630.article.A2252809.
Root, Deane L. "Music and Community in the Civil War Era." In *Bugle Resounding: Music and Musicians of the Civil War Era*, edited by Mark A. Snell and Bruce C. Kelley. University of Missouri Press, 2004.

Root, Deane L. "The Mythtory of Stephen C. Foster or Why His True Story Remains Untold." *American Music Research Center Journal* 1 (1991): 20–36.

Root, Deane L. "The Stephen Foster–Antonín Dvořák Connection." In *Dvořák in America 1892–1895*, edited by John C. Tibbetts. Amadeus Press, 1993.

Rose, Jessie Welsh. "His Widow's Memories of Foster's Life Are Recalled by Granddaughter." *Louisville Courier-Journal*, July 11, 1926.

*Rowell's American Newspaper Directory*. Rowell, 1889.

Samson, Jim. "Myth and Reality: A Biographical Introduction." In *The Cambridge Companion to Chopin*, edited by Jim Samson. Cambridge University Press, 1992.

Sanjek, Russell. *American Popular Music and Its Business: The First Four Hundred Years*. Vol. 2, *From 1790 to 1909*. Oxford University Press, 1988.

Saunders, Steven. "The Social Agenda of Stephen Foster's Plantation Melodies." *American Music* 30, no. 3 (Fall 2012): 275–89.

Saunders, Steve. "Stephen Foster and His Publishers, Revisited." *College Music Symposium* 28 (1998): 53–69.

Saunders, Steven, and Deane L. Root. *The Music of Stephen C. Foster: A Critical Edition*. Smithsonian Institution Press, 1990.

Savage, Kirk. "No Time, No Place: The Existential Crisis of the Public Monument." *Future Anterior: Journal of Historic Preservation History, Theory, & Criticism* 15, no. 2 (Winter 2018): 146–54.

Schermerhorn, Calvin. *The Business of Slavery and the Rise of American Capitalism*. Yale University Press, 2015.

Shaftel, Matthew. "Singing a New Song: Stephen Foster and the New American Minstrelsy." *Music & Politics* 1, no. 2 (Summer 2007): 1–27.

Shiras, Charles. *The Redemption of Labor and Other Poems*. W. H. Whitney, 1852.

Simpson, Joshua McCarter. *Original Anti-Slavery Songs*. J. McC. Simpson, 1852.

Slobin, Mark, James Kimball, Katherine K. Preston, and Deane Root, eds. *Emily's Songbook: Music in 1850s Albany*. A-R Editions, 2011.

Smith, Adam I. P. *No Party Now: Politics in the Civil War North*. Oxford University Press, 2006.

Smith, Christopher J. *The Creolization of American Culture: William Sidney Mount and the Roots of Blackface Minstrelsy*. University of Illinois Press, 2013.

Smith, Christopher J. "We Have Fed You All 1000 Years: 19th Century Radical Song and the Rise of North American Labor." *American Nineteenth Century History* 24, no. 3 (2023): 257–82.Smith, Gerald L. *Slavery and Freedom in the Bluegrass State: Revisiting My Old Kentucky Home*. University of Kentucky Press, 2023.

Smith, William Henry. *Complete GAR Song Book*. R. W. Haskin, 1887.

Stafford, Karen. "Binders' Volumes and the Culture of Music Collectorship in the United States, 1830–1870." PhD diss., Indiana University, 2020.

Stoler, Ann Laura. *Along the Archival Grain: Epistemic Anxieties and Colonial Common Sense*. Princeton University Press, 2009.

"Story of the Stephen C. Foster Memorial: How the Fund Was Raised by the Pittsburg Press to Honor Pittsburg's Poet Whose Songs Are Sung around the World." *Pittsburg Press*, August 5, 1900.

Sutherland, Tonia. "Archival Amnesty: In Search of Black American Transitional and Restorative Justice." *Journal of Critical Library and Information Services* 1, no. 2 (2017): 1–23.

Taruskin, Richard. *Music in the Nineteenth Century*. Oxford History of Western Music. Oxford University Press, 2010.

Taruskin, Richard. "The Poietic Fallacy." *Musical Times* 145, no. 1886 (Spring 2004): 7–34.

Taylor, Bayard. *Eldorado; or, Adventures in the Path of Empire*. G. P. Putnam, 1882.

Taylor, Bayard. *A Visit to India, China, and Japan in the Year 1853*. G. P. Putnam, 1855.

Thomas, Jean. "Bullwhips and Bad Reviews: The Colorful Career of Music Man Henry Kleber." *Pittsburgh History* 81, no. 3 (Winter 1998): 108–17.

Thurman, Kira. *Singing Like Germans: Black Musicians in the Land of Bach, Beethoven, and Brahms.* Cornell University Press, 2021.

Tick, Judith. "Passed Away Is the Piano Girl: Changes in American Musical Life, 1870–1900." In *Women Making Music: The Western Art Tradition (1150–1950),* edited by Jane M. Bowers and Judith Tick. University of Illinois Press, 1986.

Tsang-Hall, Dale Yi-Cheng. "The Chickering Piano Company in the Nineteenth Century." Doctor of musical arts thesis, Rice University, 2001.

White, Hayden. "Introduction: Historical Fiction, Fictional History, and Historical Reality." *Rethinking History* 9, no. 2/3 (June/September 2005): 147–57.

Whitmer, Mariana. "Josiah Kirby Lilly and the *Foster Hall Collection.*" *American Music* 30, no. 3 (Fall 2012): 326–43.

Whittlesey, Walter R., and Oscar Sonneck. *Catalogue of First Editions of Stephen C. Foster.* Government Printing Office, 1915.

Willis, Richard Storrs. "Pittsburgh." *Musical World and New York Musical Times* 5, no. 5 (January 29, 1853): 75.

Witt, Lynn, Sherry Thomas, and Eric Marcus, eds. *Out in All Directions: The Almanac of Gay and Lesbian America.* Warner Books, 1995.

*Wood's Minstrels Songs.* Dick & Fitzgerald, ca. 1855.

*Wood's New Plantation Melodies.* Dick & Fitzgerald, ca. 1862.

*Woodward & Rowlands' Pittsburgh Directory for 1852.* W. S. Haven, 1852.

Young, Cory James. "For Life or Otherwise: Abolition and Slavery in South Central Pennsylvania, 1780–1847." PhD diss., Georgetown University, 2021.

Young, Damon. "The Most Racist Statue in America Is in . . . Pittsburgh, and It's the Most Ridiculous Magical Negro You'll Ever See." *The Root,* August 17, 2017, https://www.theroot.com/the-most-racist-statue-in-america-is-in-pittsburgh-1797950305.

Zangwill, Israel. *The Melting Pot.* MacMillan, 1909.

Zinn, Howard. "Secrecy, Archives, and the Public Interest." *MidWestern Archivist* 2, no. 2 (1977): 14–26.

# Index

*For the benefit of digital users, indexed terms that span two pages (e.g., 52–53) may, on occasion, appear on only one of those pages.*

444 Broadway (American Theater), 158–59, 161

Adams, John, 62, 219
"After the Ball," 53–55
"Alexander's Ragtime Band," 255–56
Allegheny Arsenal, 62, 217, 218–19
Allen, Bemis, 265, 267
Allison, Young E., 264–66
American Society of Composers, Authors and Publishers (ASCAP), 258–59, 293, 294, 375
"Annie Laurie," 113
Ardilino, Edward, 6
Armour, Thomas, 245, 246
Athens, Pennsylvania, 94–95, 102–3, 221–22, 223, 253–54, 276

Balfe, Michael William, 15–16
Bampton, Rose, 346–48
*Banished Children of Eve* (novel), 353–54, 356
Bardstown, Kentucky, 211–12, 264–65, 266, 267, 290, 319, 319n.30, 322–23, 365, 366, 375
Baseball, 236, 238–39
Beabout, Maria, 247–48
Beach, Susan G., 67–69
"Beautiful Dreamer Schottische," 168, 294
Beckel, James Cox, 182
Beelen, Anthony, 62, 212
Beethoven, Ludwig van, 9–11, 62–63, 223, 340–42
Beethoven Syndrome, 9–10
Bellevue Hospital, 67, 113–14, 134, 135, 137, 139, 161, 234, 274, 281–82, 288–89, 294, 353–54
Bellini, Vincenzo, 15–16, 22–23
Benteen, F. D., 29, 51, 228
Berlin, Irving, 255–56, 259
Birdseye, George W., 44–45, 63n.4, 71–83, 136–37, 142–43, 145, 147, 160n.6, 232n.34, 249, 259, 269, 273n.6, 285, 357
Bishop, Henry Rowley, 160n.6, 343–44

Black, Samuel W., 230
Blair, J. Cust, 224
Boston Public Schools, 45–46, 256, 259–61, 262, 264, 327, 337–38, 363–64
Bowman, John G., 344–46, 375
Brower, Frank, 118n.3, 125, 128, 161–62
Brown, Nellie, 240–41, 242, 373
Brown, Samuel A., 259–60
Bryan, William Jennings, 148–49
Bryant, Dan, 39–40, 55–56, 162–63, 172
Buchanan, Ann Eliza Foster. *See* Foster, Ann Eliza
Buchanan, Edward Y., 93–94n.19, 218, 245
Buchanan Glee Club, 38, 179, 192, 195–97, 361
Buchanan, James, 28–29, 38, 43–44, 93–94, 103, 112, 182, 192, 218, 245
Butcher, Margaret Just, 363–64, 375
Butler, Robert, 158, 161

Cary, Alice, 110–11, 112
Cassidy, John H., 179–81, 322–23
"Casta Diva," 22–23
Center for American Music, University of Pittsburgh Library System, 3–4
Chadwick, George Whitefield, 256n.3
Chelf, Frank, 364
Chickering, Jonas, 19
Chopin, Frédéric, 10–11
Christy, Edwin P., 22–23, 26–28, 35–36, 64, 80, 80n.16, 91–92n.14, 98, 103, 107–8, 116, 117, 135, 138, 149, 160–61, 171–73, 231, 248, 282–83, 297–99
Christy, George, 22–23
"Church Across the Way, The," 250
Civic Club of Allegheny County, 255–56, 267–68
Civil War, 20–21, 28–31, 39–40, 50, 56–57, 80, 86–87, 141, 146–47, 153–54, 155, 159, 192–94, 206–7, 217n.9, 255–56, 259, 263–64, 288, 304, 305n.6, 353–54, 358, 359–60, 366, 367n.109, 375
"Clare de Kitchen," 91

## 394 INDEX

Clarke, Kit, 44–45, 55, 136, 157–63, 281–83, 322–23, 337–38, 357
Clay, Henry, 84, 128–29
"Coal Black Rose, The," 91, 220–21
Cohan, George M., 250
Collamore House, 157, 159, 283
Collins, LeRoy, 364
Columbian Exposition, 141–42, 150–51, 157
"Come Back Stephen," 22
Connick, Charles, 6
Cook, Will Marion, 153
Cooper, George, 38–39, 40–41, 44–45, 67, 68, 69, 72–74, 80–81, 80n.17, 131–32, 136, 137, 159, 234n.39, 249–52, 264, 274n.7, 282–83, 285–89, 322–23, 353–54, 357, 358–59, 361, 362
Copeland, Charles, 141–42
Copley, Katharine Whittlesey, 1–2
"Corcoran's Ball," 102
Cotter, Joseph, 261–62
Cotton, Ben, 55–56
Cowan, Richard, 174, 312–13
Crosman, Mary, 151–52
Cuddy, William S., 236, 238

Daly, John J, 66, 102, 109, 285–86
"Dandy Jim from Caroline," 129
Davenport, Harry J., 349
Davis, J. Harvey, 224
De Koven, Reginald, 250
De Witt, Mattie Stewart, 291n.2, 328–29, 330–33
Delany, Martin, 32–34
Dempster, William, 119–20, 226
Democratic Party, 28–29, 38–40, 45, 84, 96, 145–47, 148–50, 179, 182n.1, 192–94, 195, 224n.23, 238–39, 245, 305n.6, 361–62, 368, 370, 371–72
Denny, Ebenezer, 62, 212, 215–16
Dickens, Charles, 37
"Dimes and Dollars". *See* "Popular Credo, The,"
"Dixie," 159, 162–63, 283
Donizetti, Gaetano, 15–16
Douglass, Frederick, 31–32, 34–35, 101n.35, 235n.41, 363–64, 375
"Down By the Gate," 72–73
Dresser, Paul, 250
Du Bois, W. E. B., 152–53, 260, 261–62, 362
Dumont, Frank, 125–26, 164, 169–73, 322–23, 337–38
Duquesne Grays (militia), 245–46
Dvořák, Antonín, 147–48, 255–56, 256n.3

Earhart, Birdelle, 267–68
Eaton, B. D. M., 117–18, 279–80
Emerson, Billy, 55–56
Emmett, Daniel Decatur, 22, 55, 91–92n.14, 118n.3, 125, 128, 157, 159–60, 161–63, 283

"Father's a Drunkard and Mother Is Dead," 269
Federal Hill, 264–68, 290, 308, 319, 319n.30, 322–23, 365
Firth, Pond & Co, 20, 29, 35, 51, 55, 64, 78, 78n.14, 94n.21, 96–97, 98n.29, 102, 103, 107, 108n.5, 116, 135, 162–63, 182–83, 206–7, 225–26, 227, 231, 233–34n.36, 234, 234n.37, 332–33
Fisk Jubilee Singers, 41, 56–57, 152
Foster, Ann Eliza, 28–29, 67, 69–70, 93–94n.19, 218, 222, 245, 314, 331–32, 333, 343–44, 359, 360
Foster, Charlotte, 218, 264–65, 333, 359, 360
Foster, Dunning McNair, 44, 63, 66, 95, 137n.4, 164–65, 177, 224, 233, 266, 318–19, 336
Foster, Eliza, 98–99, 213–15, 218, 228–30, 306, 333–34, 336–37, 338, 360
Foster, Henrietta, 28–29, 144, 164–65, 205–6, 218, 266, 302, 305n.6, 306, 371–72
Foster, Henry Baldwin, 28–29, 66–70, 71, 166, 182n.1, 234, 318, 358–59
Foster, Jane McDowell, 15, 20, 41, 44, 51–55, 65, 67, 78–79, 79n.15, 99–100, 110–11, 120, 124, 136, 138, 144, 149, 164–68, 174, 175, 177, 190, 194, 203, 205–6, 228, 233, 258, 266–67, 276, 281–82, 287, 289, 291n.2, 294, 302, 303, 304, 308–21, 328–29, 330–31, 332–33, 352–53, 354–55
Foster, Marion, 20, 41, 44, 99–100, 134, 138, 142–43, 164–65, 168, 190–91, 192–94, 205–6, 234, 257–58, 263–64, 287, 290–92, 293–95, 302, 304–5, 306, 308, 313, 328–29, 330–31, 332–33, 372–73
Foster Memorial Home, 190, 256, 259, 263–64, 278, 290, 322–23, 328–29
Foster, Morrison, 36–37, 38, 44–45, 51–53, 61, 66, 67, 68, 69, 71–72, 73–74, 77n.13, 80n.16, 80n.17, 81, 84, 85–87, 93n.17, 93–94n.19, 94n.20, 94n.21, 95n.24, 95–96, 98n.31, 102–3, 110n.10, 111n.11, 119–20, 125, 131, 142–52, 155, 157, 159, 164–65, 166, 169, 174, 176n.5, 194, 195, 199, 200, 205–7, 210–35, 236, 238, 245, 246, 253, 254, 256, 259, 263–64, 269, 286–87, 289, 291n.2, 308, 311–12, 313,

314n.13, 315, 316, 318–19, 322, 327, 328, 330–31, 336, 338, 340–41, 343–44, 349–50, 358–59, 361, 365–66, 367, 369–70, 371–72

Foster, Stephen Collins
- addiction, 38–39, 41, 44–45, 61, 71–72, 75–77, 86, 99–100, 120–21, 134, 138, 142–43, 149, 206–7, 270–71, 285–86, 288–89, 300–1, 307, 317n.19, 331–32, 340, 343–44, 358, 366
- appearance, 74–76, 99–100, 134, 135, 160–61, 211, 250–51, 253–54, 271, 272, 287–88, 331–32
- death and burial, 41, 65, 67–70, 80–82, 99, 113–14, 134–35, 137, 139, 149, 161, 166, 234, 274, 281–82, 288–89, 294, 343–44, 358–61
- education, 62–63, 94–95, 137–38, 219–20, 221–22, 223, 253–54, 277
- as flageolet player, 62, 65, 76–77, 93–94, 222, 315
- as flute player, 62, 76–77, 167, 173, 176, 197, 203, 222–23, 225, 227, 254, 263–64, 277, 336
- as guitarist, 62, 167, 189, 222, 241–42, 247, 297–99, 312, 314
- finances, 20, 26, 39–40, 41, 49, 51–55, 64, 64n.5, 64n.6, 75–76, 78n.14, 80, 80n.16, 98, 98n.29, 98n.30, 103, 107–8, 108n.5, 110–11, 116, 117, 118, 123–24, 130, 135, 138, 149, 160–61, 206, 227, 228, 231, 282–83, 287–88, 306–7, 318, 330–31, 332–33
- foreign languages spoken, 63, 94–95, 176–77, 223
- musical compositions
  - "Abolition Show, The," 38, 147, 368
  - "Ah! May the Red Rose Live Alway!" 64, 98–99, 227, 320
  - "Ah! My Child!" 176n.5
  - "Angelina Baker," 355
  - "Annie My Own Love," 99n.33, 120, 142–43, 168n.8, 368
  - "Away Down Souf," 95–96, 97, 225, 318
  - "Beautiful Dreamer," 55–56, 168, 258–59, 320, 325, 355–56
  - "Better Times Are Coming," 377
  - "Bury Me in the Morning, Mother," 99
  - "Camptown Races," 55–56, 63–64, 97, 135, 343
  - "Come Where My Love Lies Dreaming," 64, 68–69, 70, 82, 98–99, 130, 133, 135, 138, 160–61, 179–80, 181, 198, 210, 227, 234, 305, 320, 321, 346, 354, 356–57
  - "Come with Thy Sweet Voice Again," 55–56, 64
  - "Comrades Fill No Glass for Me," 64, 108, 320
  - "Dearer than Life!" 72–73
  - "Don't Bet Your Money on de Shanghai," 38–39, 55–56, 97, 99n.34, 320
  - "Dream of My Mother and My Home, A" 99, 320
  - "Ella Is an Angel," 64
  - "Ellen Bayne," 36n.77, 64, 78, 113, 160–61, 172–73, 197, 227
  - "Eulalie," 99n.33
  - "Fairy-Belle," 114–15
  - "Farewell My Lillie Dear," 64
  - "Farewell! Old Cottage," 240
  - "Farewell Sweet Mother," 320
  - "For the Dear Old Flag I Die!" 39–40
  - "For Thee, Love, for Thee," 99n.33, 240
  - "Gentle Annie," 69, 113, 123–24, 227, 233, 320
  - "Give the Stranger Happy Cheer," 320
  - "Glendy Burk, The," 20–21n.38, 135, 343
  - "Hard Times Come Again No More," 36–37, 44–45, 53–56, 76–77, 97, 111, 130, 160–61, 232, 233–34n.36, 320
  - "Hurrah for Buchanan of the Keystone State," 43–44, 196–97
  - "I Cannot Sing To-Night," 99n.33, 320
  - "I Dream of My Mother" (see "Dream of My Mother and My Home, A")
  - "If You've Only Got a Moustache," 38–39, 99n.34, 320
  - "I'll Be Home To-Morrow," 99
  - "I'll Be True to Thee," 55–56
  - "I See Her Still in My Dreams," 64, 70, 98–99
  - "I Would Not Die in Spring Time," 179, 195n.3, 320–21
  - "Jeanie with the Light Brown Hair," 55–56, 64, 98–99, 320, 325, 346, 353–54
  - "Jenny June," 80, 285–86, 320
  - "Jenny's Coming o'er the Green," 79, 108–9, 160–61, 168, 320
  - "Kiss Me Dear Mother Ere I Die," 55–56, 320
  - "Laura Lee," 227
  - "Leave Me with My Mother," 99
  - "Lilly Dale," 55–56, 369
  - "Linda Has Departed," 99n.33, 240
  - "Linger in Blissful Repose," 55–56

Foster, Stephen Collins (*cont.*)
   "Little Belle Blair," 109
   "Little Ella," 64, 176
   "Little Jenny Dow," 78–79, 160–61
   "Little Mac! Little Mac! You're the Very Man," 192–94
   "Lou'siana Belle," 63–64, 96–97, 116, 182, 224
   "Lula Is Gone," 55–56
   "Maggie by My Side," 64, 98–99, 157, 176
   "Massa's in de Cold Ground," 27–29, 31–32, 41, 56–57, 63–64, 78, 97, 133, 135, 141–42, 160–61, 230, 255–56, 259–60, 265, 319, 321, 344, 346, 348–49, 369, 372
   "Meet Me Tonight Dearest, Down by the Gate," 72–73
   "Mine Is the Mourning Heart," 108, 320
   "Molly Do You Love Me?" 64
   "Mr. and Mrs. Brown," 99n.34, 320
   "My Angel Boy," 99n.33
   "My Old Kentucky Home, Good-Night!" 7, 28–29, 37, 41, 49n.4, 50, 53–55, 56, 63–64, 78, 97, 130, 138, 141–42, 155, 157, 160–61, 210, 232n.35, 247–48, 250–51, 255–56, 258–62, 264–66, 267, 280, 294, 303, 310, 319, 325, 344, 346, 348–50, 353–54, 362, 364, 369, 372
   "My Wife Is a Most Knowing Woman," 99n.34
   "Nelly Bly," 63–64, 116, 138, 240–41
   "Nelly Was a Lady," 15–16, 18, 19, 20–26, 27–28, 53–56, 63–64, 97, 141–42, 182–83, 225–26
   "None Shall Weep a Tear for Me," 99n.33, 320
   "Oh! Boys, Carry Me 'Long," 63–64, 97, 172–73, 232
   "Oh! Lemuel!" 97
   "Oh! Susanna," 16–19, 20, 26, 31–32, 34, 37–38, 44, 63–64, 76–77, 85, 90n.10, 95n.26, 96–97, 98, 105–6, 123–24, 138, 147, 160–61, 176, 182, 224, 258–59, 306–7, 318, 322, 343, 346, 353–54
   "Old Black Joe," 38–39, 41, 55–57, 97, 138, 152–53, 250–51, 255–56, 259–60, 265, 267, 306, 307, 310–11, 321, 325, 344, 346, 348–49, 353–54, 362, 364–65, 372
   "Old Dog Tray," 36n.77, 64, 78, 133, 160–61, 186–87, 203, 227, 231, 247–48, 315
   "Old Folks at Home" (Swanee River), 26–29, 31–33, 41, 51–55, 56–57, 63–64, 78–79, 80, 80n.16, 92n.15, 97, 98, 99, 103, 105–6, 107–8, 111–12, 113, 116, 117, 118, 122, 123, 124, 133, 138, 141–42, 143–44, 146, 153, 155, 157, 158–59, 160–61, 174, 202, 203, 208–9, 210, 230–31, 234, 241, 248, 250–51, 255–56, 263–64, 272, 282–83, 294, 306, 310, 319, 322, 344, 345–46, 348–50, 353–54, 364, 369, 372
   "Once I Loved Thee, Mary Dear," 99n.33
   "Open Thy Lattice Love," 63–64, 76–77, 95, 99n.33, 138, 160–61, 167, 174, 176, 223, 284, 314, 356
   "Our Bright, Bright Summer Days Are Gone," 109
   "Our Darling Kate," 102, 112–13
   "Our Willie Dear Is Dying," 109, 305n.7
   "Parthenia to Ingomar," 99n.33, 113, 197, 240
   "Sadly to Mine Heart Appealing," 94, 99n.33, 240, 241
   "She Was All the World to Me," 269–70
   "Soirée Polka," 356–57
   "Soldier in the Colored Brigade, A" 40–41, 99n.34, 147
   "Some Folks," 53–55
   "Song of All Songs, The" 158–59
   "Sound the Rally," 192–94
   "Spirit of My Song, The," 99n.33
   "Stay Summer Breath," 64, 227
   "Suffer Little Children to Come unto Me," 64, 133, 320
   "Summer Longings," 99n.33
   "Swanee River" (*see* "Old Folks at Home")
   "Tears Bring Thoughts of Heaven," 320
   "That's What's the Matter," 39–40, 55, 99n.34, 147
   "There Are Plenty of Fish in the Sea," 320
   "There Is a Land of Love," 320
   "There's a Good Time Coming," 99n.33, 240
   "There's No Such Girl as Mine," 55–56, 109
   "Thousand Miles from Home, A," 109
   "Tioga Waltz, The," 94, 223, 254
   "Turn Not Away!" 15, 16
   "Under the Willow She's Sleeping," 114, 305, 310–11, 332–33, 372–73
   "Uncle Ned," 6, 33–34, 50, 63–64, 76–77, 85, 90n.10, 93n.17, 96–97, 98, 105–6, 113, 123–24, 138, 160–61, 182, 185, 186, 210, 224, 237–38, 318
   "Way Down in Ca-i-ro," 355
   "We Are Coming, Father Abraam," 39–40, 99n.34, 146–47, 308, 310, 322, 343

"We'll All Meet Our Savior," 320
"We've a Million in the Field," 99n.34
"When Old Friends Were Here," 269–70, 274
"When the Bowl Goes Round," 109, 285–86
"Where Is Thy Spirit Mary?" 240, 241, 310, 319
"White House Chair, The," 38, 131, 192–94, 196–97, 322, 361n.86
"Why Have My Loved Ones Gone?," 55–56, 75–76
"Willie Has Gone to the War," 55–56, 251–52, 287–88
"Willie My Brave," 64, 116, 174, 176
"Willie We Have Missed You," 64, 78, 79–80, 98–99, 107–8, 111–12, 113, 160–61, 227, 233, 305
"Wilt Thou Be Gone, Love?," 98–99, 174
as painter, 61, 200–1, 223
as pianist, 62, 72, 76–77, 102, 106, 112–13, 118, 134, 137–38, 139, 167, 171–72, 171–72n.3, 175–76, 183–84, 186, 222–23, 226, 227, 241–42, 243–44, 251, 285, 315, 318, 332–33
as singer, 62, 79, 81, 96–97, 106–7, 111–12, 114, 118, 161, 171, 186–87, 192, 220–21, 225, 226, 227, 238, 315
as songwriter, 110, 112–13, 133, 134, 171–72, 171–72n.3, 175–76, 183–84, 186, 190–91, 205–6, 227, 228, 241, 251, 273, 288, 291, 318
as violinist, 139, 317
Foster Jr, William B, 66, 174, 205–6, 205n.1, 221–22, 233–34n.36, 245–46, 266, 276, 333–35, 360
Foster Sr, William B, 62, 65n.7, 93–94, 195, 211–12, 216, 236, 266, 306, 319, 328, 333–34, 335–36
Foster Hall Collection, 1–7, 11–14, 71–72, 117–18, 119, 125, 131–32, 136, 142, 144, 157, 169, 179, 182, 185, 188, 200, 202, 205, 206, 210–11n.1, 236, 243, 245, 247, 267, 276, 279, 302–3, 308, 333–39, 360, 361
Foster Hall Reproductions, 300n.10, 340–42
Franklin, Benjamin, 326
Fremont, John, 192, 197
Frost, Madge Rowan, 264–65

Garner Jr., George R, 261–62
Gaskill House, 302, 303, 304n.4, 305n.6, 305, 305n.7, 305n.8, 332–33
Gershwin, George, 255–56

Gist, Christopher, 217
Gradual Abolition Act, 240–41, 335–36
Grand Army of the Republic, 141n.2, 141n.3, 143–44
Gray, William B., 250
Green, Paul, 365
Greenfield, Elizabeth Taylor, 23, 51–53, 57–58
Grubbs, Thomas Fletcher, 243, 244
Guzman, Luis, 344

"Hail Columbia," 222, 315
Hall of Fame of Great Americans, 12, 346–48
Hallowell, Anna Davis, 146
Hamilton, William, 175, 192–99, 322, 336
Hampton Singers, 56–57
Hancock, Walter, 346–48, 349–50
Handy, W. C., 362
Hanson, Howard, 346–48
Harris, Charles K., 53–55
Haworth, Jehu, 188–89
Hays, Will S., 142n.6, 142–43, 210–11n.1, 235n.40
"Heart that Pines for Thee, The," 102
Herbert, Victor, 258, 259
Herz, Henri, 98
Hitler, Adolf, 7–9
Hodges Jr, Fletcher, 1–4, 302–3, 316n.17, 333, 338, 346, 349, 350, 361–62, 364
"Home Sweet Home," 78–79, 148, 157, 160–61, 343–44
Houdini, Harry, 80n.17, 157, 159, 281–83
Howard, John Tasker, 7–9, 12–13, 80n.16, 165–66, 185, 206, 243, 303, 306–7, 326, 328, 329–35, 339–41, 342–44, 346–48, 350–51, 352–53, 357, 361–62
Hutchinson Family, 28–29

"I'd Choose To Be a Daisey if I Might Be a Flower," 248
Indiana University Bloomington, 364–65
*Invisible Prince, The*, 120, 368, 369
Irving, Washington, 98, 103, 110–11, 112
Irwin, Thomas (Judge), 186–87, 225
Ives, Charles, 256n.3
Ivone, Arturo, 12

Jackson, Andrew, 93–94n.19, 215–16
Jefferson College, 84, 95n.22, 149, 174, 211–12, 221, 223
Jefferson, Thomas, 62, 219
Jenkinson, Hilary, 4, 5
"Jennie Lives but for Thee," 102
"Jim Along Josey," 91

## 398 INDEX

"Jock of Hazeldean," 113
"John Brown's Body," 113, 197
Johnson, John Rosamund, 153, 362
Johnston, Mary, 205–6
Johnston, William G., 84
Jope, William P. T., 245–46
"Judy Figg," 238
"Jump Jim Crow," 87–91, 220–21, 238, 297–99, 300–1

Kane, Patrick F., 44–45, 236, 237–39, 322–23, 337–38
Keenan Jr., Thomas, 45, 142, 143–44, 147–48, 150–51, 153–55, 157, 164, 210, 322
Keller, Mary, 240, 241, 319
Keller, Matthias, 71
Kentucky Derby, 7, 265–66
Kern, Jerome, 259
Ketterer, Gustav, 6
King, Sarah, 247
Kingsbury, William W., 263–64, 276–78
Kitty, 335–37
Klauder, Charles, 6
Kleber, Henry, 65, 198–99, 222–23, 234, 247, 248
Kneass, Nelson, 16, 92, 93, 95–96, 125–26, 161n.9, 171–72, 179–80, 181
Ku Klux Klan, 153–54

Labree, Benjamin, 265–66
Lawrence, James, 62, 217
Lawrenceville, Pennsylvania, 44, 62, 93n.18, 175–76, 177, 188, 196, 217–19, 240, 257, 280
Lawton, William A, 179–80, 181
Lee & Walker, 107–8, 109, 110–11
Lightner, Jessie, 145–46, 227, 233, 315
Lilly Endowments, 2–4, 350
Lilly Sr., Josiah K., 1–4, 5–6, 7–9, 45–46, 119, 206, 243, 266–68, 306, 323–51, 361, 375
Lincoln, Abraham, 39–40, 152, 192–94, 362, 367n.109
Locke, Alain, 363–64, 375
"Long Ago Day" ("Goin' Down De Road"), 296–301
"Long-Tail Blue," 91, 220–21
"Lord Ullin's Daughter," 254
Lost Cause, 150–51, 153–54, 155, 260–61, 308, 319n.30, 369–70
"Lucy Long," 91, 129, 297

Madison, James, 93–94n.19
Mahon, John, 43–45, 73–74, 80n.16, 80n.17, 98n.31, 102–15, 116–17, 136, 159, 160n.6, 168n.9, 291n.2, 372–73

Marie of Romania (Queen), 267
Marks, Edward B., 249–50
Marshall (Miller), Sophie, 227
Martin, Edward, 349
"Mary Blane," 118
"May Queen, The," 119–20, 226
McCarthy, William Henry, 197n.6, 240, 241
McClellan, George, 192–94
McClelland, John, 194
McClintock, Jonas R., 245–46
McDowell, Agnes, 313
McDowell, Andrew N., 32, 34, 65, 78–79, 164, 166–67, 228, 310–11, 312–13
McDowell, Robert P., 224
McKinley, William, 148–49, 182
Miller, Cons, 198
Miller, Mary, 205–6
Milligan, Harold Vincent, 44–45, 264, 267–68, 269–70, 284, 285–88, 322–23, 326–28, 361, 362
Monroe, James, 93–94n.19
Moore, Thomas, 20, 26, 155
Moretti, Giuseppe, 150–51
Morneweck, Evelyn Foster, 144–45, 151–52, 165, 210–11n.1, 276, 302–3, 326–27, 328, 329–39, 340–41, 343–44, 352–53, 361–62
Morris, Rebecca Shiras, 119, 120–21, 122–24, 142–43
Moss, Christopher Hawthorne, 354–55, 356–57
Mott, James, 146–47
Mott, Lucretia, 146–47
Mozart, Wolfgang Amadeus, 62–63, 223, 340–42
Murphy, James, 116, 117, 118
Murphy, Joseph, 16, 55–56, 92, 92n.15, 116, 117–18, 119, 124, 142–43
"My Gal Sal," 250
Mygatt, Katherine Schoenberger, 302–7, 323, 332–33
"My Story of Love". *See* "Long Ago Day"

NAACP (National Association for the Advancement of Colored People), 45–46, 256, 259–61, 262, 263–64, 322–23, 327, 337–38, 363–65, 375
"Nancy Fat," 162–63
National-Universal Myth, 7–12, 14, 41–42, 44–46, 58–59, 142, 153, 154–55, 255, 257–58, 263–68, 269, 286, 308, 322–25, 327–28, 338–39, 349–51, 365–67, 369–70, 371, 375, 376
Nevin, Ethelbert, 85

## INDEX

Nevin, Robert Peebles, 36–37, 44–45, 80n.16, 84–101, 102–3, 116, 119, 137, 142–43, 224n.23, 235, 236, 297, 300–1, 371–72, 375
Nilsson, Christine, 51–53, 57–58, 108, 133

Ogden, Lizzie, 15–16, 18–19, 20–22
"Old Dan Tucker," 129
"Old Folks Are Gone," 113
"Old Zack's Inauguration Grand March," 182
Ole Bull, 98
Oliver Ditson & Co., 51–53, 110–11, 131–32, 143–44
"On the Banks of the Wabash, Far Away," 250
"Our Nominee," 84, 85

Pan American Union, 344
Parkhurst, Susan McFarland, 136, 269–75, 281
Pastor, Tony, 158, 161n.10
Patti, Adelina, 51–53, 57, 130n.6, 208–9
Payne, John Howard, 148, 160–61, 160n.6
Pelham, Richard, 118n.3, 125, 128, 161–62
Pennsylvania Canal, 219, 221–22, 335
Pennsylvania Railroad, 65, 221–22, 234, 246, 335
Peters, W. C., 63–64, 76–77, 90–91, 93n.17, 96–97, 162–63, 224, 318
Pise, Olivia, 232, 335–37, 365–66
Pittsburgh Exposition, 154–55, 200
Poe, Edgar Allen, 137, 287
Polk, James K, 84, 128, 129
Pope, J William, 182–84
"Popular Credo, The," 120, 123, 131, 168

Quinn, Peter, 165n.4, 353–55, 356, 358

Republican Party, 38–40, 85, 86–87, 101n.35, 148–50, 155, 192, 305n.6, 368, 371–72, 375
Revolutionary War, 211–12, 213, 215–16, 311–12
Rice, Dan, 125
Rice, Dean J., 296–301, 342
Rice, Thomas D., 16, 88–91, 221n.17, 296–301
"Robin Adair," 94n.21
Robinson, Andrew, 174, 177, 224, 233, 236, 284, 315, 318–19
Robinson, John W., 284
Robinson, Susan Pentland, 167, 174–78, 202, 227, 233, 236, 263–64, 284, 314, 315, 318–19
Robinson, William ("Irish Bill"), 220n.16, 236, 238

Rogers, John, 29
Root, George F., 108n.6, 113
Rose, Alexander D., 291n.2, 328–29, 332
Rose, Jessie Welsh, 166–67, 190, 191, 263–64, 266–67, 278, 290, 294, 308–21, 328, 343
Rowan, John, 211–12, 319
Russell, Sylvester, 155
Rutherford, Mildred, 153–54

Sanford, Samuel, 35–37, 44–45, 125–30, 161–62, 172, 179–80, 322–23, 337–38
Saroni, Herrman S., 13–14
Schubert, Franz, 340–41
Scully, John D., 199, 330–31
Shilkret, Nathaniel, 325
Shiras, Charles, 28–29, 119–24, 131, 142–43, 164, 168, 176, 226n.27, 368, 369, 371
Shiras, Joan Sloan, 119–24, 142–43
"Sich a Gittin' Up Stairs," 91, 297
Simpson, Joshua McCarter, 31–32, 375
"Sittin' on a Rail," 91
Sivori, Camillo, 98
Skinner, Frances Van Arsdale, 6
"Soldier Is My Beau, A," 102
"Song of All Songs No 2, The," 158–59
*Songs of Stephen Foster Prepared for the Armed Forces by the Staff of the Foster Hall Collection of the University of Pittsburgh*, 348–49
*Songs of Stephen Foster Prepared for Schools and General Use*, 342–43, 364–65
Sonneck, Oscar, 1–2, 262–63
Sousa, John Philip, 259
*South before the War, The*, 141–42, 157
Spaeth, Sigmund, 346–48
Spalding, Albert, 346–48
Spanish-American War, 143–44
"Standard of the Free, The," 102
Stephen Foster Day, 9, 267–68, 349–50
Stephen Foster Memorial (building, Pittsburgh), 1, 2–4, 5, 12–14, 267–68, 344, 362
Stephen Foster Memorial (statue, Pittsburgh), 6, 143–44, 147–48, 150–51, 154–55, 157, 167, 175, 183–84, 185, 188, 195, 197, 201, 202–3, 204, 208–9, 210, 241, 246, 249
*Stephen Foster Story, The* (musical), 365–66
Stewart, Louisa, 316, 328–29, 332–33
Stewart, Mattie. *See* De Witt, Mattie Stewart
Stough, Martha, 302–7, 323
Stowe, Harriet Beecher, 152
"Swanee," 255–56

"Sweet Genevieve," 249, 353–54
Swisshelm, Jane Grey, 123, 124

"Ta-ra-ra-Boom-de-ay," 161
Taylor, Bayard, 49, 50
Taylor, Zachary, 66, 182
Tennyson, Alfred, 119–20, 226
Thalberg, Sigismond, 98
"This Rose Will Remind You," 296–300
Thomas, J. R., 72–73
Thornton, Montrose, 259–60
Ticknor & Co., 141–42
Tin Pan Alley, 250
"Tired Soldier, The," 113
Tod, Sally, 305
Towanda, Pennsylvania, 221–22, 253, 254, 276–78
Townsend, George Alfred, 143–44
Townsend, John Wilson, 249, 257–58
Trinity Episcopal Church (Pittsburgh), 15, 68–69, 99, 225n.25, 234, 313
Tucker, Henry, 249
Tuesday Musical Club, 2–3, 267–68, 375
Tyler, John, 93–94n.19, 128, 129, 182n.1

"Uncle Ned" statue. *See* Stephen Foster Memorial (statue, Pittsburgh)
*Uncle Tom's Cabin*, 28–29, 41, 49, 56, 57–58, 105–6, 128, 129–30, 152, 255–56, 367, 369, 371
United Daughters of the Confederacy, 153–54
United States Marine Band, 344
University of Pittsburgh, 1, 2–4, 267–68, 338, 344–45, 346, 349–50, 375

"Villikins and His Dinah," 38
"Vital Spark of Heavenly Flame," 234

"Volunteer Organist, The," 250

War of 1812, 216, 218n.11
Washington, George, 110–11, 112, 217, 228, 310
Waters, Horace, 133, 269, 275
Weber, Carl Maria von, 62–63, 223
Welles, R. M., 253–54
Welsh, Marion Foster. *See* Foster, Marion
Welsh, Walter, 142–43, 190, 234, 308
*Where My Love Lies Dreaming* (novel), 354
Whig Party, 66, 84, 85, 96, 182, 182n.1, 195
White, Charles, 172, 182
Whitlock, Billy, 118n.3, 125, 128, 161–62
Whitmer, T. Carl, 258
Whittlesey, Walter R., 1–2, 4, 262–63
Wiley, Jane Foster. *See* Foster, Jane McDowell
Wiley, Matthew D., 79n.15, 124, 166–67
William A. Pond & Co., 51–53, 55, 102, 107–8, 109, 110–11, 116–17, 234, 282–83, 330–31
Willig, George, 63–64, 76–77, 223
Willis, Richard Storrs, 35, 233–34n.36
Wilson, Butler R., 259–60
Winons, Francis, 243–44
Wohlgemuth, E. Jay, 265
Woods, Harry, 240
Wood's Minstrels, 251–52, 281–82, 287
Woods, Rachel Keller, 240–42, 247, 263–64
World War I, 45, 256
World War II, 9n.18, 348–49

Yellin, Samuel, 6
"Young Folks at Home," 158–59

"Zip Coon," 220–21
Zorer, Maximilan, 22–23